NORTHERN CALIFORNIA
WINE COUNTRY ACCESS®

W9-AXY-917

Wine Country Orientation

Many people, even some San Franciscans, don't realize how close the wine country is to the City by the Bay. **St. Helena** and the heart of the **Napa Valley** are just a little more than an hour's drive away from San Francisco, and if the traffic gods smile upon you, you can make it from one end of the valley to the other in about a half hour. Not that you should—there's so much to see and do along the way. The town of **Sonoma**, where California's wine-making history began in the mid-19th century, is also about an hour away, and although **Sonoma County's** vineyards cover a much larger area, roughly divided into the Sonoma and Russian River valleys, the entire region is close enough for an easy day trip.

Mendocino and **Lake counties'** wine country lies farther to the north—roughly a two-and-a-half to three-hour drive from San Francisco. Yet Napa, Sonoma, and Mendocino are close enough that in one weekend trip, it is possible to see parts of all three regions. While you're visiting wineries in Sonoma and Mendocino, plan on taking some time to explore the nearby coast, which is rugged, sparsely populated, and stunningly beautiful. (Please note that the Pacific Ocean here can be treacherous. Check with the ranger at local parks for weather conditions and information on high and low tides. And when you're exploring tide pools or clambering on rocks, never turn your back to the sea.)

While there is regular bus service to Napa, Sonoma, and Mendocino, once you get to the wine country you'll need a car to visit the wineries; no bus will take you around, unless you're with an organized tour. Since the closest international airport is San Francisco (or Oakland on the east side of the bay), it's actually simpler to rent a car at the airport and drive to the wine country, rather than take a bus and rent a car in the valleys. Once in the wine country, it's easy to get around and almost impossible to get lost, except when searching for small wineries in the foothills or those that require an appointment and don't have a sign out front.

When planning a trip, remember that this region, especially the Napa Valley, is one of the most popular destinations in California. The best time to go is off-season (November through May). And during the peak months, it is less crowded during the week. Of course, the most exciting time to visit is during the grape crush (generally in September), when the normally serene landscape of vineyards is animated with grape pickers moving along the rows and trucks full of grapes driving up and down the streets. (However, this is also when the winery crew has less time to spend with visitors.)

During the peak season and on weekends, most hotels and bed-and-breakfast inns require a minimum two-night stay. Be sure to reserve as early as possible; lodging is limited and can be extremely hard to find on holidays and summer weekends. It's a good idea to consider using a referral service to locate any vacancies.

Much of the pleasure of a trip like this lies in the planning. Start tasting wines at home and reading up on those that you particularly like. Taste and compare one type of wine from different producers, and sample varieties of the same types of wine from Napa, Sonoma, Mendocino, and Lake counties to begin to understand the differences in style. Don't worry if your wine vocabulary is lacking—people who work with wine every day can be just as perplexed as to how to describe wine, since, after all, it is a pure sensory experience, one to be approached with a spirit of curiosity and pleasure.

Unless otherwise indicated, all phone numbers are area code 707.

Getting to the Wine Country

Napa County:

The closest airports with commercial flights are **Sonoma County Airport, San Francisco International Airport (SFO),** and **Oakland International Airport (OAK).**

There is one airfield for private and charter planes: **Napa County Airport** ♦ 2030 Airport Rd, Napa. 224.0887, 644.1658

Sonoma County:

Sonoma County Airport American Eagle and United Airlines fly here from SFO and San Jose International Airport (SJC). ♦ 2200 Airport Blvd (six miles north of Santa Rosa) 542.3139

Mendocino County:

No commercial flights are available to Mendocino County; the airports listed below are for small private and charter planes only.

Boonville Airport ♦ Airport Blvd, Boonville. 895.9918

Mendocino County Airport ♦ 43001 Airport Rd, Little River (three miles east of Little River) 937.5129

Ukiah Municipal Airport ♦ 1411 S. State St, Ukiah. 463.6293

Lake County:

These are both private airfields for small planes:

Lampson Field ♦ 4773 Highland Springs Rd, Lakeport. 263.4345

Pierce Field ♦ 7140 Old Hwy, Clearlake. 994.3470

Getting around the Wine Country

Boats

Napa Riverboat Company Tours ♦ 1200 Milton Rd, Napa Valley Marina 226.2628

Buses/Shuttles

Greyhound (to Napa, Sonoma, Lake counties) ....
....415/558.6789

Napa County:

Evans Airport Service (from SFO to Napa and Yountville) 255.1559

Sonoma County:

Airporter (from SFO to Santa Rosa) 545.8015
Sonoma Airport Shuttle 938.4246

Mendocino County:

Mendocino Transit Authority 462.1422
  recording 884.3723

Lake County:

Clearlake Dial-a-Ride 994.8277
Lakeport Dial-a-Ride.................................277.9422

Taxis

Napa County:

Napa Valley Cab 257.6444
Napa Yellow Cab 226.3761

Sonoma County:

County Cab Co 546.0370
George's Taxi..546.3322

Mendocino County:

Fort Bragg Dial-a-Ride 964.1800
Ukiah Dial-a-Ride......................................462.3881

Lake County:

Clear Lake Taxi 994.6511

FYI

Drinking The legal age for drinking in California is 21. Liquor is sold in a wide variety of venues, from supermarkets and gourmet food markets to all-night convenience stores and specialized liquor and wine shops. Bars generally stay open until 2AM, but many close earlier in the wine country.

Driving Tips There are not many roads in the regions included in this book, and most of them are quite narrow, so the mix of tourist vehicles with local people trying to go about their business can be a frustrating combination. Try to watch your rear-view mirror frequently, and if you have one or two cars following closely behind, clearly wanting to go faster, pull over to let them pass. This is especially important on roads such as Hwy 128 to the Anderson Valley or anywhere along the coast; many of the roads have just one lane of traffic on either side. Also, the shoulder is not very wide, so watch for bicyclists, particularly when coming around a blind curve.

If you're following an intensive schedule of wine tasting, make sure you don't drink too much before getting behind the wheel of a car. Either conscientiously spit the wines out after you taste them as the professionals do (see "Making the Most of Your Winery Visits" on page 14) or appoint a designated driver. Eat breakfast before visiting your first winery, drink water often, and never go without lunch if you're going to continue tasting. Bear in mind that the heat will only intensify the effects of alcohol. Unfortunately, most wineries do not offer food along with their wines, although some provide crackers to clear the palate. Many are now stocking some picnic supplies so you can purchase cheese, crackers, packaged cold cuts, etc., without having to drive back to town.

Foreign Money Exchange The wine country is somewhat backward when it comes to exchanging money. It is advisable to change it at the point of embarkation—that is, at the airport or in San Francisco—before heading to the wine country. In an emergency, **Thomas Cook Foreign Exchange** has an office in Corte Madera (in Marin County), about a 40-minute drive from the town of Napa. Most banks will exchange travelers checks written in American dollars; it is much more difficult to exchange travelers checks written in foreign currency.

American Express ♦ M-F 9AM-5PM; Sa 10AM-5PM. 237 Post St, San Francisco. 415/981.5533

Thomas Cook Foreign Exchange ♦ M-F 9AM-6PM. 100 Grant Ave, San Francisco. 415/362.3452

Thomas Cook Foreign Exchange ♦ M-F 10AM-9PM;

Orientation

Sa 10AM-6PM. The Village Shopping Center, Corte Madera. 415/924.6001/6009

Thomas Cook Foreign Exchange ♦ Daily 7AM-11PM. San Francisco International Airport, second level. 415/583.4029

Money

Napa County: The major banks include Bank of America, Citibank, Security Pacific, and Wells Fargo.

Sonoma County: Most major banks have branches in Sonoma County, including Wells Fargo, California First, Bank of America, and Security Pacific.

Mendocino and Lake counties: The major banks are Bank of America and Wells Fargo.

Occupancy Tax All hotel and overnight lodging (including bed-and-breakfast establishments) is subject to a county- and/or city-imposed tax. The taxes in the wine country are currently as follows:

Napa County: 10 1/2 percent countywide

Sonoma County: 8 percent countywide, except for: Rohnert Park and Petaluma which have a 10 percent tax

Mendocino County: 10 percent countywide, except for Ukiah, which has an 8 percent tax

Lake County: 6 percent countywide, except for Lakeport, which has an 8 percent tax

Parking Parking meters generally allow for either 30-minutes, one-hour, or two-hours of parking and operate from 9AM-6PM every day except Sunday. There are exceptions to this rule, so watch for the occasional meter that is monitored on Sunday. Certain parking zones may not have meters, but nevertheless are marked a 20-minute, one-hour, or two-hour zone.

Fortunately, few places in the wine country have to worry about a lack of parking spaces. Most wineries offer ample parking (with designated handicapped spaces), and often have special areas reserved for buses or RVs. In town, usually getting a half-block or a block off the main street is sufficient to ensure a parking spot.

Smoking More and more Californians are becoming nonsmokers, and the sensitivity to smoking is acute. The best strategy is to ask before you smoke anywhere indoors. Many restaurants are entirely nonsmoking, as are some inns. When smoking is allowed, it's generally restricted to a special section of the restaurant or to certain rooms of the hotel. If you smoke, be sure to inquire about the establishment's policy when you make your reservation.

Telephone Local calls from pay phones are 25 cents, but because the 707 area code encompasses all of Napa, Sonoma, Mendocino, and Lake counties, many calls within that area code cost more. Find out what is considered a local call before holding any lengthy phone conversations. Also inquire about any of your hotel's extra phone charges.

Tipping In northern California, it is customary to tip 15 to 20 percent of your restaurant bill including the tax (CA tax is now 8 1/4 percent), depending on your satisfaction with the service. Some restaurants automatically tack on a 15 percent gratuity for parties of five or more. A taxi driver is usually tipped about 15 percent, while whoever carries your bags at a hotel might expect $1 to $2 per bag. Whether you tip the housekeeper at your hotel is up to your discretion, but a few dollars per day is typical.

Wine Publications

The Food & Wine Companion **David Rosengarten** and **Joshua Wesson** have put together a bi-monthly newsletter on food and wine and how the two go together. Sold at select retailers and by subscription ($36 per year) from Context Communications, Inc., 250 E 73rd St, Suite 14-H, New York NY 10021. 212/734.1961

San Francisco Focus The monthly city magazine published by public television station KQED has a good wine column. Also look for **Gerald Asher's** well-written column in *Gourmet* magazine and **Anthony Dias Blue's** lively column in *Bon Appétit*.

The Wine Advocate This is a bi-monthly guide to fine wine based on research by one of the most influential wine critics and writers in the business, **Robert M. Parker, Jr.** Available only by subscription ($35 one year; $60 two years). Write to *The Wine Advocate*, Box 311, Monkton MD 21111. 301/329.6477

The Wine Spectator A bi-weekly magazine offering serious coverage of wines and wine regions the world over. Widely available at newsstands and wine shops. Subscription is $40 per year; call 800/622.2062

Phone Book

Emergencies

Ambulance/Fire/Police 911

AAA, Emergency Road Service

Napa County:

Napa 253.2082

Calistoga, St. Helena, and Yountville ...963.5018

Sonoma County:

Santa Rosa, Healdsburg 523.1144

Sonoma, Glen Ellen 996.5208

Cloverdale 894.4988

Mendocino County:
Mendocino 937.3040

Lake County:
Lakeport 263.5088

Children's Emergency Services (to report child abuse; 24 hours) 800/422.4453

Handicapped Crisis Line (24 hours)..800/426.4263

Poison Control Center (24 hours)
Sonoma, Napa, and Mendocino.......800/523.2222
Lake County....................................800/342.9293

Sexual Assault Crisis Line
Napa County: 252.6227

Sonoma County:
Rape Crisis Center of Sonoma County
(24 hours)..545.7273

Mendocino/Lake counties:
Rape Crisis Hotline (24 hours).............462.4988
Youth Crisis Hotline (24 hours) 800/448.4663

Suicide Prevention (24 hours)
Napa 255.2555
Sonoma 800/833.3376
Mendocino/Lake counties 263.0160;
(evenings and weekends) 800/222.8220

Service/Referrals

Better Business Bureau
Napa 552.0186
Sonoma 577.0300

Dental Referral
Napa-Solano Dental Society 643.4870
Sonoma 575.7905
Redwood Empire Dental Society, Mendocino/
Lake 546.7275

Highway Patrol
Lake County 279.0103
Mendocino Coast 937.0808
Santa Rosa 576.2175
Ukiah 463.4717

Medical Referral Service
Physicians Referral Service, Napa 257.4004
Physicians Referral Service, Sonoma 544.2010
Physicians Referral Service, Mendocino/
Lake 462.1694

Road Conditions

Vallejo Highway Patrol (local only) 643.8421

California Highway Patrol 585.0326

Northern California Highway Patrol 462.0155

Time
....................POP.CORN (or 767 and any four digits)

Weather
San Francisco Bay Area 415/936.1212
Wine Country....................................415/364.7974

Visitor Information

American Youth Hostels
Marin County and Sacramento 415/331.2777
San Francisco 415/771.7277

Passport Information 415/744.4444

Traveler's Aid
San Francisco 415/255.2252
San Francisco Int'l Airport 415/877.0118
Oakland...510/444.6834

The Wine Institute
Information on the wine industry, including referrals to classes on related subjects. ♦ 425 Market St, Suite 1000, San Francisco CA 94105.
....415/512.0151

How to Read this Guide

WINE COUNTRY ACCESS® is arranged by region so you can see at a glance where you are and what is around you. The numbers next to the entries in the following chapters correspond to the numbers on the maps. The paragraphs are color-coded according to the kind of place described:

Restaurants/Clubs: Red	Hotels: Blue
Shops/ Outdoors: Green	Wineries/Sights: Black

Rating the Restaurants and Hotels

The restaurant ratings take into account the service, atmosphere, and uniqueness of the restaurant. An expensive restaurant doesn't necessarily ensure an enjoyable evening; however, a small, relatively unknown spot could have good food, professional service, and a lovely atmosphere. Therefore, on a purely subjective basis, stars are used to judge the overall dining value (see star ratings below). Keep in mind that the chefs and owners sometimes change, which can drastically affect the quality of a restaurant. The ratings in this book are based on information available at press time.

The price ratings, as categorized below, apply to restaurants and hotels. These figures describe general price-range relationships between other restaurants or hotels; they do not represent specific rates.

★ Good	$ The price is right
★★ Very good	$$ Reasonable
★★★ Excellent	$$$ Expensive
★★★★ Extraordinary	$$$$ A month's pay

Map Key

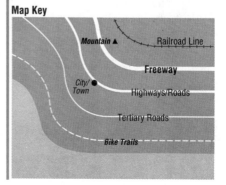

Napa Valley

The name of this verdant sliver of a valley, inhabited by six Indian tribes before white settlers arrived in the 1830s, comes from an Indian word meaning "plenty." Just over an hour north of San Francisco, the world-renowned wine-growing region is bounded by the Mayacmas Mountains to the west and the Vaca range to the east. It extends some 25 miles from San Pablo Bay to the foot of the extinct volcano Mount St. Helena to the north. Within these boundaries are some world-famous grape-growing districts: the Carneros (west of the town of Napa to the Mayacmas), Stag's Leap (east of Yountville), and the Rutherford Bench (a corridor of vineyards lying west of Hwy 29 between Yountville and St. Helena). Other small districts include Spring Mountain, Diamond Mountain, Howell Mountain, and Mount Veeder. The Napa Valley is an agricultural paradise, a ravishing landscape of gentle rolling hills, and an assortment of wineries that consistently muscle out their European counterparts in international competitions. Add to that a wealth of fine restaurants, intrigu-

Main Street Building, Napa

DRAWING BY KATHLEEN FITZGERALD

ing shops, sites of literary and historic interest, recreational opportunities galore—and you've got "plenty" indeed.

The tradition of winemaking in the Napa Valley goes back 150 years—a mere blink of the eye by European standards. In 1838 the trapper, explorer, and Napa Valley pioneer **George C. Yount** planted vines he obtained from **General Mariano Vallejo's** estate in Sonoma on part of the huge land grant he had received from the Mexican government. Yount produced his first wine in 1841; the grape was not the Chardonnay or the Cabernet Sauvignon the valley is known for today, but the Mission grape brought to Northern California by the Franciscan fathers in 1823.

By 1880 the wine business was booming; Napa Valley wines were poured in the best restaurants in San Francisco and New York. More than 10,000 acres were planted with vines and the number of wineries had quickly grown to an astonishing 175—together they produced the equivalent of one million cases of wine a year. The valley's pioneering winemakers, from France, Italy, and Germany, had laid the foundations for today's thriving wine industry, using grape varietals and skills borrowed from their homelands.

Now Napa's wines, particularly Chardonnay and Cabernet Sauvignon, are known and respected all over the world. The vineyards cover 32,000 acres and the valley boasts more than 200 wineries, ranging from tiny mom-and-pop establishments where the cellar is practically part of the house, to immense operations owned by corporations and holding companies. In recent years the international presence in the Napa Valley has grown. Some wineries are owned outright by Europen families and companies, while many others are joint ventures with European wineries.

As celebrated as it is, the Napa Valley, surprisingly, accounts for just five percent of the wine grapes harvested in all of California. The valley's wineries, for the most part, have made every effort to concentrate on quality over quantity. As a new generation of winemakers takes the helm, many of them trained at the School of Enology at the prestigious University of California at Davis, they continue to learn from each other, making improvements in both wine production techniques and viticulture.

In three decades, the Napa Valley has grown from a sleepy country outpost, a paradise enjoyed by the privileged few residents of the valley, to a prime vacation destination that attracts 1.5 million visitors each year. Driving along either of the valley's two main arteries, Hwy 29 or the Silverado Trail (one of California's most beautiful drives), you'll pass tractors chugging along at their own pace and trucks stacked with oak barrels from the forests of Burgundy or premium wines on their way to fine shops and restaurants. Sleek sports cars race along behind pick-ups, while bicyclists cling to the edge of the road.

Wineries vie with each other to attract visitors by creating lavishly appointed tasting rooms, award-winning architecture, informative tours, special tastings, displays on Napa Valley history, and world-class art collections. There is just as much friendly competition among the restaurants. Chefs here have developed a distinctive wine-country cuisine based on premium local ingredients and dishes carefully designed to showcase the wines. Elegant establishments such as the **Domaine Chandon Restaurant**, the **Auberge du Soleil**, and **The Restaurant at Meadowood Resort** rub shoulders with sassy bistros like **Mustards, Tra Vigne**, and **Brava Terrace**. And you can still find intimate restaurants where handcrafted personal cuisine is the rule, such as **The French Laundry** in Yountville or **Trilogy** in St. Helena, along with down-home spots like **The Diner** in Yountville.

One Napa Valley experience not to be missed is a wine-country picnic. You can collect the makings at a number of spots, including the granddaddy of the Bay Area gourmet shops, the **Oakville Grocery**, or **Tra Vigne's Cantinetta**. Many of the wineries provide picnic areas for their visitors; one of the best, **Chateau Montelena's** Chinese pagodas located on tiny islands in the middle of a small lake, require reservations. But spots along the Silverado Trail and parks in Yountville, St. Helena, and Calistoga, along with **Bothe-Napa Valley State Park** and the rugged **Robert Louis Stevenson State Park**, offer more secluded sites.

It's no secret that on many weekends, especially in the summer, Hwy 29, Napa Valley's main artery, is one big traffic jam. The truth of the matter is a few dozen of the prominent wineries along this road receive the majority of visitors. Some people never manage to get off the main drag, and most never make it to what the

Napa Valley

locals call the up-valley (the section of the valley north of St. Helena). To avoid the crowds, a good strategy is to head

north first and work your way south, cutting over to the parallel (and much more scenic) Silverado Trail whenever possible. If you want to visit popular wineries such as **Robert Mondavi, Inglenook, Christian Brothers,** and **Beringer**, plan a trip early in the day.

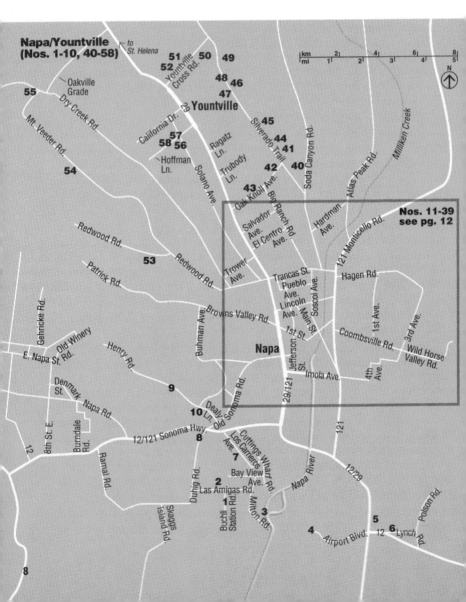

Many visitors try a different method of exploration and map out an itinerary by bicycle. You won't be able to cover as much territory, of course, but you'll experience the tranquil landscape close up, stopping along the way for winery visits and tastings. And then there is the rather controversial **Napa Valley Wine Train** (residents feared increased traffic and the circus-like atmosphere it would bring), which carries passengers in luxurious Pullman lounge cars; riders sip Napa Valley wines, enjoy an elegant meal, and view the region only from the windows of the passing train.

A recent Napa County ordinance meant to control development and tourism in the Valley limits drop-in public tours and tastings primarily to those wineries that were already doing so before 1991. Everyone else is restricted to tours and tastings *by appointment only*. But don't let this requirement dissuade you from visiting. By appointment means simply calling ahead. More than a hundred small wineries offer tours and tastings that are intimate and unrushed. Your tour guide may well be the winery owner or winemaker, and often the tour can be custom-tailored to your interests, perhaps including a vineyard walk or a barrel tasting of the newest vintage. Remember: for the best wine country experience, get off the beaten track.

1 Bouchaine Vineyards Perched on a hillside overlooking San Pablo Bay, this small, modernized winery tucked into an existing older building specializes in Carneros-district Pinot Noir and Chardonnay made by traditional Burgundian methods. They have also recently begun producing a small amount of Alsatian-style Gewürztraminer. The original wine estate at this site dates from 1899; Bouchaine was founded in 1980 and is now owned by **Gerret Copeland**. ◆ Tasting, sales, and tours by appt M-F 11AM-2PM. 1075 Buchli Station Rd, Napa. 252.9065

2 Acacia Winery A Carneros-district winery with a fine reputation for Chardonnay, especially from its Marina Vineyard. Also offers single-vineyard Pinot Noir, and a small amount of Merlot and Cabernet Sauvignon. ◆ Sales M-Sa 8AM-4:30PM; tasting and tours by appt. 2750 Las Amigas Rd, Napa. 226.9991

3 Napa Riverboat Company Tours Hop onboard for a two and one-half hour excursion down the Napa River to the Third Street Bridge and back on an original 19th-century steamboat. Three-hour Friday and Saturday night dinner cruises feature Dixieland and jazz bands; Sunday brunch cruises, too. ◆ Call for information on prices, departure times, and special charter programs. 1200 Milton Rd (Cuttings Wharf Rd) Napa Valley Marina. 226.2628

4 Bridgeford Flying Service Fly over the wine country in a Cessna Skyhawk or Centurion that seats one to five passengers for bird's-eye views of vineyards and historic wineries. The Napa tour heads north along one side of the valley as far as Calistoga, returning down the other side. An alternate coastal tour flies over the Golden Gate Bridge along the coast to Point Reyes, Bodega Bay, and Jenner, returning via the Russian River wine district and the Napa Valley. ◆ Tours by appt only. Napa County Airport. 2030 Airport Rd, Napa. Reservations required. 224.0887, 644.1658

5 Hakusan Sake Gardens It's ironic that the first wine-tasting room along Hwy 29 doesn't serve wine made from grapes, but sake, Japan's traditional rice wine. At this $21 million facility, a short video explains how their sake is made from the inner kernel of short-grained rice grown near Sacramento. It is followed by a tasting of warm and cold sake. Spend a quiet moment in the beautiful raked-sand Japanese gardens before heading up the valley. ◆ Tasting and sales daily 9AM-6PM. Hwy 29 and 12 East (entrance from N. Kelly Rd) Napa. 258.6160

6 Chardonnay Club Semi-private 18-hole championship golf course (5,300-7,150 yards, par 72, rated 73.5), rated 15th in the state by *California Golf* magazine. Golf shops, snack bar, and practice range. Reservations must be made at least a week in advance. ◆ Daily 7AM-3PM. 2555 Jamieson Canyon Rd (Hwy 12) Napa. 257.8950

The favorite grape of bootleggers during Prohibition was Alicante Bouschet because its thick skin could well withstand transportation.

Restaurants/Clubs: Red   **Hotels:** Blue
Shops/ ◆ Outdoors: Green   **Wineries/Sights:** Black

GARNET
1989
Carneros Pinot Noir

SAINTSBURY

PRODUCED AND BOTTLED BY SAINTSBURY
NAPA, CALIFORNIA, USA   ALCOHOL 12.9% BY VOLUME

7 Saintsbury Named in honor of the 19th-century wine connoisseur and writer **George Saintsbury**, who is best known to wine lovers

as the author of *Notes on a Cellar Book*, this Carneros-district winery is housed in a weathered redwood building. Owners **Richard Ward** and **David Graves** are dedicated to making Burgundian-style Pinot Noir and Chardonnay. The Chardonnay is fermented and aged in barrels coopered in France. They make two styles of Pinot Noir: the fresh and lively Garnet and the more classic Carneros Pinot Noir. All their wines are top-notch and sold at excellent prices. ♦ Tours by appt M-F 9AM-5PM. 1500 Los Carneros Ave, Napa. 252.0592

8 Domaine Carneros Founded in 1987 by the French champagne house **Taittinger**, Domaine Carneros is devoted to making sparkling wines by the traditional méthode champenoise. Managing director and winemaker **Eileen Crane** has extensive experience making

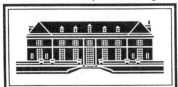

sparkling wine in California. Designed by **Thomas Faherty & Associates** of St. Helena, the massive winery was inspired by the **Château de la Marquetterie**, a historic 18th-century residence owned by the Taittinger family in Champagne. A grand cement staircase leads from the parking lot to the elegant reception and tasting room where visitors can relax with a glass of Domaine Carneros Brut at tables set with flowers. Downstairs is a gallery with views of the bottling line and fermentations, along with historical photos of the harvest in Champagne. On Friday mornings, they offer a sparkling wine and hors d'oeuvres tasting by reservation only. ♦ Admission. Tasting, sales, and tours daily 10:30AM-5:30PM, summer; 10:30AM-4:30PM, winter. 1240 Duhig Rd, Napa. 257.0101

9 Codorníu Napa Napa Valley's newest premium sparkling winery opened in September 1991. The wine and the dramatic $22 million winery bear the same name, Codorníu Napa, in honor of the Spanish owner, the **House of Codorníu**, which has been making wines in the

Catalán region of Spain for more than 400 years. Codorníu's ultra-modern winery, designed by Barcelona architect **Domingo Triay**, who also designed the firm's Raimat estate in Spain, fits snugly into its site at the foot of Miliken Peak. From a distance, it's hard to make out the modernistic structure, for Triay built the ecologically sound winery right into the hillside and covered the top with an earthen berm planted with drought-resistant California grasses to create the cool, stable conditions ideal for producing and storing fine quality sparkling wine. A series of terraces leads into the winery past columns and reflecting pools; and from the windows inside, a stunning panorama of the Carneros district unfolds. The winemaker is a young San Franciscan, **Janet Pagano**, who honed her skills at several other California wineries, including Domaine Mumm. Tours of the winery, which are designed to give an overview of méthode champenoise winemaking, are followed by a tasting of their first premium sparkling cuvée. ♦ Fee. Tasting and tours M-Th 10AM-5PM; F-Su 10AM-3PM. 1345 Henry Rd, Napa. 224.1668; fax 224.1672

10 Carneros Creek Winery A barn-like winery building just off Old Sonoma Rd marks this small Carneros-district producer. The emphasis is on Chardonnay and Pinot Noir, though they also make Cabernet Sauvignon and Merlot. A few picnic tables are set under a pergola (overhead trellis) twined with trumpetvines. ♦ Tasting and sales W-Su 9AM-5PM; tours by appt. 1285 Dealy Ln, Napa. 253.9463

Best Cellars

Some of the best wine tastings take place not at the wineries, but in the wine-country restaurants. Listed below are the restaurants with the best rosters of wines. This is where to look for those hard-to-find bottles, wines from vintners with a very limited production, and some older vintages.

All Seasons Café, Calistoga..........................942.9111

Ambrose Heath, Oakville.............................944.0766

Auberge du Soleil, Rutherford....................963.1211

California Café Bar & Grill, Yountville 944.2330

Domaine Chandon Restaurant, Yountville. 944.2892

Heritage House, Little River.........................937.5885

John Ash & Co., Santa Rosa 527.7687

Matisse, Santa Rosa 527.9797

The Restaurant at Meadowood Resort,
St. Helena...963.3646

Silverado Tavern, Calistoga 942.6725

Terra, St. Helena 963.8931

Trilogy, St. Helena.......................................963.5507

The first woman to found and build a winery in the Napa Valley was **Josephine Tychson**. Her first grape crush was near St. Helena in 1886.

Winemaking: From the Grape to the Bottle

There are almost as many methods for making wine as there are winemakers. And the differences in winemaking procedures can produce totally different wines—even when they're made from the same grapes. This basic chart outlines the major stages for making white and red wine.

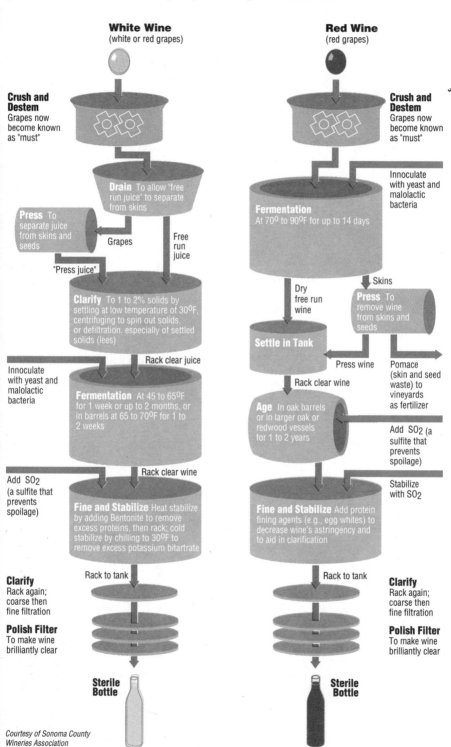

White Wine
(white or red grapes)

Red Wine
(red grapes)

Crush and Destem
Grapes now become known as "must"

Crush and Destem
Grapes now become known as "must"

Drain To allow "free run juice" to separate from skins

Innoculate with yeast and malolactic bacteria

Press To separate juice from skins and seeds

Grapes

Free run juice

Fermentation At 70° to 90°F for up to 14 days

"Press juice"

Clarify To 1 to 2% solids by settling at low temperature of 30°F, centrifuging to spin out solids, or defiltration, especially of settled solids (lees)

Dry free run wine

Skins

Press To remove wine from skins and seeds

Settle in Tank

Rack clear juice

Innoculate with yeast and malolactic bacteria

Fermentation At 45 to 65°F for 1 week or up to 2 months, or in barrels at 65 to 70°F for 1 to 2 weeks

Press wine

Pomace (skin and seed waste) to vineyards as fertilizer

Rack clear wine

Age In oak barrels or in larger oak or redwood vessels for 1 to 2 years

Add SO2 (a sulfite that prevents spoilage)

Add SO2 (a sulfite that prevents spoilage)

Rack clear wine

Stabilize with SO2

Fine and Stabilize Heat stabilize by adding Bentonite to remove excess proteins, then rack; cold stabilize by chilling to 30°F to remove excess potassium bitartrate

Fine and Stabilize Add protein fining agents (e.g., egg whites) to decrease wine's astringency and to aid in clarification

Clarify
Rack again; coarse then fine filtration

Rack to tank

Rack to tank

Clarify
Rack again; coarse then fine filtration

Polish Filter
To make wine brilliantly clear

Polish Filter
To make wine brilliantly clear

Sterile Bottle

Sterile Bottle

Courtesy of Sonoma County Wineries Association

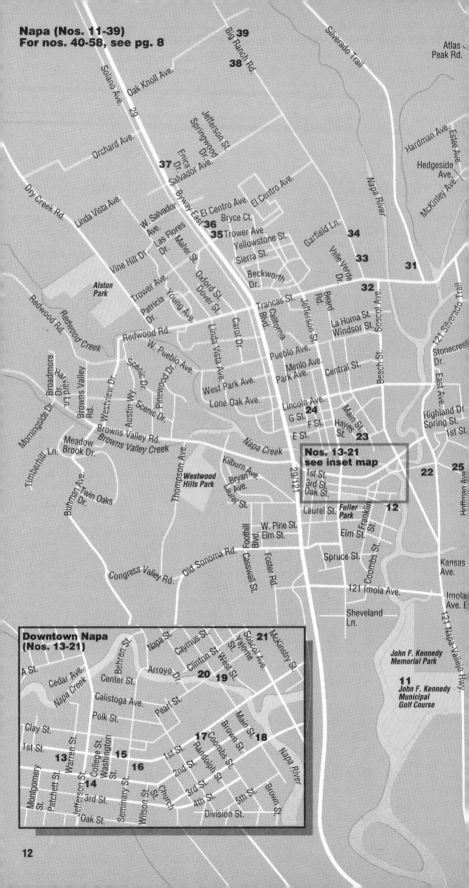

Napa (Nos. 11-39)
For nos. 40-58, see pg. 8

Atlas Peak Rd.

Big Ranch Rd.
39
38

Silverado Trail

Oak Knoll Ave.
Solano Ave.
29
Orchard Ave.

Jefferson St.
Springwood Dr.
Erica Dr.
Salvador Ave.
37

Dry Creek Rd.
Linda Vista Ave.

Byway East
W. Salvador Ave.
Las Flores Dr.
Maher St.
36
35
Bryce Ct.
El Centro Ave.
El Centro Ave.
Trower Ave.
Yellowstone St.
Sierra St.

Hardman Ave.
Estee Ave.
Hedgeside Ave.
McKinley Ave.

Garfield Ln.
34
33
31

Napa River

Vine Hill Dr.
Alston Park
Trower Ave.
Patricia Dr.
Oxford St.
Dover St.
Young Ave.
Beckworth Dr.

Valle Verde Dr.
Beard Rd.
32

121 Silverado Trail

Redwood Rd.
Redwood Creek
Redwood Rd.
W. Pueblo Ave.
Linda Vista Ave.
Carol Dr.
Trancas St.
California Blvd.
Jefferson St.
La Homa St.
Windsor St.
Stonecrest Dr.

Broadmore Dr.
Harr Dr.
Browns Valley Rd.
Westview Dr.
Scenic Dr.
Austin Wy.
Scenic Dr.
Pinewood Dr.
West Park Ave.
Lone Oak Ave.
Pueblo Ave.
Menlo Ave.
Park Ave.
Central St.
Beach St.
East Ave.
Highland Dr
Spring St.
1st St.

Morningside Dr.
Browns Valley Rd.
Browns Valley Rd.
Browns Valley Creek
Lincoln Ave.
G St.
24
F St.
E St.
Main St.
Hayes St.
23

Meadow Brook Dr.
Timberhill Ln.
Buhman Ave.
Twin Oaks Dr.
Thompson Ave.
Westwood Hills Park
Napa Creek
Kilburn Ave.
Bryan Ave.
Laurel St.
29/121
Nos. 13-21
see inset map
1st St.
3rd St.
Oak St.
22
25
Hoffman St.

Congress Valley Rd.
Old Sonoma Rd.
Foothill Blvd.
Casswall St.
Foster Rd.
W. Pine St.
Elm St.
Laurel St.
Fuller Park
Franklin St.
Elm St.
Spruce St.
Coombs St.
12
Kansas Ave.

121 Imola Ave.
Sheveland Ln.
Imola Ave. E.
121 Napa-Vallejo Hwy.

John F. Kennedy Memorial Park

11
John F. Kennedy Municipal Golf Course

Downtown Napa
(Nos. 13-21)

A St.
Cedar Ave.
Napa Creek
Behren St.
Center St.
Calistoga Ave.
Polk St.
Clay St.
1st St.
13
Warren St.
College St.
Washington St.
15
16
14
Jefferson St.
Seminary St.
3rd St.
Oak St.
Montgomery St.
Patchett St.
Napa St.
Caymus St.
Arroyo Dr.
Clinton St.
Soscol Ave.
Yajome St.
West St.
21
20
19
McKinstry St.
Pearl St.
Wilson St.
Church St.
1st St.
2nd St.
3rd St.
4th St.
Division St.
17
Randolph St.
Coombs St.
Brown St.
Main St.
18
5th St.
Brown St.
Napa River

12

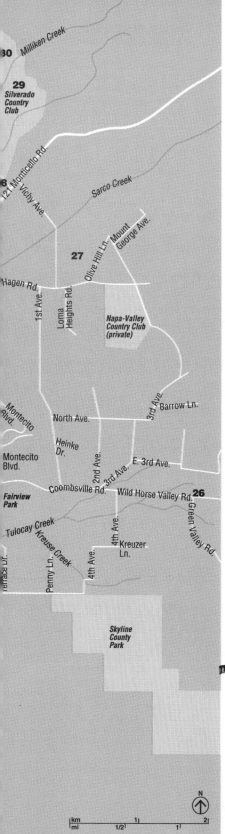

Napa

The city of Napa was founded by **Nathan Coombs**, a member of the infamous Bear Flag Party that declared independence from Mexico in 1845. Two years later Coombs surveyed Napa's original town site. The first building went up in 1848, but its owner rushed off to the gold fields to seek his fortune, returning disillusioned a year later to open the **Empire Saloon.** By the mid-19th century, the wine business was flourishing and a steamship line carried the valley's wines from Napa to San Francisco. Because of its location at the head of the Napa River, the city of Napa controlled the valley's trade for almost a century. Today it is a riverfront city of some 60,000 people with a rich heritage of Victorian domestic architecture. Stroll through the restored downtown district, passing Victorian mansions, a Gothic-style church, historic bridges, and 19th-century commercial buildings. Five self-guided walking tours of Napa's historic downtown are available for a nominal fee through the **Napa Chamber of Commerce.** Next on the books for Napa: development of the Napa River, with plans for public docks, inlets, walking paths, and restaurants overlooking the riverbanks.

Fourth Street Building, Napa
DRAWING BY KATHLEEN FITZGERALD

Short of uprooting the vines, burning every trace of them, and sterilizing the soil, there was no cure for the root louse phylloxera that devastated much of the world's vineyards in the late 19th century. Scientists finally discovered that a certain type of American rootstock, *vitis riparia,* was resistant to the pest, whereas the European *vitis vinifera* was not. And so the solution was to graft the European grape varieties onto the disease-resisitant American rootstock. This is still the practice today.

11 **John F. Kennedy Municipal Golf Course** A public 18-hole championship golf course (6,400 yards, par 72, rated 71.5). Driving range, pro shop, rental clubs and carts, plus coffee shop and snack bar. Reservations can be made a week in advance or every day before 1PM; after that, play is on a first-come, first-serve basis. No spectators. ♦ Daily dawn-dusk. Kennedy Park, 2295 Streblow Dr (Hwy 221) Napa. 255.4333

"Not only does one drink wine, but one inhales it, one looks at it, one tastes it, one swallows it. . .and one talks about it." **King Edward VII**

12 **Churchill Manor** $$ This spectacular three-story Colonial Revival-style mansion with stately columns and a spacious veranda was built in 1889 for the Napa banker **Edward S. Churchill** and is listed in the National Historic Register. Now an elegant B&B run by innkeeper **Joanna Guidotti**—who planted 7,600 bulbs on the beautifully manicured grounds—it has 10 guest rooms, all with private baths. The largest is Edward's room, the original master bedroom, with a carved French armoire and king-sized bed, plus a fireplace framed with gold-laced tiles. A full breakfast (fruit tray, fresh-squeezed orange

Making the Most of Your Winery Visits

The number of wineries in Napa or Sonoma can be daunting to the first-time visitor. From the highway, the names of famous wineries whiz by and it's natural to want to stop at all of them, but too many visits in one day—particularly too many tours—can leave you exhausted and ready to head for the nearest beer. You should take one or two tours just to get the gist of how wine is made. But more than that and the rows of stainless-steel fermentation tanks, presses, and bottling lines quickly become redundant.

In choosing an itinerary, keep in mind that some wineries present information better than others. For example, **Robert Mondavi's** tours always include well-thought-out educational components, and the winery offers several different tours, depending on your interests. **St. Supéry** has a good self-guided tour that presents information on soil types and pruning methods. And it's definitely worth visiting one of the historic wineries such as **Beringer** or **Buena Vista** to get a glimpse of 19th-century winemaking practices.

However, the focus of most visits should be tasting the wines. The general procedure is to start with the simplest white wines (such as Chenin Blanc and Colombard) and move up the ladder through the more complex Sauvignon Blanc and Chardonnay to the red wines, finishing with a dessert wine. Sampling all of them may be too much for one set of tastebuds; your palate can quickly become fatigued and no longer able to distinguish the differences. And as a driver, you risk becoming a potential hazard on the highway.

The best strategy is to limit your winery visits to only a few per day and to choose the wines you'd like to taste rather than opting to sample the winery's entire lineup. Another essential is to spit out the wine after you've had a chance to let it register on your palate, or to pour out the remaining sample after you've taken a sip (special buckets are usually provided for this purpose). These are practices the professionals engage in all the time, so be assured, no one will be offended by such actions.

If you're hoping to find bargain prices at the wineries, you'll most likely be disappointed. Wineries don't want to compete against the shops that sell their wines, so prices at the winery are generally higher than in the stores. The only time it's worth buying wines from the source is if the winery is offering selections from their "library"— that is, older vintages that are no longer available in wine shops. Also, some producers have one or two wines made in such limited quantities that they are sold only at the tasting room.

There is absolutely no obligation to buy a bottle of wine when you visit a tasting room. The rooms are there to promote brand recognition, not push bottles; this is evident from the number of non-wine-related objects bearing the name and logo of the winery that are for sale in many tasting rooms: T-shirts, baseball hats, umbrellas, refrigerator magnets, and pasta sauces—you name it.

A good tactic for visiting the wine country is to include a mix of large and small wineries in your itinerary and to set an easy pace (you're here to relax, remember?). If you like Chardonnay, for example, you might want to organize your itinerary around top Chardonnay estates. Your hotel concierge or innkeeper should be able to advise you, but you'll have to carefully assess any suggestions: Not everybody living in the wine country is well informed about wine. Before you begin planning your trip, it's always a good idea to ask a wine merchant you know and trust what wineries and estates he or she suggests visiting. Read up on the latest new wineries in wine magazines such as *The Wine Spectator,* study the wine column in your local newspaper, and start buying the Wednesday edition of *The New York Times* for **Frank Prial's** informative column written with the layperson in mind.

If you really have a strong interest in wine, a visit to a small premium winery that requires an appointment may be the highlight of your tour, since you'll get the winery's story straight from the source, often from the winemaker who has created the wine. Understandably, small wineries that have no tasting-room staff or even formal tasting rooms have a limited amount of time to receive visitors, but it doesn't hurt to ask.

Finally, keep in mind that you don't have to do all your tastings at the wineries. You can take a bottle on a picnic or visit one of the local restaurants to try a fine wine with food—which, after all, is the way wine is supposed to be enjoyed.

juice, homemade blueberry muffins or crois-sants, and a quiche or egg dish, plus herb teas and coffees) and afternoon tastings of Napa Valley wines take place in the light-drenched solarium. Bicycles, including two tandems, and croquet equipment are availa-ble for guests. ♦ 485 Brown St (Oak-Laurel Sts) Napa. 253.7733

13 Beazley House $$ In the heart of a fine old neighborhood of dignified homes and tree-lined streets, this Colonial Revival house has had few owners since it was built in 1902, helping to maintain its original character and half-acre grounds. There are 10 large

guest rooms with high ceilings, comfortable period furnishings, and handmade quilts. Five of the rooms are in the main house and the rest are in the newly built carriage house at the rear. All have private baths. The master bedroom in the main house and several rooms in the carriage house have fireplaces and Jacuzzis. The **West Loft,** a favorite with many guests, features a 15-1/2 foot cathedral ceiling and a stained-glass window with a grape motif over the king-sized bed. Innkeepers **Jim** and **Carol Beazley** will sit down with guests to map out a customized itinerary of the best the Napa Valley has to offer. Breakfast here includes fresh fruits, home-baked muffins, and a special Beazley House coffee blend sold at the **Napa Valley Coffee Roasting Company**. No smoking; no children under 12. ♦ 1910 First St (Warren-Seymour Sts) Napa. 257.1649

14 La Boucane ★★$$$ In a fine old house with burgundy awnings, **Jacques Mokrani** offers classic French cuisine at both lunch and dinner. Specialties range from prawns provençale (sautéed with cognac, tomatoes, lemon, and garlic) and salmon poached in champagne and cream to sweetbreads in a port sauce and duck à l'orange. For dessert, try the strawberries in red wine or the soufflé glacé praline. With its flowered wallpaper, beautifully set tables, and dark bistro chairs, La Boucane feels like a French provincial restaurant set down in the California wine country. ♦ M-Sa 5:30-10PM. Closed Jan. 1778 Second St (Jefferson-College Sts) Napa. 253.1177

Restaurants/Clubs: Red   Hotels: Blue
Shops/ ♥ Outdoors: Green
          Wineries/Sights: Black

15 Napa Chamber of Commerce Represents both Napa County and Napa Valley and delights in making information available to visitors on wineries, hotels, restaurants, and other activities. Ask for copies of the self-guided walking tours of old Napa prepared by the Napa Landmarks organization. ♦ Nominal fee for walking tour. 1556 First St (School-Seminary Sts) or write to Box 636, Napa 94557. 226.7455

16 Napa Valley Conference and Visitors Bureau This new office provides informa-tion on restaurants, wineries, lodging, attrac-tions, and activities, plus transportation and travel in the Napa Valley. ♦ M-F 9AM-5PM.

1556 First St (School-Seminary Sts) Suite 103, Napa. 226.7459

17 Napa County Historical Society Conceived on a pioneer picnic at the Old Bale Mill in 1948, the historical society has a library of books on Napa Valley history, manuscripts,

and hundreds of old photographs of pioneer settlers and historical sites, plus an archive of historic newspaper clippings. Housed in the **Goodman Library Building,** designed by the local architect **Luther M. Turton** at the turn of the century, it also includes a small museum of valley artifacts. Pick up their inexpensive short guide to California Historic Landmarks of Napa County, along with notecards and posters of noteworthy sites. ♦ Tu, Th noon-4PM. Goodman Library Building, 1219 First St (Randolph-Coombs Sts) Napa. 224.1739

18 Veterans Memorial Park This grassy slope overlooking the Napa River at the Third Street Bridge makes an impromptu city picnic spot. ♦ Main St (Second-Third Sts) Napa

18 Willett's Brewing Co.

★$$ Nibble on quesadillas, prawns in lemon cayenne sauce, or fried calamari with a serrano chile sauce as you sample the beer and ale brewed at this riverfront brew pub. After a day of wine tasting, a cool glass of Tail Waggin' Ale or Old Magnolia Stout is a refreshing change,

Napa

especially enjoyed at an outdoor table overlooking the Napa River. The menu, which is offered all day, also includes salads, pizzas, burgers, and beer-cured baby back ribs. Entrées range from grilled chicken breast marinated in tequila and lime juice, to chicken fajitas and German-style sausages steamed in beer and served with sauerkraut, braised red cabbage, and potato pancakes. They also make their own ale bread. ♦ M-Sa 11:30AM-10PM. 902 Main St (First-Second Sts) Napa. 258.2337

18 Fine Aromas A small cafe offering a pastry case of luscious treats, sandwiches, fine teas, coffee, and espresso drinks. ♦ M-Sa 7AM-6PM. 912 Main St (First-Second Sts) Napa. 226.1031

18 Napa Valley Coffee Roasting Company Established in 1985, this establishment, owned by partners **Denise Fox** and **Leon Sange,** is housed in a beautifully restored brick building in downtown Napa. The cozy space is decorated with old-time coffee tins, signs, and other memorabilia. Faithful patrons settle in at marble bistro tables to enjoy an espresso or a cappuccino made from freshly roasted beans. The roaster is right in the store; sacks of green coffee beans imported from plantations all over the world lean against it waiting their turn. In addition to espresso drinks and the house coffee, which changes several times throughout the day so you can sample different types, they have a stash of freshly baked goodies from local bakeries: blueberry muffins, dynamite chocolate-coconut macaroons, lemon poppy-seed cake, and, sometimes, crunchy biscotti to dip into your coffee Italian-style. ♦ Daily 7AM-6PM. 948 Main St (First-Second Sts) Napa. 224.2233

19 Napa County Landmarks, Inc. The city of Napa has a rich heritage of carefully restored historic buildings. Self-guided Landmark Walks explore the City Hall and the Old Courthouse, along with well-preserved Victorian neighborhoods. Maps for these self-guided tours in Napa as well as Yountville, St.

Helena, and Calistoga are available here and at the Napa Chamber of Commerce for a nominal fee. The organization offers guided walks through Napa neighborhoods for a small charge on Sunday from 1:30-3PM, April through September; refreshments are served afterwards. ♦ M, W, F 9AM-1PM. 1144 Main St (First-Pearl Sts) or write to Box 702, Napa 94559. 255.1836

19 Napa Valley Opera House The Italianate-style late 19th-century Napa Opera House, designed by architects **Joseph** and **Samuel Newson** and **Ira Gilchrist,** is one of the last second-story theaters left in California. A City of Napa Landmark, it is listed on the National Register of Historic Places. Built in 1879, it

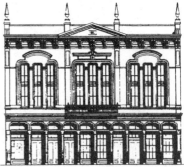

opened in 1880 with a performance of *HMS Pinafore*, but since "opera house" at that time was synonymous with a vaudeville hall, minstral shows, political rallies, and dog-and-pony shows also put in their appearances. The opera house is now undergoing extensive renovation, with plans calling for a 500-seat multi-disciplinary theater and an exhibition hall/gallery downstairs. The gallery is slated to open May 1992, and the restored theater in late 1993. ♦ 1018 Main St (First-Pearl Sts) Napa. 226.7372

20 Witter's Tea & Coffee Co. A friendly shop offering well-made coffee and espresso drinks. Plan your wine-country trip seated at one of the tables made from French oak barrels once used in valley wineries. Their coffee beans come from the quality San Francisco roaster, **Mountanos Bros**. ♦ M-Sa 9AM-5:30PM. 1202 Main St (Pearl-Clinton Sts) Napa. 226.2044

21 Napa Valley Wine Train Napa Valley's answer to the Orient Express barely made it out of the station, as it was fought by many locals who feared the traffic jams and carnival-like atmosphere it might engender. The train finally got underway in September 1989, and there are now three excursions daily. Passengers do not leave the train during the three-hour ride, but relax in luxurious Pullman lounge cars and dining cars replete with etched glass, fine fabrics, shiny brass, and mahogany. You can board for a champagne brunch, lunch, or dinner run, with both fixed-price menus and à la carte items. A good selection of Napa Valley wines are available during the trip. Be forewarned: riding the wine train will not win you favor in the eyes of many locals. Call for timetables, rates, and reservations. No smoking on board. Back at the station, their shop stocks more than 200 Napa Valley wines, which they'll gladly ship anywhere in the US. ♦ Daily excursions. Wine shop is generally open daily 9:30AM-noon, 2:30-3:30PM, 4-6PM (whenever trains are leaving or arriving) 1275 McKinstry St (Soscol Ave-First St) Napa. Reservations required. 253.2111, 800/427.4124

Within the Napa Valley Train Station:

Galleria dei Gigli Printmakers **Ruggero** and **Gina Gigli**, known throughout the Napa Valley for their wine etchings, have opened a gallery to showcase local artists in the lobby of the Napa Valley Train Station. The Giglis also have a working studio in their gallery. As passengers wait to board the Wine Train, they can watch Ruggero ink metal plates etched by Gina and print the limited-edition etchings. ♦ Daily 10AM-6PM. 226.5466

22 Napa Fairgrounds The Spring Fair in May features a fiddling contest, 4-H animal husbandry exhibitions, Highland dancers, a high school rodeo, a horse show, Renaissance games for children, a demolition derby, and a children's circus.

The five-day Napa Town & County Fair held here every August ranks among the best in the country, with a destruction derby, a rodeo, live entertainment, and building after building of floral, arts-and-crafts, and, of course, baking and jam exhibits—all that good country stuff, plus a livestock and animal exhibit. The highlight is the wine tasting where you can sample libations from almost every Napa Valley producer. ♦ 575 Third St (Silverado Trail) Napa. 253.4900

23 Hennessey House Bed & Breakfast $$ Formerly the residence of a local physician, this Eastlake Queen Anne Victorian is on the National Register of Historic Places, and is run as a gracious B&B by **Laurianne Delay** and **Andrea Weinstein**, who ran away from New York's Wall Street to Napa's Main Street in late 1990. It has nine rooms, each with private baths, queen-sized beds with old-world featherbeds and quilts, period antiques, and many other details of Victorian comfort and elegance. The four large rooms in the carriage house feature whirlpool tubs; some have fireplaces or private patios. An old-fashioned country breakfast (homemade granola and yogurt, fruit, and a hot entrée such as pancakes, baked eggs, or French toast) is served in the dining room, with its rare, hand-painted, stamped-tin ceiling. No smoking; no children under 14. ♦ 1727 Main St (Yount-Jackson Sts) Napa. 226.3774

24 Arbor Guest House $$ This white-frame home built in 1906 makes for a charming B&B, with three guest rooms in the main house and two in the restored carriage house out back. All have private baths and queen-sized beds with handmade quilts and graceful

period furnishings; three rooms also have fireplaces. In the main house, **Winter Haven** features a two-person spa in the corner, velvet Victorian chairs pulled up to the fireplace, and an Amish quilt on the bed. In the carriage house, **Rose's Bower** has a carved mahogany bed, ribboned wallpaper, cut-glass lamps, and rose-patterned French fireside chairs by the hearth. Enjoy breakfast (homemade scones or coffee cake, a baked egg dish, and fruit) in the garden, where a walkway twined with lavender trumpet vines leads from the main house to the carriage house. No smoking; no children under 10. ♦ 1436 G St (York-Marin Sts) Napa. 252.8144

25 Tulocay Winery A good small producer of rich and intense Cabernet Sauvignon, plus Chardonnay and Pinot Noir. The winery is adjacent to the family home and so small they have the same telephone number for both. ♦ Sales, tasting, and tours by appt only. 1426 Coombsville Rd, Napa. 255.4064

26 Wild Horse Valley Ranch Pack up your picnic lunch and go horseback riding at Wild Horse Valley Ranch. The well-equipped horseback riding facility not only boasts more than 50 miles of trails, it also has a race track, a polo field, and a cross-country jumping course. Classes for beginning and advanced riders are available. Three-and-a-half-hour trail rides are offered mornings and afternoons; overnight rides are occasionally scheduled. ♦ Wild Horse Valley Rd (end of Coombsville Rd) Napa (20 miles SE of town on Hwy 121) 224.0727

27 John's Rose Garden Allow at least an hour to visit **John Dallas'** garden and nursery, with more than 500 kinds of roses, many of them old varieties. The best time to visit is in May and June when most roses are in full bloom. ♦ Daily by appt 10AM-4PM. 1020 Mt. George Ave (Olive Hill Ln) Napa. 224.8002

Restaurants/Clubs: Red   **Hotels:** Blue
Shops/ ♥ Outdoors: Green   **Wineries/Sights:** Black

17

Napa

28 Quail Ridge The ivy-covered, hand-hewn stone buildings date from the late 19th century, when the winery was known as **Hedgeside Winery** and owned by California legislator **Morris M. Estee.** Today Quail Ridge is known for its barrel-fermented Chardonnay, Sauvignon Blanc, Cabernet Sauvignon, and Merlot. The winemaker is **Elaine Wellesley**. Their wines are also available for tasting at **Christian Brothers Greystone Cellars**. ♦ Tasting and tours by appt. 1055 Atlas Peak Rd, Napa. 257.1712

29 Silverado Country Club $$$$ An extensive luxury resort complex and country club now occupies the 1,200-acre estate purchased in 1869 by Civil War General and US Senator **John Miller**. His imposing mansion (built around an old adobe house) has a new life as the resort's clubhouse, and from the back terrace offers views of huge oak trees, palms, and the surrounding hills and mountains.

Clusters of studios and one-, two- and three-bedroom apartments (275 total) designed with privacy in mind are grouped around eight swimming pools and garden areas. The most popular units are on the clubhouse side, an easy walk to the tennis courts, clubhouse, and golf courses, while **Oak Creek East,** the newest area, is the most secluded. The rental units are individually owned by members but furnished according to club guidelines, with contemporary furniture, private baths, deck furniture, and full kitchens. They feel just like home—if home is a cushy condo with room service.

The club is a paradise for golf and tennis buffs. Its two challenging 18-hole championship golf courses designed by **Robert Trent Jones Jr.** are among the best in the country, and the club's 20 plexipaved tennis courts—the largest complex in northern California—make it one of the nation's top ten tennis facilities. An added bonus: head concierge **Laurie**

Gordon is a native and knows the area as only an insider could. ♦ Deluxe ♦ 1600 Atlas Peak Rd, Napa. 257.0200, 800/227.1117

Within the Silverado Country Club:

Vintner's Court ★★$$$$ This formal restaurant has a grand dining room featuring an oversized chandelier, potted palms, and a dramatic white grand piano. The walls are lined with wine lockers where prominent Napa Valley vintners stash their private reserves. Start with one of the simple appetizers, such as grilled marinated vegetables with buffalo mozzarella or cold poached asparagus and belgian endive. Then move on to an entrée, which might include grilled ahi tuna with a macadamia nut-cilantro pesto, and chicken breast stuffed with goat cheese, chorizo sausage, and anaheim chile, or pork tenderloin topped with a raspberry-peppercorn sauce. The menu reads like textbook California cuisine, but all too often something gets lost in the translation from concept to table. If you're splurging on a bottle of top California red, play it safe and stick with the herb-encrusted rack of lamb, mixed grill, or mesquite-grilled New York steak. Friday night is popular for the elaborate seafood buffet. ♦ California/French ♦ W-Sa 6:30-10PM; Su 10AM 2:30PM. Reservations recommended. 257.0200 ext 5304

Royal Oak Restaurant ★$$$ An old-fashioned steak and seafood house complete with antlers that features an open kitchen where cooks throw broiled prawns, swordfish, salmon, extra-thick Porterhouse steaks, and triple-cut lamb chops on the grill. The steaks and seafood are fine, but the side dishes disappoint (though the potato skin fad peaked years ago, they still have them on the menu, along with French onion soup), and the desserts seem designed for kids with a sweet tooth rather than adults on a night out. ♦ American ♦ Daily 6-10PM. Reservations recommended. 257.0200 ext 5363

Silverado Bar & Grill ★$ The best bet at the club is this casual restaurant, which serves breakfast all day long, plus burgers and salads. If you want the classic club sandwich, they know how to do it. ♦ American ♦ Daily 6:30AM-4:30PM. 257.0200

30 William Hill Winery This Napa winery, founded in 1974, has consistently made well-crafted wines, and produces both regular and reserve bottlings of Chardonnay and Cabernet Sauvignon. With the 1989 vintage, the winery began producing Pinot Noir and Chardonnay from grapes grown in Oregon. ♦ Tasting and sales by appt only. 1761 Atlas Peak Rd (about 1/2 mile N of Silverado Country Club) Napa. 224.6565

31 Hoffman Farm Pick your own organically grown boysenberries, pears, prunes, plums, table grapes, and walnuts in season. ♦ 8AM-dusk, Aug-Oct. 2125 Silverado Trail (Trancas St) Napa. 226.8938

La Residence Country Inn

32 Von Uhlit Ranch Harvest your own apples, pears, prunes, pumpkins, almonds, and walnuts in season. Also offers grapevine wreaths and fresh and dried flowers. ♦ Daily noon-4PM. 3011 Soscol Ave (Trancas St) Napa. 226.2844

33 Bucher Ranch Do-it-yourself Christmas trees: choose and cut Douglas fir and Scotch pine. ♦ Daily 9AM-dusk, Dec only. 2106 Big Ranch Rd, Napa. 224.5354

34 Napa Valley Christmas Tree Farm More Christmas trees to cut yourself: Douglas fir, Scotch pine, Monterey pine, pre-cut Noble fir, Silver Tip fir, and White fir. ♦ Daily 10AM-dusk, Nov-24 Dec; tours by appt. 2134 Big Ranch Rd, Napa. 252.1000

35 The John Muir Inn $$ Contemporary inn at a busy crossroads on Hwy 29 at the south end of the Napa Valley. The 59 guest rooms have modern decor, cable TVs, and private baths (some with whirlpool spas). Relax in the swimming pool and hot tub after the day's excursion. Continental breakfast. ♦ 1998 Trower Ave (at Hwy 29) Napa. 257.7220, 800/522.8999

36 Bryan's Napa Valley Cyclery Rent your wheels here: 15-speed mountain-style ATBs (all-terrain bikes), 21-speed touring bikes and tandems, plus burly trailers that will carry two children and gear. Delivery and one-way rentals available, too. The shop also offers leisurely treks with **Napa Valley Bike Tours** that cater to beginner and recreational riders as well as experienced cyclists. Tours include rental of a mountain-style bicycle and helmet, a catered picnic overlooking the valley, and a support van to carry wine purchases or too-pooped-to-pedal riders. Led by tour director **Lori Townsend,** the 9AM-4PM bike excursion covers nearly 25 miles of the Silverado Trail, stopping off at four wineries along the way for tours and tasting. Reservations required. ♦ M-Sa 9AM-6PM; Su 10AM-5PM. 4080 Byway East (off Hwy 29 at Trower Ave) Napa. 255.3377

37 La Residence Country Inn $$$ A country inn with 20 rooms on a two-acre estate just off Hwy 29. The 1870 Gothic Revival mansion has

Napa

nine rooms with private or shared baths. All are handsomely furnished in period American antiques, with patterned wallpaper, sweeping drapes, and queen-sized beds; some rooms, such as No. Six, have fireplaces and entrances onto the second-floor veranda. The remainder of the rooms are in Cabernet Hall, a new building styled after a French barn. These airy, spacious rooms are comfortably furnished with French and English pine antiques and queen-sized beds and designer prints, such as **Laura Ashley** and **Pierre Deux**. The large swimming pool between the two buildings is flanked by an arbor and a gazebo twined with wisteria. Guests sit down to a full breakfast (orange juice, a fresh fruit course, and an entrée such as French toast with berries and jam or scrambled eggs served with caramel nut rolls) in the inn's French country-style dining room. ♦ 4066 St. Helena Hwy, Napa. 253.0337

37 Table 29 $$$ This new restaurant (too new to give a star rating) may prove to be one of the valley's best. Partners **Jonathan Waxman** and **Steven Singer** bring a unique perspective to their venture. Waxman is one of the country's most talented chefs; he worked at **Michael's** in Santa Monica and later opened New York's **Jams** and **Bud's,** along with a Jams in London. He is one of the few chefs who has had a longtime interest in wine, and his eclectic cooking always incorporates the best local ingredients available. Singer owns **Singer & Foy,** San Francisco's savvy wine shop, and has put together an extensive wine list that includes many bottles from his personal cellar and a list of more than 250 labels from around the world. In addition to wine, the duo plans to focus on seafood, grilling, and deep-frying—always with an inventive twist. The menu will change daily, and, like the food, the setting is casual, yet sophisticated. The light, airy space features a terracotta tile floor, rustic plastered walls, and maple tables. The marble-topped bar should be a great spot to relax with a glass of wine and an appetizer. ♦ American/Eclectic ♦ Daily 11:30AM-10:30PM. 4110 St. Helena Hwy, Napa. 224.3300

Restaurants/Clubs: Red   Hotels: Blue
Shops/ ♣ Outdoors: Green   Wineries/Sights: Black

38 Domaine Montreux Vintage sparkling wine from an establishment founded in 1983 by a group of prominent Napa Valley vintners. Their 32-acre vineyard is planted with 40 percent Chardonnay and 60 percent Pinot Noir, grown in the proportion these premium grapes will be used in the cuvée blend. Domaine's first release was the 1983 Napa Valley Brut. ♦ Sales and tours by appt. 4101 Big Ranch Rd (near Oak Knoll Ave) Napa. 252.9380

39 Monticello Cellars Virginian **Jay Corley** pays tribute to **Thomas Jefferson,** a great lover of wines, at this brick replica of his famous estate. Jefferson would certainly have appreciated the wines, especially the two dis-

Napa

tinguished Cabernet Sauvignons—Jefferson Ranch and Corley Reserve. Corley also makes an excellent Chardonnay. The tasting room sells books about Jefferson, Monticello, and the former President's travels through the French wine country. Visitors can picnic at several tables set out on a lawn beside the Jefferson House. ♦ Fee. Tasting, sales, and tours daily 10AM-4:30PM. 4242 Big Ranch Rd, Napa. 253.2802

40 Altamura Winery and Vineyards A tiny winery concentrating on handcrafted Chardonnay since its founding in 1985. Vintner **Frank Altamura,** a Napa Valley native who picked up his winemaking skills at Caymus Vineyards, has recently introduced a Cabernet Sauvignon. ♦ Tasting and tours by appt daily 10AM-4PM. 4240 Silverado Trail, Napa. 253.2000

41 Signorello Vineyards Owned by San Francisco native **Raymond E. Signorello,** this small winery in the Stag's Leap district (east of Yountville) produces Chardonnay and Sauvignon Blanc, along with limited quantities of Cabernet, Pinot Noir, Merlot, and the white Rhône variety, Viognier. ♦ Tasting and tours by appt only. 4500 Silverado Trail, Napa. 255.5990

42 The Oak Knoll Inn $$$ This luxurious, well-run B&B is set amidst 600 acres of Chardonnay vines. Built of field stones collected from nearby vineyards, the impressive French country-style inn has three spacious rooms with high wooden ceilings, lush carpeting, and king-sized beds. Each has a full fireplace, with a comfortable sofa pulled up in front, and a private bath tiled in granite. Tall French doors open onto a broad wooden veranda with a view of the vineyards and the mountainous Stag's Leap district beyond. To make this wine-country retreat even more appealing, there is a large outdoor pool (unheated in winter), an outdoor Jacuzzi, and a gazebo for poolside picnics. Another nice touch is the croquet setup on the front lawn. A full breakfast (juice, home-baked pastries, an egg dish or quiche, fresh fruit, and coffee) is served on the veranda or in your room. Innkeepers **Jan** and **Tom Bird** enjoy planning two- or three-day itineraries for guests, which include winery visits, spas, horseback riding, bicycling, and glider rides. Discuss your interests with them when you call to reserve. ♦ 2200 E. Oak Knoll Ave, Yountville. 255.2200

43 Trefethen Vineyards Built in 1886, the tall, rust-colored winery building, shaded by centuries-old oak trees, is the last example of a three-level gravity-flow winery in California built entirely of wood. The Trefethen family, who restored the vineyards and winery in the early seventies, has set up an outdoor exhibition of antique farm equipment near the building. All the wines, including a fine oaky Chardonnay and well-made Cabernet, Pinot Noir, and Riesling, are produced from grapes grown exclusively on this 600-acre estate at the cool southern end of the Napa Valley. Special Library Selections of older vintages are sometimes available. For everyday drinking, the Eschol Red and Eschol White are always good values. ♦ Daily 10AM-4:30PM; tours by appt. 1160 Oak Knoll Ave, Napa. 255.7700

44 Chimney Rock Golf Course Privately owned nine-hole golf course surrounded by vineyards; it can also be played as an 18-hole course. Par 36. ♦ Daily 6:30AM-dusk. Open to the public; reservations recommended. 5320 Silverado Trail, Napa. 255.3363

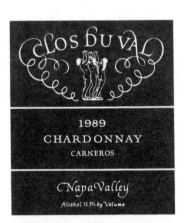

45 Clos du Val Winery Known for its Cabernet Sauvignon (especially the reserve), a velvety Merlot, and graceful Zinfandel, Clos du Val has had a French winemaker, **Bernard Portet,** at the helm since its founding in 1972. Portet grew up at Château Lafite Rothschild in Bordeaux, where his father was cellarmaster, and successfully combines Bordeaux tradition with California technological innovation. The tasting-room staff is friendly and personable. An added attraction: the series of witty wine-related postcards and posters on wine themes by artist **Ronald Searle.** Relax at the picnic tables under old oak trees. ♦ Tasting and sales daily 10AM-4PM; tours by appt. 5330 Silverado Trail, Napa. 252.6711

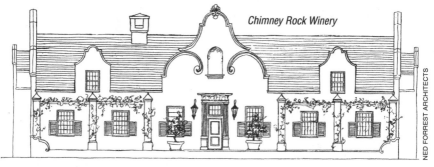

Chimney Rock Winery

NED FORREST ARCHITECTS

45 Chimney Rock Winery After decades in the international soft drink and hotel business, **Hack** and **Stella Wilson** decided to become Napa Valley vintners and in 1980 planted nine of the 18 holes of the Chimney Rock golf course, which just happened to be on prime vineyard land. Nestled in a grove of poplar trees, the distinctive Cape Dutch architecture of the hospitality center and winery features gracefully curving arched gables and steep roofs. The frieze of Ganymede (cupbearer to Zeus) adorning the cellars is a copy of the original created by 18th-century German-born sculptor **Antón Anreith**. Sculptor **Michael Casey,** resident artist for the California State Capital restoration in Sacramento, recreated the frieze here. The winery produces a supple Bordeaux-style Cabernet and a barrel-fermented Chardonnay, as well as a Fumé Blanc. ♦ Fee. Tasting and sales daily 10AM-4PM; tours 11AM-2PM by appt. 5350 Silverado Trail, Napa. 257.2641

46 Stag's Leap Wine Cellars In the now-famous Paris tasting of 1976, California wines were participants in a blind tasting with top French wines. Much to the French tasters' chagrin, the wine that won out over all the pedigreed Bordeaux was a California wine—the '73 Cabernet Sauvignon from Stag's Leap Wine Cellars, a winery founded in 1972. Vintners **Warren** and **Barbara Winiarski** have continued to consistently produce world-class Cabernets; their Cask 23 is among the most coveted and expensive California wines. They also make Chardonnay, Johannisberg Riesling, Sauvignon Blanc, Petite Sirah, and Merlot. The tasting room often has some older vintages for sale. Their lovely winery is set in a terraced hillside sheltered by trees. The new cellar next door was completed just in time for the 1991 harvest. ♦ Fee. Tasting and sales daily 10AM-4PM; tours by appt. 5766 Silverado Trail, Napa. 944.2020

47 Pine Ridge Winery Sample Cabernet Sauvignon, Merlot, Chardonnay, and a crisp Chenin Blanc in the small, rustic tasting room

on the western edge of the Stag's Leap area. If you have time, you can tour the aging cellars dug into the terraced hillside. Pine Ridge also has a shady picnic area and swings for the kids. A trail leads up to the ridge that gives the winery its name. ♦ Fee. Tasting and sales daily 11AM-4PM; tours by appt at 10:15AM. 5901 Silverado Trail (Yountville Cross Rd) Napa. 253.7500

48 Silverado Vineyards Set high on a knoll west of the Silverado Trail, this Spanish-style fieldstone winery with a tiled fountain and an entrancing view of the valley is known for its Cabernet and Chardonnay, notably the special reserves produced only in outstanding vintages. They also make Sauvignon Blanc and a Merlot. The regular Cabernet is a great value. The winery is owned by the **Walt Disney** family, who sold grapes from their vineyards before constructing their winery in 1981. ♦ Tasting and sales daily 11AM-4PM; no tours. 6121 Silverado Trail, Napa. 257.1770

49 Shafer Vineyards Another grower-turned-vintner, **John Shafer** produces excellent Cabernet, Merlot, and Chardonnay from hillside vineyards in both the Stag's Leap and Carneros districts. His top wine is the Hillside Select Cabernet Sauvignon. ♦ Tasting and sales M-F 9AM-4PM; tours by appt only. 6154 Silverado Trail, Napa. 944.2877

49 Robert Sinskey Vineyards One of the original partners in Acacia Winery, **Robert Sinskey** founded his own Stag's Leap district winery in 1986 and has been garnering a fine reputation for his well-crafted Pinot Noir, Merlot, and Chardonnay. Completed in 1989, the modern stone-and-redwood winery with a 35-foot-high cathedral ceiling and columns twined with wisteria was designed by **Oscar Leidenfrost**. It's nice to stop and sit on the edge of the koi pond or walk around the small rose garden before heading inside for some serious tasting. A deck to one side offers picnic tables and a view of the valley. ♦ Fee. Tasting and sales daily 10AM-4:30PM; tours by appt. 6320 Silverado Trail, Napa. 944.9090

21

50 S. Anderson Vineyards Founded in 1971, this small, family-owned winery reminiscent of a one-room schoolhouse specializes in Chardonnay and sparkling wines made by the traditional méthode champenoise. In 1983, a spectacular 7,000-square-foot aging cave was tunneled out of a volcanic rock hillside overlooking the estate's vineyards. ♦ Fee. Tasting and sales daily 10AM-4PM; tours by appt. 1473 Yountville Cross Rd, Napa. 944.8642

51 Napa River Ecological Reserve Picnic in a cool grove of oak, elm, and sycamore trees beside the Napa River. ♦ Yountville Cross Rd (Silverado Trail-Hwy 29)

52 Patchwork Produce Stop here for organic vegetables and fruit from **Jennifer Harris'** garden plot. ♦ Call ahead; hours vary. One Cook Rd (Yountville Cross Rd) Yountville. 944.2241

Harvesttime in Napa

Although lush vineyards appear to blanket the entire Napa Valley, grapes are not the only crop harvested here. Small plots are still devoted to fruit orchards, vegetable gardens, and berry patches. And from May through November, you can visit the Napa Valley Farmers Markets on Tuesday and Friday mornings from 7:30AM to noon (see page 47) to sample and purchase the fruits of these farmers' labors. During the summer months there are also a few produce stands set up along the Silverado Trail. For a free map and list of farms that sell their produce directly to visitors, send a self-addressed, stamped envelope to Napa County Farming Trails, 4075 Solano Ave, Napa CA 94558, or call 224.5403.

What's in Season When

	Jun	July	Aug	Sep	Oct	Nov	Dec
Apples		✔	✔	✔	✔	✔	✔
Basil		✔	✔	✔	✔		
Berries	✔	✔					
Figs				✔	✔	✔	
Grapes				✔	✔		
Kiwi						✔	✔
Melons	✔	✔	✔	✔	✔		
Nectarines	✔	✔	✔	✔			
Peaches		✔	✔				
Pears					✔	✔	
Persimmons						✔	
Plums		✔	✔				
Pumpkins					✔		
Tomatoes			✔	✔	✔		
Vegetables	✔	✔	✔	✔	✔		
Walnuts					✔	✔	✔
Xmas Trees							✔

53 The Hess Collection Winery This restored, historic stone winery is not to be missed, despite the 15-minute drive from the main road. In 1978, Swiss mineral-water magnate **Donald Hess** took a long lease on the old Christian Brothers Mont LaSalle Cellars on Mount Veeder and charged from the starting gate with a spectacular 1983 Reserve Cabernet Sauvignon. His elegant estate-bottled Chardonnay is just as impressive. A passionate art collector, Hess stored much of his extensive collection of contemporary European and American art at his headquarters in Bern, Switzerland, until he had the idea of showcasing his wines and art under one roof. In 1989, the old stone building was completely renovated to house both the winery and a private museum of contemporary art. The 130-piece collection is devoted to the work of 29 artists, including **Francis Bacon, Robert Motherwell, Frank Stella, Theodoros Stamos,** and **Magdalena Akabanowitz.** A well-designed self-guided tour takes you through the museum, and includes glimpses of the cellars where Hess' Chardonnays and Cabernets ferment and age; the tour ends in the handsome tasting room, where wines and mineral water are served. Highly recommended. ♦ Fee. Tasting, sales, and self-guided tours daily 10AM-4PM. 4411 Redwood Rd, Napa. 255.1144

54 Mayacamas Vineyards A formidable road takes you to this historic property with terraced vineyards high on the slopes of the extinct volcano, Mount Veeder. The three-story stone building, set in the volcano's crater, was built in 1889 by **John Henry Fisher,** a native of Stuttgart, Germany. The winery was re-established in 1941 when the British chemist **Jack Taylor** restored it and replanted the vineyards. It has been owned by banker-turned-vintner **Bob Travers** and his wife **Nonie** since 1968. Mayacamas is known for its rugged and intense Cabernet and rich, oaky Chardonnay, both of which age remarkably well. They also make a small quantity of port-like late-harvest Zinfandel.
♦ Sales M-F 8AM-3PM; tasting and tours by appt only M, W 10AM, F 1PM. 1155 Lokoya Rd (Mt. Veeder Rd) Napa. 224.4030

Restaurants/Clubs: Red   Hotels: Blue
Shops/ 🌳 Outdoors: Green   **Wineries/Sights: Black**

55 Château Potelle Established in 1983, Château Potelle on scenic Mount Veeder produces Chardonnay, Sauvignon Blanc, Cabernet, and Zinfandel from grapes grown on the estate's mountain vineyards. French proprietors **Jean-Noël** and **Marketta Fourmeaux du Sartel** named the winery after the family's 900-year-old castle in France. Reservations are required for the winery's picnic area, which has a panoramic view of mountains and vineyards. Call for directions; it's much faster via the Oakville Grade. ♦ Tasting and sales M, Th-Su noon-5PM; tours by appt. Closed Nov-Apr. 3875 Mt. Veeder Rd, Napa. 255.9440; fax 255.9444

56 Lakespring Winery Impressive Merlot and pleasant Cabernet Sauvignon, Sauvignon Blanc, and Chardonnay from a small winery owned by San Francisco's **Battat** brothers. ♦ Sales daily 10:30AM-3:30PM; tours by appt. 2055 Hoffman Ln, Napa. 944.2475

57 Château Chèvre Winery The name means Goat Castle, after the herds that once roamed the property. The concrete winery building used to be the barn, and the bottling line has taken over the milk room. Best known for their Cabernet Franc and Merlot, Château Chèvre also produces Sauvignon Blanc, the classic accompaniment to goat cheese. ♦ By appt only. 2030 Hoffman Ln, Yountville. 944.2184

58 Bernard Pradel Cellars Owner/wine-maker **Bernard Pradel** hails from Burgundy, where Pinot Noir is king. But here he eschews that noble red grape for another: Cabernet Sauvignon, the favored grape of Bordeaux. He also makes Chardonnay and an unusual late-harvest Sauvignon Blanc. ♦ Sales by appt daily 10AM-5PM. 2100 Hoffman Ln, Napa. 944.8720

The oldest grape seeds discovered came from Soviet Georgia; carbon dating has revealed them to date from 7,000 to 5,000 BC.

André Tchelistcheff
Enologist

A Sunday brunch or lunch on the **Napa Valley Wine Train** in the spring.

Also in spring, a leisurely drive from Napa to Calistoga on the **Silverado Trail.**

A tour of **Domaine Chandon** and lunch or dinner at the Domaine Chandon Restaurant.

A visit to the **Hess Collection** art gallery and winery.

The excitement, hopes, and anxieties of harvest season mid-September through October in Napa Valley, and the fall colors in the vineyards after harvest.

Napa

Chris Phelps
Winemaker, Dominus Estate Winery, Yountville

Waking up at the **White Sulphur Springs Resort** in St. Helena with the birds and the deer, followed by a quick walk through the surrounding redwoods. Best when the waterfalls are full!

A piping hot bowl of café mocha crème at the **Napa Valley Coffee Roasting Co.,** a great place to read the paper and meet people.

A leisurely bicycle ride with a good friend through **Pope Valley** (stop to see the rattlesnakes at the Pope Valley Garage), on up to Middletown, looping back over Mount St. Helena.

Three hours with a good book in the pools at the **Calistoga Spa.**

Hiking through the vineyards in St. Helena to a dinner at **Brava Terrace** with a bottle of Cabernet, followed by a movie at **Liberty Theatre.**

What is Wine?

Courtesy of Sonoma County Wineries Association

The grape's contribution:

Skin = 8 percent
Adds color, flavor (bitterness and astringency), and aroma. Much of the tannins in red wine and all of the color comes from the skins

Seed = 4.3 percent
Crushing these adds tannins and oils

Pulp = 80 percent juice and 4.2 percent suspended solids

Stems and Stalk = 3 percent of cluster

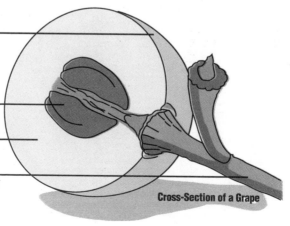

Cross-Section of a Grape

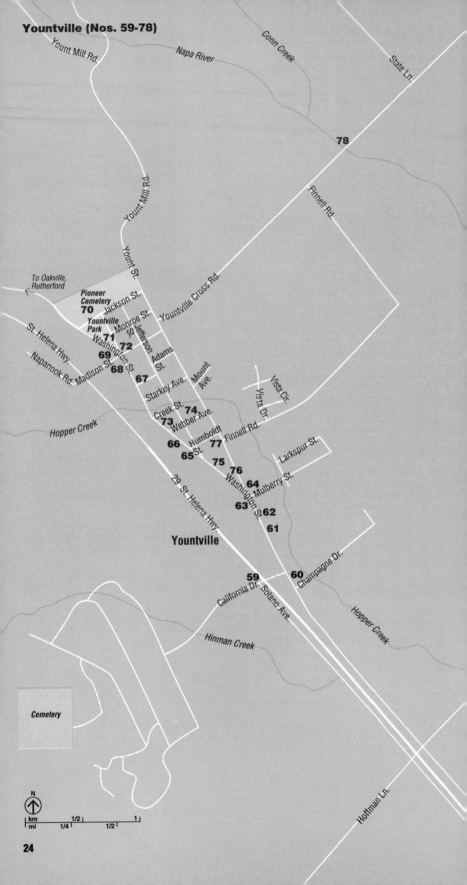

Yountville (Nos. 59-78)

Yount Mill Rd.

Napa River

Conn Creek

State Ln.

78

Finnell Rd.

Yount Mill Rd.

Yount St.

To Oakville, Rutherford

Pioneer Cemetery
70

Yountville Cross Rd.

Jackson St.

Monroe St.

Jefferson St.

Yountville Park
71

69

72

Washington St.

Adams St.

68

Madison St.

67

St. Helena Hwy.

Napanook Rd.

Starkey Ave.

Mount Ave.

Vista Cir.

Vista Dr.

Creek St.

74

73

Webber Ave.

Hopper Creek

66

Humboldt St.

77

Finnell Rd.

65

Larkspur St.

75

76

64

Washington St.

Mulberry St.

29 St. Helena Hwy.

63

62

61

Yountville

59

60

Champagne Dr.

California Dr.

Solano Ave.

Hopper Creek

Hinman Creek

Cemetery

Hoffman Ln.

N

| km | | 1/2 | | 1 |
| mi | 1/4 | | 1/2 | |

24

Yountville/Oakville/Rutherford

Just after the outskirts of Napa give way to vineyards, Yountville appears to the east of the highway. Founded by **George Calvert Yount**, a pioneer and adventurer who traveled to California overland from North Carolina, it is now a town of 3,500. Yount, who had visited **General Mariano Vallejo** at his Sonoma ranch, was the first American to settle in the Napa Valley and the first to receive a land grant from the Mexican government—the 12,000 acres

Washington Street Building, Yountville

in the heart of the valley called **Rancho Caymus**. With the help of local Indians, he also planted the first grapevines in the valley with cuttings he obtained from General Vallejo. By 1855, a town had grown up on the southern borders of Rancho Caymus, which Yount dubbed Sebastopol (not to be confused with the Sebastopol in Sonoma County). In 1867, two years after Yount's death at age 71, the town's name was changed to Yountville in his honor.

A short jaunt from Yountville up Hwy 29 are the twin towns of **Oakville** and **Rutherford,** where some of the world's best Cabernet Sauvignon vines thrive in a microclimate similar to France's Bordeaux region. This area should not be treated as a quick drive-through on the way to St. Helena, for this is the home of such great wineries as **Robert Mondavi, Inglenook,** and **Beaulieu.** And if their beautiful buildings and highly touted wines aren't enough to draw you in, then dinner or drinks at **Auberge du Soleil,** one of the valley's best restaurants, surely is.

59 Domaine Chandon The French champagne house **Moët et Chandon,** with more than two centuries of experience, has been making sparkling wine in the Napa Valley for 20 years. Their local winery pioneered the use of exclusively classic varietals in their California sparkling wines as well as certain production techniques. Domaine Chandon's top of the line is the toasty Reserve; the best value is their Blanc de Noirs. Winemaker **Dawnine Dyer** also produces very limited quantities of Chandon Club Cuvée, aged a minimum of six years on the yeast, a process that gives it a more complex flavor. Tours explain how sparkling wine is made by the traditional méthode champenoise and include a visit to a museum devoted to the history of champagne. Come just to stroll around the extensive, beautifully landscaped gardens or enjoy their informal champagne bar and cafe, Le Salon, where Domaine Chandon sparkling wine is sold by the glass and by the bottle, along with sparkling-wine cocktails, mineral water, and juice. ♦ Fee. Tasting, sales, and tours daily 11AM-6PM, May-Oct; W-Su 11AM-6PM, Nov-Apr. One California Dr (at Hwy 29) Yountville. 944.2280

Within Domaine Chandon:
Domaine Chandon Restaurant ★★★$$$
Chef **Philippe Jeanty,** a native of Champagne,

has headed the kitchen staff since the restaurant opened in 1977. With its candlelit tables and sweeping views of the vineyards, the restaurant is still one of the most romantic settings in the valley. In warm weather you can dine outdoors. Jeanty favors a light, flavorful style of cooking based on prime local ingredients and is committed to the simple idea that food should go with wine. With a glass of brut, try his alder-and-hickory-smoked Norwegian salmon with caramelized onion brioche or the home-smoked red trout filet drizzled with olive oil and served on a crisp potato salad. For red wines, he offers a dry-aged sirloin of beef, charred rare, or Sonoma-farm lamb cooked three ways and served with a roasted shallot-and-garlic tart. The venison tournedos wrapped in pancetta are perfect with a more robust wine. Another thoughtful touch: a cheese course, the ideal way to finish off that fine bottle of Cabernet. The desserts can be disappointing and too sweet, but the crème brûlée scented with lavender is fine. The service is attentive without being pretentious, and the extensive wine list offers a number of Napa Valley's best wines at good prices. The fare is more casual at lunch: several soups, inventive salads, even a pizza on occasion, and entrées such as grilled Sonoma rabbit, homemade sausages, and braised lamb shanks with spring vegetables. ♦ French/California ♦ Tu-Su 11AM-9PM. Reservations recommended. 944.2892

60 The Massage Place Therapeutic massage in a combination of Swedish/Esalen techniques. ♦ By appt daily 9AM-9PM. 6428 Washington St (Champagne Dr-Mission St) Yountville. 944.1387

61 The Diner ★★$/$$ There's lots to like about this down-home restaurant, with its colorful collection of vintage Fiesta-ware pitchers, roomy booths, and long stretch of counter where you can settle in with the morning paper and a plate of cornmeal pancakes and smoky links. Breakfast, which includes a particularly fine rendition of huevos rancheros, is enough to put this unpretentious place on the map. Lunch brings on an array of hearty sandwiches and oversized enchiladas, burritos, and tostadas, while dinner focuses on fresh fish and south-of-the-border-inspired dishes. Stop in any time of the day for their superlative but-

termilk shake. The power behind this appealing diner is **Cassandra Mitchell**, a fourth generation San Franciscan. ♦ American/Mexican ♦ Tu-Su 8AM-9PM. 6476 Washington St (Mission-Oak Sts) Yountville. 944.2626

61 Piatti ★★★$$$ One of the most popular restaurants in the valley, Piatti (which has already expanded to locations in Sonoma and Montecito) serves soul-warming Italian fare in a casual setting. With lavish garlic braids and garlands of hot red peppers, witty trompe l'oeil paintings of food on the walls, and a wood-burning pizza oven, it feels like an idealized trattoria. But what impresses most is the menu, filled with gutsy regional dishes that are hard to find even in Italy these days: real Roman bruschetta (toasted bread topped with garlic, olive oil, basil, and tomato), black risotto cooked with cuttlefish ink, and wide ribbon noodles sauced with braised rabbit, chard, and wild mushrooms. Always a good bet: the chicken breast *al mattone*, cooked under a hot brick and served with Tuscan beans and chard. Great appetizers, grilled fish, and pizzas from the wood-burning oven are available—and do save room for dessert. The well-edited wine list includes the best of both California and Italy. ♦ Italian ♦ M-F 11:30AM-2:30PM, 5-10PM; Sa noon-11PM; Su noon-10PM. 6480 Washington St (Mission-Oak Sts) Yountville. Reservations recommended. 944.2070

62 Napa Valley Tourist Bureau Stop here for free information on reservations for lodging, balloon flights, mud baths, etc., in Napa Valley. They've got the up-to-date information on which wineries have tasting fees or require

appointments for tours, and they'll help you decide which ones best suit your interests. Maps, books, and guides are also available. Busiest season? Summer and harvesttime, which extends from August through October. ♦ 6488 Washington St (Oak-Mulberry Sts) Yountville. 258.1957

63 The Whistle Stop Center The old Southern Pacific train station, built in 1889, has been restored and now houses several shops. ♦ 6505 Washington St (Yount St) Yountville. 944.9624

Within the Whistle Stop Center:

Overland Sheepskin Co. Superb sheepskin coats, hats, mittens, and slippers from a company that makes all their products in Taos, New Mexico. Coats are made from entre fino, the finest European sheepskin, in a variety of styles, but only one price range—high. The shearling gloves and the beautifully crafted shearling-lined booties are more down-to-earth. You'll find men's, women's, and children's styles, plus authentic Panama hats (which aficionados know actually come from Ecuador), oilskin raincoats from Australia, and handsome leather luggage for world-class adventurers. ♦ W-Su 10AM-6PM. 944.0778

63 Napa Valley Railway Inn $$ Three turn-of-the-century cabooses and six railcars have been spruced up and now house nine suites with queen-sized brass beds, sitting areas, and private baths. The idea has its merits, but this inn is a miss, since the touted view is actually of a parking lot with a few rows of vines beyond. ♦ 6503 Washington St (Yount-Humboldt Sts) Yountville. 944.2000

64 Vintage 1870 When **Gottlieb Groezinger** built his Yountville winery in 1871, it was hailed as the largest and best equipped in the valley. The brick winery and the old train station next to it are now a handsome shopping complex, with more than 35 specialty stores, gift shops, and boutiques (which seem to change every few months). With Muzak piped even outside the building and many shops concentrating on silly souvenirs, it takes determination to find the few interesting shops inside. The overpowering scent of popcorn and cheap snacks doesn't exactly add to its appeal. ♦ Daily 10AM-5:30PM. 6525 Washington St (Yount-Humboldt Sts) Yountville. 944.2451

Within Vintage 1870:

Adventures Aloft Balloon flights above Napa Valley with a catered light brunch and champagne. ♦ Reservations required. 255.8688

A Little Romance For lovers of Victoriana: battenberg-lace duvet covers, flowered chintz coverlets, antique quilts, old-fashioned hat boxes, a profusion of pillows, reproductions of Victorian tea sets, and books on the country house and related subjects. ♦ 944.1350

Basket Bazaar Check this shop for unusual picnic baskets, wine carriers, wicker silverware baskets, even folk-art whisk brooms

from Kentucky. The international collection includes birch-bark baskets made by Ojibwe Indians and baskets from the Philippines, South Africa, Zambia, and Indonesia.
♦ 944.8266

Drums ★★$$ Open only for lunch, Drums offers an appealingly simple menu of salads, sandwiches, and pasta dishes served inside or on the Vineyard Terrace. Executive chef **John Ellsworth** worked at **Matisse** and **Meadowood Resort** before moving to Vintage 1870. Best bets on the menu are the grilled chicken salad tossed with sugar-toasted pecans, Oregon blue cheese, and mixed greens, and the Cajun-spiced sirloin-and-chicken salad on a bed of fresh spinach. Don't miss the sandwich of snow crab, avocado, and mozzarella on a baguette spread with dill-lemon mayonnaise. One popular pasta dish pairs sun-dried tomatoes and mushrooms with tri-colored fusilli and mixed sausages from Gerhard's sausage company next door. For dessert, Ellsworth makes fresh fruit cobblers such as blackberry-lime and peach-cinnamon and a dynamite Belgian chocolate-and-bourbon cheesecake. ♦ M-Sa 11:30AM-3PM; Su 10:30AM-3PM. 944.2788

Gerhard's Napa Valley Sausage ★★$ **Gerhard Twele** learned to make sausages in Germany's famed Rhine Valley, and in 1985 he opened his own Napa Valley sausage company. Most popular are his lean chicken-apple sausage and the chorizo spiked with brandy and red chile pepper, but he makes more than 20 kinds, including fresh kielbasa, Thai chicken with ginger, and a Syrian lamb sausage perfumed with cumin. For picnics and barbecues, Twele prepares several fully cooked smoked sausages, including a spicy Cajun-style andouille, and a smoked duck sausage with morel mushrooms and red wine—of course, he slips a little wine into many of his recipes. ♦ 944.1593

Vintage Red Rock Cafe ★$ Burgers, salads, and sandwiches served in a restored, old railroad depot with an outdoor deck. The concept here is American-style pub grub. At breakfast, the kitchen turns out classic egg dishes and omelets. Lunch brings on fish and chips, fried calamari, and more. And at dinner they offer all of the above plus barbecued ribs and steaks. There's a good selection of domestic beers and ales, including San Francisco's own Anchor Steam and Sierra Nevada Pale Ale. ♦ Daily 8AM-8PM. 944.2614

Wee Bit O' Wool Wee bit o' everything Celtic, including kilts and tartans, classic wool-and-cashmere-blend sweaters, and intricate hand-knit fishermen's sweaters.
♦ 944.8184

65 Compadres ★★$$ The building that was once vintner **Gottlieb Groezinger's** home is now a Mexican restaurant and cantina (part of a chain with several restaurants in Northern California and Hawaii). Compadres makes a terrific margarita and features south-of-the-border dishes with an interesting twist. Try executive chef **Alfonso Navarro's** cilantro-laced tortilla soup, green corn tamales, seafood tacos or enchiladas, and the *pollo boracho*—a whole drunken chicken, marinated in tequila and flattened on the grill. The Mexican hot chocolate makes a great dessert. Short, well-priced wine list and a fine selec-

Yountville/Oakville/Rutherford

tion of tequilas. Some low-calorie items. Takeout. ♦ Mexican ♦ M-Th 11AM-9:30PM; F 11AM-10:30PM; Sa 8AM-10:30PM; Su 8AM-9:30PM. Vintage Estate, 6539 Washington St (Yount-Humboldt Sts) Yountville. 944.2406

66 Vintage Inn $$$ This 80-room inn is located on a 23-acre estate that was once part of the Spanish land grant that pioneer **George C. Yount** received from **General Vallejo.** Designed by **Kipp Stewart,** who also created the sybaritic **Ventana Inn** in Big Sur, the inn boasts 20 villas, each with four rooms or suites. Fireplaces in every room, pine armoires, Jacuzzi tubs, ceiling fans, refrigerators, and private patios or verandas make this a comfortable base for exploring the wine country. Other amenities include a 60-foot lap pool and spa heated year-round, two tennis courts, their own seven-passenger hot-air balloon, and bikes to rent. The concierge will arrange for private tours of wineries, mud baths, and hot-air balloon rides. Champagne Continental breakfast. ♦ 6541 Washington St (Humboldt St-Webber Ave) Yountville. 944.1112, 800/351.1133 (CA), 800/982.5539 (US)

67 Mama Nina's ★★$$$ Mama's takes great pride in their housemade pasta (a dozen different shapes for which you choose the sauce) and tried-and-true dishes such as eggplant Parmesan, lasagna, and cannelloni, plus a standard array of pizzas. The fresh-grilled fish is good, too. Chef **Michel Cornu** is also culinary director for **Far Niente Winery.** On summer nights, the outdoor patio is filled with family groups enjoying the casual ambience. ♦ Northern Italian ♦ Daily 11:30AM-3PM, 5-10PM. 6772 Washington St (Pedroni-Madison Sts) Yountville. Reservations recommended. 944.2112

68 Washington Square A small shopping center with a dozen shops and restaurants. ♦ Daily 10:30AM-5:30PM. 6795 Washington St (Pedroni-Madison Sts) Yountville. 944.0637

Within Washington Square:

Yountville Chamber of Commerce Information on Yountville and the Napa Valley. ♦ M-Sa 10AM-4PM. 944.0904

Yountville/Oakville/Rutherford

California Café Bar & Grill ★★★$$/$$$ The strong suit here is the creative California-style cuisine from the gleaming open kitchen, where **Andrew Trieger** oversees the action at the stoves. Dynamite sandwiches (try the grilled Ahi tuna with sage aioli and onions) grace the lunch menu and the pasta dishes are always well conceived. But the stars of the menu are the grilled and roasted meats, most from local farmers. The hickory-smoked baby-back ribs alone are worth the trip. Also try the grilled tandoori marinated breast of chicken, pork tenderloin in wild-mushroom sauce, and Black Angus steak with Cabernet butter. The generously proportioned dining room with walls sponged a soft peach, blonde bistro chairs, and lots of light, looks across the highway to the vineyards of Domaine Chandon. The outdoor patio is lovely in warm weather. The wide-ranging and moderately priced wine list includes many up-and-coming producers. ♦ California ♦ M-Th 11:30AM-9:30PM; F-Sa 11:30AM-10PM; Su 10AM-9:30PM. Reservations recommended. 944.2330

La Tavolozza ★★$$$ A sweet little Italian restaurant with faux marble walls, trompe l'oeil scenes of northern Italy, and tables dressed in crisp white linens. The chef is from Florence and excels at antipasti and first courses—soups (such as a vegetable-laden minestrone) and pasta. But his interest seems to flag on the main dishes. Several renditions of veal scallopine are several too many. Limited wine list. ♦ Italian ♦ Tu-Sa 6-9:30PM; Su 5-9:30PM. Reservations recommended. 944.9509

Massage Werkes Hour-long body massages given either in a combination Swedish/Esalen technique or in Chuaka, a very deep-to-the-skeleton rubdown. Herbal facials as well. ♦ By appt M-Sa 10AM-9PM. 944.1906

69 Napa Valley Lodge $$$ A very pleasant, well-run 55-room inn, built in the Spanish-hacienda style with wooden balconies and a terracotta roof, and tucked into the quiet north end of Yountville. Many rooms have vineyard views, and they have special two-room suites for families. There's also a large pool, a sauna, and a small fitness room. The helpful staff will arrange for bicycle rentals and other wine country activities. ♦ Hwy 29 and Madison St, Yountville. 944.2468

70 Pioneer Cemetery and Indian Burial Grounds The early history of the valley can be traced in the tombstones here, which include a monument to town founder **George C. Yount**, who died in 1865. Part of the cemetery, founded in 1848, serves as the burial grounds for the local Wappo Indian tribes. ♦ Off Jackson St, Yountville

71 Yountville Park A small park with shaded picnic tables, barbecue grills, and a children's playground. ♦ Washington St (Lincoln-Jackson Sts) Yountville. 944.8851

72 Yountville Market ★$ An old-fashioned country store and deli from 1916, with vintage music and good smells from the stove setting the mood. You can sit at tables covered with hand-stencilled tablecloths from the thirties, and indulge in fresh-baked muffins, scones, and croissants, along with espresso drinks made with San Francisco's legendary Graffeo coffee (roasted in North Beach). The crusty loaves of Acme bread for sale are used for sandwiches, croutons, and even a stuffing mix. In winter, a couple of soups simmer on the back of the stove. They'll put together some picnics-to-go, too. Stop in for fresh-cut flowers, fine wines and beers, and local produce. ♦ Daily 7:30AM-11PM. 6770 Washington St (Pedroni-Madison Sts) Yountville. 944.1393

73 The French Laundry ★★★★$$$$ Situated in a historic stone building that was once a laundry, **Sally Schmitt's** cozy restaurant has long been one of the favorites of the valley's food connoisseurs. A meal here is a leisurely affair; the table is yours for the evening. The prix-fixe menu, which changes daily, is generally five courses. The soup (which could be a mixture of fennel, potato, and apple) and main course (maybe braised lamb shanks, sliced rib eye of veal) as well as the salad and cheese courses are all set; you choose the appetizer and dessert. Appetizers, such as sautéed scallops with sun-dried tomatoes and oranges or smoked rabbit loin on braised leeks, are almost always intriguing. Homey desserts include a coffee pot de crème, persimmon cake, and apple and huckleberry clafoutis (batter cake). The exemplary wine list concentrates on Napa Valley's best, all fairly priced, with a few older Cabernets. Reserve well ahead for this small, popular restaurant, and be sure to go early enough to tour the beautiful herb garden. ♦ French ♦ W-Su 6-9PM. 6640 Washington St (Webber Ave-Creek St) Yountville. Reservations required. 944.2380

73 Bordeaux House $$ This unusual red-brick inn on a quiet residential street, was designed by owner/architect **Robert Keenan** in the 1970s. The six rooms, which feature tall platform beds with carpeted sides and modern furniture in tones of gold and burgundy, look somewhat dated now. Each has its own fireplace and private bath; the best one is the **Chablis Room** upstairs, which has its own balcony. An adequate Continental breakfast (muffins or other pastries, juice, and coffee) is laid out each morning in the cluttered common room. ♦ 6600 Washington St (Webber Ave-Creek St) Yountville. 944.2855

74 The Webber Place $/$$ Built in 1850 at the edge of old Yountville, this red farmhouse enclosed by a white picket fence is now a homey and unpretentious B&B owned by artist **Diane Bartholomew**. In the morning, her comfortable farmhouse kitchen smells of

good coffee, biscuits, and bacon, and on sunny afternoons, she serves tea and homemade cookies on the front porch. The four lovely guest rooms have ornate brass beds covered with antique quilts. Two of the rooms share a deep, old-fashioned tub; the other two have similar tubs tucked in alcoves. The view from the upstairs rooms is of treetops and sky. The large **Veranda Suite** downstairs boasts a queen-sized featherbed and down comforter, its own entrance, and a shady private veranda. ♦ 6610 Webber Ave (Jefferson-Yount Sts) Yountville. 944.8384

75 Napa Valley Vignerons This tasting room for **Merlion Vineyards** and **Newlan Vineyards & Winery** opened in 1991 with a tasting of current vintages and older wines for sale, along with Napa Valley food products and gift items. They'll schedule winery tours and ship any wines you buy. ♦ Daily 10AM-6PM, Mar-Nov; 10AM-5PM, Dec-Feb. Beard Plaza, 6540 Washington St (Mulberry-Humboldt Sts) Yountville. 944.0532

75 Maison Rouge ★$$$ Open for dinner only, this serene country restaurant features French cooking with an occasional Italian or California touch. Chef/owner **Marc Dullin's** small seasonal menu includes classic pâtés, escargots, housemade soups, and substantial main courses such as fricasée of rabbit in Cabernet, roasted rack of lamb with thyme-honey sauce, or a rosemary-scented grilled veal chop served with polenta. Desserts include crème caramel, warm apple tart, and profiteroles with chocolate sauce. Fairly small wine list. ♦ French ♦ M-Tu, Th-Su dinner only. 6534 Washington St (Mulberry-Humboldt Sts) Yountville. Reservations recommended. 944.2521

75 Groezinger's Wine Co. This shop offers a good selection of current Napa Valley releases along with some older wines. The tasting bar is at its busiest in summer and may offer up to

a hundred wines by the glass. The staff is helpful and knowledgeable. They'll ship wines almost anywhere in the US, too. ♦ Daily 10AM-5PM, until 7 or 9PM in summer. 6528 Washington St (Mulberry-Humboldt Sts) Yountville. 944.2331

75 The Depot Gallery A local artists cooperative showcasing everything from folk-art scenes of valley life to watercolor landscapes, handcrafted ceramics, and note cards. ♦ Daily 10AM-5PM. 6526 Washington St (Mulberry-Humboldt Sts) Yountville. 944.2044

76 Anestis' ★$$/$$$ A large restaurant with an uninspired modern decor, Anestis' offers a mixed bag of Greek specialties (stuffed grape leaves, Greek salad, and souvlakia) along with Italian pasta, Cajun calamari, and poultry and meats roasted on an imported French rôtisserie. At lunch, stop in for a quick mesquite-grilled burger or pita bread sandwich. There's a larger selection of spit-roasted items such as duckling, leg of lamb, and prime rib for dinner. Perfunctory wine list. ♦ Greek/American ♦ M-F 11:30AM-3PM, 5-10PM; Sa-Su 11AM-10PM. 6518 Washington St (Mulberry-Humboldt Sts) Yountville. 944.1500

77 Magnolia Hotel $$/$$$ This cozy old stone building has been operating as a hotel since 1873. The balcony once graced the old French Hospital in San Francisco. Rooms in the main building and the newer annex all have private baths and are furnished with antiques, dolls, and bric-a-brac. There is also a large swimming pool and a Jacuzzi for hotel guests. Innkeeper **Bruce Lochen**, former manager of San Francisco's Clift Hotel serves a full breakfast in the dining room. No children under 16 and no smoking. ♦ 6529 Yount St (Finnell-Humboldt Sts) Yountville. 944.2056

Restaurants/Clubs: Red   Hotels: Blue
Shops/ ♥ Outdoors: Green   Wineries/Sights: Black

"By making this wine vine known to the public, I have rendered my country as great a service as if I had enabled it to pay back the national debt."
Thomas Jefferson

78 Napa River Ecological Reserve Shady picnic spots under a grove of oak and sycamore trees beside the Napa River. ♦ Off Yountville Cross Rd at the bridge

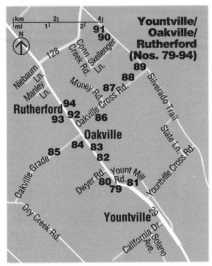

Yountville/ Oakville/ Rutherford (Nos. 79-94)

79 S. Claus It's Christmas year-round at this roadside shop where, by all rights, the helpers should be elves. Take a deep breath and make your merry way through hundreds of Christmas ornaments organized by style and theme. Categories include angels, Santas, houses, occupations, country, Victoriana, and, yes, teddy bears. The loveliest are shimmering handblown glass ornaments from Germany. Should your energy flag, step over to the espresso and dessert bar for a pick-me-up. ♦ Daily 10AM-6PM. 7331 St. Helena Hwy (1.5 miles north of Yountville) 944.XMAS

80 Mustards Grill ★★★$$$ Mustards has been a smash hit since the hot young team of **Cindy Pawlcyn** (who devises all the menus), **Bill Upson,** and **Bill Higgins** opened this roadside grill in 1983. (They also created **Fog City Diner** in San Francisco and **Tra Vigne** in St. Helena, among others.) Mustards is the quintessential wine-country restaurant, with a savvy, well-priced wine list and a menu that always induces you to order far more than you intended—plus it's open all day long for late lunches and California-style grazing. The menu changes frequently, but you can count on a superlative burger and ethereal onion rings (order them with homemade ketchup). Consider rabbit and pistachio sausages with pear chutney and a potato-shallot pancake or grilled stuffed pasilla peppers with a tomatillo salsa to start; then move on to calf's liver with caramelized onions and bacon (a great dish with a robust Napa Valley red); braised oxtail

with sun-dried tomatoes and caper sauce; or the grilled Sonoma rabbit with red peppers, fennel, and saffron. The side dishes—don't overlook the mashed potatoes or roasted garlic—are all terrific. And if you have room, by all means go for the desserts. ♦ Daily 11:30AM-10PM. 7399 St. Helena Hwy, Yountville. Reservations recommended. 944.2424

81 McAllister Water Gardens Recreate scenes from Monet's paintings in your own backyard with the help of this nursery, which specializes in water lilies and pond plants. ♦ F-Su 9AM-4PM, Mar-Sep. 7420 St. Helena Hwy, Yountville. 944.0921

82 Oleander House $$ The four rooms at this B&B in a contemporary French, country-style home just off Hwy 29 are furnished in Laura Ashley fabrics and antiques. Each has a queen-sized bed, private bath, fireplace, and balcony. A bonus: it's virtually next door to Mustards Grill, so you can stroll home to bed after a filling dinner. Innkeeper **Louise Packard** prepares a full breakfast of fresh orange juice, fruit, homebaked pastries, and an entrée such as an herb-flecked omelet or French toast with raspberries. No children or smoking. ♦ 7433 St. Helena Hwy, Yountville. 944.8315

83 Robert Pepi Winery In this contemporary winery, **Robert Pepi** and family produce a range of good wines. Their best are the Sauvignon Blanc and a Cabernet from Vine Hill ranch. ♦ Tasting and sales daily 10:30AM-4:30PM. 7585 St. Helena Hwy, Oakville. 944.2807

84 Pometta's Delicatessen ★$ Biking expeditions make pit stops at this unassuming, roadside Italian deli for barbecue chicken sandwiches, whole roasted barbecue chicken, and Pometta's Napa Valley Muffaletta sandwiches (ham, salami, two cheeses, and their special olive spread), along with an array of Italian deli salads. Outdoor patio. ♦ W-Sa 10AM-6PM; Su 10AM-4PM; closed Sa-Su Jan-Apr. 7787 St. Helena Hwy (Oakville Cross Rd) Oakville. 944.2365

85 Vichon Winery This Spanish colonial-style winery, owned by the **Robert Mondavi** family, produces wines from Chardonnay, Cabernet Sauvignon, and Merlot grapes. There are several picnic tables in a small grove and a boccie ball court for visitors. ♦ Fee for tasting older vintages. Tasting and sales daily 10AM-4:30PM; tours by appt. 1595 Oakville Grade, Oakville. 944.2811

86 Silver Oak Wine Cellars A small winery specializing in the production of only one varietal, a rich, powerful Cabernet Sauvignon from three different sites: the Napa Valley, Alexander Valley, and the small Bonny's Vineyard. The result is three knockout Cabernets, aged three years in oak and two years in the bottle before they're released. It's worth a special trip to taste these beauties. ♦ Fee. Tasting and sales M-F 9AM-4:30PM;

Sa 10AM-4PM; tours by appt M-F 1:30PM. 915 Oakville Cross Rd, Oakville. 944.8808

87 Villa Mount Eden Winery Founded in 1881, this property, now managed by **Château Ste. Michelle** in Oregon, concentrates on limited-production wines: Chardonnay, Chenin Blanc, and a usually excellent Cabernet Sauvignon. Talented winemaker **Mike McGrath** has been at Villa Mount Eden since 1982. No frills or hype here—it's like stepping back in time in this setting where real country life goes on. There's standup tasting in the small, functional tasting room, once the third bedroom of the caretaker's cottage. Bring a picnic lunch to eat at one of the tables facing the vineyards. Drive in past a hillside seeded with wildflowers and the label comes alive: you'll pass the same cream wooden farm buildings trimmed in cornflower blue and swathed in wisteria and old red roses. ♦ Tasting and sales daily 10AM-4PM; tours by appt only. 620 Oakville Cross Rd, Oakville. 944.2414

Wine-Tasting Tips

1 If you're drinking a white wine, the wine should be chilled, but not icy. If it's too cold, the flavors and aromas will be suppressed. Conversely, a red wine should not be too warm. Reds should be at room temperature, but if a room is 80 degrees F or higher, the wine will definitely be too warm. When red wine is too warm, the alcohol is accentuated and the wine tastes coarser and harsher than it should.

2 Before pouring a bottle of wine, sniff the wineglass to make sure it hasn't picked up any odors of wood from the cupboard and that there's no soap residue that will affect the wine's taste.

3 Pour the wine into a wineglass until the glass is a quarter to a third full. Don't fill up the glass; if it's too full, the wine cannot aerate (mix with air) properly, and it will be difficult to swirl the glass and experience the wine's aroma, which is part of the pleasure.

4 Hold the glass by the base or stem up to the light, and look at the *clarity* of the wine. It should be anywhere from clear to brilliant. Then note its *color*. Whites range from pale yellow to golden, rosés from pink to orange-pink, and reds from light purple to deep ruby.

5 Swirl the wine around in the glass. This aerates it, which releases the aromas. Hold the glass under your nose and breathe deeply. Smell the wine's *aroma,* which should be reminiscent of the grape from which it was made. Then note the *bouquet,* which results from the aging process and is stronger in older red wines and dessert wines.

6 Take a sip and swirl it around your mouth. Keeping a sense of the wine's aroma and bouquet in mind, try to determine its *texture* and *balance.* Is it dry or sweet? Soft or tart? Full-bodied?

Groth

1988
Napa Valley
Cabernet Sauvignon

ESTATE BOTTLED BY
GROTH VINEYARDS, OAKVILLE, CALIFORNIA, USA
ALCOHOL 12.5% BY VOLUME

Yountville/Oakville/Rutherford

88 Groth Vineyards and Winery Home of a top-ranking Cabernet Sauvignon from Atari computer maven **Dennis Groth,** his wife **Judith,** and partner and manager **Nils Venge** (who made wines at Villa Mount Eden for many years). Their Cabernets are among the most sought after in California. They also produce Sauvignon Blanc and Chardonnay. ♦ Tasting and sales by appt Tu-Sa 10AM-4PM. 750 Oakville Cross Rd, Oakville. 944.0290

89 Girard Winery One of California's best wineries. This family-owned property, which has supplied grapes to a number of top Napa Valley vintners, now produces its own rich, barrel-fermented Chardonnay. They also make an impressive Cabernet Sauvignon, including a notable reserve, a small amount of Sémillon, and a Pinot Noir that is from Oregon grapes, available only at the winery. ♦ Tasting and sales daily noon-4:30PM; tours by appt. 7717 Silverado Trail, Oakville. 944.8577

90 ZD Wines Former aerospace engineers **Gino Zepponi** and **Norman de Leuze** took the first letters of their last names to form their logo when they started making wine in Sonoma in 1969. A decade ago, they moved their operation to the Silverado Trail in the Napa Valley. The star here is opulent barrel-fermented Chardonnay. Also look for their Pinot Noir and powerful Estate Cabernet Sauvignon. ♦ Fee. Tasting, sales, and tours M-F 9AM-noon, 1-4:30PM. 8383 Silverado Trail, Napa. 963.5188

91 Mumm Napa Valley This joint venture between the French Champagne producer **G.H. Mumm** and the **Seagram** wine company, Domaine Mumm, directed by French winemaker **Guy Devaux** and his American counterpart **Greg Fowler,** produces several pleasant sparkling wines made by the traditional méthode champenoise. The winery building, with its steep-pitched roof and redwood siding, is reminiscent of the traditional Napa Valley barn. You can taste either the Brut Prestige or the Blanc de Noirs in the salon overlooking the vineyard, where they also sell Champagne flutes and crystal wine buckets. There is a large porch open to the vineyards with views across to the Mayacmas Mountains, and, in warm weather, a patio area is set with shaded tables. Domaine Mumm has recently released a Prestige Cuvée called Mumm Grand Cordon. In certain years, they also make a vintage-dated reserve, a blend of Chardonnay and Pinot Noir, that's aged two years on the yeast. ♦ Fee. Tasting and sales daily 10:30AM-6PM; tours every hour on the half hour 10:30AM-3:30PM. In addition, private tours and tastings are available by appt. 8445 Silverado Trail, Napa. 963.1133

Yountville/Oakville/Rutherford

92 Ambrose Heath Sandwich and Oven
★★$ Stop here for inventive sandwiches prepared on light sourdough rolls from the **Sciambra Bakery** in Napa. **Paul Nicholson** has 40 or so sandwiches in his repertoire, including fresh-roasted turkey with tomato, watercress, and spinach; pan-fried eggplant layered with artichoke hearts, roasted peppers, Teleme cheese, and sun-dried tomatoes; and Italian meatballs with onions marinated in bourbon. Desserts include chocolate-raspberry torte, cheesecake, and fresh fruit tarts. He also has an extraordinary wine list at very good prices. Sit on the terrace or ask Nicholson to pack your sandwiches to go. He has recently started serving breakfast, as well as an eclectic dinner menu on the weekends (try a plate of the baby-back ribs in a pomegranate and spice marinade). ♦ Continental ♦ M-Th 8AM-3PM; F-Su 8AM-3PM, 5:30-9:30PM. 7848 St. Helena Hwy (Oakville Cross Rd) Oakville. 944.0766

92 The Oakville Grocery ★★★$$ The place to shop for a sumptuous picnic. Oakville Grocery is stocked with a vast array of gourmet—and pricey—goodies: wonderful pâtés, cold cuts, caviar, crusty country breads, crackers, and carefully tended cheeses, including local jack and goat. You can also opt for the prepared sandwiches, such as turkey and pesto or roast beef with blue cheese on Italian flat bread. A small

produce section stocks tender leaf lettuces, fresh herbs, and ripe summer fruit. Also check out the top-quality olive oils and vinegars, and don't miss the desserts, many of them from the **Model Bakery** in St. Helena. The clerks will walk you through the store, building a picnic to go with a particular wine. With a day's notice, they will put together any kind of picnic fantasy: everything from bicycle box lunches to lavish honeymoon picnics. A top-notch grocery store and granddaddy of all the gourmet shops in the Bay Area. ♦ Daily 10AM-6PM. 7856 St. Helena Hwy (Oakville Cross Rd) Oakville. 944.8802

93 Robert Mondavi Winery If there's one person who has put California on the international wine map, it is the ebullient **Robert Mondavi,** who seems to have spread the gospel of Napa Valley wine to every country in the world. Even in the early years he held fast to the idea that California was capable of making world-class wines, and his vision has shaped much of the success of the Napa Valley image both in this country and abroad. In his own winery, Mondavi has been an innovator in technology, viticulture, and marketing. His greatest coup may have been the joint venture he formed with the late **Baron Philippe de Rothschild** of Mouton-Rothschild in Bordeaux to produce Opus One, a Bordeaux-style Cabernet blend with cachet to burn. (A new Opus One winery is under construction, but no plans have been made to open it to the public.) Mondavi's mission-style winery building, designed by **Cliff May** in 1986, is a familiar image from the ubiquitous Mondavi label, and the firm turns out a vast range of benchmark Napa Valley wines, from straightforward varietals to exquisite reserves. Mondavi is the first stop on everyone's wine route, and as a consequence, the tasting room and tours are packed with visitors all year round. A recently introduced reservation system for tours has helped to manage the crowds. In addition to the usual one-hour tour given by well-prepared guides, Mondavi gives a three- to four-hour in-depth tour and tasting several times a week (less often in winter). Special tastings are scheduled one evening a week, too. Both require reservations. ♦ Tasting, sales, and tours daily 9AM-5PM, May-Oct; 9AM-4PM, Nov-Apr. Reservations recommended for tours. 7801 St. Helena Hwy, Oakville. 963.9611

Robert Mondavi Winery

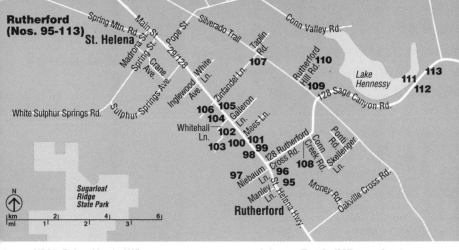

Rutherford (Nos. 95-113)

St. Helena

Sugarloaf Ridge State Park

Rutherford

Within Robert Mondavi Winery:

The Great Chefs at Robert Mondavi Winery This first-class cooking school sponsored by Robert Mondavi Winery invites the top chefs from France and the US to teach master classes ranging from two or three days to one week in a posh wine-country setting. The school originated in 1976 as the Great Chefs of France. In 1983 a Great Chefs of America series was added, and in 1986 the two were merged under the present name. Most of France's Michelin three-star chefs have taught at the school at one time or another, as have home-grown stars such as **Alice Waters** of Chez Panisse in Berkeley, **Wolfgang Puck** of Spago's in Los Angeles, **Jeremiah Tower** of Stars in San Francisco, and **Mark Miller** of The Coyote Café in Santa Fe. Each year four to seven Great Chefs programs of varying length are scheduled. Classes are deliberately kept small and students are a mix of cooks, chefs, and die-hard food fans from around the world. After each class, participants sit down to a meal based on the cooking demonstrations. Fine china and linen and Christofle silverware are the order of every day, and the decor of the Vineyard Room is transformed to match the theme of each meal, often with live music. Needless to say, the wine flows freely—and **Robert Mondavi** and his wife **Margrit Biever** are generous with the good stuff. For most classes, accommodations and local transportation are provided. ♦ For further information, contact Axel Fabre, Director, The Great Chefs at Robert Mondavi Winery, Box 106, Oakville CA 94562. 944.2866

94 Evensen Vineyards & Winery A half-timbered, Alsatian-style building houses the cellar where **Richard Evensen** and family produce a wine to match the architecture: Gewürztraminer. ♦ Tasting and sales by appt. 8524 St. Helena Hwy, Oakville. 944.2396

94 Johnson-Turnbull Vineyards A small winery in an award-winning, barn-like structure designed by San Francisco architect **William Turnbull,** who is also a partner in this venture with San Francisco attorney **Reverdy Johnson.** Their first vintage was in 1979; in 1985, **Kristin Belair** signed on as winemaker. The winery produces a Cabernet Sauvignon with a pronounced minty, eucalyptus character. Vineyard Selection 67 comes from the last block of old vines on the property. ♦ Tasting, sales, and tours by appt Tu-Sa 9AM-4PM. 8210 St. Helena Hwy, Oakville. 963.5839

95 Peju Province Winery This family-owned winery, founded in 1983, produces Cabernet Sauvignon, White Cabernet, and French Colombard, as well as Chardonnay and Sauvignon Blanc. ♦ Tasting, sales, and self-guided tours daily 10AM-6PM. 8466 St. Helena Hwy, Rutherford. 963.3600

95 St. Supéry Vineyards and Winery Winemaking enthusiasts will enjoy the walk-through display vineyard, where you can see different grape varietals and various examples of pruning and trellising. Inside the functional modern winery building, an informal exhibition is devoted to promoting arts in the Napa Valley. Shows change every two months and range from exhibits by individual local artists to group shows with participating Napa Valley galleries; occasionally artisans may demonstrate fabric painting or a variety of other textile crafts. The Queen Anne Victorian farmhouse on the property has been recently restored in period furnishings as a living museum of 1880s viticultural life in the Napa Valley. Also part of the self-guided tour are exhibits on different types of soils, growing conditions, and climate, along with an interactive lesson in wine jargon. St. Supéry's wines include Chardonnay, Sauvignon Blanc, and Cabernet Sauvignon. ♦ Tasting, sales, and tours daily 9:30AM-4:30PM; W-Su only, Nov-Apr. Reservations recommended for tours. 8440 St. Helena Hwy, Rutherford. 963.4507

Restaurants/Clubs: Red   Hotels: Blue
Shops/ ♥ Outdoors: Green   Wineries/Sights: Black

95 Sequoia Grove Vineyards A small winery owned by the **James Allen** family in a century-old barn shaded by hundred-year-old Sequoia trees. Three generations of the family work the vineyards and the winery, producing Chardonnay and Cabernet Sauvignon. Old Chardonnay vines by the river provide grapes for its estate bottlings. ♦ Tasting, sales, and self-guided tours daily 11AM-5PM. 8338 St. Helena Hwy, Rutherford. 944.2945

95 Cakebread Cellars This small, family-owned winery housed in a simple redwood barn was designed and built in 1986 by the San Francisco architect **William Turnbull. Jack** and **Dolores Cakebread,** with sons **Bruce** as winemaker and **Dennis** as business manager, specialize in regular and reserve Cabernet Sauvignon, Chardonnay, and Sauvignon Blanc. ♦ Tasting and sales daily 10AM-4PM; tours by appt. 8300 St. Helena Hwy, Rutherford. 963.5221

Yountville/Oakville/Rutherford

96 Rutherford Square This small complex of buildings on land that was once part of **Rancho Caymus,** the original land grant given to pioneer **George Yount** by **General Vallejo** more than a hundred years ago, was developed by local sculptress **Mary Tilden Morton**. It now includes a post office, bar, and two houses. ♦ St. Helena Hwy and Rutherford Cross Rd, Rutherford. 963.2617

Within Rutherford Square:

The Corner Bar $ Hot dogs, pizzas, wines. ♦ Daily 11AM-midnight or later. 963.7744

96 Rancho Caymus Inn $$$ Sculptress **Mary Tilden Morton** of the pioneer **Morton Salt** family), built this $4-million, rustic 26-unit Spanish Colonial-style inn. The two-story building is constructed around a central

courtyard with a fountain and wisteria-covered balconies. Morton planned each room as a separate work of art, hiring local carpenters and craftspeople skilled at creating stained glass, wrought iron, and ceramics. She designed and built the adobe fireplaces herself, and collected crafts from Ecuador, Peru, and Mexico to decorate the rooms and suites. The four master suites, each named for a local historical figure, feature Jacuzzi tubs, full kitchens, and large balconies, and are ideal for long stays. A hacienda breakfast (orange juice, coffee, and freshly baked muffins) from the **Caymus Kitchen** is included, and can be served in your room or on the balcony or gardens. In 1991 Morton sold the

inn to Flora Springs winery owner **John Komes**. ♦ 1140 Rutherford Rd, Rutherford. 963.1777

Within the Rancho Caymus Inn:

Caymus Kitchen ★$ This small restaurant with both indoor and outdoor seating offers breakfast and lunch every day. For breakfast, try the stacks of buttermilk pancakes with real maple syrup, sourdough French toast, or the ranch eggs scrambled with guacamole, Sonoma jack cheese, and chiles. Sunday brunch is more elaborate, with eggs Benedict, corned beef hash, and homemade waffles with chicken-apple sausage. For lunch, there are quesadillas filled with black beans and cheese, sandwiches, excellent burgers served with homemade mayonnaise and potato salad, a great tostada with smoked chicken, black beans, and avocado, and good soups. Wines by the glass. ♦ Mexican/American ♦ Daily 8AM-2PM. 963.1777

97 Niebaum-Coppola Estate Winery The Niebaum-Coppola estate dates back to 1879, when winemaking pioneer **Captain Gustave Niebaum,** a Finnish fur trader and founder of **Inglenook,** first established his winery at the foot of Mount St. John. After Niebaum's death, his grand-nephew **John Daniel, Jr.** took over the estate; in 1964 he sold off the Inglenook name and the winery buildings, keeping the Victorian mansion and a large block of prized vineyards in the heart of the prime Rutherford Bench area. In 1975 filmmaker **Francis Ford Coppola** purchased the estate and, under the guidance of renowned enologist **André Tchelistcheff,** one of the seminal figures in California winemaking, began producing a deeply colored, full-bodied Bordeaux-style blend of Cabernet Sauvignon, Merlot, and Cabernet Franc called Rubicon. Coppola is serious about making a first-class wine and it shows, with each vintage a personal and well-crafted success. ♦ By appt only. 1215 Niebaum Ln, Rutherford. 963.9099

98 Inglenook Vineyards This handsome stone winery building dating from the 1880s, is now romantically cloaked in ivy. The exhibition of photos and memorabilia tracing the history of Inglenook and Napa in the lobby includes an 1881 map of the valley; 19th-century books on Napa and the wines and

vines of California; portraits of Inglenook's founder, Finnish sea captain and fur trader **Captain Gustave Niebaum**; and pictures of the first vintage and crush in 1882. Of special interest: a page of an 1890 Sunday *San*

Francisco Examiner extolling Inglenook's modern cellars, and a December 1933 article from the *St. Helena Star* hailing the end of Prohibition. Wines produced at this historic winery include Chardonnay, Sauvignon Blanc, Cabernet, Merlot, Zinfandel, and Pinot Noir. Ask about tasting the special Reserve bottlings (for which there is a fee). ♦ Tasting, sales, and tours daily 10AM-5PM. 1991 St. Helena Hwy, Rutherford. 967.3300

99 Beaulieu Vineyard Tasting Center This historic Rutherford estate should not be missed. Founded by the French emigré **Georges de Latour** in 1900, who named it Beaulieu (beautiful place), the winery is now known for its Chardonnay, Sauvignon Blanc, Riesling, and especially its Cabernet Sauvignon. The Rutherford and Georges de Latour Private Reserve are the benchmark California Cabernets, which have a long track record for their aging potential. They also make Gamay Beaujolais, Zinfandel, and a sweet Muscat de Frontignan. Note the informal exhibition of old barrel-making tools and corkscrews from the 1700s to the present. In 1991 a small tasting room opened next door showcasing their library wines, namely three vintages of the Private Reserve and an occasional older Rutherford Cabernet. Wine tasting in the main room is free; there is a small charge for this one. ♦ Tasting and sales daily 10AM-4PM; tours until 3PM. 1960 St. Helena Hwy, Rutherford. 963.2411

100 Grgich-Hills A dapper emigré vintner from Yugoslavia, **Miljenko (Mike) Grgich** is one of the pioneers who made the reputation of Napa Valley wines in the early seventies. He began his career at **Château Montelena** (he made the 1973 Chardonnay that won the famous Paris Tasting of 1976 and then opened his own winery with partner **Austin Hills** of the **Hills Bros. Coffee** family in 1977 in a functional Spanish Colonial building alongside Hwy 29. Grgich is an undisputed master of Chardonnay and has priced his wines accordingly. He also makes a distinguished Fumé Blanc, a full-bodied Cabernet, and a Zinfandel from old vines. On weekends you can taste older library wines (for a small fee) and wines from selected older vintages are for sale. A definite stop on your wine itinerary. ♦ Tasting, sales, and tours daily 9:30AM-4:30PM. 1829 St. Helena Hwy, Rutherford. 963.2784

101 Napa Valley Grapevine Wreath Company Wreaths made from twined grapevine cuttings in many shapes (hearts, or, at Christmas, trees and reindeers) and sizes (up to 36 inches across or even larger by special order). Also sells fresh produce from May through October. ♦ M-Tu, Th-Su 10AM-5PM. 1796 St. Helena Hwy, St. Helena. 963.0399

---

102 Rutherford Vintners Alsace-born **Bernard Skoda** worked for 15 years as a manager at **Louis M. Martini** before leaving to open his own small winery in 1976. He produces Riesling, Chardonnay, Cabernet, and Pinot Noir, plus a special sweet Muscat of Alexandria sold only at the winery. ♦ Tasting and sales daily 10AM-4:30PM; tours by appt. 1673 St. Helena Hwy, Rutherford. 963.4117

103 The Ink House $$$ This Italianate Victorian B&B was built in 1884 by **Theron H. Ink,** a wealthy local landowner. Now owned by **Ernie Veniegas,** a former director of the Honolulu symphony and the Hawaii opera theater, the inn has understated period decor and antique furnishings. The four guest rooms of varying sizes all have private baths and antique brass and iron beds. The breezy observatory on the third floor is a perfect spot to watch hot-air balloons floating over the

valley. Continental breakfast with fresh-baked bread and herb teas. ♦ 1575 St. Helena Hwy (at Whitehall Ln) St. Helena. 963.3890

104 Whitehall Lane Winery Good Cabernet and Merlot from winemaker **Arthur Finkelstein,** who founded this small winery on the northern edge of the Rutherford Bench district in 1979. He also produces Chardonnay and special bottlings of Pinot Noir and Cabernet Franc. ♦ Tasting and sales daily 11AM-5PM; tours by appt. 1563 St. Helena Hwy, St. Helena. 963.9454

105 Franciscan Vineyards The state-of-the-art motherhouse of four Napa Valley properties where you can stop and taste wines from Franciscan Vineyards, Estancia, Pinnacles, and Mount Veeder wineries. Franciscan's flagship wine is the Franciscan Oakville Estate Meritage, a blend of red Bordeaux varietals, and Cuvée Sauvage, a Chardonnay fermented in French oak barrels by the naturally occurring wild yeast present in the vineyard. The winery is owned by the **Eckes** family of Germany, who have been involved for five generations in winemaking and brandy distilling in Germany, and by **Agustin Huneeus,** president of Franciscan. In 1991 Franciscan

Oakville Estate released their first Grappa di Nappa, a fiery spirit distilled in the Italian tradition from grape pressings, in this case of Merlot or Zinfandel. ♦ Fee on weekends. Tasting and sales daily 10AM-5PM. 1178 Galleron Ln, Rutherford. 963.7111

106 Flora Springs Wine Company Founded in the 1880s by the **Rennie** brothers from Scotland, the old stone winery building now houses a state-of-the-art cellar. The present

winery, owned and run by three generations of the **Komes** and **Garvey** families, produces top-rated Chardonnays in a French Burgundy style and an exceptional Sauvignon Blanc. Winemaker **Ken Deis'** blend of Cabernet Sauvignon, Merlot, and Cabernet Franc is called Trilogy. Depending on visitors' interests, tours may include the vineyards as well as the cellar. Picnic area. ♦ Tasting and tours by appt. 1978 W. Zinfandel Ln, St. Helena. 963.5711

107 Mario Perelli-Minetti Winery A very small, family-owned winery producing only Cabernet Sauvignon and Chardonnay. Owner **Mario Perelli-Minetti** comes from one of California's oldest wine families. He was actually born in the Sonoma County winery built by his father, **Antonio,** who graduated from the Royal Academy of Viticulture and Enology at Conegliano, Italy. From 1902 until his death in 1976, Antonio was active in viticulture and winemaking in California and Mexico. ♦ Tasting and sales daily by appt. 1443 Silverado Trail, Rutherford. 963.8762

108 Caymus Vineyards
Charlie Wagner and his son **Chuck,** second- and third-generation winemakers, have created a no-nonsense operation that just happens to turn out some of California's best Cabernets. Drive past the ranch-style house to the small tasting room. The chalkboard hung out front is a reference to their less expensive second label, Liberty School. Caymus was one of the first vintners to produce *oeuil de perdrix* (partridge eye) from Pinot Noir, and is best known for their outstanding Cabernet Sauvignon (the Special

Selection is always one of California's greatest). They also make a good Sauvignon Blanc and Zinfandel. ♦ Fee. Tasting and sales daily 10AM-4PM. 8700 Conn Creek Rd, Rutherford. 963.4204

109 Auberge du Soleil $$$$ The breathtaking setting for this French country inn is an old olive grove overlooking Napa Valley. The team of architect **Sandy Walker** and designer **Michael Taylor** built 11 maisons on the 33-acre site, each named after a region of France; indeed, once inside one of these very private villas, you feel as if you've been transported to a hill town in southern France. Every suite or room has its own entrance, along with tall wooden shutters and French doors opening onto a completely private veranda that runs the length of the room. Windows are set deep into earth-toned stucco walls, much like a Provençal farmhouse. Terracotta tiles cover the floor, frame the fireplace, and even top bureaus and counters. The queen- or king-sized beds are covered with thick cotton chenille in sizzling pinks and yellows. The bathrooms, most with oversized tubs, are opulently large. The most romantic rooms are the deluxe bedrooms, which are a third larger than standard rooms and have fireplaces and Jacuzzi whirlpool baths. Two full-time gardeners tend the extensive grounds planted with rosemary, lavender, and a profusion of flowers. Because of the privacy it affords, the Auberge has become a honeymoon haven. In fact, the complimentary Continental breakfast can be left outside the door if you like. The large swimming pool has a heartstopping, panoramic view, and there's also a basic spa with a steam room, showers, and a massage room, and two tennis courts. The bar is the best place in the valley to linger over a glass of wine at sunset. Full concierge service. ♦ Deluxe ♦ 180 Rutherford Hill Rd, Rutherford. 963.1211

Within Auberge du Soleil:

Auberge du Soleil Restaurant ★★$$$
When the Auberge's restaurant first opened in 1981 with the late Japanese chef **Masa Kobayashi** at the helm, it became an instant hit with both restaurant critics and romantics. Since he left to open his own restaurant, San Francisco's **Masa's,** a few years later, Auberge du Soleil has had its ups and downs, but things have taken a strong turn for the better since Swiss-trained **Udo Nechutnys** (former owner/chef at **Miramonte** in St. Helena) signed on as executive chef in 1989. The dining room, with its sculptural bouquets of seasonal flowers, comfy banaquettes, and seemingly endless views of the valley, has always been the most romantic in the area—and is often booked months ahead on the weekends.

Nechutnys' seasonal menu is appealingly unfussy. Start with the sautéed Sonoma duck liver on an herb brioche; the lamb's tongue salad with curly endive; or freshly cracked Dungeness crab accompanied by an artichoke and Belgian endive salad. Main courses are designed to show off selections from their extensive list of Napa Valley and California wines: seared rare Ahi tuna served with tender polenta; Peking duck with green onion pancakes; roasted rack of lamb simply prepared with parsley and garlic, accompanied by sublime buttermilk mashed potatoes; or a grilled New York steak served with roasted shallots and rich, creamy scalloped potatoes. Desserts are winning, too, with choices like warm chocolate-pistachio brownies with peach sherbet and vanilla sauce; a benchmark crème brûlée; and warm peach cobbler with vanilla bean ice cream. The Sunday brunch menu is also intriguing. ♦ French/California ♦ Daily 11:30AM-2PM, 5-9PM. Reservations required. 963.1211

RUTHERFORD HILL

1978
Napa Valley
CABERNET SAUVIGNON

PRODUCED AND BOTTLED BY RUTHERFORD HILL WINERY
RUTHERFORD, CALIF. USA • ALCOHOL 12.7% BY VOLUME

110 Rutherford Hill Winery Take an informative tour through this contemporary wood winery, including a walk through their extensive aging caves carved half a mile into the cliffs behind the winery. Tunnel specialist **Alf Burtleson** spent 13 months on the job, using an English drilling machine to burrow into the hard-packed earth and rock. Winemaster **Jerry Luper** focuses on Merlot, Chardonnay, and Cabernet Sauvignon; the winery also produces Sauvignon Blanc and Gewürztraminer. The picnic grounds are spectacularly situated under the oaks and in the olive grove—and share the same panoramic view as Auberge du Soleil. ♦ Tasting and sales daily 10:30AM-4:30PM; tours 11:30AM, 1 and 2:30PM. 200 Rutherford Hill Rd, Rutherford. 963.7194

111 Lake Hennessey Recreation Area A picnic area, complete with barbecue pits. If the lake has been stocked with trout, as it generally is each spring, you could even catch a fish and fry it up right here. This is a reservoir for local drinking water so no swimming is allowed; however, you can take a dip in the creek that runs alongside the picnic area. ♦ Off Hwy 128

112 Long Vineyards A tiny family winery on Pritchard Hill east of the Silverado Trail. Long Vineyards was founded in 1978 by **Zelma Long,** one of California's most prominent women winemakers and president of **Simi Winery** in Sonoma County, and her former husband **Bob Long**. Still partners, they continue to produce first-class Chardonnay, Riesling, and Cabernet Sauvignon, all of which are hard to find because quantities are so limited and sought after by connoisseurs. Another Long Vineyards bottle to covet: their opulent late-harvest Johannisberg Riesling, produced only in years when conditions are right. ♦ Tours by appt only. 1535 Sage Canyon Rd, St. Helena. 963.2496

113 Chapellet Vineyard Founded in 1967, **Don** and **Molly Chapellet's** pyramid-shaped winery located on a spectacular site on Pritchard Hill is devoted to just three wines: a crisp Chenin Blanc, Chardonnay, and a very good Cabernet. ♦ Fee. Tasting and sales at Vintners Village

Yountville/Oakville/Rutherford

north of St. Helena daily 10AM-5PM; tours at the winery by appt only. 1581 Sage Canyon Rd, St. Helena. 963.7136

Bests

Helen M. Turley, Winemaker
John P. Wetlaufer, Owner, All Season's Wine Shop

An hour's massage by **Frank Hughes,** owner of **Nance's Hot Springs** in Calistoga—the ultimate in pain-and-tension relief.

Lunching at **River's End** in Jenner—completely undiscovered original food with an emphasis on just-caught fish.

Climbing **Mount St. Helena**. On a clear day you can see the ocean and the snow-topped Sierra.

Jeremiah Tower
Restaurateur/Stars and Starmart, San Francisco

After dinner, the steam room at **Auberge du Soleil,** with a bottle of Krug rosé in an ice bucket. The only way to recover after a long day in Napa.

An early fall lunch at **Mondavi Winery** during the Great Chefs' program. They do it all (wine, food, flowers) the best.

Madeleine Kamman's week-long classes at **Beringer Vineyards**—only Madeleine knows that much and would work you that hard.

Any event at **Jordan Winery** in the Alexander Valley, especially if you try their new "*J*" sparkling wine.

Joseph Phelps' birthday-party barbecues and any of the small lunches serving French and California wines.

Restaurants/Clubs: Red	Hotels: Blue
Shops/ ♦ Outdoors: Green	Wineries/Sights: Black

St. Helena

This small town in the heart of Napa Valley got its start when **Edward Bale**, an impoverished British surgeon who sailed to California aboard a whaling vessel and later married into General Vallejo's family, built a flour mill beside a creek three miles north of the present town in 1846. The land was part of Rancho Carna Humana, an immense Spanish land grant covering some 20,000 prime acres—virtually all of northern Napa Valley—which Bale received in 1839. He later sold a hundred acres to a fellow Englishman, **J.H. Still**, who promptly opened a general store. That became the nucleus of the town, which took its name from Mount St. Helena. Here you will find several of the best restaurants in the wine country, a number of historic wineries, and the Napa Valley Wine Library, which preserves the history of the area in its books, papers, and oral histories.

Main Street, with its stately, 19th-century stone buildings, is a portion of the valley's main highway, and has been a significant thoroughfare since the days of the horse and buggy. The infamous **Black Bart**, who taught school and wrote

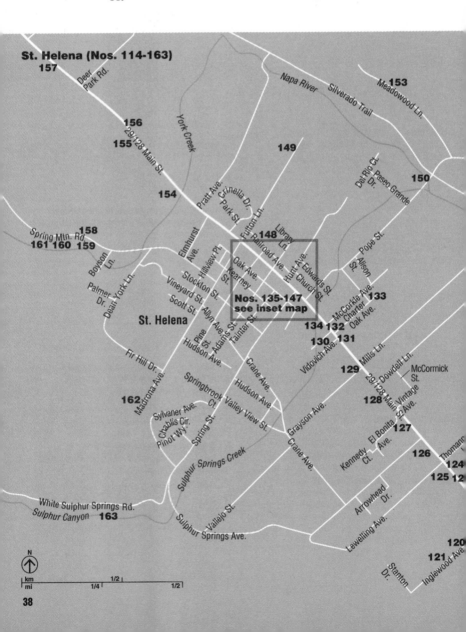

St. Helena (Nos. 114–163)

Nos. 135–147
see inset map

St. Helena

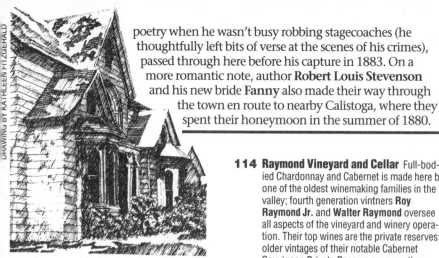

poetry when he wasn't busy robbing stagecoaches (he thoughtfully left bits of verse at the scenes of his crimes), passed through here before his capture in 1883. On a more romantic note, author **Robert Louis Stevenson** and his new bride **Fanny** also made their way through the town en route to nearby Calistoga, where they spent their honeymoon in the summer of 1880.

St. Helena Building

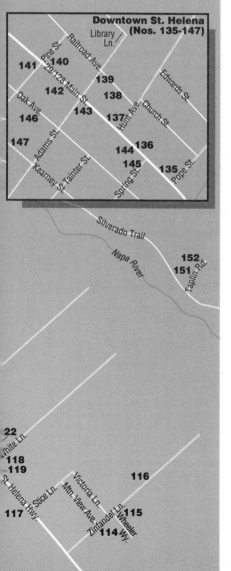

Downtown St. Helena (Nos. 135-147)

Library Ln.
Railroad Ave.
Pine St.
141
140
29/128 Main St.
142
139
Edwards St.
Oak Ave.
143
138
146
137
Hunt Ave.
Church St.
147
Adams St.
144
136
145
Kearney St.
Tainter St.
Spring St.
135
Pope St.

Silverado Trail

Napa River

152
151
Taplin Rd.

22

White Ln.

118
-119

St. Helena Hwy

116

Victoria Ln.

E Stice Ln.
Mtn. View Ave.
Zinfandel Ln.
Wheeler
115

117
114 Wy.

114 Raymond Vineyard and Cellar Full-bodied Chardonnay and Cabernet is made here by one of the oldest winemaking families in the valley; fourth generation vintners **Roy Raymond Jr.** and **Walter Raymond** oversee all aspects of the vineyard and winery operation. Their top wines are the private reserves; older vintages of their notable Cabernet Sauvignon Private Reserve are sometimes available at the winery. ◆ Tasting and sales daily 10AM-4PM; tours by appt. 849 Zinfandel Ln, St. Helena. 963.3141

115 Shady Oaks Country Inn $$ This inn features two guest rooms in a 1920s house and two in an 1800s stone winery building, all with private baths and furnished with country antiques. A champagne breakfast including eggs Benedict and Belgian waffles is served in the parlor or on the patio overlooking the garden and vineyards, which is shaded with a century-old wisteria. ◆ 399 Zinfandel Ln, St. Helena. 963.1190

116 Shadow Brook Winery Housed in an old barn, this tiny winery is known for its Chardonnay. A picnic area is available. ◆ By appt only. 360 Zinfandel Ln, St. Helena. 963.2000

117 Milat Vineyards A small winery producing Chardonnay, Chenin Blanc, White Zinfandel, and Cabernet. ◆ Fee. Tasting and sales daily 10AM-6PM. 1091 St. Helena Hwy, St. Helena. 963.0758

118 V. Sattui Winery The fourth generation of the Sattui family offers ten of their wines to taste at this 1885 winery with yard-thick stone walls, hand-hewn timbers, and four underground cellars. It's also a busy stop for picnic fare: their large, well-organized cheese shop and deli offers more than 200 imported and domestic cheeses, a variety of cold cuts, straightforward salads, and desserts such as truffles and oversized cookies. Enjoy your booty at the shady picnic area alongside the highway. Wine- and cheese-related gifts, too. ◆ Tasting daily 9AM-6PM, summer; 9AM-5PM, winter; tours by appt. 1111 White Ln, St. Helena. 963.7774

In 1889, France allowed American wines to compete for the first time in the international wine competition at the World's Fair in Paris. Thirty-four awards and medals were given to California wines and brandies, and 20 of these went to entries from the Napa Valley.

119 St. Helena Wine Merchants A large wine shop with a broad range of California and imported wines at good prices. They specialize in wines from small-production wineries that can be hard to find outside California. At any given time, you can choose from 400 to 500 estates (more than 300 Cabernets alone). The knowledgeable staff is ready to advise. Expect to find the latest releases from up-and-coming new wineries, too. Out-of-state shipping is available. ♦ Daily 10AM-6PM. 699 St. Helena Hwy, St. Helena. 963.7888; fax 963.7839

120 Villa Helena Winery This small producer specializes in Chardonnay. ♦ Tasting and sales by appt 10:30AM-4:30PM. ♦ 1455 Inglewood Ave, St. Helena. 963.4334

121 La Fleur Bed and Breakfast $$ There are three guest rooms in this 1882 Queen Anne Victorian which is surrounded by vineyards. Each room is individually decorated in designer prints, has a fireplace and a private

St. Helena

bath, and views of the vineyards or rose garden. A full breakfast is served in the sunny solarium, where most days you can see hot-air balloons drifting in the distance. ♦ 1475 Inglewood Ave, St. Helena. 963.0233

122 Sugarhouse Bakery For 20 years **Rudy** and **Therese Frey** have been turning out delicious cross-hatched loaves of Swiss farmhouse bread, coarse rye, and potato bread. They also make sweet cinnamon rings, strudels, and stollens, plus Swiss leckerli cookies, gingerbread, and brownies. For picnics, order sandwiches on their own fresh-baked rolls. Special breads and sweets are available at Christmas and Easter. ♦ W-Sa 7:30AM-6PM; Su 8:30AM-5PM. 587 St. Helena Hwy, St. Helena. 963.3424

123 Heitz Wine Cellars

A Napa Valley old-timer. Established in 1961 by **Joe** and **Alice Heitz,** this winery is known for its big, full-bodied Cabernets, especially those made from two specially selected Cabernet Sauvignon vineyards—Bella Oaks and Martha's Vineyard. The latter is noted for its unique bouquet of eucalyptus and mint. ♦ Tasting and sales daily 11AM-4:30PM; tours by appt M-F. 436 St. Helena Hwy, St. Helena. 963.3542

124 Louis M. Martini Winery This is one of the oldest wineries in the Napa Valley, and was founded in 1922 by **Louis M. Martini** and is still run by the Martini family. The founder's granddaughter, **Carolyn,** is now president; his grandson, **Michael,** is the winemaker. After a period of decline, Martini is making a strong comeback. Los Niños is a Cabernet

Sauvignon from the oldest vines on Monte Rosso; the wine is meant to age until los niños —the children born the year of the vintage— are at least 21 years old. Their benchmark wine is the Cabernet Monte Rosso from a vineyard high in the Mayacmas Mountains; the regular bottling is called North Coast Cabernet. ♦ Tasting and sales daily 10AM-4:30PM; tours five times daily. 254 St. Helena Hwy, St. Helena. 963.2736

SUTTER HOME

1988 CALIFORNIA
WHITE ZINFANDEL

VINTED AND BOTTLED BY SUTTER HOME WINERY
ST. HELENA, NAPA VALLEY, CALIFORNIA BW 1007
ALCOHOL 9% BY VOLUME. CONTAINS SULFITES

125 Sutter Home Winery This winery was founded in 1874 by Swiss-German immigrant **John Thomann,** purchased by the Sutter family in 1906, and it has been under the sole ownership of the **Trinchero** family since 1947. Housed in a complex of gussied up Victorian buildings, Sutter Home is best known for its Zinfandels, especially their Amador County Zinfandel and their White Zinfandel, a wine tailor-made for a mass audience. They also make Chardonnay, Cabernet, and a slew of other wines. Their visitor's center is a big operation: T-shirts, baseball jackets, Victorian gift tins of Sutter Home wines, umbrellas—they've got it all. ♦ Tasting and sales daily 9AM-5PM. 277 St. Helena Hwy, St. Helena. 963.3104

126 Harvest Inn $$$ If the Catalán Modernist architect **Antoni Gaudí** worked in brick, he might create something like this fantasy hotel just off Hwy 29. The bricks came from turn-of-the-century San Francisco houses, old cobblestones were used to build the myriad fireplaces, and more than a million dollars was spent on antiques (mostly oak refinished to look brand new). Alas, the effect is just a bit ho-hum. Rooms with names such as Romeo and Juliet, King of Hearts, the Earl of Ecstasy, and the Count of Fantasy are scattered over several buildings on the spacious grounds, and feature ornate fireplaces, hardwood floors, and decks or patios. West-facing rooms have hillside views. Overstuffed leather sofas are pulled up around a baronial fireplace in the main hall, which sports a wine bar with a dozen wines by the glass. Two swimming pools; Jacuzzis in some deluxe rooms. ♦ One Main St, St. Helena. 963.9463, 800/950.8466

127 El Bonita Motel $ An Art Deco, thirties motel right out of the pages of hard-boiled detective novels. It may not be deluxe, but it's a real wine country bargain with a convenient location to boot. The 16 small, neat rooms have French louvered windows, cable TVs, and vintage tile bathrooms with showers. Sunbathe at the classic kidney-shaped pool while traffic whizzes by on Hwy 29. For families, they have six bungalow units with kitchenettes—the best deal in the valley. ♦ 195 Main St, St. Helena. 963.3216, 800/541.3284

128 Vintage Hall The temporary home of the Napa Valley Museum. Located in the St. Helena High School Building, the museum presents changing exhibits on Napa Valley culture and history. Previous exhibits have included prints of California native plants by the late artist **Henry Evans,** a photography exhibit of rare plants of the Napa Valley from The Native Plant Society Collection, and an exhibit devoted to the Wappo Indian tribe. One of the museum's most important services is the Trunk Program; docents travel to schools to present programs about the cultural and agricultural heritage of the Napa Valley. In 1988 the Napa County Museum acquired a four-acre site adjacent to Domaine Chandon in Yountville as the future home of the museum and the board of directors devote much of their time and effort raising funds for the proposed building (slated to open in 1995). ♦ M-F 9AM-noon, 1-4PM; Sa 1-4PM. 473 Main St. St. Helena. 963.7411

129 A&W Restaurant & Ice Cream Parlor $ Burgers, hot dogs, chili dogs, sandwiches, onion rings, French fries, and old-fashioned root-beer floats in frosted mugs. In short, the high school hangout. ♦ American ♦ Daily 10AM-9PM. 501 Main St, St. Helena. 963.4333

130 Dansk Factory Outlet Save up to 60 percent on seconds, discontinued patterns, overstocks, and limited editions of Dansk dinnerware, flatware, crystal wine glasses, wooden salad bowls and carving boards, cookware, and gifts. They'll ship throughout the US, too. ♦ Daily 10AM-6PM. Dansk Square, 801 Main St, St. Helena. 963.4273

131 Tra Vigne ★★★$$/$$$ The name means "among the vines," and since the day it opened, Tra Vigne has been one of the hottest restaurants in the wine country. It's spacious and lively with a stylish ambience, popular with visitors and residents alike. Garlands of pepper and garlic, hanging sausages and hams, and a broad terrace shaded with a black-and-white awning give it the look of a postmodern Italian movie set. The large menu is constantly changing (and admittedly the cooking is sometimes uneven, but when this place is on, it is a memorable wine country experience). The list of antipasti, salads, pasta, and pizzas from the wood-burning oven is quite long. While you can have just a dish or two at the bar or regroup over a glass of wine on the terrace, it's more fun to gather with friends and sample everything on the table: warm spinach-and-escarole salad with pancetta, goat cheese, and sliced grilled pears; polenta with wild mushrooms in aceto balsamic sauce; grilled rabbit with mustard, sage, and grappa-soaked cherries; and rustic pizzas with caramelized onions and gorgonzola, or chef **Michael Chiarello's** house-cured sausage and mozzarella, from a wood-burning oven. Dolci (sweets) include

St. Helena

anise-almond biscotti to dip in a Tuscan dessert wine, freshly made Italian-style ice creams and sherbets, and a winning semifreddo (hazelnut and vanilla ice cream doused with espresso). The wine list features an all-star selection of Italian wines and a big array of great grappas. ♦ Italian ♦ Daily noon-10:30PM, summer; noon-9:30PM, winter. 1050 Charter Oak Ave, St. Helena. Reservations recommended. 963.4444

Within Tra Vigne's courtyard:

Cantinetta ★★★$ Have a light bite and a glass of wine or an ice-cold draft beer and shop for hard-to-find Italian groceries at this classy, upscale Italian deli and wine shop. The wood-paneled bar on one side serves aperitifs, strong espresso drinks that taste like the real thing, and their own special campari. They also have a wonderful selection of wines by the glass. Step up to the counter to order panini (Italian sandwiches), focaccia (pizza bread), savory pies, whole roasted garlic heads to spread on bread Italian-style, and other items to go. Every night there's a different take-out entrée. And from the deli counter look for goat cheese from **Laura Chenel's Chèvre** in Sonoma, handmade Calabrese-style salami, fresh wild mushrooms, dried porcini mushrooms, and special dried beans for *pasta e fagioli* (a bean-and-pasta soup). The perfect wine country gift? Tra Vigne's own dried tomato conserves, virgin olive oil, and flavored wine vinegars. They also have a nice selection of top California, Oregon, and Italian wines, plus books on Italian wines and cooking. ♦ Italian ♦ M-Th, Su 11:30AM-6PM; F-Sa 11:30AM-7PM. 963.8888

Restaurants/Clubs: Red **Hotels:** Blue
Shops/ 🌳 Outdoors: Green **Wineries/Sights:** Black

132 Merryvale-Sunny St. Helena Winery
Visit this winery in the historic stone St. Helena building and try their award-winning, barrel-fermented Chardonnay. Profile is a blend of the Bordeaux varietals Cabernet Sauvignon, Cabernet Franc, and Merlot from vineyards in and around the Rutherford Bench area. Under winemaker **Bob Levy,** a special Merryvale Vineyards label has been established to designate premium varietal wines. For picnics, pick up a bottle of the Sunny Picnic Rosé. The tasting room also sells a Zinfandel-spiked pasta sauce and catsup, a Dijon Chardonnay mayonnaise, and other goodies under the winery label. Olive oil from the Tra Vigne restaurant next door is also on sale here. On Saturday morning the winery offers a component tasting in which participants learn how to taste tannin, sugar, and tartaric acid in wines. ♦ Admission. Tasting and sales daily 10AM-5:30PM; tours by appt. Reservations required for component-tasting class. 1000 Main St, St. Helena. 963.7777

133 Napa Valley Olive Oil Co. Osvaldo Particelli and Policarpo Lucchesi have been selling their dark golden-green California olive oil (regular or extra-virgin) for almost 60 years at a very modest price. In addition, stock up on jars of homemade antipasto, bags of freshly grated imported Parmesan, the sharper pecorino Romano, and boxes of imported De Cecco pasta and dried porcini mushrooms. For picnics, they have Sciambra bread from Napa, cheese at good prices, whole salami, prosciutto, and mortadella. The hand-rolled grissini (bread-sticks) and focaccia (pizza bread) come from **Cuneo Bakery** in San Francisco's North Beach. Fresh mozzarella drizzled with their extra-virgin olive oil makes a terrific first course. For dessert try the torrone (nougat), biscotti, amaretti cookies, or the famous chocolate baci (kisses) from the Italian chocolate firm Perugina. ♦ Daily 8AM-6PM, summer; 8AM-5PM, winter. 835 McCorkle Ave, St. Helena. 963.4173

134 Taylor's Refresher $ Since 1949 this roadside stand has been dishing out burgers (and now veggie burgers), hot dogs, corn dogs, French fries, and homemade burritos and tacos. Shakes, malts, and floats, too. ♦ American ♦ Daily 11AM-6PM. 933 Main St, St. Helena. 963.3486

135 St. Helena Chamber of Commerce
Information on St. Helena and the Napa Valley, including lodging, restaurants, wineries, and bike routes. ♦ M-F 10AM-noon, 1-4PM. 1080 Main St, St. Helena. 963.4456, 800/767.8528

135 Spratt's Candy, Nuts, and Confectionery
Kids will like Spratt's chocolate turtles, chocolate-dipped Oreo cookies and almond clusters, plus there are a dozen flavors of San Francisco's own **Bud's** ice cream to choose from for malts, shakes, and old-fashioned banana splits. ♦ M-Th 11AM-5:30PM; F-Sa 11AM-8PM; Su noon-5PM. 1152 Main St, St. Helena. 963.1956

135 St. Helena Cyclery Rent hybrid bikes (a mountain/touring cross) complete with helmets, side bags, and a lock. They don't take reservations, so arrive early, especially on weekends. Colorful biking togs, accessories, and books on biking in the wine country are for sale, too. ♦ M-Sa 9:30AM-5:30PM; Su 10AM-5PM. 1156 Main St, St. Helena. 963.7736

136 The Noble Building The hipped roof and double dormers mark this 1903 landmark as an example of Dutch Colonial architecture. Designed by **Luther Mark Turton,** who created more than 50 homes and buildings in the valley, it has housed a furniture store, an undertaking establishment, and a chicken hatchery at various times in its history. Now it's home to several small businesses. ♦ 1200-04 Main St, St. Helena

136 Calla Lily Debra Caselli has special sources in Europe for her luxury table and bed linens. Among the treasures here are exquisite Italian linen tablecloths with matching napkins handwoven in Renaissance patterns; silky Belgian cotton percale sheets (300 thread count), which can be monogrammed in more than 200 thread colors; Egyptian-cotton towels; wool-filled bed pads; and bedcoverings and pillow shams in jacquard cotton or subtle Marseille piqué. Caselli will make custom sheets and bedcoverings in her quality fabrics, too. ♦ M-Sa 10AM-5PM; Su and other hours by appt. 1222 Main St, St. Helena. 963.8188

136 Stillwaters This unique shop features owner **Ron Sculatti's** IFS (Innovative Fishing Systems) designs: padded packs with movable compartments and pockets for fishers on their way to Baja or Alaska; state-of-the-art graphite poles that telescope down to 26 inches; and elegant bamboo rods that come apart in two sections. The theme here is adventurous toys for those on the sporting edge, which means "Gone Fishing" signs, fish cookbooks, out-of-print fishing classics, hand-crafted decoys, tropical duds—and picnic baskets for two (with wineglasses). The pocket fish knives are a handy item. Catalog. ♦ Daily 10AM-6PM. 1228 Main St, St. Helena. 963.1782; fax 963.2567

136 Trilogy ★★★$$$ Chef/owner **Diane Pariseau** keeps her restaurant small so she can personally cook almost every dish. The graceful, spare dining room with just eight tables is especially lovely at lunch, and a good deal of wine-country business is conducted at this unpretentious spot. The broad, well-priced list of California wines is just as big a draw as Pariseau's light and flavorful cooking, which is always beautifully presented. Her appetizers are intriguing, especially her signature wild mushroom ragout served with fresh corn crepes, and the grilled fennel, eggplant, and red bell pepper. The soup is always wonderful, and she has a sure hand with fish dishes such as steamed salmon with lemongrass, ginger, garlic, and sesame oil or chilled rock shrimp and couscous with red-bell-pepper puree. Red-wine lovers will find dishes such as pheasant with chanterelle mushrooms, roast rack of lamb with whole-grain mustard and rosemary, and sautéed medallions of veal with shiitake mushrooms and sage. Pariseau also offers a four-course prix fixe menu with two main-course choices that changes daily. The restaurant has a small patio area where you can stop in for a glass of wine and a couple of appetizers. ♦ French/California ♦ Tu-F noon-2PM, 6-10PM; Sa 6-10PM. 1234 Main St, St. Helena. Reservations recommended. 963.5507

137 Avant-Garden Early birds who can't get a cup of coffee at their hotel until 7 or 8AM can head for this combination florist/espresso bar for a cappuccino or latté and at 6AM pastry in an indoor garden setting. You'll find all sorts of flower arrangements, from country style to high style and ikebana. Pick up some fresh-cut flowers for your room or a dried wreath or dried flower arrangement to take home. Ponder your choice as you munch on home-made chocolate truffles, a fruit tart, and other desserts. ♦ Daily 6AM-10PM. 1118 Hunt Ave, St. Helena. 963.5300

137 La Placita ★★$ This small, cheerful Southwestern restaurant with a soothing fountain and bright mission murals offers a nice twist on familiar dishes. Try the grilled chicken wings with Rio Grande Mole; the Yucatán quesadilla filled with corn, black olives, and cheese and served with lime-drenched guacamole; or the grilled chicken salad with orange-lime dressing. The grilled marinated shrimp or chicken is tasty, too, and once a week they have taco specials. Short wine list. Takeout. ♦ Southwestern ♦ Daily 11:30AM-9PM; F-Sa 11:30AM-10PM. 1304 Main St, St. Helena. 963.8082

137 Green Valley Café ★$$ With its long green bar and vintage opera posters, this feels like a trattoria somewhere in the Italian countryside. The day's specials are chalked on the board: fried calamari, gnocchi in Gorgonzola sauce, ravioli with meat and porcini mushroom sauce. Generous portions are the rule. Skip the cappuccino, though—it's too weak and foamy. ♦ Italian ♦ W-Sa 11:30AM-3PM, 6-9:30PM; Su 11:30AM-3PM, 5:30-9:30PM. 1310 Main St, St. Helena. 963.7088

137 St. Helena Star Building Home to St. Helena's only local newspaper since 1900. ♦ 1328 Main St, St. Helena. 963.2731

137 Liberty Theatre Though this cozy small-town theater dates from 1918, the original facade and interior were remodeled in the fifties. Today the theater, which seats 172, shows current releases and classic films in runs of two days to one or two weeks. Niceties include comfortable rocking lounge

St. Helena

chairs, dolby stereo sound, and fresh popcorn with real butter. 1340 Main St, St. Helena. 963.5813

DRAWING BY MARY R. MOFFITT

137 Steve's Hardware & Housewares Since 1878 this old-fashioned hardware store has been a fixture in St. Helena, offering picnic supplies and inexpensive cooking equipment, such as knives, styrofoam coolers, enamel coffeepots for the campfire, wineglasses (in plastic versions, too), pocket corkscrews, and other handy necessities. ♦ M-F 7:30AM-6PM; Sa 7:30AM-5PM; Su 10AM-3PM. 1350 Main St, St. Helena. 963.3423

137 I.O.O.F. Building Built in 1885, this remains one of the largest stone buildings in town. The brick facade boasts details such as lions' heads, brackets, and rosettes. Part of the base is painted cast iron. The upstairs area still houses the **Odd Fellows** meeting hall. ♦ 1350 Main St, St. Helena

According to **William F. Heintz,** author of *Wine Country—A History of Napa Valley,* when the 1906 San Francisco earthquake hit, an estimated 45 to 50 million gallons of wine were stored in San Francisco warehouses, which easily could have been used to put out the fire that devastated nearly 500 city blocks.

138 Showley's at Miramonte ★★$$$

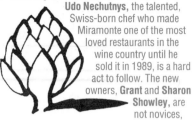

Udo Nechutnys, the talented, Swiss-born chef who made Miramonte one of the most loved restaurants in the wine country until he sold it in 1989, is a hard act to follow. The new owners, **Grant** and **Sharon Showley,** are not novices, however; they previously ran a gourmet take-out in Orange County. Their menu features local ingredients and clear, uncomplicated flavors from Californian, French, and Italian traditions: risotto of duck, Parmesan, and pine nuts; grilled pizza topped with roasted garlic, ham, and Fontina; fresh fettuccine with grilled chicken and garden vegetables; veal sweetbreads in Madeira and whole-grain mustard sauce. Desserts include berry cobbler and Queen of Sheba chocolate-

St. Helena

almond torte. A big attraction here is the brick patio shaded by a century-old fig tree. ♦ California ♦ Tu-Su 11:30AM-3PM, 6-10PM. 1327 Railroad Ave, St. Helena. Reservations recommended. 963.1200; fax 963.8864

TERRA

138 Terra ★★★★$$$ **Lissa Doumani** and her husband, **Hiro Sone,** a Japanese chef who worked with **Wolfgang Puck** at **Spago** in Los Angeles, have created one of the highest-quality restaurants in the Napa Valley. If you enjoy truly fine food and wine, Terra is a *must* on your wine-country itinerary. The fact that it's a favorite with local winemakers says it all. Sone's cooking is subtle and marvelously flavorful, featuring well-crafted, intelligently conceived dishes such as Nantucket bay scallop tartare with caviar, wonton of duck liver with wild-mushroom sauce, grilled medallion of lamb with anchovy-and-black-olive sauce, and roasted sea bass with shallot-butter sauce and chanterelle mushrooms. The setting in a historic stone building with two dining rooms is elegant and understated. Doumani is warm and welcoming, and the service is professional and unobtrusive. Extensive California wine list featuring many hard-to-find selections from small estates. ♦ California ♦ M, W-Su 6-9:30PM. 1345 Railroad Ave, St. Helena. Reservations recommended. 963.8931

139 Stratford Winery Good quality Chardonnay at a reasonable price. ♦ Sales daily 9AM-4PM. 1472 Railroad Ave, St. Helena. 963.3200

140 Rissa Oriental Café ★★★$ The second restaurant of **Terra** owners **Hiro Sone** and **Lissa Doumani** is a charming, serene haven with just the kind of inexpensive, tasty fare you really want to eat any time, any place: spicy fried calamari, pan-fried dumplings, warm soups spiked with chiles and coconut, and vegetarian Thai curry. For hot summer days, try the Japanese-style, cold buckwheat noodles dipped in a fiery sauce or spicy Thai barbecue beef salad. For dessert, opt for ginger cake and ice cream. The short wine list includes sake (rice wine) from Hakusan at the foot of the Napa Valley. A welcome addition to the roster of Napa Valley restaurants. ♦ Thai/Chinese/Japanese ♦ M-Sa 11:30AM-9PM. 1420 Main St, St. Helena. 963.7566

140 Lyman Park Gazebo, picnic tables, barbecue pits, and a playground for kids. ♦ Main St (Adams-Pine Sts) St. Helena

141 Ambrose Bierce House $$ The modest exterior of this 1872 Victorian home hides a hospitable, superbly restored guesthouse/mini-museum crammed with memorabilia of 19th-century writer **Ambrose Bierce** and friends (the likes of **Lillie Langtry, Edward Muybridge,** and **Lillie Coit**). Bierce lived here for 13 years, plotting ghost stories before his mysterious disappearance in Mexico in 1913. (**Gregory Peck** played Bierce in the 1989 film *Old Gringo.*) The inn has two suites for rent upstairs, both with a queen-sized bed and private baths. The largest and most comfortable is, of course, named for Bierce. Innkeeper **Jane Gibson** has complimentary bicycles for guests, and serves a sumptuous Continental breakfast featuring a special blend of coffee, freshly squeezed juice, fruit, and homemade scones or croissants. ♦ 1515 Main St, St. Helena. 963.3003

142 Vanderbilt and Company For the stylish picnic, this housewares-and-garden shop has a great collection of paper plates and matching napkins in grape, flower, or lettuce patterns; nifty Italian plastic plates that mimic old majolica pottery (cracks and all); plastic champagne flutes and wine glasses (a necessity around pool areas); and handsome wicker picnic baskets. If you really want to go whole hog, they have lovely jacquard linens from Le Jacquard Français, hand-painted tablecloths, rustic terra-cotta, Italian handblown wineglasses, and white-on-white grapeleaf majolica pottery from Deruta, a town in Umbria, Italy, which has specialized in majolica since the Middle Ages. ♦ Daily 9:30AM-5:30PM. 1429 Main St, St. Helena. 963.1010

143 Main Street Books This shop features a small, well-edited selection of wine books, including *Norman's Napa Valley Adventures*, a coloring-and-activity book for children. Good California travel section, too. ♦ M-Sa 10AM-5:30PM.1371 Main St, St. Helena. 963.1338

143 The Gallery on Main Street **Barbara Ryan** concentrates on local artists and wine-related art in this Napa Valley gallery. Check the portfolio for **Sebastian Titus** prints of grape varieties suitable for framing. ♦ M-Sa 10AM-5PM. 1359 Main St, St. Helena. 963.3350

143 Model Bakery The best bread in the valley comes from Model's old-fashioned brick oven. Look for *pain de campagne* (half-wheat, half-white sourdough), sour rye, crusty sweet or sourdough baguettes, plus terrific poppy- or sesame-seed sandwich rolls. If you're thinking of a picnic, owner **Karen Mitchell** stuffs croissants with ham and cheese or spinach and feta, sells Brie by the slice, and bakes several types of pizza every day—call to reserve a slice of pizza to go. For dessert, she's got chocolate-chocolate chip cookies, oatmeal-raisin cookies, almond-studded biscotti and, in summer, lovely fruit tarts. Bring in your thermos and she'll fill it with coffee or espresso brewed from freshly roasted beans. ♦ Tu-Sa 7AM-5:30PM. 1357 Main St, St. Helena. 963.8192

143 Mosswood One of Main Streets newest shops is this garden-and-nature store. Look for top-of-the-line tools, most imported from England, plus French galvanized watering cans, garden gloves, and other essentials for the upscale gardener. They also have a small line of unusual, limited-edition garden furniture. The store features a large selection of bird baths, fountains, and statuaries in various materials, plus hand-crafted accents for the home and garden. In the solarium out back, you can find exotic orchids, ivy and myrtle topiaries, and other ornamental plants. The children's section devoted to toys and educational games with a nature focus is quite good. ♦ Daily 10AM-5:30PM. 1239 Main St, St. Helena. 963.5883

143 The St. Helena Bottle Shop Few bargains here, but you can find rare, hard-to-come-by wines at high-ticket prices, including several vintages of **Dominus,** a California Cabernet produced by **Christian Moueix,** proprietor of Chateau Pétrus in Bordeaux. Shipping is available. ♦ Daily 9:30AM-6PM.1321 Main St, St. Helena. 963.3092

The Benedictine monk **Dom Pérignon** is credited with perfecting the secondary fermentation stage of champagne making, which took place at the abbey of Hautvillers near Epernay in the Champagne region of France in the late 17th century.

Restaurants/Clubs: Red   **Hotels:** Blue
Shops/ 🍃 Outdoors: Green   **Wineries/Sights:** Black

DRAWING BY MARY R. MOFFITT

143 Masonic Building The most elaborate building on Main Street, this fancy Victorian structure was erected in 1892 by **M.G. Ritchie** and bought by the Masons in 1972. The influence of British architect Charles Eastlake is obvious in such repetitive motifs as turned spindles and concentric circles. The facade is brick over structural stone, the bays

St. Helena

are wood, and the sides show the use of stone repeating some of the wood designs. ♦ 1327-37 Main St, St. Helena

143 Michael's Attic An interesting mix of Crabtree & Evelyn soaps, bound journals to fill with your travel or wine-tasting notes, charming tin toys, and hooked rugs. The back room displays thatched-roof mail boxes, bird houses, verdigris chimes, a farmhouse dinner bell, and whimsical garden sculptures. A pig in chef's whites, anyone? ♦ Daily 10AM-5:30PM. 1317 Main St, St. Helena. 963.0300

143 Art & Wine Shop Artist **Gaye Frisk** uses a combination of sandblasting and hand-painting to decorate wine bottles. Most are commissioned by corporations and wineries with their own logo, but she also sells her own series of designs (mostly on magnum-sized bottles) with wines from Dunn, Bernard Pradel, Flora Springs, and others inside. ♦ M-Sa 10AM-5PM; call first, as hours vary. 1315 Main St, St. Helena. 963.5352, 944.1655; fax 944.0359

143 Doidge's ★★$ A branch of the San Francisco Doidge's with a solid reputation for generous, American-style breakfasts. At this storefront restaurant, it's easy to tuck away overstuffed omelets, home fries, stacks of pancakes, and other hearty dishes—all the more reason for an afternoon bike ride. At lunch, they make a variety of sandwiches on their own fresh-baked bread. No wine list. ♦ American ♦ Daily 7:30AM-2PM. 1313 Main St, St. Helena. 963.1788

143 Hotel St. Helena $$ Built in 1881, this inn celebrated its first hundred years with a total refurbishing and a return to respectable comfort. The 18 old-fashioned rooms are decorated with period wallpapers, fabrics, and accessories, and every effort is made to make

45

guests feel at home. Some rooms share generous-sized bathrooms; others have private baths. Continental breakfast included. ◆ 1309 Main St, St. Helena. 963.4388

144 My Favorite Things Handwoven throws, wooden arks, and children's carved wooden trains, plus nostalgic picture frames and needlepoint pillows. ◆ M-Sa 10AM-5:30PM; Su noon-4PM. 1289 Main St, St. Helena. 963.0848

144 St. Helena Antiques Among the finds here are antique corkscrews, 19th-century French bottle-drying racks and wine carriers, crystal decanters, old ice cream and butter molds in the shape of a cluster of grapes, as well as handmade English basketry wine carriers for four or six bottles, and garden furniture. ◆ M-Sa 11AM-5PM; Su noon-4PM. 1231 Main St, St. Helena. 963.5878

St. Helena

144 The Valley Exchange Head towards the back of this store—past the bird feeders, terra-cotta pots, baskets, and more—for the divine chocolate truffles from **Cocolat** in Berkeley and the crunchy, almond-studded biscotti from San Francisco's **La Tempesta** bakery. ◆ M-Sa 10AM-5:30PM; Su 11AM-4PM. 1201 Main St, St. Helena. 963.7423

145 St. Helena Fish Market Cooked crab, shucked oysters, smoked salmon and trout, plus bouillabaisse and other freshly-made soups for those who can heat them up in a kitchenette. ◆ Tu-F 10:30AM-6PM; Sa 10:30AM-3:30PM. 1232 Spring St, St. Helena. 963.5331

146 Napa Valley Coffee Roasting Company Only open since June of 1991, this attractive corner cafe, with light flooding through the French windows, is a great spot for breakfast or whiling away the afternoon. Settle in at one of the marble bistro tables for some of the best espresso drinks in the valley. Partners **Denise Fox** and **Leon Sange** roast all the coffees at their downtown Napa location, and offer more than 20 varieties. (Forget the Napa Valley T-shirts and take home a pound or two of great coffee for a different kind of wine country souvenir.) They open at a wide-awake 7:30AM and offer freshly squeezed orange juice, the cappuccino of your dreams, bagels with cream cheese and chutney, crumbly scones, flaky Danishes, and toasted bread from the popular Berkeley bakery, **Acme Baking Company.** And if that isn't enough, they have outdoor seating on the porch, a shelf of good reads provided by Main Street Books, and live music from 8 to 10PM on Friday and Saturday night. If the weather's toasty, stop in for their refreshing double espresso granita, a rough slush of frozen coffee crystals topped with panna (whipped cream)—now that's truly *la dolce vita.* ◆ Daily 7:30AM-10PM. 1400 Oak Ave, St. Helena. 963.4491

147 The Cinnamon Bear $$ Teddy bears—the best plaything ever invented—is the motto at this B&B, with teddies of every size and description scattered throughout the 1904 bungalow where St. Helena's longtime mayor **Walter Mezner** lived for many years. Willow furniture graces the broad veranda, and the four guest rooms (three upstairs and one down) have 1920s antiques, queen-sized beds, and private baths. Innkeepers **Carla Dolson** and **Brenda Cream** serve a breakfast of orange juice, fruit, Spanish soufflé or broccoli quiche, and hot muffins. ◆ 1407 Kearney St, St. Helena. 963.4653

147 Chestelson House $$ Just off Main St, this small 1904 Victorian offers the welcoming ambience of a family home. Owner **Jackie Sweet** draws on her success as a caterer and cooking instructor to plan creative, mouth-watering meals, which might include bran muffins with praline butter, peach shortcake, her signature baked stuffed eggs, French toast filled with ricotta, and jam, fruit, juice, and coffee. The three light, spacious bedrooms are elegant and unfussy, with queen-sized beds, Roman blinds or French shutters, and private baths. Each room is named for a different verse in **Robert Louis Stevenson's** *Child's Garden of Verses.* Sweet also keeps picnic baskets for guests' use. ◆ 1417 Kearney St, St. Helena. 963.2238

"Why look you now; 'tis when men drink they thrive, grow wealthy, speed their business, win their suits, make themselves happy, benefit their friends."
Aristophanes

Brother Timothy, a member of the Christian Brothers order and an avid corkscrew collector, credits **Samuel Hensall,** an English parson, with designing the first patented corkscrew in 1795.

148 Silverado Museum This museum is devoted to the beloved **Robert Louis Stevenson,** author of *A Child's Garden of Verses* and *Treasure Island*, who spent his honeymoon in an abandoned bunkhouse at the old Silverado Mine on Mount St. Helena in 1880. Founded by bibliophile **Norman Strouse,** it has a touching and quirky collection of more than 8,000 items acquired from heirs and friends of Stevenson: original letters, manuscripts, first editions, paintings, sculpture, photographs, and memorabilia. You'll see the copy of *A Child's Garden of Verses* that he presented to his wife **Fanny**; the Parmesan cheese case his father used to carry (which later turned up in *Treasure Island)*; a lead toy soldier and the miniature tea set he played with more than a century ago; and the name board from the ship *Equator*, which carried the Stevenson family from Hawaii to Samoa in 1889. Also on view: the gloves that fellow author **Henry James** forgot during a visit, which Fanny gleefully appropriated and put in an envelope with the note: "Henry James' gloves left in my house and dishonestly confiscated by me. FS." ♦ Tu-Su noon-4PM. 1490 Library Ln, St. Helena. 963.3757

148 Napa Valley Wine Library For anyone interested in wine lore, this 6,000-volume collection of books, tapes, and reference materials on wine and viticulture is definitely worth a visit. Browsers and borrowers alike are made to feel welcome. ♦ M-W 10AM-9PM; Th-F 10AM-6PM; Sa 10AM-2PM. 1492 Library Ln, St. Helena. 963.5244; fax 963.5264

Associated with the Napa Valley Wine Library:

Napa Valley Wine Library Association The $20 annual membership fee gives you access to the specialized wine library, a subscription to a newsletter listing new wine books in the collection, and an invitation to the gala tasting in August—in itself well worth the price of membership. ♦ Box 328, St. Helena. 963.5145

Napa Valley Wine Library Association Courses Weekend courses in May and June, including an informal introduction to wine appreciation presented by wine professionals from Napa Valley wineries. Lectures, field trips, and tastings cover sensory evaluations of wines, grape varieties, and production. The fee includes a year's membership in the association. ♦ Box 207, St. Helena. 963.5145

148 Napa Valley Farmers Market Shop for exotic leaf lettuce, vine-ripened tomatoes, and handmade cheeses and breads at this once-a-week farmers market in the parking lot behind Dansk Square. It's a certified farmers market, which means each farmer grows the produce he or she sells. This is a great chance to see some of the top-notch ingredients that go into wine-country cooking firsthand. It's also fun to rub elbows with innkeepers, chefs, vintners, and other local folk who make a point of shopping here every week. ♦ F 7:30AM-noon, May-Nov. Old Railroad Depot, Railroad Ave. 963.7343

149 Calafia Cellars Named for an Amazonian Queen, Calafia produces small quantities of Cabernet and Merlot. ♦ By appt. 629 Fulton Ln, St. Helena. 963.0114

150 Stonesbridge Park A small park on the banks of the Napa River where you can sit and enjoy a picnic lunch. ♦ Pope St (near Silverado Trail) St. Helena

St. Helena

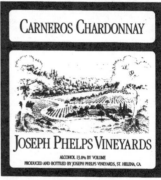

151 Joseph Phelps Vineyards Construction magnate Joseph Phelps built a couple of wineries for other people before he decided to construct his own in 1974 on the former Connolly Hereford Ranch in Spring Valley. The redwood winery is so cleverly designed that it almost disappears into the hillside to the east of the Silverado Trail. Under general manager **Bruce Neyers** and winemaker **Craig Williams,** Phelps makes quite a few excellent wines, including an outstanding late-harvest Riesling, a Bordeaux-style blend called Insignia, and several vineyard-designated Cabernet Sauvignons. In 1990 they added a new Vin du Mistral label for Rhône-style wines. These include a Syrah, a violet-scented Viognier white, a Grenache, and a blend of Mourvedre, Grenache, and Syrah they've dubbed Rouge—for red. ♦ Sales daily 8AM-5PM; tasting and tours by appt. 200 Taplin Rd, St. Helena. 963.2745

Restaurants/Clubs: Red   Hotels: Blue
Shops/ ♥ Outdoors: Green   Wineries/Sights: Black

152 The Farmhouse $$ In the midst of **Joseph Phelps'** vineyards sits this graceful farmhouse B&B, built around an inner courtyard draped with wisteria. Decorated in an understated country style, the three guest rooms, all with private baths, have queen-sized beds with cheerful duvets and plump pillows, and Southwest-inspired furniture. The **Blue Room** is the largest, and has windows across two sides and a view of vines with wildflowers at their feet. The spring-fed swimming pool is in a spectacular setting framed by fruit trees and a gnarled olive tree. Breakfast, prepared by innkeeper **Hannah Nunn,** might feature homemade pear or fig jam from the farm's own trees, and in the evenings, she and her husband **Ron,** an architect who has designed several wineries, may serve Phelps' wine and some cheese in front of the fire. There are several nice walks through Spring Valley; as a guest you can hike through acres of Phelps' vineyards. ♦ 300 Taplin Rd. St. Helena. 963.3431

153 Meadowood Resort $$$$ A luxurious retreat of great charm and style that was originally a private country club for well-to-do Napa Valley families. After a 1984 fire destroyed the old clubhouse, Sausalito architect **Kirk Hillman** rebuilt it, using elements of New England's grand turn-of-the-century cottages in his design. Trimmed in white, with tiers of gabled windows and wrap-around porches, the main lodge and the 13 smaller lodges scattered over the 250-acre property evoke a feeling of old money and tradition. General manager **Maurice Nayrolles** honed his craft at the Plaza Athenée in Paris and other top-flight European hotels, and his professionalism is evident in the staff's attention to detail and the old-world sense of service. The 85 rooms range from one-room studios (with fireplaces) to large suites; all have private porches, beds covered in chintz with matching pillows and plump down comforters, robes, wet bars, coffeemakers, and toasters. The grounds include six championship tennis courts strung along a hillside, two pools, a nine-hole executive golf course, and an English croquet court where whites are de rigeur.

Meadowood and **Domaine Mumm** host the **Domaine Mumm Napa Croquet Classic** here each year, and the resort is also the site of the elegant annual **Napa Valley Wine Auction**. In addition to golf, tennis, and croquet pros, Meadowood has **John Thoreen,** an unpretentious and down-to-earth resident wine expert, to advise guests on winery itineraries or to conduct tastings for groups. Book well ahead

for summer stays and weekend getaways. ♦ Deluxe ♦ 900 Meadowood Ln, St. Helena. 963.3646, 800/458.8080; fax 963.3532

Within the Meadowood Resort:

The Restaurant at Meadowood
★★★$$$/$$$$ The restaurant at Meadowood boasts an elegant, understated dining room in the main lodge overlooking the golf-course green. The executive chef is **Henri Delcros,** a French Catalán, who worked at several two- and three-star restaurants in France before moving to the US. He's recently added gutsier, country-style dishes to the menu, moving away from a strictly French nouvelle approach, with the confidence and the craft to back it up. The bright, unfussy dishes such as the baked farm-hen breast with Spanish olive oil, garlic, potatoes, and fresh herbs, and his Paul Bocuse grilled New York steak with hand-cut garlic French fries and Roquefort butter are a tribute to the celebrated chef. One of the best dishes is Delcros' Paella Catalán studded with lamb sausage, chicken, shellfish, and calamari. And how about mint ice cream with chocolate sauce for dessert, or the ginger-spiked crème brûlée? The service is exemplary and the wine list offers a treasure trove of Napa Valley's finest. ♦ California/French ♦ M-Sa 11:30AM-2:30PM, 6-9PM; Su 10:30AM-2PM, 6-9PM

The Grill at Meadowood ★★$$ This informal restaurant overlooking the golf course offers breakfast and lunch, and in summer, light dinners. In warm weather, the terrace outside is a glorious spot for a meal. Breakfast includes a tropical fruit compote, pancakes, and French brioche toast, along with the usual eggs, bacon, and potatoes. It's the lunch menu that really shines, with lots of inventive sandwiches and salads, along with a great burger, a Coney Island Dog with chili and cheese, and updated classics such as a clubhouse sandwich made with grilled Atlantic salmon, capers, and onions. You can always find a freshly made soup or an interesting salad, and for dessert, there's rocky road fudge cake, milk shakes, and a superlative carrot cake. Sample wine by the glass from a well-edited California list. On the weekends they offer an inexpensive prix-fixe, three-course dinner. ♦ California ♦ M-Th 7AM-8:30PM; F-Su 7AM-9PM

154 Beringer Vineyards The oldest continuously operating winery in the Napa Valley received its bond in 1876. Founder **Frederick Beringer** built the landmark **Rhine House** as a tribute to the home he left behind when he emigrated from Germany in the mid-19th century. A popular tour of the vineyards includes the house and the extensive caves tunneled out by Chinese laborers a century ago. Today Beringer is owned jointly by the Swiss food conglomerate **Nestlé** and the French **Labruyère** family. Since 1977 the winery has been known for its extraordinary private reserve Chardonnay and Cabernet. Winemaker **Ed Sbragia** also produces a roster of other wines, all well made. The old Beringer family home, known as the **Hudson House,** is now Beringer's Culinary Arts Center, where French chef, cookbook author, and PBS television personality **Madeleine Kamman** hosts a variety of seminars and special weekends for food-and-wine lovers. It's also the home of the **School for American Chefs,** a graduate program for professional chefs. ♦ Tasting, sales, and tours daily 9:30AM-4:30PM. 2000 Main St, St. Helena. 963.7115

155 Christian Brothers-Greystone Cellars

Thousands line up each year for the grand tour of Christian Brothers' impressive and historic cellars, which date from 1888 (though the Roman Catholic teaching order didn't acquire the property until 1950 and it was sold a few years ago). Even if you've already taken the tour, **Brother Timothy's** fascinating and wacky corkscrew collection is worth a second look. Go around to the south side of the immense, century-old Greystone building, following the signs for sales and barrel tasting. Just past the tasting room, hundreds of corkscrews are displayed in glass cases, organized by theme. The display called "Animal Farm," for example, includes corkscrews in the shape of piglets, dachshunds, sea horses, monkeys, owls, hippos, bulls, and ladybugs. A display of pocket corkscrews traces the waiter's corkscrew in all its permutations, including the ingenious Screwpull. ♦ Tasting (with tour) 10AM-4PM; sales daily 10AM-5PM. ♦ 2555 Main St, St. Helena. 967.3112

156 Charles Krug Winery

Pioneer winemaker **Charles Krug** founded this winery in 1861, though it's been run by a branch of the **Mondavi** family since 1943. Long known for its generic table wines, the Krug winery has recently jumped on the quality bandwagon with its benchmark Cabernet Sauvignon Vintage Select. The winery makes three vineyard-designated reserve wines: Slinsen Ranch for Cabernet, Brown Ranch Los Carneros for Pinot Noir, and Cabral Ranch Los Carneros Chardonnay. ♦ Fee for tasting. Tasting and sales daily 10AM-5PM; tours by appt. 2800 St. Helena Hwy, St. Helena. 963.5057

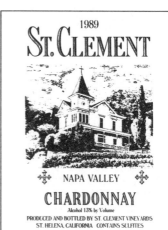

157 St. Clement Vineyards

The elegant mansion that appears on St. Clement's label was built in 1878 by San Francisco

St. Helena

glass merchant **Fritz Rosenbaum,** and its stone cellar became one of the earliest bonded wineries in the valley. After years of neglect, the cellar was restored in time for the 1975 vintage. In 1990 the lovely Victorian mansion now used as the Visitor's Center was opened to the public for the first time in a century. Napa Valley native and winemaker **Dennis Johns** concentrates on a limited production of flavorful Sauvignon Blanc, Chardonnay, and a rich complex Cabernet. ♦ Tasting, sales, and tours by appt daily 10AM-4PM. 2867 St. Helena Hwy, St. Helena. 963.7221

158 Spring Mountain Vineyards

Television fans the world over will recognize the exterior of this winery as the fictional *Falcon Crest* mansion, and, as a result, the tasting room is often crowded. Chardonnay, Cabernet, and Sauvignon Blanc. ♦ Tasting and sales daily 10AM-4:45PM; tours by appt. 2805 Spring Mountain Rd, St. Helena. 963.5233

159 Robert Keenan Winery

This family-owned winery, perched on Spring Mountain, where a 1904 winery used to be, produces just three wines: Chardonnay, Merlot, and a sturdy and tannic Cabernet. Picnic area. ♦ Tasting and sales by appt M-Sa 10AM-4PM. 3660 Spring Mountain Rd, St. Helena. 963.9177

160 Philip Togni Vineyard

Renowned vintner **Philip Togni** (who has acted as winemaker and consultant for a slew of top estates including Mayacamas, Chalone, Chapellet, and Cuvaison) has been producing wine under his own label since 1985. Most notable are a rich and intense Cabernet Sauvignon, and a crisp, lean Sauvignon Blanc. He continues to consult for Chimney Rock Winery. ♦ Tours by appt only. 3780 Spring Mountain Rd, St. Helena. 963.3731

161 Smith-Madrone Vineyard Founded by brothers **Charles** and **Stuart Smith** in 1977, this winery on Spring Mountain produces Chardonnay, Cabernet, and Riesling. The '78 Riesling won the top award at the French wine-and-food magazine *Gault-Millau's* tasting in 1979. ♦ Sales and tours by appt. 4022 Spring Mountain Rd, St. Helena. 963.2283

161 Ritchie Creek Vineyards Located up a winding road at the very top of Spring Mountain, this tiny winery produces small quantities of Chardonnay and Cabernet Sauvignon from steeply terraced vineyards on the Sonoma border. ♦ Tasting and sales by appt only. 4024 Spring Mountain Rd, St. Helena. 963.4661

162 Newton Vineyards A winery designed by owners **Su Hua Newton** and **Peter Newton**, founders of Sterling Vineyards, that sits on a high knoll overlooking the valley and features a spectacular formal roof garden of old roses and boxwood. Newton's steeply terraced vineyards on Spring Mountain produce consistently good Chardonnay, Sauvignon Blanc, Cabernet, and Merlot. The cellar is laid out along classic French lines, with the oak barrels all housed underground. Until he left to found his own small winery, **Ric Forman,** one of the hot young stars of California winemaking, was the winemaker here; **John Kongsgaard** is the current winemaker. ♦ Sales M-F 8AM-5PM; tours by appt F 11AM. 2555 Madrona Ave, St. Helena. 963.9000

163 White Sulphur Springs Resort $$ The oldest hot springs resort in California, established in 1852, is just three miles west of St. Helena on a 330-acre estate in a quiet valley. The family-owned resort offers rustic lodging in either the 13-room inn (with shared kitchen and shower, and private toilets and sinks), a carriage house that sleeps 30 (with individual rooms, and shared bath and kitchen), or eight cabins (with private bath; most have kitchens). This really feels like the country and for the times when racing around the valley is too taxing, you can settle in for a soak in the outdoor mineral spring pool, picnic in the secluded redwood grove, or take on your fellow guests in a game of basketball or horseshoes. It's a great spot for bicycling, too. An

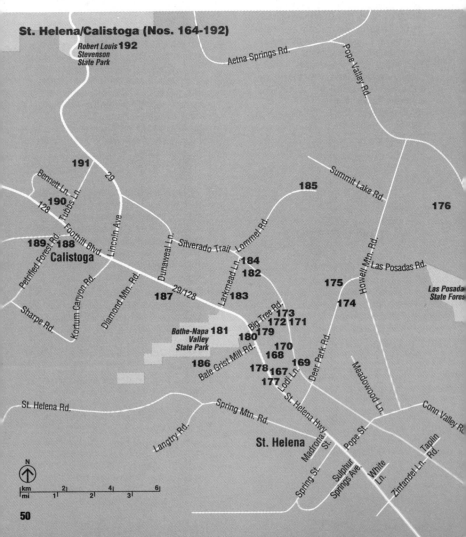

St. Helena/Calistoga (Nos. 164-192)

Olympic-sized pool is slated to be completed in the spring of 1992. No smoking. ♦ 3100 White Sulphur Springs Rd, St. Helena. 963.8588, 944.1915

Within the White Sulphur Springs Resort:

White Sulphur Springs Historical Museum A small museum with memorabilia of the historic hot springs and the surrounding area. ♦ M-F 9AM-6PM; Sa-Su 8AM-10PM. 963.8588

164 Green and Red Vineyard At this minuscule winery founded in 1977, former sculptor and professor of art **Jay Heminway** specializes in Zinfandel. His wines can be found on the lists of top Bay Area bistros. ♦ Tours by appt only. 3208 Chiles Valley Rd, St. Helena. 965.2346

165 Rustridge Ranch and Winery $$ This 442-acre vineyard, winery, and thoroughbred-horse breeding facility opened as a five-room B&B in 1989, with guests bunking down in the 1940s ranch house. Seemingly lost in the hills above the Silverado Trail, the site is actually an old Wappo Indian camp, and

innkeepers **Jim Fresquez** and **Susan Meyer Fresquez** have a collection of arrowheads, leather grinding bowls, and pestles that they've found on the property. The ranch has become a popular getaway for San Franciscans who prefer a serene retreat over wine-country glitz. The entire ranch house can also be rented to families and groups of friends. Four of the neat, pleasant rooms are in the left wing of the ranch house. The largest is the sunny **Rustridge Room,** which has its own fireplace, bath, and dressing room and is flanked by the **Oak Rooms,** two smaller rooms that share a bath and look onto a deck situated above ancient oak trees and a stream. **The Chiles Valley Room** is off to itself, with the sauna and hot tub just outside the door. The entire inn is decorated in an updated Santa Fe style. Guests have the run of the ranch house, which includes a large comfortably furnished living room with a fireplace, pressed straw roof, and skylights. The innkeepers offer the unusual—and very

welcome—option of using the professionally equipped kitchen to make a salad or even cook dinner for yourself. The ranch also has a tennis court and a swimming pool. The horses on the ranch are not available for riding, but you can bring your own and keep them in the stables here. There are miles of nearby trails for either riding or hiking. ♦ 2910 Lower Chiles Valley Rd, St. Helena. 965.9353

166 Lake Berryessa Creek Canyon was dammed at one end to create 26-mile-long Lake Berryessa, the largest human-made lake in Northern California. Oak Shores Park and resorts around the lake offer an array of recreational opportunities. Fishers will find lots of trout, bass, catfish, and silver salmon. The lake's marinas have docks, berths, and boat launches; most will rent fishing or ski boats, jet skis, sailboards—and one rents houseboats. Tent and RV camping, picnic areas, and barbecue facilities are available at the lake's resorts. ♦ For more information call Lake Berryessa Chamber of Commerce at 800/726.1256

167 Freemark Abbey Winery A lovely room with a wood-beam ceiling and sofas pulled up in front of a fieldstone fireplace welcomes you to the tasting area, where you can sample not only new releases, but an occasional older vintage. Winemaking here dates from 1866, the year **Josephine Tychson** established Freemark Abbey, which made her the first woman to build a winery in California. She was succeeded by **Antonio Forni** who built the present stone structure circa 1900. After the repeal of Prohibition, it changed hands several times until the present owners bought it in 1967. Headed by third-generation Napa Valley resident **Chuck Carpy,** the winery is best known for its Cabernet from Bosché Vineyard near Rutherford, considered one of

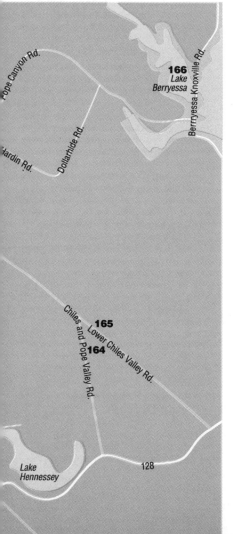

the finest vineyards in California. They also produce oaky Chardonnays and Johannisberg Riesling, which in certain years develops into Edelwein, a rich and extravagantly perfumed late-harvest dessert wine. ♦ Fee. Tasting and sales daily 10AM-4:30PM; tours at 2PM. 3022 St. Helena Hwy, St. Helena. 963.9694

Within the Freemark Abbey complex:

Hurd Beeswax Candles You can watch candlemakers roll, dip, and cut pure beeswax into fanciful shapes, such as treble clefs, flames, and spirals. Classic forms are decorated with leaves or wildflowers. Kids will love peering through a little window to see an actual beehive at work. You can also buy natural beeswax candles here, from slender tapers and votive lights to tall, hefty candles big enough for a cathedral. ♦ M-F 8:30AM-5PM; Sa-Su 10AM-5:30PM. 3020 St. Helena Hwy, St. Helena. 963.7211

St. Helena

167 Brava Terrace ★★★$$ A welcome addition to the restaurant scene in Napa Valley. **Fred Halpert,** who was head chef at the highly regarded restaurant in San Francisco's Portman Hotel, pulled up his stakes to open this California/Mediterranean bistro in 1991. The light, spacious room has a large fieldstone fireplace, bright textiles on the seats and banquettes, and a shady outdoor terrace facing the woods for al fresco dining. Halpert's love of the vibrant, sun-drenched flavors of Provence and Italy—with a soupçon of California country thrown into the mix—is obvious: Provençal salad of wild greens and herbs with warm Sonoma goat cheese, a skewer of locally smoked sausage with vegetables and a Catalán romesco dip, and a *soupe de poissons* (Provençal fish soup with garlic croutons) are just a few of the first courses on his menu. He's got some great sandwiches, too, including a burger made with naturally raised beef, topped with tomatoes and basil on a potato bun. Ask about the risotto and pasta of the day; a pasta dish made without butter or oil is always on the menu. And the minute it gets a little chilly outside order the cassoulet de Puy, a hot, hearty French dish of lentils simmered slowly with pork tenderloin, lamb, and smoked duck sausage. For dessert, there's no question: order the vanilla bean chocolate chip ice cream accompanied by chocolate cookies.

Well-edited wine list, too. ♦ California/Mediterranean ♦ Daily 11:30AM-9PM. 3010 St. Helena Hwy, St. Helena. Reservations recommended. 963.9300

168 Folie à Deux Winery The name of this winery is from a French term used by psychiatrists in this country to describe a fantasy or delusion shared by two people—the duo in this case being **Larry** and **Evie Dizmang** (a psychiatrist and psychiatric social worker, respectively). Everyone told them they were crazy to start a winery, hence the name. And they contend that a bottle of wine shared on a special occasion provokes a spirit of folly and fantasy all its own. Founded in 1981, the winery produces wonderful Chenin Blanc, perfect for apértifs, along with Chardonnay and Cabernet. Their Muscat Canelli dessert wine, available only at the winery, is called *à Deux*. Note the Rorschach inkblot on the winery's label; it represents the designer of the label and her twin sister. The tasting room is in the original turn-of-the-century farmhouse. Oak-shaded picnic grounds. ♦ Tasting and sales daily 11AM-5PM; tours by appt. 3070 St. Helena Hwy, St. Helena. 963.1160

169 Wine Country Inn $$ This small hotel was designed in the tradition of the inns of New England and is located off the highway in the midst of a quiet meadow. All 25 rooms have private baths and views of the serene countryside; most have private patios or balconies and/or fireplaces. Country furniture (carved wooden beds, wicker chairs, and pine armoires) is balanced with coverlets, curtains, and carpeting in autumnal or spring colors. Continental breakfast with homemade bread and granola. ♦ 1152 Lodi Ln, St. Helena. 963.7077

170 Duckhorn Vineyards Margaret and **Daniel Duckhorn** founded this winery with ten other families, all friends, in 1976; their first wines from the 1978 vintage, a Cabernet and a Merlot, were immediately acclaimed, and they remain their best. The Merlots, in fact, come from two specific vineyards: the one from Three Palms Vineyard needs time to tame its tannins, while the Merlot from Vine Hill Vineyard tends to be more supple and elegant. They also make a Sauvignon Blanc. ♦ Tasting and sales by appt. M-F 9AM-4PM. 3027 Silverado Trail, St. Helena. 963.7108

171 Rombauer Vineyards Founded in 1982 by **Joan** and **Koerner Rambauer,** the great-nephew of **Irma Rombauer,** author of *Joy of Cooking,* this well-equipped young winery custom-crushes wines for a number of aspiring winemakers and also produces a crisp Chardonnay, Cabernet Sauvignon, and a proprietary red wine of Cabernet blended with Cabernet Franc and Merlot under the name Le Meilleur du Chai ("the best of the cellar"). ♦ Tasting daily 9AM-5PM; tours by appt. 3522 Silverado Trail, St. Helena. 963.5170

172 Tudal Winery Consistently well-made Cabernet from a small family-owned property where two generations of the **Tudal** family work side by side. ♦ Tasting and tours by appt daily 10AM-4PM. 1015 Big Tree Rd, St. Helena. 963.3947

173 Charles F. Shaw Vineyard & Winery Among other offerings, this family estate produces a new-world Gamay Beaujolais Nouveau, inspired by its French counterpart. ♦ Tasting and tours by appt daily 10AM-5PM. 1010 Big Tree Rd, St. Helena. 963.5459

DEER PARK WINERY

1983
Napa Valley
SAUVIGNON BLANC

PRODUCED & BOTTLED BY DEER PARK WINERY
DEER PARK, NAPA VALLEY, CALIFORNIA, USA
BW 4931 — ESTABLISHED 1891
PROPRIETORS R. & L. KNAPP AND D. & K. CLARK
ALCOHOL 12.7% PER VOLUME

174 Deer Park Winery A small, state-of-the-art winery housed in a venerable, two-story stone building that dates from before Prohibition. The winery, owned by the **Robert Knapp** and **David Clark** families, produces Sauvignon Blanc and Zinfandel from a rocky hillside vineyard. They also produce Chardonnay and a small amount of Petite Sirah. ♦ Tasting and sales by appt M-Sa 10AM-4:30PM. 1000 Deer Park Rd, St. Helena. 963.5411

175 Burgess Cellars In a two-story wood-and-stone winery building on the site of a vineyard planted around 1880, former airline pilot **Tom Burgess** and winemaker **Bill Sorenson** produce big bold wines from Burgess' Chardonnay, Cabernet, and Zinfandel vineyards. The Cabernet Vintage Selection and the barrel-fermented Chardonnay from Triere Vineyard both age well. ♦ Tasting and tours daily by appt 10AM-4PM. 1108 Deer Park Rd, St. Helena. 963.4766

176 La Jota Vineyard Co. This unassuming winery, built from huge stone blocks quarried nearby, dates from 1892 and won several medals at the Paris Exposition of 1900, but was abandoned by the end of Prohibition. Present owners **Bill** and **Joan Smith** released their first wine in 1984, and today the small winery is respected for its long-lived Cabernet and rich, spiced Zinfandel from Howell Mountain. Seek out their lovely,

hauntingly perfumed Viognier, a white wine made from the same grape that goes into the Rhône Valley's famed Condrieu. ♦ Tasting and tours by appt only. 1102 Las Posadas Rd, Angwin. 965.3020

177 Vintners Village A glitzy complex that houses tasting rooms for four wineries: **Audubon, Chappelle, Charles F. Shaw,** and **Dunwood.** The tasting fee includes a souvenir wineglass and if you buy food or beverages here, they'll waive the charge for using the hillside picnic site. The remainder of the complex is taken up with shops (including a London Fog outlet), antique stores, galleries, a deli, and a restaurant. ♦ Daily 10AM-5PM. 3111 St. Helena Hwy, St. Helena. 963.4082

Within Vintners Village:

Vines ★$$/$$$ The cornerstone of Vintners Village is this informal California cuisine restaurant. Lunch includes freshly made soups, sandwiches of roasted meats and

poultry, mesquite burgers, Black Angus steaks, and pizzas from the wood-burning oven. Dinner offers a broader menu, including prime rib from the rôtisserie and mesquite-grilled fish and game. ♦ California ♦ M-Sa 11:30AM-3PM, 5-9PM; Su 1:30-3PM, 5-9PM. 963.8991

178 Bale Grist Mill State Historic Park Believe it or not, Napa Valley's economy was once based on wheat, not grapes. This historic flour mill was designed and built by the young British surgeon **Edward Turner Bale** in 1846, who served under **General Vallejo,** married Vallejo's niece, and settled in Napa Valley. In 1988 the handsome mill was restored to working condition, complete with a 36-foot wooden waterwheel and huge millstones. On weekends at 1 and 4PM, the immense wheel turns and you can watch the ranger/miller grind grain with the French buhrstone; sometimes you can linger in the granary to see baking demonstrations. It's an invigorating walk to the mill from **Bothe-Napa Valley State Park** along the well-marked **History Trail** (1.2 miles), which passes through a pioneer cemetery and the site of the first church in Napa County, built in 1853. A bit of movie trivia: this site may look familiar as it was used by Walt Disney in the 1960 film *Pollyanna.* ♦ Admission; children under age 6 free. Daily 10AM-5PM. 3369 St. Helena Hwy, St. Helena

179 Frog's Leap Winery Named for the frogs that once were raised in this spot along Mill Creek. An old ledger discloses that at the turn of the century, the critters went for 33 cents a dozen—destined, no doubt, for the tables of San Francisco restaurants. This small winery has been using organic farming methods since **Larry Turley** and partners founded it in the early eighties. Their best wine is a

Sauvignon Blanc, but the Chardonnay and Cabernet Sauvignon are not far behind. They also make a spicy Zinfandel. ♦ Sales by appt M-F 10AM-4PM; tours by appt. ♦ 3358 St. Helena Hwy, St. Helena. 963.4704

180 Bale Mill Classic Country Furniture

Owner **Tom Scheibal** designs about 80 percent of the handsome country pine furniture, stylish iron garden chairs, beds, and chaise longues for sale here. More portable are the rustic willow baskets, and wire baskets. They also have some lovely lamps and weathered iron signs. Scheibal has a second shop, called **Palladio,** in Healdsburg. ♦ M, W-Su 10AM-6PM. 3431 St. Helena Hwy, St. Helena. 963.4595

St. Helena

181 **Bothe-Napa Valley State Park** An 1,800-acre park with more than a hundred picnic sites, all with tables and barbecues situated under huge maple and Douglas fir trees. After lunch, you can swim in the park's pool or work off your picnic by taking a hike. The **History Trail,** rated as moderately strenuous, leads past a **Pioneer Cemetery** and the site of Napa County's first church, built in 1853, to the **Old Bale Grist Mill**.

Originally a country retreat built in the 1870s by **Dr.** and **Mrs. Charles Hitchcock,** the estate was bought by **Reinhold Bothe** after Hitchcock's daughter **Lillie Coit** died in 1929. Bothe deeded it to the state in 1960, and today the park is a haven for wine-country vacationers, offering the ultimate bargain in Napa Valley budget accommodations. There are 50 family campsites including 10 remote, walk-in sites suitable for tent camping. The remaining 40 sites can accommodate tents or RVs. Campsites have flush toilets, hot showers, laundry sinks, picnic tables, and barbecues, plus use of the swimming pool. Evening campfire programs and talks about the stars and planets are held on Wednesday and Saturday. Fifteen-day limit. Reservations for campsites accepted eight weeks in advance. ♦ Fee. Open year-round; pool daily 10:30AM-7PM, mid-June through Labor Day. 3801 St. Helena Hwy, Calistoga. 942.4575, 800/444.PARK

182 **Rancho Maria Louisa** This farmstand sells seasonal organic garden produce and fresh herbs, plus wine vinegar, and dried fruit. ♦ Daily 9AM-6PM. 3911 Silverado Trail, Calistoga. 942.6941

Louis Pasteur's discovery of yeast as the source of fermentation provided the key to consistency in winemaking.

183 Larkmead Inn $$ This delightful country inn and the Hans Kornell Champagne Cellars located next door were once part of Larkmead Winery, owned in the late 1880s by the flamboyant heiress **Lillie Coit.** The Palladian-style farmhouse with an octagonal loggia flanked by two wings is built on two levels, with the main part of the house upstairs—the better to oversee the vineyards and catch the afternoon breezes. Four guest rooms, all with private baths and vineyard views, are in one wing of the house. The **Beaujolais Room** has a queen-sized bed, vintage wicker-and-cane chairs with cushions covered in a **William Morris** print, and a private veranda; the airy Chenin Blanc room features an antique, queen-sized bed and a chaise longue covered in a flowered print; and the **Chablis Room** has its own little solarium. Innkeeper **Joan Garbarino** serves an excellent breakfast (fruit plate, croissants, scones, and coffee) on her Imari china and heirloom sterling. Smoking permitted. ♦ 1103 Larkmead Ln, Calistoga. 942.5360

184 Hans Kornell Champagne Cellars Specializing in sparkling wines made by the traditional méthode champenoise used in the French region of Champagne, this cellar was founded in 1958 by German immigrant **Hans Kornell,** who worked in Germany and Europe before settling in America. In fact, Kornell was Napa Valley's first producer of méthode champenoise champagne. An instructive guided tour of the two-story, stone winery takes you through every aspect of sparkling wine production, and is followed by a tasting of Kornell's broad range of sparkling wines. Among the best: the Blanc de Blancs and Blanc de Noirs Cuvées. ♦ Tasting, sales, and tours daily 10AM-4:30PM. 1091 Larkmead Ln, Calistoga. 963.1237

185 **Calistoga Ranch Campgrounds** A 168-acre park with 144 campsites accommodating tents, campers, and RVs (full and partial hookups). Barbecue pits, swimming pool, picnic area, and trails. ♦ Open year-round. 580 Lommel Rd, Calistoga. 942.6565

186 Stony Hill Vineyard Founded in 1951 by the late **Fred** and **Eleanor McCrea,** this small vineyard on the rocky hillside of the western ridge of the Napa Valley has a cult following for their voluptuous Chardonnay. Despite the high quality and the difficulty in finding this wine, which is sold to a mailing list of faithful customers, the prices remain uncommonly moderate. ♦ Sales by mailing list only. Tours by appt only. 3331 St. Helena Hwy, St. Helena. 963.2636

A French immigrant from Bordeaux by the apt name of **Jean-Louis Vignes** planted the first non-Mission grapes in California at his Los Angeles ranch in the mid-19th century.

Restaurants/Clubs: Red Hotels: Blue
Shops/ ♦ Outdoors: Green Wineries/Sights: Black

187 Schramsberg Vineyards Follow the footsteps of **Robert Louis Stevenson,** who paid a visit in the late 1880s to this historic winery founded by itinerant barber **Jacob Schram** in 1862. The place was virtually a ruin by 1965, when **Jack** and **Jamie Davies** fell in love with it and restored it as a producer of sparkling wines. The original stone winery building still stands next to the old Schram family home, and the tunneled-out hillside is now a modern wine-production cellar. In 1972 the White House served Schramsberg champagne at the banquet **President Richard Nixon** gave for **Premier Chou En-lai** in Peking. The Davies make half a dozen sparkling wines in all, including Blanc de Blancs, Blanc de Noirs, and a rosé called Cuvée de Pinot. ◆ Tours by appt M-Sa. 1400 Schramsberg Rd, Calistoga. 942.4558

188 Meadowlark $$ An 1886 farmhouse recently remodeled into a B&B set on a wooded, 20-acre estate with a swimming pool and sun deck. Innkeeper **Kurt Stevens** raises horses, too (though not for guests' use). The four upstairs guest rooms all have queen-sized beds, private baths, and contemporary furniture and art. Guests share the downstairs area, which includes a living room, refrigerator, and a shady veranda overlooking an English garden. The California Continental breakfast includes orange juice, fruit, muffins, and scones, along with a more substantial dish such as quiche. No smoking. ◆ 601 Petrified Forest Rd, Calistoga. 942.5651

189 Storybook Mountain Vineyards A small winery entirely devoted to producing Zinfandel—and owner **Bernard Seps** does a knock-out job, consistently producing one of the top California Zinfandels in both a regular bottling and an age-worthy reserve. ◆ Tasting, sales, and tours by appt M-F. 3835 Hwy 128, Calistoga. 942.5310

190 Old Faithful Geyser Just two miles north of Calistoga, you'll find one of the town's prime attractions, one of three faithful geysers (so-called because of regular eruptions) in the world. Every 50 minutes, thar she blows—a column of 350-degree water and vapor comes roaring more than 60 feet into the air. Old Faithful became a paying attraction at the turn of the century, when people would arrive in their Model Ts, spread picnic cloths and lavish lunches on the grounds, and settle in for the show. A video explains to visitors how geysers are formed. There is also a wishing well and picnic facilities nearby on Tubbs Ln. ◆ Admission. Daily 8AM-sundown. 1299 Tubbs Ln, Calistoga. 942.6463

"A Californian vineyard [has] nothing to remind you of the Rhine or Rhône, of the low Côte d'Or, or the infamous and scabby deserts of Champagne; but all is green, solitary, covert."
Robert Louis Stevenson, *The Silverado Squatters.*

CHATEAU MONTELENA
ESTABLISHED 1882

ALEXANDER VALLEY
Chardonnay
1984
PRODUCED & BOTTLED BY CHATEAU MONTELENA
WINERY · CALISTOGA, NAPA VALLEY, CALIFORNIA · BW 4525
ALCOHOL 13.6% BY VOLUME

191 Chateau Montelena Winery Don't miss this historic winery secluded at the foot of Mount St. Helena. It was built of local stone in a grandiose Italian-palazzo style in 1882 by **Alfred L. Tubbs,** one of California's first state senators. A Chinese engineer bought the property in 1947 and added the five-acre lake with four islands and a floating Chinese junk.

St. Helena

In 1972 the **Barrett** family and partners replanted the vineyards, restored the cellars, and hired **Mike Grgich** (now at his own winery, Grgich-Hills) as winemaker. His second vintage, the 1973 Chardonnay, brought Chateau Montelena fame and fortune in the famous 1976 Paris competition, when expert French tasters rated it first among world-famous French Burgundies in a blind tasting. The winery, with **Bo Barrett** as winemaker now, continues to produce classic Napa Valley Chardonnay and Cabernet Sauvignon with plenty of aging potential. Chateau Montelena takes only one reservation per day for their two spectacular picnic sites, each under the shelter of a Chinese pagoda on Jade Lake. Don't rule out this lovely spot in fall and winter; it can be nice even on a rainy or misty day. ◆ Fee for tasting. Picnic facilities by reservation. Tasting and sales daily 10AM-4PM; tours by appt. 1429 Tubbs Ln, Calistoga. 942.5105

192 Robert Louis Stevenson State Park

This largely undeveloped area at the northern end of the valley contains an abandoned silver mine where Stevenson and his wife **Fanny** spent their honeymoon in 1880, staying in a rustic, abandoned bunkhouse. He later wrote about his experiences and the area's beauty in *The Silverado Squatters.* He also modeled Spyglass Hill in *Treasure Island* after Mount St. Helena, which at 4,343 feet is the highest of the Bay Area's peaks. A rigorous five-mile trail to the top of the mountain offers unsurpassed views of the wine country below—on a *very* clear day, you can see all the way to Mount Shasta and the Sierra Nevada. Plan your hike for the cool morning hours and bring plenty of water. The park has no developed facilities. ◆ Daily dawn-dusk (five miles north of Calistoga on Hwy 29) 942.4575

Calistoga

As its legacy of geysers, hot springs, and lava deposits attests, the Calistoga area began life with a bang—a volcanic bang, that is. Some of the eruptions formed the gray stone used in local landmarks such as the **Christian Brothers Greystone Cellars** and various bridges. Local Indian tribes healed their sick in steam baths they constructed around the hot springs at the northern end of the valley. And when **Sam Brannan,** California's first millionaire, visited the area in the mid-19th century, he immediately envisioned a first-class spa and set to work designing a lavish hotel to attract wealthy San Franciscans to the site of what is now **Indian Springs Resort.** Brannan also brought the first railroad to the valley and dubbed the town "Calistoga," a hybrid of California and Saratoga (the famous New York resort).

Set in the midst of rolling vineyards with extinct volcano Mount St. Helena standing guard in the distance, this small country town (population 4,450), with its Old West-style main street, is famous for its mineral water and mud baths. The spas offer the rare bargain in wine-country lodging; and the pools and mineral baths are a welcome diversion, especially in summer.

Cedar Street Building, Calistoga

DRAWING BY KATHLEEN FITZGERALD

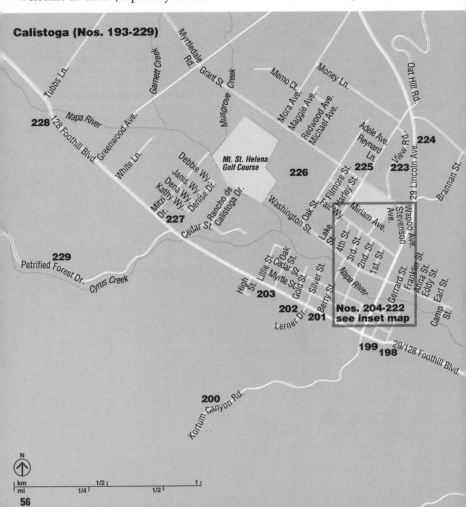

Calistoga (Nos. 193-229)

193 Stonegate Winery Founded in 1973 by **Jim** and **Barbara Spaulding** to produce wine from hillside vineyards near Diamond Mountain, Stonegate produces consistently good Cabernet and Merlot, especially from the **Spaulding** vineyard. Winemaker **David Spaulding** also crafts both a regular and a late-harvest Sauvignon Blanc. ♦ Fee. Tasting and sales daily 10:30AM-4:30PM; tours by appt. 1183 Dunaweal Ln, Calistoga. 942.6500

194 Sterling Vineyards The flagship winery of the Seagram Corporation, this dazzling white, Mediterranean-style winery on a 300-foot knoll just south of Calistoga, is approached by way of an aerial tramway with breathtaking views from the suspended cars. At the end of the ride, follow the self-guided tour of the winery at your own pace. Then settle in at a table in the panoramic tasting room to sample Sterling's top-flight wines: Chardonnay, Merlot, and especially their Cabernet reserve and Diamond Mountain Cabernet. In addition, winemaker **Bill Dyer** makes limited bottlings of Chardonnay from the Diamond Mountain vineyard, Pinot Noir from the legendary Winery Lake vineyard in the Carneros district, and a blend of Cabernet Sauvignon, Cabernet Franc, and Merlot. ♦ Fee for aerial tramway includes wine tasting. Tasting, sales, and self-guided tour daily 10:30AM-4:30PM. 1111 Dunaweal Ln, Calistoga. 942.3300

Within Sterling Vineyards:

Seagram Classics School of Service and Hospitality This professional school for training restaurant employees in the expert service of food and wine is directed by **Evan Goldstein**—who in 1987 was the youngest person ever to pass the prestigious Master Sommelier exam, making him one of only 31 master sommeliers in the world at the time. In addition to three-day seminars for professionals, the school also offers a comprehensive one-day session for non-professionals. Filled with fun and information about everything from grape growing and winemaking to wine tasting and developing a personal cellar, the class includes a visit to Sterling's vineyards and a first-hand look at what goes on in the cellar. At lunch students practice pairing a variety of wines with selected dishes. ♦ For more information, write to

Calistoga

Evan Goldstein, Seagram Classics School of Service and Hospitality, Box 365, Calistoga 94515, or call 942.0832

CLOS PEGASE: COURTESY MICHAEL GRAVES

195 Clos Pegase **Michael Graves** designed and built the Clos Pegase Winery and house in 1986. The commission resulted from a major architectural design competition sponsored by the owner, wealthy international businessman **Jan Schrem,** and the **San Francisco Museum of Modern Art**. And it was won by the architect/artist team of Graves and **Edward Schmidt**. Widely recognized for his post-modernist architectural designs as well as household objects, Graves built the Shrem's house on a secluded wooded knoll overlooking the winery just south of Calistoga.

What visitors will see are the stunning earth- and russet-colored winery buildings that take their inspiration from ancient Mediterranean sources; rows of tall columns (distressed to look ages-old) are arranged around a central

197
Rosedale Rd.
Silverado Trail

Rosedale Rd.
Pickett Rd.
Simmons Canyon

Downtown Calistoga (Nos. 204-222)

Wapoo Ave.
Stevenson Ave.
222
Miriam Ave.
Fairway St.
219
221
220
3rd. St.
2nd. St.
218 **217**
Lincoln Ave.
216
212
1st. St.
210 **215**
Washington St.
211
196
Spring St.
Cyrus Creek
208
Gerrard St.
214
Franklin St.
Anna St.
Eddy St.
207
Cedar St.
209 **213**
Hazel St.
Pine St.
Napa River
195
206
Myrtle St.
205
Dunaweal Ln.
194
Elm St.
204
193

courtyard. Outdoor sculptures are set into the landscape; the most remarkable is an over-sized bronze thumb that appears to be planted in the vineyard. The highlight of a tour of the building is the cylindrical room that Schmidt has covered with frescoes depicting allegorical scenes of winemaking. Visitors can also watch a slide show called "Wine in Art," which covers images of winemaking in art ranging from Egyptian reliefs and medieval illuminated manuscripts to Cubist works. The winery produces straightforward Chardonnay, Cabernet, and Merlot. ♦ Fee. Tasting, sales, and outdoor self-guided tours daily 10:30AM-4:30PM; guided tours of the winery, art collection, and caves M-F 10AM. 1060 Dunaweal Ln, Calistoga. 942.4982

196 Cuvaison Winery Founded in 1969, this Spanish Colonial-style winery is Swiss owned and specializes in Chardonnay, although winemaker **John Thacher's** Cabernet and Merlot are first-rate, too. The tasting room has an incisive collection of wine books for sale, plus insulated wine bags and picnic carriers, corkscrews, and local jams and condi-

Calistoga

ments. Picnic tables are set out under moss-covered oaks. ♦ Fee. Tasting and sales daily 10AM-5PM; tours by appt. 4550 Silverado Trail, Calistoga. 942.6266

197 Silver Rose Inn $$ Five spacious rooms, all with a private bath, are featured at this inn on a knoll overlooking the Silverado Trail just south of Calistoga. **Sally Dumont** has had a lot of fun decorating the rooms and suites, each with a different theme such as teddy bears, period dolls, and cats. Shoji screens, Oriental rugs, a Japanese lacquer bed, and a private Jacuzzi make the Oriental Suite the most popular. The swimming pool was carved out of the natural rock hillside and has an adjoining Jacuzzi in the shade of a tremendous, 300-year-old oak tree. At breakfast time, Dumont dishes up lots of fresh fruit and homemade bread. Reserve the whole inn with a group of friends and the Dumonts will organize a poolside barbecue and wine tasting party. No smoking. ♦ 351 Rosedale Rd (at the Silverado Trail). Calistoga. 942.9581

198 Calistoga Pottery Traditional functional stoneware. **Jeff Manfredi** and his wife **Sally** specialize in oven-proof dinnerware decorated with lead-free glaze. Custom work, too. ♦ Tu-Su 11AM-5PM. 1001 Foothill Blvd (Pine St) Calistoga. 942.0216

199 Wine Way Inn $$ This Craftsman-style inn, built as a family home in 1915, has been a B&B for more than ten years. The five rooms upstairs, all with a private bath, vary in size, and each is named for a wine-country town.

A secluded guest cottage adjoins the huge, three-level deck at the rear. Guests can enjoy breakfast or an aperitif in the gazebo at the very back of the steeply terraced wooded property. A full breakfast is served, which might include French toast, fruit crepes, or a frittata. ♦ 1019 Foothill Blvd (Hazel St) Calistoga. 942.0680

200 Falcon's Nest $$ It's only a quarter mile up steep Kortum Canyon Rd from Calistoga, but it feels like a world away at this B&B with a panoramic view of the valley from three guest rooms (all with spare modern decor, private bath, and sliding glass doors) on the lower floor of a spacious contemporary home. The outdoor Jacuzzi and tub have the same heart-stopping view. Continental breakfast might include pastries, fruits, and juice. ♦ 471 Kortum Canyon Rd, Calistoga. 942.0758

201 The Pink Mansion $$ Built in 1875 by the pioneer **William F. Fisher,** who founded Calistoga's first stagecoach line, this extravagant mansion is now a five-room inn run by **Jeffrey Seyfried,** nephew of **Alma Simic,** the mansion's last longtime owner, who painted it pink sometime in the thirties. Each room has its own bath and views of the valley or forest behind. The **Rose Room** suite has a sunken sitting room and a private redwood deck, while the **Angel Room** holds some of his aunt's treasured collection of

The Pink Mansion

decorative angels. Heated indoor pool, Jacuzzi, and substantial breakfast. ♦ 1415 Foothill Blvd (Spring-Berry Sts) Calistoga. 942.0558

202 **Calistoga Wayside Inn** $$ This Spanish-style twenties house set on a wooded hillside has three rooms, only one with a private bath. The two upstairs rooms share a large bath. Down comforters and feather pillows, a small library of reading material, and an outdoor terrace where breakfast is served all contribute to a feeling of well-being. ♦ 1523 Foothill Blvd (Terrace-Lerner Drs) Calistoga. 942.0645

203 **Culver's Country Inn** $$ A beautifully restored Victorian house built by **Major John Oscar Culver,** a Milwaukee newspaperman, in the early 1870s. The period decor is refreshingly understated in the six rooms, all with shared baths and comfortable custom-made mattresses. What's more, there's a medium-sized swimming pool and sauna.

Innkeeper **Meg Wheatley** prepares a full-country breakfast such as homemade scones, sour-cream coffee cake, and more. ♦ 1805 Foothill Blvd (Oak-High Sts) Calistoga. 942.4535

204 **The Pine Street Inn** $$ On a quiet Calistoga side street, this inn and spa consists of several stucco bungalows with flower boxes and parking in front. Bedrooms are on the small side, but they have pine armoires and are prettily decorated in pastels with matching curtains and drapes; some have real kitchenettes with a stove. Guests can relax in the patio coffee bar, where a Continental breakfast (pastries, donuts, and coffee) is served. To cool off, there's an outdoor kidney-shaped pool surrounded with a small, grassy, shaded area. Badminton court, too. ♦ 1202 Pine St, Calistoga. 942.6829

Adjoining the Pine Street Inn:

Eurospa A spa specializing in a very different sort of mud bath. For their European fango mud bath, they fill a private tub with a dehydrated compound that is added to water; it has a looser consistency than a regular mud bath and is taken in a double Jacuzzi so you also get the benefits of hydrotherapy. (Hygiene-conscious clients might like to know that the tub is completely drained and cleaned between each treatment.) Herbal oils and extracts can be added to the mud if you

like, and the spa also offers seaweed or herbal body wraps. Masseuses will give either a one-hour full-body massage or a half-hour massage that concentrates on back, neck, and shoulders. Eurospa also has their own line of natural facial products; made from plants and herbal extracts, they contain no alcohol or abrasives. ♦ M-Th 10AM-6PM; F 10AM-7PM; Sa 9AM-9PM; Su 9AM-8PM. 942.6829

205 **Jules Culver Bicycles** Sales and rentals of mountain bikes, road bikes, and bicycles for two. Owner **Jules Culver** will advise on the best routes for your energy level and abilities. He will also deliver rental bicycles to northern valley locations, and in peak season, offers one-way rentals. His popular downhill cruises—maximum coasting, minimum pedaling—are catching on, too. He plans to add rental mopeds and scooters soon. ♦ Daily 9:30AM-6PM. 1227 Lincoln Ave (Myrtle-Cedar Sts) Calistoga. 942.0421

Cafe Pacifico

205 **Cafe Pacifico** ★$$ Terracotta floors, potted palms, and patterned oilcloth-covered tables set the Southwest theme here. For breakfast, you can order huevos rancheros, blue-corn buttermilk pancakes, and machaca con huevos (scrambled eggs with shredded beef, black beans, and a fresh salsa all wrapped up in a flour tortilla). Tacos, tostadas, enchiladas, chile rellenos, fajitas, and grilled chicken are also for the asking. Fiesta hour daily 4:30-6PM with special prices on well-made margaritas, tacos, and taquitos. ♦ California/Mexican ♦ M-F 11AM-10PM; Sa-Su 10AM-3PM. 1237 Lincoln Ave (Myrtle-Cedar Sts) Calistoga. 942.4400

206 **La Chaumière** $$ This turn-of-the-century house remodeled in the thirties in a Cotswold Cottage Revival style features two guest rooms, each with queen-sized beds and private baths. The spacious upstairs suite has its own sitting room, while the downstairs room has French doors leading to a secluded private deck with potted plants and flowers. Innkeeper **Gabriele Ondine** graduated from the **California Culinary Academy** and now works as a chef and restaurant consultant, and the two-course breakfasts she serves are designed to showcase her passion for cooking. You can expect something like freshly squeezed orange juice, her own yeast breads and rolls, and bananas flambéed in rum and served with a raspberry-lime sauce. Hold on, that's just the first course. Then might come a mixed vegetable timbale scented with fresh dill and served with smoked salmon and sautéed vegetables. ♦ 1301 Cedar St, Calistoga. 942.5139

Restaurants/Clubs: **Red**
Shops/ 🎋 Outdoors: **Green**

Hotels: **Blue**
Wineries/Sights: **Black**

Getting Down and Dirty in Calistoga

A Guide to the Famous Mud Baths

Say "mud bath," and some people will fall into a fit of giggles at the idea of lying in a tub naked, covered in warm, gooey mud. Well, keep in mind this is not just any mud, this is Calistoga's famous volcanic-ash mud mixed with mineral water and, in some cases, imported peat. The mud is first heated to sterilize it and then cooled down to just over one hundred degrees. The mud bath itself, taken in individual tubs, lasts only 10 to 12 minutes. It's followed by a warm, mineral-water shower and a whirlpool bath, then a steam bath. At that point, relaxation sets in as attendants swathe you in warm blankets, leaving you to rest and slowly cool down.

If soaking in a mud bath is just not your idea of a good time, the spas also offer a full array of auxiliary treatments, starting with massages given in a variety of techniques. You can get a full-body massage or a neck-and-shoulder massage, which can be combined with seaweed or herbal body wraps. Or perhaps you'd prefer to be scrubbed with a loofah or

Calistoga

to soak in a fragrant herbal bath after indulging in a facial. Every spa has its specialties and will explain them in detail. Don't plan on doing anything too rigorous immediately after; you'll probably feel so relaxed you won't be able to move.

Calistoga Spa Hot Springs ♦ 1006 Washington St. 942.6269

Calistoga Village Inn & Spa ♦ 1880 Lincoln Ave. 942.0991

Dr. Wilkinson's Hot Springs ♦ 1507 Lincoln Ave. 942.4102

Golden Haven Hot Springs ♦ 1713 Lake St. 942.6793

Indian Springs ♦ 1712 Lincoln Ave. 942.4913

International Spa ♦ 1300 Washington St. 942.6122

Lincoln Avenue Spa
♦ 1339 Lincoln Ave. 942.5296

Nance's Hot Springs
♦ 1614 Lincoln Ave.
942.6211

**Pine Street Inn and
Eurospa** ♦ 1202 Pine St.
942.6829

Roman Spa ♦ 1300
Washington St. 942.4441

207 The Elms $$ Built in 1871 by **Judge A.C. Palmer,** this truly elegant three-story French Victorian house with a formal parlor and tall windows overlooking Cedar St is furnished with grace and style. The new owners have remodeled it to create a private bath for each of the four bedrooms, and added a small upstairs parlor with a credit-card phone. Some B&Bs have just one exceptional room; here all four have something special—for example, there is a magnificent, one hundred-year-old Swedish sleigh bed converted to a king-sized bed in one room and a view of the mountains in another. Innkeeper **Lee Marks** prepares a full gourmet breakfast, such as creamed spinach and scrambled eggs with toast or fresh biscuits. The cottage in back is ideal for honeymooners. ♦ 1300 Cedar St (Elm-Spring Sts) Calistoga. 942.9476

207 Pioneer Park A shady park with picnic tables scattered around a white Victorian gazebo. ♦ Cedar St (Elm-Spring Sts) Calistoga

THE ARTFUL EYE

208 The Artful Eye An inspiring crafts gallery featuring top West-Coast work in glass, ceramics, jewelry, wood, and textiles, including exquisite handblown glasses and wine goblets and an entire case of handmade marbles from a number of craftspeople. Also glass paperweights, intricately painted little scarves, handwoven shawls, and mufflers. Prices match the quality. ♦ M-Th, Su 10AM-6PM; F-Sa 10AM-7PM. 1333-A Lincoln Ave (Cedar-Washington Sts) Calistoga. 942.4743

208 Lincoln Avenue Spa This spa features herbal-mud treatments with 34 herbs imported from India, herbal blanket wraps and facials, Swedish/Esalen massages, acupressure face-lifts, and foot reflexology. Special deluxe spa packages are also available. No accommodations. ♦ Daily 9AM-9PM. 1339 Lincoln Ave (Cedar-Washington Sts) Calistoga. 942.5296

208 The Calistoga Bookstore A comfortable place to browse through books on wine and California travel and history, with a nice section of paperback mysteries, children's books, and art supplies. The inviting sofa at the back comes complete with a sleeping cat. ♦ M-Th, Su 10AM-6PM; F-Sa 10AM-9PM. 1343 Lincoln Ave (Cedar-Washington Sts) Calistoga. 942.4123

209 Calistoga Inn $ For travelers on a budget, this turn-of-the-century building on Calistoga's main street offers 17 clean, basic rooms with a bathroom down the hall (something like a French one-star hotel). There are no TVs or phones in the rooms, but there's complimentary beer or wine. The rooms, which can be noisy until the bar below settles down at night, include portable electric fans in the summer and small heaters in the winter. Includes Continental breakfast (juice, coffee, and fresh pastries). ♦ 1250 Lincoln Ave (Cedar-Washington Sts) Calistoga 942.4101

Within the Calistoga Inn:

Calistoga Inn Restaurant ★★★$$/$$$
Dine either in the large garden area with tables set under a pergola (overhead trellis) beside the river or in the comfortable dining room with jazz playing on the stereo. Kitchen partners **Leo Kleinhanz** and **Rosie Dunsford** have been turning out appetizing California cuisine since 1986. A mix of tourists and locals come here to enjoy homey dishes such as Barney's chicken, a boned half-chicken roasted with grilled onions and savory olives; Cajun peel-and-eat prawns cooked in the inn's own lager beer; and a hearty pan-fry of Italian sausage, peppers, and new potatoes. Steamed clams and mussels, Caesar salad, and interesting soups, too—and everything is served with their country bread. For dessert, go for the homemade brownies with vanilla ice cream and hot fudge sauce. Short wine list. Well-crafted ale from the brew pub next door. ♦ California ♦ M-Th, Su 11:30AM-3PM, 5:30-9PM; F-Sa 11:30AM-3PM, 5:30-10PM. Reservations recommended for dinner

Napa Valley Brewery The valley's first brewery since Prohibition, housed in an old water tower at the back of the garden. Brewmaster **Todd Scott** will draw you a cool glass of Calistoga Golden Lager, Calistoga Red Ale, or Old Water Tower Barley Wine (a malted barley ale brewed to the strength of a wine). The beer served with the inn's lunch and dinner menus is also available in 22-ounce bottles to go. Special happy hour M-F, Su 4-6PM. ♦ Daily 11:30AM-10PM

209 Las Brasas ★$ Mesquite-grilled chicken, fajitas, pork chops, steaks, and carnitas (Jalisco-style roasted leg of pork) served with tortillas and *frijoles borachos* (beans cooked with beer). ♦ Mexican ♦ Daily 11AM-9:30PM. 1350 Lincoln Ave (Cedar-Washington Sts) Calistoga. 942.4056

209 Silverado Tavern ★★$$$ The wine cellar here, noted for its tremendous breadth and scope, is owner **Alex Dierkhising's** special passion. What's curious is that the food isn't better. Not that he would have to do much. He could keep the spirit of the place and simply offer the best steak and prime rib in the valley and it would be a big hit. Instead, the lowbrow, retro decor and the kitchen's inconsistencies distract from the wine. Opt for the roast prime rib with creamed horseradish sauce and garlic mashed potatoes or the range-fed veal scallops. ♦ Daily 5-10PM; bar 8AM-midnight or later. 1374 Lincoln Ave (Washington-Fairway Sts) Calistoga. Reservations recommended. 942.6725

210 Loneoak & Co. Outlet Store This firm's handmade terracotta and porcelain dinnerware has been featured in food and design magazines. Here seconds of their Country-French, Southwest, and sleek modern designs sell at a sharp discount in white porcelain or natural terra-cotta glazed with color. The bowls are ideal for pastas and soups, and the oversized serving platters are a real find. Also sells napkins, glassware, and extra-virgin olive oil from Sparta, Greece. ♦ M, W-Su 10AM-5PM. 1226-A Washington St (Lincoln Ave-First St) Calistoga. 942.9704

211 The Sharpsteen Museum and Sam Brannan Cottage After 30 years at Walt Disney Studios, **Ben Sharpsteen** retired to Calistoga and created this museum. With the help of a few friends from his Disney days, he designed and constructed elaborate dioramas recreating the arrival of the railroad, Calistoga's former Chinatown, and more. The largest depicts Calistoga as it looked when millionaire

Sam Brannan opened the town's first spa in 1865. Hailing it as the "Saratoga of the Pacific," his Calistoga included a hotel, dining hall, stables, and racetrack, plus an indoor pool, a pavilion for dancing and roller skating, a distillery, a winery, and a cooper's workshop. One of the 14 original cottages is also part of the museum, furnished as it would have been in 1860 (that is, with no kitchen; guests were expected to take meals in the hotel). Books on the history of the Napa Valley are for sale, too. ♦ Daily noon-4PM; 10AM-4PM in summer. 1311 Washington St (First-Second Sts) Calistoga. 942.5911

212 Roman Spa $ You'll find motel-like accommodations at this no-frills spa. A lounge and chairs are set out on AstroTurf around a mineral pool. Finnish sauna and outdoor Jacuzzi, too. ♦ 1300 Washington St (First-Second Sts) Calistoga. 942.4441

Within the Roman Spa:

The International Spa Mud baths for couples, plus Japanese enzyme baths, Swedish/Esalen massages, foot reflexology, acupressure, herbal facials, herbal blankets —all in an unassuming bungalow directly behind the Roman Spa. ♦ Daily 9AM-9PM, 1 May-31 Oct; M-Th 9AM-5PM, F-Su 9AM-9PM, 1 Nov-30 Apr. 942.6122

213 Palisades Mountain Sport Mountain bike rentals by the hour or the day. Bike repairs, rugged outdoor wear and climbing equipment, too. No tours are available, but they will provide a map of suggested routes. ♦ M, W-Su 10AM-6PM. 1330-B Gerrard St (Cedar-Washington Sts) Calistoga. 942.9687

214 Calistoga Spa Hot Springs $ This is the people's spa: relaxed, fun, unpretentious, and a great base for exploring the wine country. It has all the amenities of a resort at budget prices, including kitchenettes and cable TVs. The best rooms have king-sized beds, high ceilings, and a muted pastel decor, plus a larger kitchen area. All of them open onto the attractive pool area that boasts four outdoor mineral pools: a giant pool for lap swimming, a 100-degree soaking pool, a 105-degree pool with Jacuzzi jets, and a wading pool with a fountain. Barbecues are set up on the outskirts of the pool area.

Make an appointment in advance for a volcanic ash mud bath, mineral bath, steam bath, blanket wrap, or massage. Exercise equipment and aerobic classes are also available. Families are welcome. If you plan to stay elsewhere and still want to enjoy the pool, they have a day-use pass; stop by early in the day to buy one, as they book up quickly. ♦ Spa daily 8:30AM-4PM. 1006 Washington St (Gerrard-Fairway Sts) Calistoga. 942.6269

Calistoga

215 All Seasons Café ★★$$/$$$ This take-out deli-turned-cafe is a favorite because of its great wine list and enlightened pricing policy. Instead of doubling or tripling the retail price of the wine (which is what most restaurants do), they simply add a small fee to each bottle. It works on a sliding scale; the higher the retail price, the smaller the added fee, and for bottles costing more than $30, there's no added charge. Needless to say, they sell a lot of wine from a list of top-notch Burgundy, Bordeaux, and Napa Valley producers.

Wine is so much on chef/owner **Mark Dierkhising's** mind that he divides the menu into dishes appropriate to different styles of wines. The menu changes every month and is particularly strong in first courses such as fresh dungeness crab cakes or grilled marinated shiitake mushrooms with smoked fresh mozzarella and a roasted garlic vinaigrette. More complex wines are shown off with entrées such as roast chicken with whole garlic cloves and potatoes, grilled center-cut pork chops with sun-dried cherry and port glaze, or grilled salmon with braised white beans, tomatoes, and spinach. The cafe is a wonderful spot for lunch, too, offering a menu of pasta dishes, pizzas, and excellent sandwiches. For picnics, with a morning's notice, the cafe can have a box lunch or a more lavish spread ready to go. It might include their terrific "Beyond the BLT," made with pancetta (unsmoked bacon), tomato, local lettuces, and sweet basil leaves on a homemade cheese-and-onion roll, and one or more appealing salads. ♦ M, W-Su 11:30AM-4PM, 5-10PM; Tu 11:30AM-4PM. 1400 Lincoln Ave (Washington-Fairway Sts) Calistoga. Reservations recommended for dinner. 942.9111

Within All Seasons Café:

All Seasons Wine Shop Go all the way to the back of the cafe and turn left for the wine shop that manager **John Wetlaufer,** a winemaker and scholar, has stocked with an astute array of Burgundies and top California wines from small producers. He loves to talk wine and will put together a mixed case of hard-to-find wines at very good prices and then arrange to ship them all home to you. He also produces a well-written, informative newsletter. For picnics, he has a nice selection of white wines already chilled. ♦ Daily 10AM-6PM. 942.6828

215 Checkers $/$$ A trendy, informal spot with a polished wood floor, black-and-white tile details, and bright abstract paintings, offering a dozen pizzas with thin, California-style crust. Choices include a sun-dried-tomato-and-artichoke pizza scattered with fresh thyme and pine nuts, or an unusual Thai pizza with marinated chicken, cilantro, and peanuts. The calzone (pizza turnovers) are large enough for two. Add a salad—Greek, Italian, Chinese, Thai, or Californian—for a casual lunch or dinner. At night, they also serve pasta and several chicken dishes. For dessert, make your own frozen yogurt creation at the bar. Espresso drinks; short wine list. No smoking. Takeout and free evening delivery in Calistoga. ♦ M-Th, Su 11:30AM-9PM; F-Sa 11:30AM-10PM. 1414 Lincoln Ave (Washington-Fairway Sts) Calistoga. 942.9300

215 Silverado Ace Hardware Hardware, garden supplies, housewares—and used wine barrels for planters. ♦ M-F 8AM-6PM; Sa 8AM-5PM; Su 9AM-5PM. 1450 Lincoln Ave (Washington-Fairway Sts) Calistoga. 942.4396

215 Depot Railroad Station Established in 1868 and restored a century later, this historic landmark is believed to be the oldest railroad depot remaining in California. The clapboard building is now a mini-shopping gallery that houses the **Chamber of Commerce,** a restaurant, and several shops. Six restored Pullmans are parked alongside the station. ♦ Shops daily 10AM-6PM. 1458 Lincoln Ave (Washington-Fairway Sts) Calistoga. 942.6333

Within the Depot Railroad Station:

Calistoga Candy Co. More than 200 kinds of old-fashioned candies, from candy sticks and saltwater taffy to jelly beans and licorice drops, all priced by the pound. ♦ 942.6838

Once in a Lifetime Balloon Co., Inc.
Hot-air balloon flights take off shortly after sunrise. Watch the crew inflate the balloon and step aboard for a gentle ride high above the vineyards, floating down about an hour later wherever the wind decides. A catering truck races to meet you with a champagne brunch. Complimentary photo and flight certificate. Gift certificates available. ♦ 942.6541, 800/722.6665 (CA only)

Up, Up, and Away: Where to See Napa from the Air

Whether you drift in a hot-air balloon or soar in a helicopter, glider, or small plane, there's nothing like an aerial view of one of the world's most scenic wine regions. Here's where you can get that high in the sky:

Hot-Air Balloons

One-hour flights in the Napa Valley cost about $145 to $165 per person.

Above the West Ballooning Hot-air balloon flights over the Napa Valley followed by a champagne breakfast. Transportation from San Francisco can be arranged. ♦ Daily by reservation. Box 2290, Yountville CA 94599. 944.8638, 415/776.6382, 800/627.2759

Adventures Aloft Balloon trips topped off with a champagne brunch. ♦ Daily by reservation. Vintage 1870, Box 2500, Yountville CA 94599. 255.8688

American Balloon Adventures Flights followed by a champagne toast. ♦ Daily by reservation. 7321 St. Helena Hwy, Yountville CA 94599. 944.8116, 800/333.4359

Balloon Aviation of Napa Valley, Inc. Trips over the Napa Valley with a Continental breakfast before and a champagne brunch after. ♦ Daily by reservation. Vintage 1870, Box 2500, Yountville CA 94599. 252.7067, 800/367.6272

Balloons Above the Valley Flights from Domaine Chandon followed by a champagne barbecue. ♦ Daily by reservation. 1812 Soscol Ave, Napa CA 94559. 253.2222, 800/233.7681

Bonaventura Balloon Company Rides from the St. Helena area followed by a champagne toast or brunch. ♦ Daily by reservation. 133 Wall Rd, Napa CA 94558. 944.2822

Napa's Great Balloon Escape Flights followed by a full champagne brunch at the Silverado Country Club. ♦ Daily by reservation. Box 4197, Napa CA 94558. 253.0860

Napa Valley Balloon Safaris Flights over the Napa Valley. ♦ 3377 Solano Ave, Suite 305, Napa CA 94558. 800/255.0125

Napa Valley Balloons, Inc. Trips from Domaine Chandon followed by a full champagne breakfast at Marie Callender's in Napa. ♦ Daily by reservation. Box 2860, Yountville CA 94599. 253.2224, 800/253.2224; fax 253.2719

Once in a Lifetime Balloon Co., Inc. Flights and champagne brunch. ♦ Daily by reservation. The Depot, Box 795, Calistoga CA 94515. 942.6541, 800/722.6665 (CA only)

Small Planes, Helicopters, and Gliders

For two to three people, 30- to 60-minute flights cost about $95.

Bridgeford Flying Service Fly over the wine country in a Cessna Skyhawk or Centurion; accommodates one to five passengers. ♦ Daily by reservation. Napa County Airport, 2030 Airport Rd, Napa CA 94558. 224.0887

Calistoga Gliders of Napa Valley One- or two-passenger glider rides over the Napa Valley. ♦ Daily 9AM-sunset. 1546 Lincoln Ave, Calistoga CA 94515. 942.5000

Napa Valley Helicopter Tours Half-hour tours in a four-passenger Jet Ranger helicopter. ♦ Daily by reservation. Napa County Airport, 2030 Airport Rd, Napa CA 94558. 255.0809, 800/622.6886

The Gold Treasury Jewelry Here you can pick up some old pieces as well as sterling silver jewelry from local designers. 942.6819

Calistoga Wine Stop A bright yellow train car trimmed in green parked right in the middle of the Depot makes an ingenious space for a serious, small wine store with more than 1,000 Napa and Sonoma wines. Some rare and older bottles are available, and they ship out of state. ♦ 942.5556

Chamber of Commerce Information available here on Calistoga and the Napa Valley. ♦ M-Sa 10AM-5PM; Su 10AM-3:30PM. 942.6333

Bed & Breakfast Exchange No-fee reservation service for the wine country with more than 150 B&Bs and inns in Northern California listed. You can buy a gift certificate for a friend here, too. ♦ 942.5900

Adela's Yarn North A tiny cottage crammed with European yarns, knitting books, and supplies for needlepoint and embroidery. And Adela is ready to advise on any needlework project. ♦ 942.4872

216 **Bosko's Ristorante** ★$$$ This casual restaurant with oilcloth-covered tables and sawdust on the floor offers a dozen fresh pasta dishes—everything from that old familiar spaghetti and meatballs to fettuccine with a seafood sauce of bay shrimp and tomatoes. The style and the portions are definitely Italian/American. Order cafeteria style; they'll cook your pasta to order. (And do speak up if you prefer it al dente.) The best deal at lunch is a half order of any fresh pasta with a green salad. There are generous Italian club sandwiches (made with pancetta instead of bacon), too. Takeout available. ♦ Italian ♦ Daily 11AM-10PM. 1403 Lincoln Ave (Washington-Fairway Sts) Calistoga. 942.9088

216 **Evans Ceramics Gallery** Exotic handmade pottery, many pieces oversized or one-of-a-kind, and all discounted by 40 to 90

Calistoga

percent at this factory outlet. Notice the gaudy New Age twist on the subtle art of raku (an ancient Japanese method of firing pottery) from **Tony Evans** and company, the world's largest producer of raku ware. ♦ Daily 10AM-5PM. 1421 Lincoln Ave (Washington-Fairway Sts) Calistoga. 942.0453

216 **Mount View Hotel** $$ Built in 1917 on the site of the old European hotel, the 30-room Mount View, which is on the National Register of Historic Places, has been restored in the Art Deco style of the twenties and thirties. Nine fantasy suites are furnished with handsome period pieces. The standard doubles, all with private baths, are less glamorous—Deco on a budget. But everybody gets to enjoy the pool and Jacuzzi out back, and the new spa with facials, massages, and body wraps is for hotel guests only. The chrome-and-black Art Deco bar is one of the few places in the valley with live music in the evenings. Continental breakfast. ♦ 1457 Lincoln Ave (Washington-Fairway Sts) Calistoga. 942.687

Within the Mount View Hotel:

Valeriano's Ristorante ★★$$$ Featuring la cucina creativa—creative cooking with a Northern Italian bent, this restaurant tries to straddle the fence, offering trendy pasta dishes such as the cannelloni stuffed with artichokes, prosciutto, and mozzarella, and chicken ravioli served in a pine-nut sauce. Main courses come with polenta and vegetables; stick with the simplest (grilled lamb chops or baked scampi), and finish your meal with crema cotta (a Piedmontese version of crème brûlée) or *tiramisu* (a Venetian dessert of rum-soaked lady fingers, mascarpone, espresso, and cocoa). All-California wine list. ♦ Italian ♦ Daily 11:30AM-3PM, 5:30-10PM. Reservations recommended. 942.0606

217 **Palisades Market** A ranch market with good-looking produce, a small wine section, and imported chocolate bars, teas, and gourmet groceries. ♦ M-W, Su 9AM-7PM; Th-Sa 9AM-8PM. 1506 Lincoln Ave (Fairway-Brannan Sts) Calistoga. 942.9549

217 **The Tin Barn** It's fun to browse through the hodge-podge of old furniture, vintage hats and clothing, costume jewelry, collector's items, and bric-a-brac at this antique dealers' collective behind Palisades Market. ♦ M, W-Su 10AM-6PM. 1510 Lincoln Ave (Fairway-Brannan Sts) Calistoga. 942.0618

217 **Calistoga Gliders of Napa Valley** The valley's warm, up-currents of air, called lifts, are perfect for gliding. Calistoga Gliders' exhilarating rides over the Napa Valley last about 20 minutes; two can go up, provided the combined weight is not more than 340 pounds. Be sure to bring your camera to capture the views. They have only seven gliders, so reserve ahead in peak season (June through September). Unlike hot-air balloons, glider flights are scheduled all day. Spectators can settle into garden chairs at the top of the airfield to watch tiny planes tow the graceful gliders into the sky. Picnic tables and a Weber barbecue are available, too. ♦ Daily 9AM-sunset. 1546 Lincoln Ave (Fairway-Brannon Sts) Calistoga. 942.5000

217 **Nance's Hot Springs** $ Indulge in an indoor, hot mineral pool or mud and steam bath, which you can top off with a wonderful therapeutic massage. Motel accommodations include kitchenettes and cable TVs. ♦ M-Th

9AM-3:30PM; F-Su 9AM-5PM. 1614 Lincoln Ave (Fairway-Brannon Sts) Calistoga. 942.6211

218 Dr. Wilkinson's Hot Springs $ The salon at Dr. Wilkinson's features a wide variety of treatments, including facials, acupressure face lifts, back and shoulder treatments, mud baths, natural mineral steam baths, blanket wraps, Swedish/Esalen massage, and special spa packages (the mid-week "Stress-Stopper" includes an overnight stay). Accommodations range from motel-like rooms to Victorian rooms in the building next door. All of the rooms have mini-refrigerators, drip-coffee makers, color TVs, and the use of three mineral-water pools (indoor whirlpool, outdoor soaking pool, and outdoor cool swimming pool); several rooms have full kitchens. The patio area is furnished with chaise longues and tables. ♦ Spa M-F 8:30AM-3:30PM; Sa-Su 8:30AM-5:30PM. 1507 Lincoln Ave (Fairway-Stevenson Sts) Calistoga. 942.4102

219 Hideaway Cottages $ On a quiet residential street off Lincoln Ave, Hideaway Cottages offers alternative overnight lodging, mostly for clients of Dr. Wilkinson's Hot Springs spa around the corner. The 15 cottages on the property all have air-conditioning and TVs, but no telephones. Some have kitchenettes, and all have picnic tables and barbecues outside. The somber forties decor could use a little brightening up. The bonus here is the outdoor, hot mineral Jacuzzi and a large, heated mineral swimming pool with chaise longues, tables, and umbrellas in a shady lawn and garden area. No children allowed. ♦ 1412 Fairway St (Third St) Calistoga. 942.4108

220 The Body Works Massage Clinic Deep-tissue massage and body work is offered here, as well as a private mineral-water Jacuzzi hot tub. ♦ M-Tu, Th-Su 9AM-5PM. 1631 Lincoln Ave (Stevenson-Wapoo Sts) Calistoga. 942.6316

221 Brannan Cottage Inn $$ When **Sam Brannan** opened his Calistoga Hot Springs Resort in 1860, he built 14 cottages where the Indian Springs resort now stands. Of the three cottages remaining today, only the demure, highly recommended Brannan Cottage Inn remains on its original site. Listed in the National Register of Historic Places, this charming B&B was once owned by the **Winn** sisters, cousins of Sam Brannan. Its restoration has been a long labor of love for original innkeepers **Jay** and **Dottie Richolson** (they have since sold the inn). The townspeople got interested in the project along the way. One man donated the matching porch lights, others provided the turn-of-the-century photos that were enlarged to make templates for the intricate gingerbread gable. Each of the six rooms and suites is stenciled with a different wildflower border and furnished with antiques and wicker. All have private entrances and baths and queen-

sized beds with down comforters. On sunny mornings the lavish breakfast (such as Grand Marnier-scented French toast with chicken-and-apple sausage) is served in the courtyard under the lemon trees. No smoking. ♦ 109 Wapoo Ave (Lincoln Ave-Grant St) Calistoga. 942.4200

222 Indian Springs $$$ Originally founded in 1860 by millionaire **Sam Brannan,** the spa is called Indian Springs because local Native Americans built sweat lodges around the springs long ago. To the left of the spa building, you can see the three active geysers that provide the spa with a constant supply of hot mineral water. Services include mud baths, massages, facials, skin-glow rubs, and mineral baths in a thoroughly professional setting. Indian Springs also boasts an Olympic-sized hot-spring pool, built in 1913 and restored in 1988. Owner **Jim Merchant** has furnished the 15 bungalow suites with summery wicker and cool cotton. Each one-bedroom suite has a queen-sized sofa bed in the living room, along with a vintage tile kitchen set up for light housekeeping. Barbecues are also available.

Calistoga

Families welcome. ♦ Spa daily 9AM-5:30PM; Sa 9AM-7:30PM. 1712 Lincoln Ave (Wapoo-Brannan Sts) Calistoga. 942.4913

223 Comfort Inn Napa Valley North $$ A comfortable motel with its own hot mineral-water swimming pool and spa, and a sauna and steam room. The 54 rooms have modern decor, private baths, and cable TVs; rooms upstairs have decks with views of the hills. Continental breakfast. ♦ 1865 Lincoln Ave (Brannan St-Silverado Trail) Calistoga. 942.9400, 800/228.5150

224 Calistoga Village Inn & Spa Another full spa/inn combo. The spa offers mud baths, mineral baths, steam and blanket wraps, body massages, natural facials, and skin-glow rubs. The accommodations are in pleasant white bungalows trimmed in blue, and include use of the mineral-water swimming pool, spa, sauna, and steam rooms. Bungalows have cable TVs and private baths, and suites have private whirlpools. Continental breakfast. Families welcome. ♦ Spa M-Th 9AM-8:30PM; F-Su 8AM-9PM. 1880 Lincoln Ave (Brannan St-Silverado Trail) Calistoga. 942.4636, 800/543.1094 (CA only); fax 942.5306

Within the Calistoga Village Inn & Spa:

Jamee's Restaurant ★★$$$ Fresh seasonal food in a light, airy dining room with white tablecloths. Choose from a couple of appetizers, the chef salad, and straightforward fare such as chicken-apple sausages cooked in cider, marinated grilled pork chops, or roasted rack of lamb in a Pinot Noir sauce. ♦ Tu-Su 5:30-9PM. 942.0979

225 Golden Haven Hot Springs It's not Southern California's luxurious Golden Door Spa, but it does have the requisite mud bath that you can take with your honey. Also offered are a deeply relaxing hot mineral Jacuzzi, European body wraps, massages, acupressure treatments, herbal facials, and a whole slew of other treatments. The mineral pool is in a makeshift building with a fiberglass roof and is often filled with Europeans who understand the tradition of spas and don't think of it as a luxurious extra to their everyday lives. Day-use fee for the swimming pool and hot-mineral pools; free with a spa appointment.

The spa's accommodations, like most in Calistoga, are hardly glamorous and are more akin to motels. This one has rooms with sliding-glass doors opening onto a minuscule

Calistoga

patio in front of a parking place; some have kitchenettes and/or a private Jacuzzi and sauna. Guests have use of the swimming pool, hot mineral pools, and sun deck. No children allowed on weekends and holidays. ◆ Daily 9AM-9PM. 1713 Lake St (Grant St-Reynard Ln) Calistoga. 942.6793

226 Napa County Fairgrounds Each Fourth of July weekend the Napa County fair kicks off for five fun-packed days. Choose between live music and entertainment or auto racing at night; leave the day for touring exhibits on domestic arts and checking out the homemade wine competition. ◆ 1435 Oak St (Fairway-Fisher Sts) Calistoga. 942.5111

At the Napa County Fairgrounds:

Public Campground Camping for 55 RVs and 10 tent sites on a lawn area; hot showers. First come, first serve. Maximum two-week stay. ◆ 942.5111

Calistoga Speedway Half-mile oval track with small, open-wheel sprint-car races May through September. ◆ 942.5111

Mount St. Helena Golf Course Nine-hole golf course. ◆ Daily 8AM-dusk. 942.9966

227 P.J.'s Tote Cuisine ★$ These busy Napa Valley caterers (that's **Nicholas Johnson** and **Terri Piper Johnson**) opened this take-out spot in 1991, which is perfect for picnickers and meals around the pool. Stop here for fresh-baked breads (onion-sage focaccia, rosemary and garlic bread) and sandwiches, plus

half-a-dozen light or main-course salads and an ever-changing array of entrées-to-go (some may need to be heated), including seafood brochettes with black-bean sauce, barbecued veal short ribs, lasagna, manicotti, and grilled duck breast with rice pilaf. Desserts include everything from dainty tartlets and a chocolate Cabernet cake to poppy-seed pound cake and white-chocolate-and-macadamia-nut brownies. ◆ Daily 11AM-6PM. 2450 Foothill Blvd (Mitzi Dr) Calistoga. 942.5432

228 Foothill House $$ **Susan** and **Michael Clow** took a small, turn-of-the-century farmhouse nestled in the foothills of Calistoga and turned it into a romantic, comfortable, tastefully decorated, and soothing hideaway. They continue to show up on the short list of best B&Bs in the country. Their secret? Superb attention to detail and service while maintaining respect for a guest's privacy—a combination not easy to achieve. The three large guest suites, each with a private entrance and bath, take their color scheme from intricate handmade quilts on the antique beds. Each room has a radio/cassette player, refrigerator, wood-burning fireplace, and soundproofed walls. The **Evergreen Suite** features a Jacuzzi tub and a private sun deck with table and chairs. An even more private cottage has a fireplace and a kitchenette so you can settle in for a longer stay. Breakfast includes Susan's homemade baked goods. ◆ 3037 Foothill Blvd (Greenwood Ave-Tubbs Ln) Calistoga. 942.6933

229 The Petrified Forest Six miles from Calistoga are gigantic redwoods that turned to stone more than six million years ago when Mount St. Helena erupted and molten lava coursed through the valley that is now the Petrified Forest. Silicates in the ash that blanketed the area seeped into the tree fibers, replacing wood cells with crystalized silica and turning the trees to stone. Highlights along the well-marked trail include the Giant (a 60-foot-long and six-foot-in-diameter tree that was 3,000 years old when it was petrified 3.4 million years ago, the 300-foot Monarch tunnel tree, a wishing well, a museum, and a nature store. A bronze plaque marks the meadow where **Charles Evans** discovered the first stump of petrified wood in 1870. His meeting in 1880 with **Robert Louis Stevenson** is immortalized in Stevenson's book, *The Silverado Squatters.* Wheelchair access for part of the trail. ◆ Admission; children under age 10 free. Picnic tables on a first-come, first-serve basis. Route well marked from town. North of Petrified Forest Road on Hwy 128. 942.6667

James Conaway
Author, *Napa: The Story of an American Eden*

Breakfast at **The Diner** in Yountville (cafè lattè and corn cakes).

A stroll around **Inglenook Winery** in Rutherford, avoiding the tour.

Lunch at **Piatti** in Yountville (a glass of Chardonnay and capellini with fresh tomatoes, garlic, and basil).

A dip in any of the hot springs in Calistoga, without the mud bath (herbal wrap optional).

A glass of Domaine Mumm on the deck of the **Auberge du Soleil** in Rutherford.

Dinner at **Mustards Grill** in Yountville (grilled asparagus and Sonoma rabbit, accompanied by an honest Napa red).

Madeleine Kamman
Director, School for American Chefs, Beringer Vineyards, St. Helena

Sunset on the **Silverado Trail** in Napa Valley.

Picking grapes for the vintage at **Schramsberg Vineyards** in Calistoga.

Meditating in **Chabot Vineyards**, Glass Mountain Rd in St. Helena.

A massage in Calistoga.

Dinner at **Terra** in St. Helena.

Lunch on the terrasse of **Domaine Chandon** in Yountville.

Chamber music concerts in the cellars at **S. Anderson Vineyard** in St. Helena.

New Year's Eve at **Meadowood Resort** in St. Helena.

Touring the art galleries of the Napa Valley.

Sunday breakfast at **Ambrose Heath** restaurant in Oakville.

Sandi S. Belcher
Winemaker/Grapegrower, Long Vineyards, St. Helena

The view from the **St. Helena Hospital** on the northeast side of the upper Napa Valley.

Onion rings at **Mustards Grill** in Yountville.

Watching the cormorants nesting in a lone Digger pine tree on the south shore of Rutherford's **Lake Hennessey** each night at dusk.

Breakfast at **The Diner** in Yountville.

A glass of wine on the deck of **Auberge du Soleil** in Rutherford during frost season.

Lunch, dinner, drinks—anything at **Tra Vigne** in St. Helena.

Hiking to the top of **Bothe-Napa Valley State Park** on Hwy 29 north of St. Helena (with a camera) for a view up and down the valley.

Rafting the **Russian River** to **Memorial Beach** in Healdsburg.

Sauntering through the caves of **Beringer Winery** in St. Helena for the wonderful smells. And visiting their **Rhine House** for a look at the stained-glass windows and the sensual wooden staircase—a nicely preserved touch of history.

Taking a peek at the fountain at **Franciscan Winery** in Rutherford.

A springtime stroll through the **St. Helena Cemetery** to look at the flowering bulbs and trees and the good view of the east side of the valley.

A visit to the **Napa Valley Wine Library** in St. Helena.

Daniel H. Baron
General Manager, Dominus Estate Winery, Yountville, and Owner, Salmon Creek Cellars

A mud bath at **Indian Springs** in Calistoga.

Monday night concerts at **Domaine Chandon** in Yountville.

Walking in a vineyard just after sunset on a summer evening.

Noodles at **Rissa Oriental Café** in St. Helena.

The view from the **Auberge du Soleil** bar in Rutherford with a winter storm coming in.

Napa's **Skyline Park,** with its off-road bike trails and Civil War re-enactment.

Hiking to **Louis Stevenson Park** on Mount St. Helena.

Dinner at the **Foothill Cafe** in Napa.

Waking up at 4AM to a spring frost with the smudge pots on.

The **Greek Wine Festival** in the summer at Macedonia Park near St. Helena.

Bruce and Barbara Neyers
Joseph Phelps Vineyards, St. Helena

A round of golf on the short but tricky nine-hole executive golf course at **Meadowood Resort,** St. Helena.

A drink at sunset on the veranda of **Auberge du Soleil** in Rutherford.

A late lunch on Sunday afternoon at **Tra Vigne** in St. Helena.

A bicycle ride along **Conn Valley Road** from the Silverado Trail to its dead end at Lake Hennessey.

A hike up the fire trail on Mount St. Helena.

Some barbecued ribs or Mongolian pork chops at **Mustards Grill** in Yountville.

The steak fajitas at **Las Brasas** in Calistoga.

Breakfast or lunch at **The Diner** in Yountville.

A leisurely stroll along Main Street in St. Helena with a visit to **Steve's Hardware & Housewares.**

Soaring over the north end of the valley in a glider based at **Calistoga Gliders.**

A mud bath and massage at **Dr. Wilkinson's Hot Springs** in Calistoga.

Sonoma Valley

The birthplace of the California wine industry, this crescent-shaped valley extends from San Pablo Bay through the town of **Sonoma** and a small cluster of old hot-springs towns, past tiny, bucolic **Glen Ellen** and **Kenwood,** and stops just short of **Santa Rosa.** Bounded to the east by the Mayacmas range and to the west by the Sonoma Mountains, the valley is an easy hour's drive from San Francisco—close enough for a one-day jaunt through the wine country. It is also ideal for a long weekend of winery visits paired with a stroll through the town of Sonoma and an unhurried drive through the pastoral **Valley of the Moon.**

The earliest vineyards on the North Coast were planted in 1824 by the Franciscan fathers at the **Mission San Francisco Solano de Sonoma,** which had been founded the year before. The fathers planted the Mission grape, which they used to produce sacramental wines. When Mexican *comandante* **General Mariano Vallejo** closed down the mission in 1834 under orders from the Mexican government, he took over the vineyards, planted more vines behind the presidio barracks, and in 1841 became Sonoma's first commercial vintner. His cellar, wine presses, and sales outlet were housed in the barracks, and he bottled his wines under the **Lachryma Montis** (tear of the mountain) label. A decade later, when the flamboyant Hungarian count and political exile **Agoston Haraszthy** arrived in Sonoma, he quickly realized the possibilities this fertile valley held for winemaking, having already tried and failed to grow grapes in Wisconsin, San Diego, and San Francisco. In 1857 he planted the first major vineyard of European grape varietals in California at his **Buena Vista** estate on the eastern outskirts of Sonoma. Today, Haraszthy, who cultivated 300 varieties of grapes, is widely known as the father of

Sonoma Valley

California wine. Other wine-savvy immigrants soon followed, such as **Jacob Gundlach** of **Gundlach-Bundschu.** By 1870 Sonoma was already considered the center of California's burgeoning wine industry.

Today the Sonoma Valley is home to more than 150 grape growers and 33 wineries, including some of the most familiar names in California winemaking: **Buena Vista, Sebastiani,** and **Glen Ellen.** Together they produce about 25 types of wines, ranging from crisp Sauvignon Blancs and buttery Chardonnays to robust Cabernets and spicy Zinfandels. Some vintners are experimenting with Sangiovese from Tuscany, and Syrah and Viognier from the Rhône valley in southern France. And you can also find premium sparkling wines and luscious late-harvest dessert wines made from Johannisberg Riesling. Both the large and small wineries here tend to be much more casual than those in the Napa Valley about drop-in visits. Few charge for tastings and most can be visited without calling ahead; those who ask for an appointment do so only because they want to make sure someone will be around when you arrive.

As in the Napa Valley, Sonoma producers have taken special pains to provide visitors with lovely picnic spots. Many wineries have some sort of picnic supplies on hand; most notably, **Sam** and **Vicki Sebastiani** go all out with an upscale Italian marketplace and deli at **Viansa,** their hillside property at the gateway to the Sonoma Valley. With its red-tile roof and grove of olive trees, Viansa resembles a little bit of Italy set down in Sonoma—and indeed, the countryside here is reminiscent of Tuscany. The stretch of Hwy 12 (the Sonoma Highway) from the town of Sonoma north past Kenwood is a state-designated scenic route, marked with signs depicting an orange poppy (the California state flower) on a blue background. The half-hour drive runs along the old stagecoach and railroad route linking Sonoma to Santa Rosa, past rolling hills, neatly manicured vines, and old barns and farmsteads.

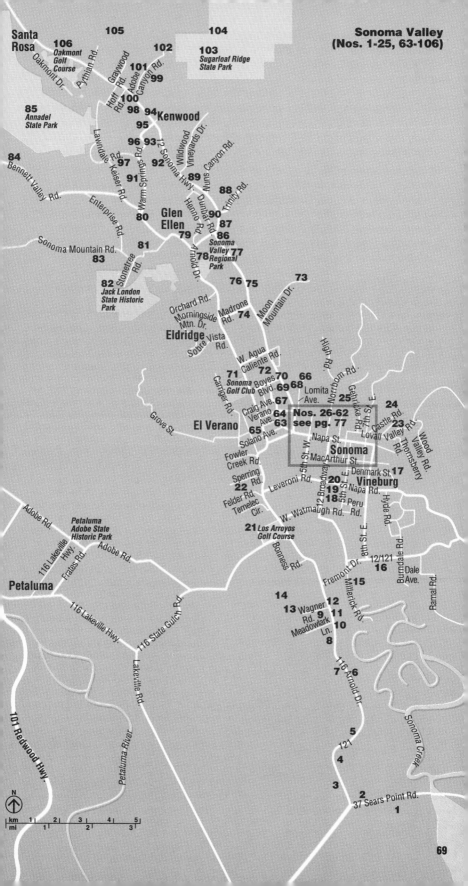

Santa
Rosa

105

104

106
Oakmont
Golf
Course

102

103
Sugarloaf Ridge
State Park

101
99

100
98 **94** **Kenwood**
95

85
Annadel
State Park

96 **93**
97 **92**
91

80 **Glen**
Ellen
79

84

81

83

82
Jack London
State Historic
Park

90
87
86
Sonoma
77
78 *Valley*
Regional
Park

88

76 **75**

73

Orchard Rd.
Morningside
Mtn. Dr. **74**
Eldridge
Sobre Vista
Rd.

71 **72**
Sonoma *Boyes*
Golf Club **70**
69 **68**
67
El Verano
64
65 **63**
Sonoma

66

25
24
23
Nos. 26-62
see pg. 77

17
Vineburg

22

20
19
18

21 *Los Arroyos*
Golf Course

Petaluma

Petaluma
Adobe State
Historic Park

16

15

14
13 *Wagner* **12**
Rd. **9** **11**
Meadowlark **10**
Ln.
8

7 **6**

5

4

3

2 *Sears Point Rd.*
37 **1**

N

km 1 2 3 4 5
mi 1 2 3

69

Fetters Hot Springs, Boyes Hot Springs, El Verano, and Agua Caliente, all popular hot-springs resorts at the turn of the century, now rub up against the outskirts of Sonoma, while Glen Ellen, the site of **Jack London's** beloved **Beauty Ranch,** is a sleepy little town with the feeling of bygone times. London's old ranch has been turned into the spectacular **Jack London State Historic Park,** just one of several Sonoma Valley nature preserves and parks where you can wander through fields of wildflowers and groves of redwoods, spend the afternoon basking in the sun, or go for a vigorous hike or horseback ride. The valley is also compact enough to make bicycling a great way to see the wine country.

The deluxe **Sonoma Mission Inn,** on the site of an old hot-springs resort, combines a first-class spa with luxury lodgings. The valley also has a posh Italian-style pensione, a number of intimate bed-and-breakfasts ranging from Victorian elegance to farmhouse funky, and several restored Gold Rush-era hotels and contemporary inns. When it comes to food, you'll find that Italian cuisine dominates, a legacy from the Italian stonecutters who originally immigrated to the valley in the 19th century to quarry stone and then often turned to winemaking. You can choose from both hearty, old-fashioned Italian-American fare and a newer generation of restaurants concentrating on Italian regional cuisine and California wine-country cooking.

Sonoma Valley

1 San Pablo Bay National Wildlife Refuge

This largely undeveloped 332-acre marsh on San Pablo Bay is popular with bird-watchers and wildlife photographers. Park your car at the locked gate at Tolay Creek and Hwy 347, then hike in two and three quarters miles to the bird sanctuary on Lower Tubbs Island; from there more trails lead down to the bay and the salt marshes (where critters like the opossum shrimp, pictured above, live). Bring your binoculars and a good field guide to identify canvasback ducks, the endangered California clapper rail, and the more than 280 species of other resident and migrating birds that call this preserve home. It might be a good idea to pack a few sandwiches in case you want to stay longer than anticipated in this unspoiled spot. The best time to visit is in winter, when the weather is cool and the birds are plentiful. From certain points along the trail, you can see the San Francisco skyline or the Golden Gate Bridge. Waterfowl and pheasant hunting is permitted in specified areas during the legal hunting season (months vary; please call). No restrooms or drinking water. ♦ Open year-round, daylight hours only. Hwy 37 (just past the Hwy 121 cutoff for Sears Point Raceway) Sonoma County. 415/792.0222

2 Port Sonoma Marina The diverse Port

Sonoma Marina offers a combination of open bay, tidal salt marsh, and freshwater wetlands. Complete with boat-launching facility and picnic area. ♦ Office daily 8:30AM-5:30PM. 270 Sears Point Rd, Sonoma County. 778.8055

3 Sears Point International Raceway One of the most demanding courses in the country. Sears Point offers automobile, bicycle, and motorcycle racing at their best. Pros such as **Mario Andretti** and **Al Unser** have raced frequently on the 12-turn, two-and-a-half-mile course, along with celebrities like **Tom Cruise, Paul Newman, Clint Eastwood,** and even Murphy Brown herself, **Candice Bergen.** Most events are held from March through October; call for schedules and more information. ♦ Hwys 37 and 121, Sonoma. 938.8448

At Sears Point International Raceway:

Skip Barber Racing School This school specializes in one- to three-day classes in high-performance BMW driving for amateurs, as well as professional racing courses. ♦ Call for information. 939.8000

4 Roche Winery Established in 1988, Roche Winery is surrounded by 25 acres of Chardonnay and Pinot Noir vines. Owners **Joseph** and **Genevieve Roche** believe in producing estate wines at reasonable prices, and their winemaker, **Steve MacCrostie,** also produces wines under his own label. Picnic facilities. ♦ Fee for tasting special or older wines. Tasting and sales daily 10AM-5PM; tours by appt. 28700 Arnold Dr (Hwy 121, just north of Sears Point Raceway) Sonoma. 935.7115

5 The Cherry Tree The pure, unsweetened Black Bing cherry juice sold at this white clapboard stand is a Sonoma tradition. Available in eight-ounce bottles on up to gallon jugs, this juice is so addictive you may want to pick up a case on your way out of Sonoma. The **Napoli** family's cider, made from a family recipe that originated in Germany over a century ago, is a mix of cherry juice and apple cider; they also produce their own unsweetened fruit butters and sell 100 percent Sonoma varietal wines under their own label, Napoli Cellars. And if you're heading toward Napa, look for Cherry Tree No. 2 on Fremont Dr (Hwy 12) between Sonoma and Napa. ♦ Daily 9AM-dusk. Arnold Dr (Hwy 121) Sonoma. 938.3480

6 Viansa Winery and Italian Marketplace
On a Carneros district hilltop, **Sam Sebastiani,** a third-generation vintner from one of Sonoma's oldest wine families, has created a fantasy of a Tuscan village. The russet-colored winery with terra-cotta roof tiles and green shutters is surrounded by a grove of olive trees; the Italian theme continues inside with evocative frescoes of vineyard scenes by San Francisco artists **Charlie Evans** and **Charley Brown.** Sebastiani has hired a winemaker from Tuscany and is experimenting with the Italian Sangiovese grape, but his flagship wines are still the Chardonnay, Cabernet, and Sauvignon Blanc made from a blend of premium grapes from the Napa and Sonoma valleys. His top wine, Obsidian, is a blend of Cabernet Franc and Cabernet Sauvignon.

Sebastiani and his wife, **Vicki,** an accomplished cook and gardener, offer elegant Italian picnic fare in their market-place. The produce comes from the estate's huge kitchen garden, and the food is very classy indeed—*foccacia*-bread sandwiches, country pâtés, pasta salads, imported Italian cheeses, and cold cuts. The colorful *torta rustica* is a tall, layered vegetable and cheese pie. Pay particular attention to the lovely little cookies and fig and walnut tartlets. Enjoy the informal picnic fare at a bistro table inside—or dine al fresco in the olive grove with its sweeping view of the valley. The marketplace also features an array of local food products, such as jams, mustard, olive oil, and vinegar, all handsomely packaged, plus handpainted terra-cotta and books on wines and Italian food. ♦ Tasting, sales, and guided tours daily 10AM-5PM, Jan-Mar; 10AM-6PM, Apr-Oct. 25200 Arnold Dr (Hwy 121) Sonoma. 935.4700; fax 996.4632

California's first Sauvignon Blanc grapes were planted in 1878. They came from the famous Bordeaux estate Château d'Yquem.

Restaurants/Clubs: Red   **Hotels:** Blue
Shops/ ♥ Outdoors: Green   **Wineries/Sights:** Black

7 Cline Cellars One of the newest additions to Sonoma Valley, this former Contra Costa County winery specializes in California Rhône-style wines. Owner **Fred Cline,** a University of California at Davis  graduate, makes three blends of Zinfandel with Carignane or Mourvèdre (both varietals from France's Rhône Valley), along with some terrific pure Zinfandels, a barrel-fermented Sémillon, and a lush dessert wine from Muscat of Alexandria. Some special varietals and reserves are only available at the tasting room inside the restored white-and-green 1850s farmhouse. The surrounding vineyards are planted with Syrah and the rare white Rhône varietals Viognier and Marsanne. Picnic area with views of Sonoma Valley. ♦ Tasting and sales daily 10AM-5:30PM; tours by appt. 24737 Arnold Dr (Hwy 121) Sonoma. 935.4310

8 The Fruit Basket Sandwich boards along the road mark this produce stand, where bins overflow with Sonoma's best-tasting bounty. Stop here for farm-fresh eggs, Clover-

Stornetta Farms milk, artichokes, asparagus, luscious strawberries by the flat, dried fruit and nuts, and other staples. They've also got a selection of Sonoma Valley wines, some of them chilled. ♦ Daily 7:30AM-7:30PM. 24101 Arnold Dr, Sonoma. 938.4332

9 Country Pine English Antiques A great selection of pine tables for your country kitchen (either English antiques or new reproductions) and armoires for your bedroom. Check this gracious shop for antique kitchen utensils, teapots, vases, and country-style dinnerware, too. One of the wooden plate racks would be a great addition to any kitchen. ♦ M-Th 10AM-5PM; F-Su 10AM-5:30PM. 23999 Arnold Dr, Sonoma. 938.8315

10 Aeroschellville Take an exhilarating 15- to 20-minute ride over Sonoma in a 1940 Stearman biplane once used to train WWII combat pilots. Unlike a balloon, which is dependent on wind currents, the little plane can take off anytime and 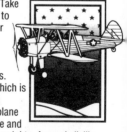 head straight for the sights. Aeroschellville offers all sorts of rides, most for just one or two people, ranging from leisurely flights over the Sonoma Valley or an extended scenic ride over both Napa and Sonoma valleys to an aerobatic ride with loops, rolls, and assorted dizzying maneuvers and—definitely not for the faint at heart—the kamikaze, described as an "intensely aerobatic" ride. Whoopee! Or you can stay safely on the ground and hire one of the pilots to skywrite a message to your honey. ♦ Daily 9AM-5PM. Schellville Airport, 23982 Arnold Dr (Hwy 121) Sonoma. 938.2444

11 World of Birds Walk into the bird room here and the cacophony is truly astonishing, as giant parrots, macaws, cockatiels, and smaller exotic birds join in the fray with warbles, honks, and chirps. World of Birds is the largest indoor breeding facility of exotic birds in the country, and, somewhat incongruously, it is also home to a herd of Peruvian llamas. Kids will want to get a close-up look, and if somebody in the family happens to fall in love with these gentle creatures...well, they are for sale, too. You'll also find wine-country and World of Birds souvenirs along with bird cages, books, and all manner of bird paraphernalia. ♦ Daily 7AM-5PM. 23570 Arnold Dr (Hwy 121) Sonoma. 996.1477

12 Angelo's Wine Country Meat & Deli Pull in here for generous sandwiches made with **Angelo Ibleto's** own roasted and

Sonoma Valley

smoked meats, plus 15 varieties of housemade sausages. Some are smoked and can be eaten as is; others are perfect for the grill. Hikers and campers swear by Angelo's flavored beef jerkies; he makes half a dozen now, including a dynamite Cajun. (They'll let you taste before you buy.) For picnics, consider their small boneless ham, about as big as two fists, or the smoked Cornish game hens. ♦ Daily 9AM-6PM. 23400 Arnold Dr, Sonoma. 938.3688

13 Gloria Ferrer Champagne Caves According to the winery's Spanish owner, **José Ferrer,** by the time America won its independence in 1776, his family had accumulated 15 generations of winemaking experience in Catalonia. (They also own the well-known cava [Catalan sparkling wine] producing house, **Freixenet.**) When Freixenet's sparkling wines became such a runaway success in this country, the firm decided to invest in their own California facility. Named for Ferrer's wife, **Gloria,** their Carneros-district winery boasts extensive subterranean aging cellars, and the design evokes Spain with its tiled roof, rows of arches, and whitewashed walls. In the **Sala de Catadores** (hall of the tasters), complimentary *tapas* (appetizers) are served with glasses of Gloria Ferrer's appealing brut. In

winter, settle in at the green-marble bistro tables in front of the massive fireplace; in warmer weather, the terrace overlooking the vineyard is an attractive spot to relax. The winery's popular cellar tour gives visitors an overview of the art of making sparkling wine. And before you leave, stock up on paella rice, Catalan oil and vinegar, olives, anchovies, and other Spanish delicacies. The winery occasionally offers Spanish cooking classes, and every July it hosts a Catalan Festival. ♦ Fee. Tasting and sales daily 10:30AM-5:30PM; tours on the hour 11AM-4PM. 23555 Hwy 121, Sonoma. 996.7256

14 Schug Cellars Walter Schug has moved his entire operation from Napa to Sonoma, building a new winery at the end of Bonneau Road just north of Gloria Ferrer. The half-timbered winery building pays tribute to Schug's German heritage and includes an underground cellar dug into the hillside for aging the casks of wine. The winery concentrates on Carneros-district Chardonnay and Pinot Noir; yet the estate's newly planted vineyard, not yet in production, consists of two-thirds Chardonnay and one-third Pinot Noir grapes. Picnic facilities on a sometimes windy site. ♦ Tasting, sales, and tours daily 10AM-5PM. 602 Bonneau Rd (Hwys 116 and 121) Sonoma. 939.9363

15 Sonoma Creek Vineyards & Winery This family-owned Carneros-district winery retains vineyards first established in the late 19th century and specializes in barrel-fermented, estate-bottled Chardonnay. Former veterinarian **Bob Larson** and his wife, **Helen,** along with their two sons and two daughters, also produce some Cabernet and Zinfandel. ♦ Tasting and sales daily 10AM-4PM; tours by appt. 2335 Millerick Rd, Sonoma. 938.3031

16 The Cherry Tree No. 2 Every other car heading down Hwy 12 seems to pull in at this large and fancier version of the original Cherry Tree (see page 70) on Hwy 121. This one features a deli and picnic area. Skip the sandwiches, but buy as much of the delicious, unsweetened cherry juice as you can carry. ♦ Daily 7:30AM-dusk. 1901 Fremont Dr, Sonoma. 938.3480

17 Gundlach-Bundschu Winery California's second-oldest bonded (state-licensed) winery was founded in 1858 by Bavarian-born **Jacob Gundlach.** He planted 400 acres of vineyards and introduced the German varietal Johannisberg Riesling to California at his Rhinefarm. Soon he and his son-in-law, **Charles Bundschu,** had created a worldwide market for their wines, sold under the Bacchus label. (Their warehouse in San Francisco covered an entire city block.) But after the 1906 earthquake destroyed the winery and Prohibition effectively ended their business, the family had to shut down their operations, though they still held on to the land and vineyards. The story does have a happy ending: In 1976 Jacob's great-great-grandson, **Jim Bundschu,** reopened the historic winery, rebuilding the original cellar and restoring Rhinefarm's vineyards. The specialty here is Kleinberger, a little-known white German varietal; he also makes Chardonnay and a crisp Riesling. Taste the Cabernet from Rhinefarm and Batto Ranch; the Rhinefarm Estate Merlot and Pinot Noir are excellent, too. And after your visit, hike up the short trail to the landmark **Towles Eucalyptus** tree and a panoramic view of the valley. The tree was planted by **Towles Bundschu,** a fourth-generation Bundschu, when he was 10 years old. Picnic tables on a grassy knoll. ♦ Tasting and sales 11AM-4:30PM. 2000 Denmark St, Sonoma. 938.5277

18 The Ranch House ★$$ A real find, this restaurant serves Yucatan-style Mexican cuisine in a relaxed, informal setting. Aficionados line up for the succulent *carne adobada* (beef braised with onions, tomatoes, and a mix of Yucatan spices) or the *puchero* (chicken in a sharp tomatillo sauce). Burritos get an interesting twist with a filling of spicy prawns spiked with bay and orange, yet you can still find well-prepared standard enchiladas and tostadas, and crisp, not soft, tortillas. ♦ Daily 11AM-10PM. 20872 Broadway, Sonoma. 938.0454

19 Sonoma Valley Visitors Bureau Information on lodging, wineries, restaurants, and activities in the Sonoma Valley. ♦ Daily 9AM-5PM. 20820 Broadway, Sonoma. 996.5793

Much of Sonoma County's highway system follows the old Indian trails.

Harvesttime in Sonoma

San Franciscans who appreciate farm-fresh foods send for their free Sonoma Farm Trails map and guide every year for an updated listing of more than 145 family farms that sell direct to the consumer. Many of these farms are near wineries, which makes it easy to stop on your wine-country excursion to buy freshly picked apples or berries. You'll often find homemade jams, jellies, and vinegars, along with handmade dried-flower or grapevine wreaths, and seasonal produce (see chart at right). The annual guide is available at chamber of commerce offices throughout Sonoma, or send a self-addressed, stamped envelope with a request for the farm guide to: Sonoma County Farm Trails, Box 6032, Santa Rosa CA 95406, or call 586.3276.

The following Sonoma County farmers markets also offer an opportunity to purchase fresh produce, and most are open a couple of days a week from May through November.

Healdsburg Farmers Market ♦ Tu 4:30-7PM, Sa 9AM-noon, May-Nov. City parking lot, North and Vine Sts, Healdsburg. 431.8409

Petaluma Farmers Market ♦ Sa 2-5PM, May-Oct. Downtown Petaluma

Santa Rosa Farmers Market ♦ Sa 9AM-noon, year-round; W 9AM-noon, Apr-Dec. Veterans Memorial Bldg parking lot, Brookwood Ave (at Hwy 12) Santa Rosa. 538.7023

Sonoma Farmers Market ♦ Tu 9AM-noon, May-Nov; F 9AM-noon, year-round. Arnold Field parking lot, First St West, Depot Park (north of W. Spain St) Sonoma

Thursday Night Market ♦ Th 5:30-7:30PM, May-Oct. Fourth St (B-E Sts) Santa Rosa. 539.0345

What's in Season When

	May	Jun	July	Aug	Sep	Oct	Nov	Dec
Apples			✔	✔	✔	✔	✔	✔
Delicious					✔	✔	✔	
Jonathan				✔	✔	✔		
Rome						✔	✔	✔
Azaleas/Rhododendrons	✔	✔						
Blackberries	✔	✔	✔					
Blueberries		✔	✔					
Bonzai					✔	✔		
Cherries	✔	✔						
Corn				✔	✔	✔		
Figs					✔	✔	✔	
Fresh Flowers	✔	✔	✔	✔	✔	✔	✔	
Grapes					✔	✔		
Japanese Maples	✔	✔	✔	✔	✔	✔	✔	✔
Kiwi						✔	✔	
Orchids	✔							✔
Peaches		✔	✔	✔	✔			
Pears				✔	✔	✔	✔	
Persimmons						✔	✔	✔
Plums		✔	✔	✔	✔			
Prunes				✔	✔			
Pumpkins				✔	✔	✔	✔	
Raspberries	✔	✔	✔					
Strawberries	✔	✔						
Succulents	✔	✔	✔	✔	✔			
Tomatoes			✔	✔	✔	✔	✔	
Vegetables	✔	✔	✔	✔	✔	✔	✔	
Walnuts						✔	✔	

20 Train Town Kids—and train buffs of all ages—will love this meticulously crafted diminutive railroad system. Every 20 minutes the scaled-down reproduction of an 1890s steam train departs with passengers in tow, chugging its way through 10 acres landscaped with miniature forests, tunnels, bridges, and lakes. At the halfway point, the little steam engine stops to take on water in **Lakeville,** a small replica mining town, where passengers can hand-feed a menagerie of farm animals. ♦ Admission. Daily 10:30AM-5:30PM, summer; Sa-Su 10:30AM-5PM, winter. 20264 Broadway (Hwy 12) Sonoma. 938.3912

21 Los Arroyos Golf Course Open to the public, this is a nine-hole course, par 29. ♦ Daily dawn to dusk. First come, first serve. 5000 Old Stage Gulch Rd, Sonoma. 938.8835

22 Happy Haven Ranch Sonoma locals favor the **Adamson** family's hot red-pepper and green-pepper jellies and stock up by the case. In season, the ranch also has an old-fashioned mix of flowers, decorative wheat sheaves, and strawberries that actually taste like they did in days past. If you like, you can get right in the strawberry patch and pick them yourself. ♦ M-Sa 10AM-6PM, Apr-Dec; by appt Su. 1480 Sperring Rd, Sonoma. 996.4260

Sonoma Valley

23 Buena Vista Winery Founded by the flamboyant Hungarian emigré and count, **Agoston Haraszthy,** Buena Vista is California's oldest premium winery and shouldn't be missed. On a visit in the 1850s, Haraszthy happened to taste the wines from **General Vallejo's** Sonoma estate (and also happened to woo his daughter). Immediately realizing the region's winemaking potential, he opened his own winery and set up housekeeping on a very grand scale in a nearby villa. Widely credited as the father of California wine, Haraszthy brought back thousands of cuttings of European grape varieties from France (for which the state never paid him) and turned Buena Vista into a showcase wine estate. A few years before phylloxera (an aphid that destroys grapevines) ravaged the region's vineyards, he disappeared somewhere in Nicaragua. His sons **Attila** and **Arpad** managed the estate until the 1906 earthquake forced the winery to close. It remained abandoned until 1943, when war correspondent **Frank Bartholomew** revived the historic property; he sold it 25 years later and founded **Hacienda** cellar on the site of Haraszthy's former villa. Buena Vista's present German owners, **Marcus** and **Anne Moller-Racke,** have continued the restoration of the huge, forested estate and massive stone cellars.

From the parking lot, follow the nature trail past rambling roses and wild blackberry bushes to the winery grounds. Picnic tables are set up in front of the cellars and in the shady grove just beside them. The original press house now serves as the tasting room, where you can sample most of the winery's current releases, including a good, commercial Chardonnay and a graceful Sauvignon Blanc produced by winemaker **Jill Davis.** The new releases of Private Reserve and Estate Cabernets are consistently top notch. For a small fee, you can taste older vintages of the Private Reserves along with Bricourt Champagne and Maison Thorin Burgundies, both from the owner's French wineries. They also stock picnic supplies: Sonoma jack and cheddar, local goat cheese, salami, pâtés, even Muscovy duck breast—and paper plates. You can take a self-guided tour of the the stone winery and hillside tunnels; weekends feature guided tours with a historical perspective. ♦ Fee for older vintages. Tasting, sales, and self-guided tours daily 10AM-5PM. 18000 Old Winery Rd, Sonoma. 938.1266

Within Buena Vista Winery:

Presshouse Gallery Once the winery presshouse, this upstairs gallery in the tasting room mounts shows of local artists. ♦ Daily 10AM-5PM. 938.1266

HACIENDA

1985
SONOMA COUNTY

Cabernet Sauvignon

24 Hacienda Winery Buena Vista's founder, **Agoston Haraszthy,** really knew how to pick a site. The first building you encounter at the end of the grand drive is not the winery, but a reconstruction of the Pompeian-style villa Haraszthy built here in 1857. A plaque commemorates a masked ball held on this site at the original building (which was destroyed by fire) on 23 October 1864, the first formal vintage celebration in California history, with **General** and **Señora Vallejo** as guests of honor. Farther along is the actual winery, a Spanish colonial building originally intended as a community hospital. Founded in 1973 by newspaperman **Frank Bartholomew** (who revived the Buena Vista

Winery in the forties), it is now principally owned by **A. Crawford Cooley,** a descendant of Bear Flagger **William B. Elliott.** In the dark, otherworldly tasting room, you can see the aging cellar just past the iron grill and taste the winery's Chardonnay, Chenin Blanc, Estate Reserve Pinot Noir, and Cabernet; Antares is Hacienda's blend of Cabernet Sauvignon, Merlot, and Cabernet Franc. If you express an interest in Port, the tasting-room manager might offer a bit of their vintage Port to taste with a chocolate truffle. ♦ Tasting and sales daily 10AM-5PM; tours by appt M-F. 1000 Vineyard Ln, Sonoma. 938.3220

25 Ravenswood A stone building with a sod roof (formerly known as the Haywood Winery) is the headquarters of this Zinfandel specialist. The tidy tasting room with a wood-burning stove and a cat cozied up to the fire has a sign that reads "No Wimpy Wines Allowed." Winemaker **Joel Peterson,** an immunologist by training, started the winery in 1976 in partnership with **W. Reed Foster,** president of the San Francisco Vintners Club. The name Ravenswood came from two ravens who scolded Peterson during his first day harvesting—and from the opera *Lucia de Lammermoor.* Ravenswood has established a reputation as one of California's great Zinfandel producers; grapes come from several very old, dry-farmed vineyards, yielding rich, concentrated wines. Peterson also makes Cabernet Sauvignon, Merlot, and a small amount of Chardonnay. The distinctive label was designed by the renowned Bay Area poster artist **David Lance Goines.** ♦ Tasting, sales, and tours daily 10AM-4:30PM. 18701 Gehricke Rd, Sonoma. 938.1960

"The first settlers arriving in Sonoma County found the valley floor covered with a growth of wild oats that could hide a man on horseback. We latecomers can only imagine that it must have been a beautiful sight."
Harvey J. Hansen,
Wild Oats in Eden: Sonoma in the 19th Century

Frank J. Prial
Wine Columnist, *The New York Times*

The breathtaking view of the Mayacmas Mountains through the archway at the **Robert Mondavi Winery** in Oakville.

The self-conducted tour of the stunning **Sterling Vineyards** winery near Calistoga (reachable only by tramway).

Any of the beautiful rooms at the tiny **Boonville Hotel** in the Anderson Valley.

Driving from Napa to Sonoma over the mountains via the **Oakville Grade** in a 5-series BMW.

The Pacific at sunset from the candlelit dining room at the **Albion River Inn,** on the ocean cliffs just south of Mendocino.

Admiring Napa Valley's blazing late-fall colors from **Philip Togni's** vineyard high up on Spring Mountain while sipping his Sauvignon Blanc.

The serene beauty of architect **Michael Graves'** inner courtyard at the **Clos Pegase Winery** near Calistoga.

The hiss of a propane burner and the sudden shadow of a multi-colored, hot-air balloon floating majestically over the vineyards.

Lunch in the garden at **Tra Vigne** in St. Helena on an early spring day, with a good Italian wine (just for a change of pace).

Sonoma Valley

Patricia Unterman
Restaurant Critic, *San Francisco Chronicle*
Chef/Owner, Hayes Street Grill

Beaulieu Winery in Rutherford—one of the oldest wineries in California and maker of elegant and long-lived Cabernets.

Clos Pegase Winery near Calistoga, which was designed by architect **Michael Graves** and has an art collection.

The caves of **Carmenet Vineyard** in Sonoma.

A snack under the trees at **Tra Vigne's Cantinetta** in St. Helena.

A prix-fixe dinner at **The French Laundry** in Yountville.

Stopping at **Oakville Grocery** to get supplies for a picnic at the **Conn Dam Reservoir.**

Visiting the **Downtown Bakery & Creamery** on Healdsburg Plaza for fabulous housemade ice creams and cookies.

Renting a canoe from **W.C. "Bob" Trowbridge** in Healdsburg for a trip down the Russian River.

Riding in a glider from Calistoga over the Napa Valley.

A dinner and overnight stay at the Victorian **Madrona Manor** outside of Healdsburg.

Restaurants/Clubs: Red	**Hotels:** Blue
Shops/ ♥ Outdoors: Green	**Wineries/Sights:** Black

Town of Sonoma

This wine-country town, whose name is said to come from a Suisun Indian word meaning "vale of many moons," had its beginnings as **Mission San Francisco Solano de Sonoma.** Founded by Franciscan **Padre José Altimira** in 1823, the mission was the northernmost and the last of the 21 missions that his order established in California. In 1834 the Mexican government sent the young **General Mariano Vallejo** to oversee the secularization of the mission and to establish a Mexican pueblo and presidio. It was Vallejo who laid out Sonoma's lovely Spanish-style plaza and the cluster of rustic adobe buildings that grew up around it. By 1845 the little town had 45 houses and a population of more than 300. Sonoma was incorporated as a city in 1850.

This was also the site of the short-lived Bear Flag revolution, in which disgruntled American settlers, who had been lured to the area by rumors of free land, rebelled against the Mexican government when they discovered noncitizens were prohibited from owning property. For 25 days in 1846, a ragtag band of immigrants, who called themselves the **Bear Flag Party,** seized control of Sonoma, jailed Vallejo, and raised their flag (the grizzly bear-emblazoned banner later adopted by the state of California) over the plaza. The revolution ended less than a month later when the American government stepped in and took over.

Today this city at the very end of **El Camino Real** (the royal Spanish road that connected the missions of California) offers visitors a glimpse into California's past. The eight-acre parklike plaza is surrounded by historic adobe buildings that house boutiques, antique stores, restaurants, and food shops, along with several renovated Gold Rush-era hotels. The **Sonoma Historical Museum** comprises half a dozen sites in and around the plaza, including the old mission, the Indian barracks, the **Toscano Hotel,** and General Vallejo's Gothic Victorian Revival home at his estate, **Lachryma Montis.**

Within walking or biking distance from the plaza are some of the Sonoma Valley's earliest wineries: **Buena Vista,** founded in 1857 by the Hungarian political exile **Agoston Haraszthy; Hacienda Winery,** perched on the site where Haraszthy had built a Pompeian-style villa; and **Gundlach-Bundschu,** another famous 19th-century wine estate. **Sebastiani,** perhaps Sonoma's best-known winery, and some smaller, new estates such as **Ravenswood,** which just happens to make one of the best Zinfandels in California, round out Sonoma's wine-tasting experience.

Sonoma

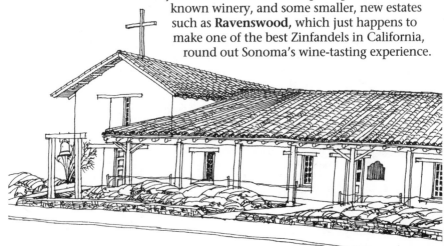

Mission San Francisco Solano de Sonoma

DRAWING COURTESY E. ROSS PARKERSON

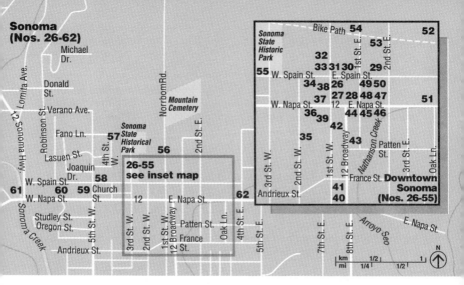

Sonoma (Nos. 26–62)

Michael Dr.

Lomita Ave.

12 Sonoma Hwy.

Donald St.

Verano Ave.

Robinson St.

Fano Ln.

Lasuen St.

Joaquin Dr.

4th St. W.

57 Sonoma State Historical Park

Norrbom Rd.

Mountain Cemetery

2nd St. E.

56

W. Spain St.

26-55 see inset map

W. Napa St. **58**

61 60 59 Church St.

12

E. Napa St.

62

Studley St.

Oregon St.

Andrieux St.

5th St. W.

3rd St. W.

2nd St. W.

1st St. W.

12 Broadway

Patten St.

France St.

Oak Ln.

4th St. E.

5th St. E.

Sonoma Creek

Sonoma State Historic Park

Bike Path **54**

W. Spain St.

55

32

33 31 30

34 38 26

37

36 39

35

E. Spain St.

1st St. E.

2nd St. E.

53

29

49 50

W. Napa St. 12 E. Napa St.

27 28 48 47

44 45 46

42

43

52

51

Nathanson Creek

Patten St.

France St. **Downtown**

41

40

Andrieux St.

Sonoma

(Nos. 26–55)

Arroyo Seo

E. Napa St.

7th St. E.

8th St. E.

km 1/2 1

mi 1/4 1/2

N

---

26 Sonoma Plaza The real heart of old Sonoma is this eight-acre Spanish-style plaza, a state and national landmark. **General Mariano Vallejo,** the Mexican *comandante,* laid it out with a pocket compass in 1835 as the nucleus of a mile-square town. At first, it was a bare, dusty place where Vallejo drilled his troops. Later it was used to graze livestock and provide soil to make adobe bricks. Then at the turn of the century, the **Ladies Improvement Club** took it over and turned it into the verdant park it is today with more than 200 trees and an intriguing mix of native and exotic plants, including a salmon-colored rose called the Sonoma rose. With its shady areas, playground, duck pond, and wooden tables, the plaza is an appealing spot for a picnic. Parking spots on the sides of the plaza have a two-hour limit; a lot behind the Sonoma barracks building permits longer stays. ♦ Spain and Napa Sts-First St West and First St East

26 Bear Flag Monument A bronze figure raises the Bear Flag to commemorate 14 June 1846. On that date, a band of American immigrants rode into Sonoma, imprisoned **General Mariano Vallejo,** and proclaimed California an independent republic. Bear Flagger **John Sears** contributed the white cloth for the banner's background; the flag's red stripe came from a petticoat; and Abraham Lincoln's nephew, **William Todd,** painted a large bear, a single star, and the name "California Republic" on the flag. The audacious band's new republic lasted just 25 days, when the US government stepped in to halt the rebellion. In 1911 the California state legislature voted to adopt the design as the official state flag. ♦ Sonoma Plaza, directly across from the Barracks, Sonoma

DRAWING COURTESY E. ROSS PARKERSON

27 Sonoma City Hall To avoid slighting any of the merchants on the plaza, when San Francisco architect **A.C. Lutgens** drew the plans for Sonoma's new city hall (pictured above) in 1906, he designed the square Mission Revival building to be identical on all four sides. Built of locally quarried basalt, the eccentric golden-stone building is the subject of Sonoma schoolchildren's drawings at the annual art show. If the courthouse looks familiar it might be because you saw it as the Tuscany County Courthouse on TV's long-running wine-country soap opera, *Falcon Crest.* ♦ The city hall is at the end of Broadway, the grand boulevard that marks the entrance to Sonoma and the end of El Camino Real, the King's Highway.

28 Sonoma Valley Visitors Bureau The Neoclassic brick building that once housed the town library is now the headquarters of the visitors bureau. Everyone on the staff here is knowledgeable about the area and ready to help visitors plan their itinerary and advise them on lodging availability. Be sure to pick up a copy of the self-guided walking tour of Old Sonoma; you can also sign up for guided tours of the city. Check the bulletin board out front for events and activities. The visitors bureau also contains the offices of the **Sonoma Valley Vintners Association** and

---

Restaurants/Clubs: Red   Hotels: Blue
Shops/ ♦ Outdoors: Green   Wineries/Sights: Black

sells the official Sonoma Valley blue-stemmed wine glasses. ◆ M-Sa 9AM-5PM; Su 9AM-3PM. 453 First St East, Sonoma. 996.1090

29 Mission San Francisco Solano de Sonoma Here is the northernmost and the last of the 21 Franciscan missions built along the length of California (see illustration on page 76). Named after a Peruvian saint, it was constructed on a site chosen by **Padre José Altimira** in 1823, when California was under Mexican rule. Construction of the original church began in 1823, but all that survives of those times are the adobe padre's quarters. (The present church was built under the direction of **General Mariano Vallejo** in 1840.) You can walk through the mission fathers' former rooms and tour blacksmith, weaving, and bread-baking workshops to get a sense of what life was like in this mission outpost. ◆ 114 E. Spain St, Sonoma

30 The Barracks Between 1836 and 1840, Native American laborers built this two-story example of Monterey Colonial adobe construction to serve as **General Mariano Vallejo's** Mexican troop headquarters. Seized by the Bear Flag Party when they set up a short-lived independent republic in 1846, it was a US military post until the 1850s. A century later, the state bought and restored it as part of the Sonoma State Historical Park. ◆ First St East and E. Spain St, Sonoma

Sonoma

30 Toscano Hotel Originally built as a general store and lending library in the 1850s, this early California wood-frame building became a hotel in 1886; its name is a tribute to the proprietors' Tuscan heritage. In 1957 a descendant of the hotel's original owners sold it to the state. The **Sonoma League for Historic Preservation** stepped in to help restore the old mining hotel, endowing it with a certain raffish charm. They've left whiskey glasses and hands of cards on the tables, as if the players had just slipped out for a minute or two, while ragtime music plays in the background. Upstairs, the six bedrooms are furnished with period antiques and authentic touches. The turn-of-the-century kitchen in back displays a quirky collection of cookware and gadgets. ◆ Tours: M 11AM-1PM, Sa-Su 1-4PM; Kitchen annex: M, Sa-Su 11AM-4PM. 20 E. Spain St, Sonoma. 938.4257

30 Casa Grande Indian Servants' Quarters This two-story Monterey Colonial, once used as a servants' quarters, is all that's left of **General Vallejo's** early Sonoma home. His imposing Casa Grande, built circa 1835, featured a three-story tower from which the general could survey the surrounding countryside. Eleven of his 14 children were born in the sprawling adobe house, but in 1853 he moved his family to **Lachryma Montis,** a new home he built on a secluded

site north of Sonoma. In 1867 a fire destroyed Casa Grande's main buildings, leaving only these servants' quarters, where a small Native American exhibit is now housed. ◆ 20 E. Spain St, Sonoma

31 Plaza Books A welcome refuge from the tourist fray. Just the smell of all the old leather- and cloth-bound books transports you back to another era. No current bestsellers here, just quality used and rare books. ◆ Daily 11AM-6PM; Sa-Su open later in summer. 40 W. Spain St, Sonoma. 996.8474

31 Marioni's Restaurant ★$$ For die-hard surf 'n' turf fans, this wood-lined canteen is the place to get all manner of steaks and seafood. The teriyaki chicken is about as exotic as it gets. ◆ American ◆ Daily 11:30AM-2:30PM, 5-10PM. 8 Spain St, Sonoma. 996.6866

31 Sonoma Cheese Factory ★$ The plate-glass windows at the back of this crowded shop offer a good view of workers in white hard hats and yellow aprons making cheese. Famous for its Sonoma jack, the factory has developed a growing line of cheeses including jack spiked with pepper, garlic, or caraway seeds, a mild cheddar, and a tender cheese called teleme. Founder **Celso Viviani's** son **Pete** and grandson **David** now run the family business; David's brother-in-law **Fred Harland** is the cheesemaker. The store is filled with all sorts of picnic fare, not only cheeses, already wrapped and priced, but also slices of pâté and cold cuts sliced to order; the prepared salads are less tempting. You can have them make you a sandwich and retire to the shady patio for lunch. They also offer crackers, local mustards, jams, and Sonoma wines—some arranged in gift baskets. ◆ M-F 8:30AM-5:30PM; Sa-Su 8:30AM-6PM. Sonoma Plaza, 2 Spain St

32 Chairhouse-Sonoma This is the place to find baskets, textiles, toys, and more—but not one chair. The gallery takes its name from the owners' original San Francisco shop (which used to sell chairs in the fifties). ◆ F-Su 11AM-5PM. 383 First St West, Sonoma. 938.0298

The exact origin of Zinfandel, which has become one of the most beloved grapes in California, is unknown. Scholars are certain it's a *vitis vinifera* (non-native) variety that somehow got to California in one of the shipments of vine cuttings that pioneer Sonoma vintner **Agoston Haraszthy** sent back from Europe. In shape and foliage, Zinfandel closely resembles Primitivo, a grape variety from the northern Italian region of Piedmont, but the wine flavors it produces are very different—and therein lies the mystery.

33 Sonoma Hotel $ Completed in 1880, this corner building has had a checkered past. As in many buildings of the era, the downstairs was used as a series of shops and saloons. Upstairs, it featured a hall and a stage for social occasions. When **Samuele Sebastiani** bought it in the twenties, he added a third floor and a balcony encircling the second floor—and he made himself a hotel, which he dubbed the **Plaza.** Those upstairs rooms, with shared baths à la the European tradition, are wine-country bargains; **Maya Angelou** wrote *Gather Together in My Name* in No. 21, a small cozy room with a pitched ceiling, a floral comforter, and lace curtains. Rooms with private baths on the first two floors have deep, clawfoot tubs. The grandest is the **Vallejo Room,** furnished with a four-piece bedroom suite of carved rosewood that once belonged to General Vallejo's daughter and is on loan from the Historical Society. ♦ 110 W. Spain St, Sonoma. 996.2996

Within the Sonoma Hotel:

Sonoma Hotel Restaurant and Saloon
★★$$ The casual restaurant, with an adjoining garden courtyard (reopened in 1991), serves a bar-and-grill menu featuring salads, sandwiches, and burgers at lunch, with daily specials added in the evening, such as roasted baby-back ribs or grilled prawns. If you just want to linger over a glass of wine from the bar, order chilled prawn remoulade or baked brie with roasted garlic to spread on some Sonoma sourdough. For a quick bite, try the grilled chicken-breast sandwich or the bacon, avocado, and tomato sandwich. The all-Sonoma wine list offers more than a hundred wines and includes a number of older vintages, too. The one hundred-year-old mahogany bar is a good spot for a drink. ♦ M, W-Su 11AM-8PM; hours may vary in winter. 996.2996

34 Thistle Dew Inn $$ This 1910 California arts and crafts house offers six guest rooms (two rooms in the main house, four in the cottage out back), all with a private bath. The **Rose Garden Room** is furnished with antique oak furniture and a fan-patterned quilt; the smaller **Cornflower Room** is, of course, blue with a matching Star of Texas quilt. Most of the original arts and crafts furniture is by Gustav Stickley or Charles Limbert; lamps, textiles, and rugs are from the same period. Guests can use the cozy parlor complete with a wood-burning stove and plump, pale green sofas. Innkeeper **Larry Barnett** cooks a full breakfast (fluffy soufflé pancakes, scrambled eggs with salmon, pancakes with fruit, or French toast with cinnamon). The inn has bicycles and picnic baskets for guests and also offers access to the best local health club with aerobics, Nautilus, and pool facilities. No smoking and no children under 12 or pets allowed. ♦ 171 W. Spain St, Sonoma. 938.2909

35 Sonoma Valley Inn $$ On a busy street one block from Sonoma Plaza, this Best Western inn has 75 comfortable rooms and suites, all with a private bath and no-nonsense modern decor; some have wood-burning fireplaces, Jacuzzis, or kitchenettes. All have use of the pool and spa. Continental breakfast. ♦ 550 Second St West, Sonoma. 938.9200, 800/334.KRUG (CA only)

36 The Cat and the Fiddle A store for romantics and subscribers to *Victoria* or *Country Life*, filled with English and French country antiques, sentimental children's

books and toys, handpainted furniture, and anything with bows or lace. ♦ M-Sa 11AM-5PM; Su noon-4PM. 153 W. Napa St, Sonoma. 996.5651

36 The Sonoma Country Store Suffused with the scent of lavender and dried flowers, this large, airy shop stocks majolica dinnerware, Mexican handblown glass, country linens and tablemats, beeswax candles—in short, everything to turn your house into Sonoma's version of Provence or Tuscany. ♦ M-Sa 10AM-6PM; Su noon-5PM. 165 W. Napa St, Sonoma. 996.0900

37 Chevy's ★$$ Sonoma County's freshest addition to the "Fresh-Mex" chain. Settle in for nachos (chips slathered in cheese, beans, and jalapeño chiles) and quesadillas (cheese-stuffed tortillas), and great margaritas made with freshly squeezed lime juice. For more substantial fare, try the fajitas *al carbon* (marinated grilled beef or chicken served with flour tortillas, guacamole, hot sauce, and rice and beans), and for four people, the giant *plato gordo* (which adds mesquite-broiled quail and jumbo shrimp to the platter). Roll it all up in the tender fresh tortillas baked on the premises. Forget about drinking wine for the moment, and have an ice-cold Mexican beer. ♦ Mexican ♦ M-Th, Su 11:30AM-10PM; F-Sa 11:30AM-11PM. 136 W. Napa St, Sonoma. 938.8009

37 Mary Stage Jewelry It's fun to browse through the collection of antique silver and gemstone jewelry from the Edwardian era up to the forties. Flatware and silver serving pieces are also sold here. ♦ Tu-Sa 10AM-5PM. 126 W. Napa St, Sonoma. 938.1818

37 Homegrown Bagel Shop ★$ Order a bagel with a cream cheese schmear or a made-to-order sandwich to eat at the counter or at any of the half-dozen tables squeezed into this small shop. Takeout. ♦ M-F 6:30AM-2:30PM; Sa-Su 7:30AM-2:30PM. 122 W. Napa St, Sonoma. 996.0166

38 Sonoma Books This false-front pioneer-era building now houses a very personal selection of literature and nonfiction books, with a large section on the healing arts. Books from local authors are prominently displayed (and there are a good many of them, too). Pick up one of Glen Ellen writer M.F.K. Fisher's musings on gastronomy, a history of Sonoma, or *A Cook's Tour of Sonoma* by Michele Anna Jordan. ♦ Tu-Sa 10:30AM-5PM; Su noon-4PM. 483 First St West, Sonoma. 935.1944

38 Batto Building A three-section, glazed-brick building in Classic Revival style dating from about 1912. ♦ 453-461 First St West, Sonoma

Sonoma

Within the Batto Building:

Sonoma Sausage Co. ★★★$ Herb Hoeser learned to make sausages in Germany, where it's not unusual for one small shop to make more than a hundred varieties. In this bustling Sonoma shop he makes more than 70 handmade sausages (though not all at the same time), as well as pâtés and gorgeous hams and meats. Don't miss the homemade German sauerkraut and the great assortment of local mustards. The wonderful sandwiches, especially those made with German cold cuts such as *laberkaese* or Black Forest-style ham, are real wine-country bargains. For picnics, there is such ready-to-eat fare as Gypsy ham (smoky and lean), cooked bratwurst, and Nürnberger bratwurst flavored with marjoram. For the barbecue: old-fashioned franks, German wieners (veal and pork), all-beef hot dogs, hot beer sausages spiked with cayenne and paprika, and Hawaiian Portuguese (made with pork, red pepper, and wine). Many of the sausages freeze well, but if you plan on buying any fresh, purchase them immediately before driving home; they'll keep well unrefrigerated for two and a half hours maximum. ♦ M-Sa 9:30AM-5:30PM; Su noon-5PM. 453 First St West, Sonoma. 938.8200

38 Kaboodle The gable-roofed building has had several lives—first as a laundry and employment office for Chinese immigrants in the latter half of the 19th century, later as a boarding house and restaurant. Today it is one of the plaza's most charming shops. Designer/owner **Beth Labelle** sits at a table right in the shop putting together her exquisite dried flower wreaths. She also decorates romantic straw hats with silk ribbon from France. Her choice selection of children's books and stuffed animals from Germany will tempt the child in anyone. The old-fashioned topiaries and graceful bird cages make wonderful gifts. ♦ Daily 11AM-5PM. 447 First St West, Sonoma. 996.9500

38 Ruggles Music & Art Supplies Here's where to pick up sketch pads and pastels or watercolors to keep the whole family busy. One wall of the long, narrow space is designated as the Sonoma Valley Art Center Gallery and shows work from local artists. Also sold here is sheet music for popular songs and showtunes, plus guitar strings, etc. ♦ Daily 11AM-5PM. 439 First St West, Sonoma. 996.2590

38 Sign of the Bear You'll find crocks for making pickles, pressed glass bottles for steeping vinegar with herbs, and all sorts of kitchen utensils and gadgets at this unpretentious, friendly cookware shop, which is not so much gourmet as it is a combination cookware and general store. Nice selection of cookbooks, too. ♦ M-Sa 10AM-5PM; Su noon-4PM. 435 First St West, Sonoma. 996.3722

38 Salvador Vallejo Adobe Under the direction of **General Vallejo's** brother **Don Salvador Vallejo,** Native Americans completed construction of this historic adobe in 1846. During the Gold Rush it became the El Dorado Hotel. The second story was probably added when it was converted to a boarding school in the late 1850s. ♦ 405, 415, 421, 427 First St West, Sonoma

Within the Salvador Vallejo Adobe:

Bendice There's always something of interest in this lovely shop, whether it's terra-cotta dinnerware from Portugal, handpainted furniture from the Southwest, or tooled leather bags and briefcases from Mexico. ♦ Daily 11AM-5PM. 421 First St West, Sonoma. 938.2775

El Dorado Hotel $$ Goose-down comforters, terry-cloth robes, and the use of a heated, outdoor swimming pool are just a few the perks at this small hotel on the plaza, newly renovated by a team led by **Claude Rouas** (of the posh Auberge du Soleil in the Napa Valley). Instead of full-tilt luxury, they've gone for simple comfort at moderate prices. The 27 rooms, all with a private bath, are fairly small, and they've wisely left them uncluttered, adding terracotta tile floors, handcrafted furniture, and textiles in pale, soothing colors. French doors lead to small balconies overlooking either the plaza or the courtyard and pool in back; cable TV and AM/FM radios are standard equipment. The heated lap pool is new and an Italian Continental breakfast (coffee, fruit, and freshly baked breads and Italian pastries) is served on the brick patio beneath an ancient fig tree. The strong suit here is the thoroughly professional concierge service; use it to arrange dinner reservations, a massage, horseback rides, picnics, or wine tours. ♦ 405 First St West, Sonoma. 996.3030, 800/289.3031; fax 996.3148

Within the El Dorado Hotel:

Ristorante Piatti ★★★$$$ Like its sister restaurant in the Napa Valley, Piatti offers regional Italian cuisine. Rustic *bruschetta* (grilled bread topped with tomatoes, garlic basil, and olive oil), carpaccio, or *bagna caûda* (a hot bath of garlic and anchovy sauce with a plate of fresh vegetables) are top choices for antipasti. The wood-burning oven turns out classic pizzas such as *margherita* (tomato, mozzarella, and basil) or marinara (fresh tomatoes, oregano, garlic, and olive oil). Pastas can be very good; try the old Roman dish *penne all'amatriciana* (pasta with a pancetta and tomato sauce spiked with chili). Main courses from the grill are always an excellent choice— particularly the marinated free-range chicken and the grilled sausage served with creamy polenta and wilted greens. Sorbetti and gelati put a chill on Sonoma's summer heat; save the richer desserts for cooler weather. But go for the *affogato al caffè* (white chocolate and Amaretto ice creams drenched with espresso) anytime. ♦ M-Th 11:30AM-2:30PM, 5-10PM; F 11:30-2:30PM, 5-11PM; Sa noon-11PM; Su noon-10PM. 996.2351

Button Down Explore this swanky men's shop featuring gorgeous ties, suspenders, and slinky armbands (to hold your sleeves up) from England. They sell a few women's items, too. ♦ M, W-Su 11AM-6PM. 996.8816

Wine Country Living Stop here to pick up ceramic and terra-cotta serving platters, bowls, jugs, and pitchers with the grape as a design motif. Most are imported from Italy and Portugal. They also have ceramic wine coolers from a local Sonoma potter. ♦ M-Sa 10:30AM-6PM; Su noon-6PM. 996.3453

39 The Feed Store Cafe & Bakery ★★$ One side of this enormous former feed store (built in 1921) is a bakery with dainty cafe tables. Everything is housemade, from oversized croissants and poppyseed muffins to pumpkin cheesecake and peaches-and-cream pie, sold whole or by the slice. For a

quick snack, order champagne biscotti or the raspberry brownie with a cappuccino made from Mr. Espresso beans (a superior blend roasted over an oakwood fire)—but ask them to make it double or it won't be strong enough. Next door, the cafe (with a sunny garden terrace in back) serves build-your-own omelets at breakfast, as well as creative egg dishes such as the Mission Solano Scrambler (three eggs with local jack and cheddar cheeses, chiles, and tomato). Lunch here means burgers, hot dogs, salads, and several inventive sandwiches. ♦ M-W 7AM-3PM; Th-Sa 7AM-9PM; Su 8AM-3PM. 509 First St West, Sonoma. 938.2122

40 Side Door Inn $$$ Conveniently located on a quiet residential street, this inn has a completely private two-bedroom suite that can be shared by two couples. It has contemporary decor, a TV, and a fully equipped kitchen. The bedrooms, each with a private bath, open onto a large redwood deck in front. There's also a room available downstairs. Through the side gate is a small, Japanese-style garden of stones and potted bamboo. Complimentary breakfast at the Feed Store Cafe & Bakery up the street. No smoking. ♦ 784 First St West, Sonoma. 938.1459

Magfiulo's

Sonoma

41 Magliulo's Restaurant ★$$/$$$ Specialties at this family restaurant in a spiffed-up Victorian include homemade minestrone, a wide variety of pasta dishes (such as angelhair with a basil, tomato, and pine nut sauce), and a hearty helping of spaghetti and meatballs. You can find familiar Italian-American dishes such as chicken marsala and a veal scaloppine that is prepared several ways. There's a New York steak and (Saturday only) a prime-rib dinner. For dessert, what else but spumoni or the frothy zabaglione. Summer evenings, ask to be seated in the brick-paved courtyard. ♦ Italian/American ♦ Daily 11AM-3PM, 5-8:30PM. 691 Broadway, Sonoma. 996.1031

41 Magliulo's Pensione $$ The proprietors of Magliulo's Restaurant next door have turned this cornflower-blue Victorian house into a B&B. They decorated it with the usual brass beds, armoires, and ceiling fans, and antique quilts are hung on the walls. Rooms have either private or shared baths. The parlor features a pink sofa and a fireplace framed in copper with cozy chairs pulled up in front. Drinks and hors d'oeuvres are available from the restaurant next door. Continental breakfast. No smoking allowed, and no minimum stay required. ♦ 681 Broadway, Sonoma (register at Magliulo's Restaurant) 996.1031

42 Bear Moon Trading Co. In an 1880s building with an Italianate false front, Bear Moon carries a good selection of natural-fiber sweaters, socks, and comfortable hot-weather clothing. Consider one of the handsome Panama hats to ward off the summer sun. ♦ M-Sa 10AM-5PM; Su 11AM-4PM. 523 Broadway, Sonoma. 935.3392

43 Marika Didn't bring enough clothes? Brought all the wrong clothes for the season? Marika can rescue your wardrobe with fashionable, discounted clothing from well-known designer lines. We're not talking Issey Miyake here, but good-looking cottons, linens, and silks, more casual than fancy. ♦ M-Sa 10AM-5PM; Su noon-5PM. 526 Broadway, Sonoma. 935.3300

43 The Craft Gallery A welcome change from tourist-oriented bric-a-brac stores, this gallery (pictured above) concentrates on fine

Sonoma

examples of contemporary crafts. Look for gilt-edged glass platters from **Annie Glass,** intricately crafted jewelry, handwoven clothing, and handpainted silk scarves. And for the practical at heart: masterful bowls created on a wood turner's lathe, shimmering ceramics, and hardwood cutting boards. ♦ M-Sa 10AM-5PM; Su noon-4PM. 548 Broadway, Sonoma. 996.2255

44 Good Day Sunshine Check out this spacious shop if you're in the market for contemporary crafts from California. The selection runs the gamut from ceramics and lots of handcrafted jewelry to handblown glass goblets and beautifully crafted hardwood wine coasters. ♦ M-Sa 10AM-5:30PM; Su 11AM-5PM. 29 E. Napa St, Sonoma. 938.4001

44 Magnifico This inviting store features imported Italian faïence (fine painted and glazed pottery) in a bright wash of colors, plus wine jugs and sleek Italian espresso and coffee makers. Distressed metal signs look as if they were lifted from a provincial French cafe. ♦ Tu-F 10AM-5:30PM; Sa 10AM-6PM; Su 11AM-5PM. 25 E. Napa St, Sonoma. 939.0431

45 Della Santina's ★★★$$ It's a trattoria, a rosticceria, and a pasticceria all in one, run by cousins of the same family that runs the

Joe's restaurant dynasty of San Francisco's North Beach. In the window, chickens coated with herbs turn in front of the Italian-style rôtisserie. They make a nice minestrone and Caesar salad, and the handmade pastas are all very good. Plump tender gnocchi come with a meat and porcini-mushroom sauce; tortellini are tossed in a fragrant pesto; and wide ribbon noodles are served with a duck sauce, just as in Tuscany. But the real stars here are the meats from the rosticceria—half chickens, Sonoma rabbit, pork loin, roast veal, and turkey breast. The plate of mixed roasted meats will go with just about any wine. At lunch they'll tuck some of that savory meat into a roll brushed with olive oil and fresh herbs and serve it with grilled radicchio and sautéed onions. Desserts are less successful. Limited list of Italian and Sonoma wines. Takeout available. ♦ Italian ♦ Tu-Sa 11AM-9:30PM. 101 E. Napa St, Sonoma. 935.0576

46 Pasta Nostra ★$$ Chef **Matteo Watkins** beat out 24 other Bay Area chefs in Viansa Winery's first pasta festival and sauce competition in 1990 with his flambéed lamb cream sauce. This restaurant in a white Victorian gingerbread cottage just off the plaza features hearty Italian-American fare. Start with prosciutto and melon, calamari salad, or the garlic bread. Homemade pastas include fettuccine carbonara, spaghetti with clams, and, yes, spaghetti and meatballs. Free-range veal and baked chicken are prepared several ways. The best seats in the house are the tables outside in the courtyard decorated with old wine barrels planted with olive trees. Portions are generous. ♦ Italian ♦ M-Th 5-9PM; F-Sa 5-10PM; Su 4:30-9PM. 139 E. Napa St, Sonoma. 938.4166

46 Bonito ★★$$$ Taking over the diminutive stone house where the French restaurant **Les Arcades** was installed, this new oyster bar and seafood grill is a welcome addition to the Sonoma restaurant scene. The small menu offers the kind of dishes that taste wonderful any time of the day. Chef **Todd Thorpe** is a veteran of San Francisco's **Anchor Oyster Bar.** Gear up for seafood cocktails and refreshing crab Louis or platters of steamed shellfish and deep-fried calamari. They've got burgers and grilled rib eye steak, but why not opt for the open-face crab, fish, and cheese sandwich or the grilled prawns? Every day brings several catch-of-the-day items, most often grilled and served with a choice of sauces. Keep an eye out for the restaurant's namesake bonito or tuna. To wash it all down, they offer an all-California wine list dominated by Sonoma wines—and every wine on the list can be ordered by the glass. In warm weather, you can eat outside in an enclosed patio twined with ivy. ♦ Mediterranean/California seafood ♦ M-Sa 11:30AM-9:30PM. 133 E. Napa St, Sonoma. 939.1266

47 **Robin's Nest** A paradise for serious cooks, Robin's Nest features an ever-changing array of cookware at a discount. Proprietor **Debra Friedman** was in the restaurant business for years and can advise on how to use everything in the shop. Sort through seconds of Spanish hardwood spoons, baking pans, and gadgets galore. Also stop here for acrylic wine glasses (perfect for picnic fare). ♦ Daily 11AM-5PM. 140 E. Napa St, Sonoma. 996.4169

47 **Peterberry's** ★★$ Billed as an espresso cafe and aviation gallery, this is a good spot to plan your day over a Continental breakfast of freshly squeezed orange juice, croissant, and a double espresso or real hot chocolate. Nostalgic old-time model airplanes fly overhead against a background of painted clouds; most of the vintage planes have been donated by customers. At lunch, they offer salads, sandwiches on croissants or whole-grain breads, and other light fare. Homemade pies and cookies, too. On occasion, owner/chef **Curtis Dorsett** gets so carried away in the galleylike open kitchen that he bursts into song. Takeout available. ♦ M-Sa 8AM-5PM; Su 10AM-6PM. 140 E. Napa St, Sonoma. 996.5559

48 **Sonoma Children's Clothing** Browse through their snappy and appealing selection of cotton clothing for kids and novelty items such as custom-painted hi-top tennies for babies and cowboy booties with a black-and-white cow pattern. ♦ Daily 10AM-5PM. 488 First St East, Sonoma. 938.1919

48 **Artifax** Proprietor **Tom Rubel** travels all over the world buying crafts for this elegant gallery with a special emphasis on offerings from Asia and Africa. Japanese flower arranging tools, African musical instruments, handsome woven platters from the Philippines, and bamboo trays from Japan all make special gifts. ♦ Daily 11AM-5PM. 148 E. Napa St, Sonoma. 996.9494

49 **Alberigi's Old Sonoma Creamery** ★$ This is a shop with a split personality: One side is an old-fashioned ice cream parlor with a row of booths; create your own sundae fantasy from the 40 flavors made here at the height of summer. Next door is an informal wine-tasting bar and deli

featuring cheeses, cold cuts, salads, and sandwiches to take out or eat inside. For dessert, try the Toscano, a fudge brownie topped with vanilla ice cream and hot fudge sauce. ♦ Daily 9AM-5PM. 400 First St East, Sonoma. 938.2938

49 **The Sonoma Wine Shop** One-stop shopping for wine paraphernalia from many of the valley's wineries, plus all sorts of corkscrews, wine carriers, picnic baskets outfitted with wineglasses—and a modest selection of wine. On weekends you can taste several wines by the glass at the little wine bar in back. ♦ M-F 11AM-5PM; Sa-Su 10AM-5PM. 412 First St East, Sonoma. 996.1230

Flights of Fancy: Where to See Sonoma from the Air

Most flights based in Sonoma travel over the Russian River Valley, and the farther north you go, the more scenic your trip will become. Here's where you can get that stunning aerial view:

Hot-Air Balloons

One-hour tours in Sonoma cost about $145 per person.

Air Flambuoyant Hot-air balloon flights over the

Sonoma

Sonoma wine country followed by a champagne brunch. ♦ Box 545, Santa Rosa CA 95402. 575.1989, 800/456.4711

Airborn of Sonoma County Balloon rides followed by a champagne brunch. ♦ Box 1457, Healdsburg CA 95448. 433.3210

Once in a Lifetime Balloon Co., Inc. These trips depart from the Piper-Sonoma or Rodney Strong vineyards and are followed by a champagne brunch at the Doubletree Hotel in Santa Rosa. ♦ Box 1263, Windsor CA 95492. 578.0580, 800/722.6665 (CA only)

Sonoma Thunder Wine Country Balloon Safaris Flights followed by a champagne celebration. ♦ 4914 Snark Ave, Santa Rosa CA 95409. 538.7359, 800/759.5638

Small Planes

For one to three people, 30- to 60-minute flights cost about $90 to $120.

Aeroschellville Rides in a Stearman plane once used to train WWII combat pilots. ♦ Schellville Airport, 23982 Arnold Dr, Sonoma CA 95476. 938.2444

Let's Fly, Inc. Scenic flights in three-passenger planes. ♦ Sonoma County Airport, 2238 Airport Blvd, Santa Rosa CA 95403. 546.9362

Petaluma Aeroventure Scenic flights in one- or three-passenger planes. ♦ 2210 E. Washington St, Petaluma CA 94954. 778.6767

The Vasquez House

DRAWING COURTESY E. ROSS PARKERSON

49 El Paseo After passing under an archway of plum stone from local quarries, you'll discover a series of small shops off a charming courtyard. Rents have increased dramatically in recent years, forcing many of

Sonoma

the longtime tenants, such as **Old City Pottery,** to find other quarters. ♦ 414 First St East, Sonoma

Within El Paseo:

The Vasquez House Built in 1855 by the Civil War hero **"Fighting" Joe Hooker,** who later sold it to early settlers **Catherine** and **Pedro Vasquez,** this steep-gabled house (pictured above) is now headquarters of the **Sonoma League for Historic Preservation.** It contains a library devoted to the town's history and a changing exhibit of historical photos gleaned from the town archives. The diminutive tea room is staffed by league volunteers who serve homebaked desserts and tea at modest prices. In summer, sit at an umbrella-shaded table outside. For eight to ten people, they'll arrange a walking tour; reserve one month in advance. You can also pick up books on Sonoma's history and copies of their guide, *Sonoma Walking Tour.* ♦ W-Su 1-5PM. 938.0510

49 Zino's Restaurant and Bar ★$$ Gino's restaurant and bar was transformed overnight to Zino's when the longtime chef bought out the owner last year. Alterations in the menu were as slight as the name change; Zino's is sticking with the tried-and-true Italian-American fare his regulars keep coming back for: fresh pasta dishes, chicken parmesan, turkey scaloppine, and osso buco (braised veal shanks). Perfunctory wine list. ♦ Daily 11AM-10PM. 420 First St East, Sonoma. 996.4466

The Mercato *Mercato* is Italian for "market," and this Post-Modernist building bathed in stylish pastels contains several new shops. Check out the 16-by-13-foot mural on the side of the building, a bird's-eye view of the Sonoma Valley by local artist **Claudia Wagar.** ♦ 452 First St East, Sonoma

Within the Mercato building:

Papyrus This stationery store has a collection of appealing cards, writing materials, and ornate wrapping papers, many from museums around the world. ♦ M-Sa 10AM-5:30PM; Su 11AM-4PM. 935.6707

The Sonoma Wine Exchange The spacious, well-organized shop offers a dynamite array of California wines selected by the knowledgeable staff. This is the place to come for some serious wine talk—or beer talk, for that matter, as they also feature a superb collection of brews from around the world. And—this is the best part—they have a comfortable, informal wine bar at the back where you can sample a dozen top wines by the taste or glass, as well as several draft beers. They give case discounts and will ship. ♦ M-Sa 10AM-6PM; Su 11AM-6PM. 938.1794

Restaurants/Clubs: Red
Shops/ 🌳 **Outdoors:** Green
Hotels: Blue
Wineries/Sights: Black

Rosebud of Sonoma Jo Anne Petro has created a feminine world of imported linens, soft pillows, and flower-bedecked comforters—in short, little luxuries for the sensualist at heart. ♦ M, W-Sa 10AM-5PM; Su 11AM-4PM. 996.6924

Breakout Art Gallery In this low-key gallery setting, **Lauren Keyson** features Bay Area artists and artisans with an emphasis on crafts at moderate prices. ♦ M-Sa 10AM-5PM; Su 11AM-4PM. 996.4103

49 Vigil's Native American Galleries This glitzy shop displays Native American jewelry, pottery, and the occasional Navajo rug. There's a gallery of lithographs, paintings, and posters on Native American themes in the back. ♦ Daily 10AM-5PM. 452-A First St East, Sonoma. 996.3763

arts guild

49 Arts Guild of Sonoma A nonprofit gallery run by artist members since 1977, the guild features both fine arts and crafts. ♦ Daily 10AM-6PM. 460 First St East, Sonoma. 996.3115/2318

49 Place des Pyrenees The arch that frames the entrance to this cobblestoned passageway was built from local stone. Inside you'll find several shops, a French restaurant, an English pub, and a coffee roaster. ♦ 464 First St East, Sonoma. 996.1996

Within Place des Pyrenees:

Hooker's Shebang A tiny shop crammed with jars of old-fashioned candies weighed out by the pound. ♦ Daily 11AM-5PM. 996.6177

Full Circle Alex Gilmore and his wife, **Emiko**, have collected lots of interesting stuff in this antique shop, from the late 19th-century wooden-shafted golf clubs to the collection of restored vintage fountain pens with gold nibs and the antique, working cameras. ♦ Daily 11AM-5PM. 996.1996

L'Esperance Restaurant ★★$$$ Hearty bistro fare stars at this small French restaurant. Start with the house pâté, the escargots in garlic butter, or the mussels in saffron cream. For the entrée, order the anise-scented scallops or the roast half duck glazed with honey and lemon. Well-edited wine list with good prices. ♦ French ♦ M-Th 11AM-2:30PM, 5-9PM; F-Sa 11AM-2:30PM, 5-9:30PM; Su 3-9PM. 464 First St, Sonoma. 996.2757

Ma Stokeld's Pie Shop & Village Pub ★$ Anglophiles will enjoy this replica of an English pub serving cool beers and typical pub grub such as bangers (a mild English

pork sausage flavored with marjoram), sausage rolls, Cornish pasties, and steak pie—all made here. Sit at the tables outside in fine weather. Takeout available. ♦ M, Su 11AM-5PM; Tu-Sa 11AM-10PM. 935.0660

Jeanine's Coffee & Tea Company Enjoy a cappuccino or espresso at tables outside in the cobblestone courtyard. Proprietors **Jeanine** and **Bruce Masonek** buy the green beans and roast their own coffees in an old-fashioned drum roaster to get the slow-roasted flavor they prefer. To compensate for flavor lost in the decaffeination process, they roast their decaf coffees a bit darker. ♦ M-Tu 10AM-5PM; W-Sa 10AM-5:30PM; Su 11AM-5PM. 996.7573

Briar Patch Smoke Shop & Coffee & Teas The other half of Jeanine's Coffee & Tea Company is devoted to handcrafted cigars and custom-blended tobaccos (some with affectionate local names: Glen Ellen, Jack London, Sonoma, etc.). ♦ M-Tu 10AM-5PM; W-Sa 10AM-5:30PM. 996.7573

Sonoma

49 Sonoma French Bakery Lili and Gratien **Guerra** emigrated from the French Pyrenees more than 40 years ago to open this popular bakery on Sonoma's town square. The doorbell never stops ringing as customers crowd in to buy their unique and delicious sourdough French bread. The bakery also makes sour French in baguettes or torpedoes (short loaves) and sandwich rolls, as well as a whole-wheat sour French in round loaves. Mornings bring plain and almond croissants warm from the oven. The Italian panettone made year-round in one-pound loaves makes excellent toast. ♦ W-Sa 8AM-6PM; Su 8AM-noon. 468 First St East, Sonoma. 996.2691. No phone

50 Blue Wing Inn The two-story Monterey Colonial adobe built by **Vallejo** to lodge troops and travelers now houses two antique stores: **Mission Antiques** and **Blue Wings & Things.** During the Gold Rush, the inn became an infamous saloon where **Ulysses S. Grant, Kit Carson,** and the bandit **Joaquin Murrietta** stopped to hoist a few. In spring, cascades of wisteria blossoms hang from the hand-hewn balconies. ♦ 125-139 E. Spain St, Sonoma. No phone

"A meal without wine is like a day without sunshine."
Anthelme Brillat-Savarin,
Physiologie du Goût, 1825

51 Victorian Garden Inn $$ The white picket fence and posies in front only hint at the carefully tended garden beyond. **Donna Lewis** has spent years cultivating her Victorian-era garden, with its sweet-scented violets, peonies, and heritage roses and ornate wrought-iron garden benches.

Her B&B, located on a quiet residential street, has just four rooms; one is in the main house; the rest are in a century-old water tower. She's left the architecture as it was, only adding private baths and decorating the rooms in period decor (visitors in the main house may occasionally share the bathroom with the owner's guests). The **Garden Room,** decorated in Laura Ashley rose-colored prints, has white wicker furniture and a clawfoot tub. Her most requested room is the **Woodcutter's Cottage,** with a private entrance and bath, sofa, and armchairs set in front of the fireplace. For breakfast she serves cherry or apple juice, farm-fresh eggs, a special granola or muffins, and fresh fruit from the garden. ♦ 316 E. Napa St, Sonoma. 996.5339

Sonoma

52 Sonoma Bike Path No cars are allowed on this path, making it ideal for walks, too. The bicycle trail takes you past the **Vella Cheese Company,** the **Depot Museum** and park, and General Vallejo's Victorian home, **Lachryma Montis.** Along the way, you can test your mettle on the parcourse, or, in season, buy fresh-picked corn from a stand set up by the path. ♦ Sebastiani Vineyards to Maxwell Farms Park (Hwy 12)

53 Vella Cheese Co. When **Joe Vella** arrived in California from his native Sicily in 1916, he sold butter, eggs, and cheese in San Francisco until he saved enough to open his own cheese-making business in Sonoma in 1931. His Monterey jack cheese and the "Bear Flag" dry Monterey jack (a grating cheese popular with local Italians) have long been wine-country favorites. Under the direction of Joe's son **Ig,** Vella Cheese Co. now makes at least half a dozen cheddars, an Oregon blue, and several flavored jacks at their headquarters in an old stone building. Sample the new pesto-flavored jack or the jalapeño version made from fresh New Mexico peppers. And if you live nearby, pick up some of Vella's sweet

butter. Call ahead to watch the entire artisanal cheese-making process; Ig Vella often conducts the tours himself. A mail order catalog is available. ♦ Daily 9AM-6PM. 315 Second St East, Sonoma. 938.3232, 800/848.0505

54 Depot Park A few old train cars are pulled up alongside the replica of an old train station, which is now a museum. The park includes a playground area, gazebo, picnic tables, and barbecue pits. ♦ 200 block of First St West, Sonoma

In Depot Park:

Sonoma Depot Museum A replica of the old Northwestern Pacific Railroad station now houses Sonoma's impromptu historical museum. The volunteer docents are eager to show off the restored stationmaster's office, where the big clock still ticks away. Show an interest and they'll conduct you around the museum, pointing out a map and a collection of memorabilia that traces the coming of the railroads in this part of the West. A recreation of the kitchen and other rooms in a typical Victorian household and photos of local historical figures (including the infamous Bear Flag Party) complete the display. The museum has a nice selection of historical books and monographs on Sonoma, plus coloring books for kids on California history. ♦ W-Su 1-4:30PM. 285 First St. 938.9765

Sonoma Farmers Market Don't miss this vibrant outdoor market, which is held twice a week for much of the year. Where better to shop for a picnic? ♦ Tu 9AM-noon, May-Nov; F 9AM-noon, year-round. Arnold Field Parking Lot, First St West

55 Natalia's Garden This self-serve produce stand puts together a surprise grab bag of organic produce—and sometimes flowers—from **Cannard Farm,** which supplies the famed Chez Panisse restaurant in Berkeley. Baby lettuces, slender zucchini, bitter greens, and more. Bags are all the same price and payment is on the honor system; you leave your money in a box on the way out. ♦ Daily 2-5PM or later. 400 W. Spain St, Sonoma. 938.8424

56 Depot Hotel 1870 Restaurant and Wine Bar ★★$$ Built in 1870 with stone from nearby quarries, this restaurant (pictured above) was originally a three-bedroom home with a saloon operating out of the living room. Once the railroad was extended and a station was built across the street, the railroad purchased the house and

Lachryma Montis

DRAWING COURTESY E. ROSS PARKERSON

saloon to use as a lodging for travelers. The present owner has transformed it into a spacious, airy restaurant; the severe stone facade gives no hint of the surprises inside. The dining room is dressed in blue and white; outside a glassed-in garden room and terrace look out to a pool and formal garden. At lunch they offer soups, salads, and sandwiches; more elaborate dishes are served at dinner. For main courses, try Tuscan-style *bistecca alla fiorentina* (prime rib grilled over mesquite), sautéed chicken with mushrooms, or prawns sautéed with white wine, garlic, and lemon. For dessert, they have *tiramisu* (espresso-soaked ladyfingers layered with *mascarpone* and cream), along with chocolate decadence, a dense, dark chocolate cake served with raspberry purée. ◆ W-F 11:30AM-2PM, 5-9PM; Sa-Su 5-9PM. 241 First St West, Sonoma. 938.2890

57 Sonoma State Historical Park There are no formal boundaries to this historical park, which includes five Sonoma sites. One ticket is good for all of them, provided you use it the same day: Mission San Francisco Solano de Sonoma, General Vallejo's barracks, the Toscano Hotel, Casa Grande Indian Servants' Quarters, and Lachryma Montis (Vallejo's home). The ticket is also good for the Vallejo Adobe in Petaluma. Perfect for a leisurely ramble through Sonoma's past. ◆ Nominal admission. Daily 10AM-5PM. 938.1519

"There is so much contained in a glass of good wine. It is a gift of nature that tastes of man's foibles, his sense of the beautiful, his idealism, and virtuosity."

Kermit Lynch,
Adventures of the Wine Route

58 Lachryma Montis A visit to **General Vallejo's** Victorian home and gardens is worth the price of the museum ticket. Set in the shelter of a hillside, the steep-gabled, yellow-and-white wood house in the Gothic

Sonoma

Revival style is twined with rambling roses. One yellow variety has climbed a 30-foot tree and is said to be the oldest rosebush in Sonoma. Inside, the curators have tried to give the feeling the family is only out for the afternoon. The table is set and a bottle of the general's wine decanted; his wife seems to have laid out her shawl on one of the beds upstairs. The former wine-and-olive storehouse has been turned into a little Vallejo museum, with the general's silver epaulets, books, cattle brand, and photos on display along with examples of his wine label: Lachryma Montis, the name of this estate. It means "tears of the mountain"—a reference to a mineral spring on the property. You can picnic at shaded tables on the terraced hillside and spend the afternoon at the 20-acre estate. ◆ W-Su 10AM-5PM. W. Spain St (Third St East) 938.1519

59 Sonoma Wine & Spirits Founded in 1976, this well-stocked wine shop has an array of wines from all over the world, including more than 60 Sonoma wines. Shipping available. ◆ M-Th 9AM-9PM; F-Sa 9AM-10PM; Su 9AM-7PM. 551 W. Fifth St, Sonoma. 996.1108

Restaurants/Clubs: Red   Hotels: Blue
Shops/ ♥ Outdoors: Green   **Wineries/Sights:** Black

60 Lainie's Cuisine To Go ★★★$ This is the take-out shop for the full-service **Elaine Bell Catering Company** (Bell is the culinary director at Sterling Winery in the

Napa Valley). Stop here on your way up the valley for delectable morning pastries: honey-bran muffins, banana-nut muffins, cappuccino brownies, chocolate chip cookies. Everything looks fresh and good, from chicken tabbouleh salad and her special red-skinned potato salad to the vegetarian lasagna and the meaty pork ribs glazed with Lainie's barbecue sauce. The menu changes every Tuesday. They'll concoct a special box lunch with 48 hours notice (choose from a half-dozen appealing menus), or come in and they'll box up whatever you want. Ask her to throw in a couple of chocolate-raspberry brownies or lemon-meringue tartlets. ♦ Tu-Sa 11AM-8PM. 682 W. Napa St, Sonoma. 996.5226

61 Trojan Horse Inn $$ Innkeepers **Susan** and **Brian Scott** have just redecorated their

Sonoma

blue, wood-frame B&B, built in 1880 as the home of a Sonoma pioneer family. They did all the plasterwork, wallpapering, and painting themselves and have made each of their six light and airy rooms, all with a private bath, quite different in character.

The spacious first-floor **Bridal Veil Room** has a wood-burning stove and a canopy bed decked out in white Battenberg lace. On the second story, the **Walden Pond Room** is painted a deep shade of green and has a lovely, carved hardwood bed. The **Grape Arbor Room,** in shades of silver, lavender, and rose, has a border of stenciled grapes and its own two-person Jacuzzi. The inn has bicycles for guests' use, an outdoor Jacuzzi on the patio beside the creek, and a large garden hidden from the street. ♦ 19455 Sonoma Hwy 12, Sonoma. 996.2430

62 Sebastiani Vineyards When **Samuele Sebastiani** arrived in the area from his native Tuscany, he first found work in the local stone quarries. He made his debut wine, a Zinfandel, around 1895; the winery that continues to bear his name, today the largest premium varietal winery in Sonoma, still has the equipment that was used to make that first batch. The third generation runs the huge winery now. **Sam Sebastiani** opened his own winery, **Viansa,** in the Carneros

district a few years ago, leaving his brother **Don** in charge of Sebastiani. The tour takes visitors through the fermentation room and the aging cellar, with its extensive collection of ornate carved cask heads, all crafted by local artist **Earle Brown.** The tasting room offers samples of Sebastiani's full line of wines, from the quaffable Italian varietal Barbera to Cabernet, Merlot, Pinot Noir, and more. Kids are served grape juice. The winery has a row of picnic tables set along the edge of a nearby vineyard. ♦ Daily 10AM-5PM. 389 Fourth St East, Sonoma. 938.5532

63 Moosettas A casual little shop offering down-to-earth fast food in the Eastern European tradition: hearty homemade soups and piroshki (a flaky turnover with a beef, vegetarian, or mushroom and cheese filling, ready to eat or frozen). Half-sized piroshki are ideal for appetizers. If your lodging includes a kitchenette, consider their Hungarian cabbage rolls, beef stroganoff, or turkey pot pies to go. For dessert, the lovely little cookies are worth a stop all on their own. Seating is available outside on the porch. ♦ Tu-Sa 10AM-7PM. 18976 Sonoma Hwy, Sonoma. 996.1313

64 Maxwell Farms Regional Park This regional park with some 85 acres of woods and meadows along Sonoma Creek offers picnic spots just minutes from downtown Sonoma, along with several hiking trails and a playground for kids. The farm once belonged to turn-of-the-century conservationist **George Maxwell,** an advocate for small farmers. A footpath runs along the creek; the Sonoma bike path that runs from Sebastiani Vineyards past Depot Park and **General Vallejo's** Gothic Revival home is a scenic route for bikers and pedestrians into the park. Shady picnic facilities. ♦ Day-use only. Entrance at Verano Ave and Riverside Dr, El Verano. 938.2794

Hot Springs Resorts

At the northwest end of Sonoma, you'll suddenly find yourself in the old resort towns of **El Verano, Boyes Hot Springs, Fetters Springs,** and **Agua Caliente** (Spanish for "hot water"). The local Indians had discovered the hot springs early on and brought their sick to bathe in the healing waters, but it was the young British naval officer **Captain Henry Boyes,** urged on by **General Mariano Vallejo,** who developed the site as a resort. By the turn of the century, San Franciscans were taking their families north by train—and later in their private cars—to spend the summer at these popular resorts. The resorts became less family oriented during Prohibition; speakeasies served bootleg liquor, the atmosphere was rowdy, and madams such as Spanish **Kitty Lombardi** set the tone. Today, only a few vestiges of the hot springs' heyday remain, notably the Sonoma Mission Inn in Boyes Hot Springs.

65 Little Switzerland $$ Kick up your heels to the live polka, tango, and waltz music at this popular weekend dance hall. All the fun people are here—they'll tell you so on the phone. A menu of beer sausages and dumplings adds to the European atmosphere. ♦ Cover. Sa 6:30-8:30PM, music 8PM-midnight; Su 2-9PM. Grove and Riverside Drs, El Verano. 938.9990

66 Hanzell Vineyards When former ambassador to Italy **James D. Zellerbach** established this boutique winery in the late fifties, he set out to emulate the wines he admired in Burgundy. He modeled the two-story winery's stone facade after the Clos de Vougeot, a famous Burgundian property, and finished off his idea by ordering a shipment of French oak barrels to age his Chardonnay. Now owned by the Australian heiress **Barbara de Brye,** Hanzell still produces the intense, full-bodied Chardonnay prized by cognoscenti, along with Burgundian-style Pinot Noir and Cabernet Sauvignon. The winemaker is **Bob Sessions,** who previously worked at Mayacamas Winery. ♦ Tasting, sales, and tours by appt M-F 10AM-4PM. 18596 Lomita Ave, Sonoma. 996.3860

67 The Fruit Basket A veritable cornucopia offering the best of Sonoma County produce at good prices, plus dried fruits and nuts, bulk foods, farm-fresh eggs, cherry juice from the Cherry Tree, and an array of Sonoma wines. ♦ Daily 7AM-7PM. 18474 Sonoma Hwy (Hwy 12) Sonoma. 996.7433

68 The Good Time Bicycle Co. Owner **Doug McKesson** will deliver his well-maintained rental bikes to your hotel or B&B by prior arrangement. Back at the shop, he sells bicycles, racing gear, accessories, and books on local biking routes. If you're pedaling down his way, stop in for updated route advice and information on guided tours. ♦ M-Sa 9AM-5PM; Su 10AM-4PM. 18315 Sonoma Hwy (Hwy 12) Sonoma. 938.0453

69 Sonoma Mission Inn and Spa $$$$ In the late 19th century, the English adventurer **Captain Henry Boyes** built a posh hot-water spa on what is believed to have been an ancient Indian healing ground. In its heyday, the spa was a fashionable summer retreat for San Francisco's wealthy Nob Hill set. The present inn was built in 1927, after a fire destroyed the original buildings, and was totally renovated in the early eighties; additional rooms were added in 1985. Today the Spanish-style Sonoma Mission Inn is Sonoma's premier luxury retreat. The 170 guest rooms (doubles and suites) are decorated in soft shades of peach and pink; each has ceiling fans, plantation shutters, and a half-canopied bed with down comforters. Room service caters to every need. The eight-acre site just off busy Hwy 12 includes a spring-fed stream (the source of the Inn's privately bottled sparkling water), an Olympic-sized pool, tennis courts, and two restaurants. And now that the Sonoma Golf Club, orginally built as part of the inn in 1926, has been restored by its new owners, guests can also enjoy this tournament-level, 18-hole golf course. But the state-of-the-art European spa (open to guests and nonguests) is still the real draw. ♦ 18140 Sonoma Hwy (Hwy 12) Boyes Hot Springs. 938.9000, 800/862.4945 (CA only)

Within the Sonoma Mission Inn:

The Spa Reserve well ahead, especially on the weekends, for a wide range of spa treatments in a glamorous, upscale setting with soft lights and soothing music. The possibilities are many, from individual treatments to custom-designed three- to five-day packages of diet and exercise. Choose from several types of massage (including

seaweed hydro massage), body scrubs, body wraps, various facials, or a go-for-broke, all-in-one treatment. Even tarot readings and dream analysis can be arranged. One favorite therapy is a purifying wrap of Irish linens infused with fragrant herbs. Afterward, relax in the Bathhouse sauna, steam room, or whirlpool bath, or tone those muscles in the weight room. The spa's large roster of famous and not-so-famous fans swear by its restorative powers. ♦ By appt daily 7AM-9PM (guests), M-F only (nonguests) 938.9000

The Grille ★★$$$ Winemakers like the sunny dining room and poolside terrace at lunchtime when chef **Michael Flynn** presents an array of pasta entrées, salads, sandwiches, and other light fare. The club sandwich (oak-smoked chicken, avocado, and tomatoes on toasted rye) is a classic, and the sorbets are usually a good bet for dessert. Dinner in the peaches-and-cream dining room is more formal, with candlelight replacing the sun that streams in the windows during lunch. While the emphasis is on fresh local products and naturally raised meats, the restaurant hasn't quite found a focus since the departure of former chef **Charles Saunders,** who brought the restaurant to national attention with his imaginative spa cuisine. (He's slated to open a Sonoma restaurant soon.) The special spa

menu continues to feature low-calorie, low-cholesterol, and low-sodium dishes.
♦ California ♦ Daily 8AM-10PM. Reservations recommended. 938.9000

Big Three Café ★★$$ Famous for its generous breakfasts and Italian-inspired lunch fare, this handsomely remodeled cafe includes a wine bar and market. At the height of summer, it's a refreshing spot for lunch with its open kitchen, cool green-and-white decor, and old-fashioned ceiling fans. And this is one restaurant where everyone in the family can find something they'll like to eat, from the Cobb salad (smoked turkey, applewood-smoked bacon, avocado, tomatoes, and blue cheese) to burgers (the Sonoma is topped with grilled onions, mushrooms, and sour cream), savvy pasta dishes, and hip California pizzas from the wood-burning oven. They've got smoothies and shakes, too, and the wine bar features more than a dozen Sonoma wines by the glass. Spa menu by request. Take home Sonoma Mission Inn sweatshirts from the marketplace, along with books and all the appurtenances of country life in the Italian-California style. ♦ Northern Italian/California ♦ Daily 7AM-3PM, 5:30-9PM. 938.9000

70 J. Noblett Gallery This gallery features contemporary fine art from around the world. Exhibits change monthly. ♦ Daily

Sonoma

10AM-6PM. 22 Boyes Blvd, Boyes Hot Springs. 996.2416

71 Sonoma Golf Club Originally designed in 1926 by **Sam Whiting** and **Willie Watson** (who also designed the Lakeside Course at San Francisco's Olympic Club), this 18-hole championship course reopened in March 1991 after a $7.5 million restoration supervised by the renowned golf-course architect **Robert Muir Graves**. It has a spectacular setting: more than 177 acres and three lakes bordered with centuries-old oak and redwood trees with the majestic Mayacmas Mountains in the background. The Japanese owners offer both a California and a Japanese menu in the clubhouse restaurant. ♦ Daily dawn to dusk; clubhouse daily dawn-2:30PM, 5-9PM. 17700 Arnold Dr, Sonoma. 996.4852; fax 996.5750

72 Agua Caliente Mineral Springs Cool off at this family swimming spot, which has a warm-water mineral pool and a cool-water diving pool, plus a special kid's pool and a picnic area with barbecue pits. ♦ M-Th, Sa-Su 10AM-6PM, mid May-Sep; Sa-Su 10AM-6PM, Oct-mid May. 17350 Valietti Dr (Hwy 12) Agua Caliente. 996.6822

73 Carmenet Vineyard This estate's steep, terraced vineyards near the crown of the Mayacmas Mountains date from the 19th century. They were reworked in 1981 when **Chalone,** a small premium wine company, which also owns top-rated Chalone Vineyard, Edna Valley Vineyard, and Acacia, bought the property. Chalone replanted the vineyard in Bordeaux varietals and began making the kind of blends the Bordelaise refer to as *carmenet,* hence the name. Cool, underground aging cellars hold French oak barrels of Carmenet estate red, a Bordeaux-style wine made from a blend of Cabernet Sauvignon, Merlot, and Cabernet Franc that consistently earns high marks. Winemaker **Jeffrey Baker's** white reserve is mostly Sauvignon Blanc blended with a small amount of Sémillon; the inexpensive, well-made Colombard comes from old vines just off the Silverado Trail in the Napa Valley. ♦ Sales and tours by appt M-Sa 10AM-4PM. 1700 Moon Mtn Dr, Sonoma. 996.5870

74 Valley of the Moon Winery In 1941, San Francisco salami king **Enrico Parducci** bought a defunct winery with 500 acres of vineyards laid out in 1851 by the Civil War hero **"Fighting" Joe Hooker.** The property was owned at one time by newspaper tycoon William Randolph Hearst's father, **Senator George Hearst,** who introduced varietals from France and enjoyed pouring his own wines at his home in the nation's capital. The original winery, a low-slung stone building with a galvanized tin roof, is still used today; the enormous California bay laurel in front (featured on the winery's label) is at least 400 years old and protected by a special city ordinance. For years Valley of the Moon was known for its jug wines; the Parducci family began making affordable estate-bottled premium wines only a decade ago. Taste them all here—Chardonnay, Sémillon, Cabernet, and Pinot Noir—or take a bottle over to their grassy picnic area beside the creek. Their 15-year-old port is available only at the tasting room. ♦ Tasting and sales daily 10AM-5PM; tours by appt. 777 Madrone Rd, Glen Ellen. 996.6941

75 Oak Hill Farm Stop here for organic summer fruits and vegetables, including vine-ripened tomatoes and fresh garlic, plus bouquets of flowers. ♦ Th-Su 10AM-4PM, mid July-mid Oct. 14805 Sonoma Hwy (Hwy 12) Glen Ellen. 996.6643

76 B.R. Cohn Winery As manager of the rock and roll band the Doobie Brothers, B.R. Cohn parleyed the group to fame and fortune. He took his share of the fortune and bought this beautiful property, then known as Olive Hill

Farm, in 1974. At first he sold the grapes, but in 1984 he released his first wines. Every year, the winery makes a highly rated Cabernet; the grapes come from the Olive Hill vineyard on the slopes of a rounded hill planted with gnarled olive trees. He also makes regular and barrel-fermented Chardonnay, and continues to manage both his music enterprises and the winery from an office in Sonoma. ◆ Tasting and sales by appt daily 10AM-4PM. 15140 Sonoma Hwy, Glen Ellen. 938.4064

77 Garden Court Cafe ★$ Hearty country breakfasts at this simple roadside cafe come with three eggs, home fries, toast or biscuits, and fresh fruit. At lunchtime stop in for straightforward burgers, sandwiches, and salads. ◆ Daily 7AM-2PM. 13875 Sonoma Hwy (Madrone Rd-Arnold Dr) Glen Ellen. 935.1565

78 Sonoma Valley Regional Park In springtime, the wildflower preserve here is a carpet of California poppy, lupine, wild iris, and other native flowers. There's also a picnic area and hiking and bike paths. ◆ Day-use only. Entrance on the east side of Sonoma Hwy, 6 miles north of Sonoma

Glen Ellen

The nucleus of early Glen Ellen was the sawmill **General Vallejo** built on Sonoma Creek in the mid-19th century. Before long, winemakers from all over Europe had followed pioneering vintner **Joshua Chauvet** to the area, planting vineyards and establishing landmark wineries in the heart of the Valley of the Moon. When the narrow-gauge railroad tracks reached the town of Glen Ellen in 1879, the rural community was invaded by scores of San Franciscans, and the saloons, dance halls, and brothels that opened to serve the city slickers turned Glen Ellen into a country cousin of the Barbary Coast. Author **Jack London** came to have a look and stayed to write at the place he dubbed Beauty Ranch (now known as Jack London State Park). The diminutive town, home to the food writer and novelist **M.F.K. Fisher,** is a quiet backwater now, and its bawdy days have been left far in the past.

79 The Gaige House $$ The brown-and-beige Italianate Queen Anne home built in 1890 for the town butcher, **A.E. Gaige,** is now a comfortable B&B in the heart of old Glen Ellen. The front parlor is furnished with red velvet sofas, oriental carpets, and potted palms; the seven bedrooms all have a private bath and cozy quilts folded over quilt racks. The largest is the **Gaige Suite,** the old master bedroom, furnished with handsome antiques, its own Jacuzzi, and a private deck. Innkeepers **Michol Tallent** and **Steve Salvo** serve a full breakfast (such as ham and eggs,

waffles, or pancakes) in the formal dining room or on the back deck. The large lawn with a brick-edged swimming pool along Calabazas Creek is an ideal spot for an afternoon of relaxation. ◆ 13540 Arnold Dr, Glen Ellen. 935.0237

79 Jody's Espresso Cafe ★$ This funky corner cafe has its charms at breakfast and lunch, when the tiny kitchen turns out homemade soups, salads, and other light fare. On Saturday afternoon over dessert and coffee, a dream consultant will sit down and interpret the dream of your choice for a modest fee. ◆ M, Th-F 7AM-3PM; Tu 7-11AM; Sa-Su 9AM-6PM. 13648 Arnold Dr, Glen Ellen. 938.3598

79 The Village Mercantile Here you will find an ever-changing selection of teapots and cups collected by owner **Raegene Africa.** Some are choice pieces from the thirties and forties; others are reproductions of antique pieces. Specialty teas available, too. ◆ Tu-Sa 11AM-5PM. 13647 Arnold Dr, Glen Ellen. 938.1330

79 Glen Ellen Inn ★★★$$$ Reserve well ahead for this romantic inn where owners **Bob** and **Lynda Rice** cook for just 18 people every night. The place is minuscule, and the open kitchen is located at one end of the simple dining room. The menus change weekly and emphasize bistro-style cooking

and fresh local ingredients. You get a choice of two or three appetizers and several entrées, which come with a salad of local greens garnished with Asiago cheese. A meal might start with house-cured salmon or a roast vegetable bisque, followed by grilled swordfish on a bed of pasta with a garlic-and-thyme-scented compote of wild mushrooms or a New York strip pepper steak with Jack Daniels sauce and oven-fried potatoes. Best bet for dessert: the dreamy espresso *pot de crème* or the lemon tart with chantilly cream and fresh blackberry sauce. On selected Tuesday nights Bob teaches informal cooking classes, which include the preparation of a four-course meal. While most are four-class series limited to eight students, he just might have an opening for one-time-only students, too. Call for information. No smoking. ◆ California ◆ Th-Su 6 PM-closing. 13670 Arnold Dr, Glen Ellen. Reservations required. 996.6409

79 Cafe Trax ★★$$ This casual spot with scrubbed tile floors and oak tables offers hefty, build-your-own omelets, homemade corned-beef hash, or eggs with chicken-apple sausage for breakfast, along with espresso drinks and freshly squeezed orange juice. Lunch and dinner menus feature pasta dishes and pizzas made from a whole-wheat dough and topped with such goodies as

Gerhard sausage, smoked mozzarella, baby clams, and pesto. For a picnic in Jack London Park, consider the sandwiches or barbecued baby-back ribs to go. Small loaves of country-style bread are baked just for Cafe Trax. Glen Ellen wineries dominate the wine list. ♦ California ♦ Tu-F 7AM-9PM; Sa-Su 9AM-9PM. 13690 Arnold Dr, Glen Ellen. 939.1350

79 Jack London Lodge $ This two-story motel set beside a creek and the entrance to Jack London State Park has just 22 fairly large guest rooms, all with private baths and functional decor brightened with country prints; ask for one of the upstairs rooms. It's hardly luxury, but it's just fine for the budget traveler and even has a creekside swimming pool. Breakfast is served in the adjoining restaurant. ♦ 13740 Arnold Dr, Glen Ellen. 938.8510

Adjacent to Jack London Lodge:

Jack London Lodge Restaurant ★$$ At this unpretentious spot, a Czech cook turns out homey Eastern European food: hearty homemade soups, fragrant paprika-spiked Hungarian goulash, and prime rib. All entrées are served with soup and salad. For dessert—you guessed it—the specialty is apple strudel. ♦ Eastern European ♦ Daily noon-3PM, 5:30-9PM. 939.0645

Jack London Saloon Plaid shirts, hiking boots, and the lumberjack look are de

Sonoma

rigueur at this historic saloon. The bar has been pouring drinks to locals and city slickers alike since Jack London's days, and the saloon seems to have saved every bit of memorabilia from those rowdy years. On warm summer evenings, it's fun to linger over drinks outside on the patio beside the creek. ♦ Daily 11AM-2AM. 996.3100

79 Shone's Country Store Now an all-purpose grocery store, Shone's dates back to Glen Ellen's pioneer days. You'll find all the basics here, plus a selection of deli meats, cheeses, and, in season, fresh cracked crab. ♦ 13750 Arnold Dr, Glen Ellen. 996.6728

79 Jack London Village Almost hidden in the hoary oaks along Sonoma Creek, this complex of ramshackle redwood buildings is home to a series of small shops and artisan's workshops. ♦ 14301 Arnold Dr, Glen Ellen

Within Jack London Village:

Spinner's Web This shop crammed with exotic fleece, weaving supplies, and spinning wheels just may inspire you to try your hand at these traditional crafts. They offer occasional classes, books on the subjects, and concentrated, natural extracts that can dye cottons, wools, and other fibers. If

you're interested in textiles, pick up a copy of Sonoma County Fiber Trails, a map that lists spinners, weavers, felters, knitters, and sources for fleeces and fibers. ♦ M, Th-Su 11AM-5PM. 935.7006

Remember When Antiques-Collectibles A collective of antique dealers has filled this large space with a grab-bag collection of pressed and cut glass, period furniture, costume jewelry, china, and toys. Who knows what a careful rummage here will turn up? There are few bargains, but an afternoon's browsing is entertaining enough. ♦ Daily 11AM-5:30PM. 938.4670

Grist Mill Inn Restaurant ★$$ You can still see **Vallejo's** mill wheel turning on the side of this historic grist mill, now a popular brunch spot because of its atmosphere. In warm weather the choice seats are outside on the broad deck overlooking the ancient oaks. The new owners have revamped the menu, focusing more on California and Greek items. Start with grilled Sonoma sausages, steamed clams, or Greek-style mussels. At lunch the Grist Mill burger or the club sandwich are good choices. The dinner menu adds mesquite-grilled filet mignon, roast leg of lamb, San Francisco-style cioppino (crab and fish stew), and Greek Island shrimp sautéed with herbs and feta cheese. ♦ California ♦ Tu-Su 11:30AM-2PM, 5:30-9PM. 996.3077

JACK LONDON BOOKSTORE

79 Jack London Bookstore Owner **Russ Klingman** knows more about Jack London than almost anybody else in America, and his bookstore is filled with works by and about Glen Ellen's famous writer. It is a resource much used by London scholars and aficionados, where you can find first-edition works by London, rare and out-of-print works, and other books not relating to London. It's a cozy, unintimidating place to spend an afternoon and is one of an endangered species: a serious small bookstore. Klingman's collection of London memorabilia, so extensive it was really a small museum, is in storage now; he plans to mount it again in the future, but the bookstore is already bursting at the seams. ♦ Daily 10AM-5:30PM. 14300 Arnold Dr, Glen Ellen. 996.2888

80 Glenelly Inn $$ Originally built as an inn for train travelers in 1916, this charming place on rural Warm Springs Rd retains the ambience of another era with its long verandas furnished with wicker chairs. The inn consists of two peach-and-cream buildings set on a hillside, with a terrace garden shaded by old oaks in back. A hot tub is sheltered by an arbor twined with grapevines and old roses. All eight rooms have private baths and private entrances—as well as a veranda in front. Pine armoires, ceiling fans, and clawfoot tubs add to the country feel; some rooms also have wood-burning stoves. Innkeeper **Kristi Hallamore Grove** pays attention to details such as reading lights, down comforters, and firm mattresses. Breakfast includes a hot dish, fruit, and fresh-baked muffins. ♦ 5131 Warm Springs Rd, Glen Ellen. 996.6720

81 Glen Ellen Winery Young winemaker **Mike Benziger** was scouting vineyard properties in Sonoma Valley when he came across this historic estate, established by the carpenter **Julius Wegener,** who received the land as payment from **General Vallejo** for constructing his Sonoma home. Benziger was so taken with the steep, terraced vineyard site that he convinced his father, the late **Bruno Benziger,** to buy it. Founder of a wine-and-spirits distributorship, the elder Benziger was an inspired marketer, and masterminded Glen Ellen Winery's astonishing growth from a small family operation to Sonoma Valley's second-largest winery in little over a decade. Their uncomplicated wines, especially the ready-to-drink, modestly priced Proprietor's Reserve Chardonnay and Cabernet Sauvignon, have won an unassailable place on the market; their best wines are the Benziger of Glen Ellen wines, made from grapes grown on their steep, terraced Home Ranch vineyard. They also make Sauvignon Blanc, Merlot, and Zinfandel. The Glen Ellen property includes a folksy tasting room and a classic California-barn winery building. Picnic grove. ♦ Tasting and sales daily 10AM-4:30PM; tours Sa-Su. 1883 London Ranch Rd, Glen Ellen. 935.3000

82 Jack London State Historic Park Just as **Robert Louis Stevenson** is associated with the Napa Valley, the Sonoma Valley is **Jack London** territory. It was London who, in his 1913 novel *The Valley of the Moon,* recounted an Indian legend that says Sonoma means "many moons." This 800-acre park, a memorial to the adventurer and writer, is located on what was once London's beloved **Beauty Ranch.** The highest-paid author of his time, with *Call of the Wild* (1903) and *The Sea Wolf* (1904) under his belt by the age of 28, London settled permanently on his Glen Ellen ranch in 1909. Here visitors can experience the unspoiled landscape much the way it was in London's time.

Just off Hwy 12 on the east side of the valley, the well-maintained park is a paradise for hikers and horseback riders, with nine miles of trails. You'll see the eerie remains of **Wolf House,** the dream home built by London and his wife, **Charmian,** that mysteriously burned down days before they were to move in. You can visit the white-frame cottage where they lived and where he wrote many of his books, as well as the log cabin and artificial lake he constructed in tribute to his Klondike days. And don't forgot to visit the remarkable **Pig Palace** with its two 40-foot-high silos. Charmian later built a scaled-down version of Wolf House, which she dubbed the **House of Happy Walls.** Now a touching museum of London memorabilia, it is filled with the furniture, art, and personal photographs the Londons had intended for Wolf House—it even includes a collection of the successful author's rejection slips. Nearby is the tranquil grove of oaks where London is buried. In the 40 years of his life, London managed to write 51 books and 193 short stories (and somehow he also fit in two lifetimes of travel and adventure in exotic locales). Bring a picnic, because you'll want to roam this magnificent park for hours. A rigorous three-mile trail leads to the summit of Sonoma Mountain and a breathtaking view of the Valley of the Moon. ♦ Admission fee per car. Park: daily 8AM-dusk; the House of Happy Walls: daily 10AM-5PM. 2400 London Ranch Rd (off Hwy 12) Glen Ellen 938.5216

Sonoma

Within Jack London State Historic Park:

Sonoma Cattle Co. One of the best ways to see the park is on horseback, riding down trails **Jack London** once used to survey his Valley of the Moon domain—past lush meadows, redwood groves, and vineyards now owned by London's descendants. The stone barn London built to house his English shire horses now stables the horses used for guided rides through the park. The Sonoma Cattle Co. provides horses for riders of all levels and takes them out in groups of two to six. If you like, you can sign on for a two-hour horseback ride followed by a personal tour and a picnic at Glen Ellen Winery. Reserve ahead. Children must be at least eight years old; no previous riding experience needed. The Sonoma Cattle Co. also offers rides in nearby Sugarloaf Ridge State Park. ♦ Reservations required. 996.8566

When Jack London bought his Beauty Ranch in Glen Ellen, improvements to the property and agricultural experiments became a passion. In the early 1900s, he devoted two hours a day to writing and 10 hours to farming.

Restaurants/Clubs: Red   **Hotels:** Blue
Shops/ ♦ Outdoors: Green   **Wineries/Sights:** Black

83 Stone Tree Ranch $$ Perfect for privacy seekers, you'll be the only guests at this B&B on a secluded 13-acre ranch. The remodeled groom's quarters are set well away from the main house; the rustic upstairs suite has a sleeping alcove, a sofa that converts to a queen-sized bed, a clawfoot tub and shower, a wood-burning stove, and a dining area. Owner **Alice Gavigan** stocks the small, fully equipped kitchen with all the makings of a country breakfast, including coffee beans and a grinder. She provides terry robes for the walk to and from the hot tub next to the main house that's perched on a deck overlooking a one hundred-year-old vineyard. You can enjoy grand views of the hills, and there's not a neighbor in sight. Children and pets are welcome, and it's a pleasant hike to Jack London Park from this privileged spot. Gavigan is also a great source for information about anything in the valley. ♦ 7910 Sonoma Mtn Rd (off Warm Springs Rd) Glen Ellen. 996.8173

MATANZAS CREEK WINERY

84 Matanzas Creek Winery For a particularly scenic drive, take Warm Springs Rd and Enterprise Dr to Bennett Valley Rd and this

Sonoma

showcase winery overlooking Bennett Valley and the Sonoma Mountains. Owned by **Bill** and **Sandra McIver,** the winery is an inviting place, with a loggia leading up to the tasting room and tables on a deck that are sheltered by a centuries-old oak. Since the beginning, when **Merry Edwards** made the wines, Matanzas Creek Chardonnays have appeared on the most discerning wine lists in the country; when she left to open her own winery in 1984, **David Ramey** took on the job. The Chardonnays are among the best in California, and his Sauvignon Blanc is also top flight. The Merlot is so much in demand that it's sold out every year a few weeks after it's released. You'll also find the Matanzas Creek poster by painter **Mary Silverwood** on sale here, and out front is the whimsical whale sculpture created by sculptor **Peter Busby,** a series of five woven-steel life-size whales in various stages of diving. ♦ Tasting, sales, and self-guided tour M-Sa 10AM-4PM; Su noon-4PM. 6097 Bennett Valley Rd, Santa Rosa. 528.6464

85 Annadel State Park The Pomo and Wappo Indian tribes gathered food and obsidian in this wilderness 3,000 years before Europeans arrived in the area. In 1837 Scottish sea captain (and General Vallejo's brother-in-law) **John Wilson** received a land grant of 18,860 acres from the Mexican government; that parcel of land included what is now Annadel

State Park. From the 1870s until the 1920s Italian stoneworkers cut paving stones from the basalt rock quarried here; production stepped up dramatically just after the 1906 earthquake, when the rebuilding of San Francisco was under way. Today this 5,000-acre park bordering the city of Santa Rosa offers nearly 40 miles of trails for hikers, horseback riders, and mountain bikers. Most of the trails interconnect and include a wide range of terrain and landscape, from rigorous mountain hiking to leisurely walks through meadows of wildflowers. You can head to Lake Ilsanjo for fishing or go bird-watching in Ledson Marsh. Camping is available in nearby Sugarloaf Ridge State Park. ♦ Day-use fee. Off Hwy 12, near Glen Ellen. 539.3911

86 Three Springs Ranch $$ It's easy to imagine staying for a week at this cottage in the Valley of the Moon. It has a large living room with a wood-burning stove and a fully equipped kitchen. Two bedrooms, one with a queen-sized bed, the other with twin-sized beds, make it ideal for two couples or a group of friends. The quilts are handmade, and owner **Bettylou Hutton** has installed baseboard heaters, air conditioners, and a TV with a VCR. A flagstone patio next to the lawn is furnished with Victorian garden furniture and an umbrella, while the front porch boasts white wicker furniture and an unbeatable view of the Sonoma Mountains. Checkout time is a civilized 4PM. No children or pets; no smoking. This place books up quickly. ♦ Th-Su only. 12851 Sonoma Hwy, Glen Ellen. 996.1777

87 JVB Vineyards $$ This pair of adobe cottages with terracotta roofs and tile floors look right at home on this grape-growing estate. Both have decks and patios, queen-sized beds, full baths, and a small kitchen area with a coffeemaker and toaster oven (but no real stove). One of the cottages is on top of a hillside overlooking the valley; the other lies at the bottom of the hill. A full breakfast is served at the farmhouse or on the patio. **Jack** and **Beverly Babb** or their daughter **Mary,** the vineyard manager, will take guests through the vineyard to explain how grapes are grown. They also have a Christmas tree farm and raise ostriches—no ostrich egg omelets for breakfast, though; one egg would be the equivalent of 24 chicken eggs! ♦ 14335 Hwy 12, Glen Ellen. 996.4533

87 Arrowood Vineyards and Winery When Chateau St. Jean's longtime winemaker **Richard Arrowood** founded his own small winery in 1987, he decided to make just one Chardonnay and one Cabernet Sauvignon, using a blend of grapes from different regions. He feels he can make better wines by blending varietals and grapes from several Sonoma Valley regions, rather than focus on single-vineyard wines as he did at Chateau St. Jean. Might be he's onto something, as you'll see when you taste both of these con-sistently excellent wines at his New England-style winery's tasting room. The Maple Leaf flag flies out front right next to the American flag because Arrowood's wife, **Alys,** who manages the winery, was born in Canada. ♦ Sales M-Sa 10AM-4:30PM; tours by appt. 14347 Sonoma Hwy, Glen Ellen. 938.5170

88 Trinity Road-Oakville Grade Buckle up for this 12-mile scenic drive from Hwy 12 near Glen Ellen over the Mayacmas Mountains to Hwy 29 in the Napa Valley at Oakville. The twists and turns, along with the panoramic views of the valley and mountains, make for an exciting ride; be sure your brakes—and stomachs—are up to the task before you set off.

89 Beltane Ranch B&B $$ This restored 1892 bunkhouse painted buttercup yellow and white once belonged to the former slave and abolitionist **Mammy Pleasant**—who, at one time or another, was also a madam, a cook, and the mistress of British millionaire **Thomas Bell.** (When Bell was murdered in their posh San Francisco home, Mammy was suspected, but she was never indicted.) Innkeeper **Rosemary Wood** inherited the place from her aunt and uncle, the **Heins,** who had raised turkeys here since the thirties, and reopened the house as a B&B in 1981. She has four guest rooms: two unpretentious and simply decorated suites (bedroom, sitting room, and private bath), another guest room upstairs, and one bedroom downstairs. (Try for the suite with a king-sized bed and wood-burning stove.) Wood keeps a library of books on local history, fauna, and flora and sets up chairs in the shade of a venerable old oak. There's a tennis court across the lawn and, for the seriously lazy, a hammock perfect for snoozing. Guests have the run of the 600-acre estate, which extends all the way to the Napa County line and includes eight miles of hiking trails. A brisk early morning walk should just about work up an appetite for the full-country breakfast. ♦ 11775 Sonoma Hwy 12, Glen Ellen. 996.6501

90 Grand Cru Vineyards Built around the 1886 stone-and-cement tanks French emigré **François Lemoine** used to ferment his wines, Grand Cru was founded in 1970 by winemaker **Bob Magnani** and partners. The wines include Gewürztraminer, Sauvignon Blanc, Chenin Blanc, and a good example of white Zinfandel. They also offer a new Carneros Chardonnay from grapes grown on the Sangiacomo Ranch, a Cabernet Sauvignon, and a thoroughly respectable *vin maison* (house wine). The view from the A-frame tasting room is of the Mayacmas Mountains, and you can picnic on the lawn. They've also opened a new tasting room in Kenwood (8860 Sonoma Hwy). ♦ Tasting and sales daily 10AM-4:30PM; tours by appt. 1 Vintage Ln, Glen Ellen. 996.8100

Kenwood

The town of Kenwood, the surrounding valley, and what is now Annadel State Park were once part of the vast Rancho Los Guilicos. The name was a Spanish corruption of Wilikos, the name the Wappo Indians had given their village. In 1834, just after **General Vallejo** established the Sonoma presidio, smallpox and cholera epidemics reduced the local Native American population by thousands; those who survived were later driven away or moved to the Mendocino reservation. **Juan Alvarado,** the Mexican governor of California, ceded the 18,883-acre ranch to **Captain John Wilson,** a Scottish sea captain who had married General Vallejo's sister-in-law, **Romona Carrillo.** Wilson sold the vast holding shortly after the 1846 Bear Flag uprising in Sonoma; the buyer was **William Hood,** another Scotsman, who had fallen in love with the valley as a young man. Hood was a shipwright, a carpenter, and a cabinetmaker who made his fortune in real estate in Australia, South America, Canada, and California. The old Indian settlement was soon renamed Kenwood. Laid out in the 1880s, Kenwood is built around a small central plaza where the Gothic Kenwood Community Church still stands. On Warm Springs Rd, you can see the valley's only stone railroad depot, built in 1887 of basalt quarried in the surrounding hills.

Sonoma

91 Morton's Warm Springs This spot is a family tradition in Kenwood for summer swimming and picnics. Morton's has three swimming pools heated by the naturally warm springs. Indians used to bring their sick to bathe in its waters, and early pioneers created an impromptu bathhouse by putting up a burlap sack around a wooden tub. At the turn of the century, Warm Springs (then called Los Guilicos Warm Springs) was a popular resort. The water still bubbles out of the ground at 87 degrees (about one hundred degrees too cool to be classified as a hot spring), and actually has to be cooled down for use in the swimming pool. Plan on spending the day here; they have 25 or so barbecues and picnic tables, plus a baseball diamond, volleyball and basketball courts, and a snack bar. ♦ Sa-Su 10AM-7PM, May; Tu-Su 10AM-7PM, June-Oct. 1651 Warm Springs Rd, Kenwood. 833.5511

92 Kenwood Inn $$$ Last year San Francisco contractor **Terry Grimm** and his wife, **Roseann,** a restaurateur who owns **Bonito** in Sonoma, turned an old antique store into a posh pensione (Italian-style inn) with just four suites. Outside, they've dabbed the stucco with pale washes of color and planted a romantic garden of old roses and wisteria. The living room and kitchen area are defined with Italianate colors—rusts and ambers—

and the full breakfast continues the Italian theme, with Mediterranean egg dishes, polenta, and freshly baked fruit tarts and pastries. Each of the suites is very different in size, decor, and feeling, though all have fireplaces and private baths. Sensualists will appreciate the down comforters and Egyptian cotton sheets; others may find the decor a bit much. Suite No. 4 features faux-marble walls in yellow and amber, a yellow comforter on the bed, and a high window that looks out on a bank of green foliage. The sunniest is suite No. 5, drenched in burgundy, peach, and rose tones and equipped with two tapestry-covered sofas. The honeymoon suite upstairs is the most private, featuring a small stone balcony overlooking the swimming pool, a separate living room, and a dramatically canopied bed in somber autumn colors. ♦ 10400 Sonoma Hwy, Kenwood. 833.1293

93 Kenwood Restaurant and Bar ★★$$
From the outdoor terrace where you can eat in the shade of large canvas umbrellas, the view is all vineyards. Inside, this California roadhouse with polished wood floors and a natural pine ceiling is simply furnished with white linens and bamboo chairs. Chef **Max Schacher** features the same apealing California wine-country menu at both lunch and dinner—and serves all through the afternoon. Check the large, reasonably priced wine list first, and then choose dishes to go with the wine. For

Sonoma

whites, he has sautéed oysters, clam chowder, or grilled swordfish with a fresh tomato salsa; there is also an excellent Caesar salad. Red-wine aficionados can select from lamb, Petaluma duck in orange sauce, a Kenwood burger with a tall pile of thick-cut fries, or braised Sonoma rabbit with mushrooms and polenta. ♦ California ♦ Tu-Th, Su 11:30AM-9PM; F-Sa 11:30AM-10PM. 9900 Hwy 12, Kenwood. 833.6326

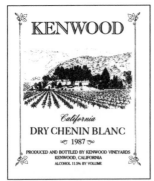

KENWOOD

California

DRY CHENIN BLANC

1987

PRODUCED AND BOTTLED BY KENWOOD VINEYARDS
KENWOOD, CALIFORNIA
ALCOHOL 11.5% BY VOLUME

94 Kenwood Vineyards Originally built in 1906 by the Italian **Pagani** brothers, who peddled their jug wines from door to door, the name changed to Kenwood when the **Martin Lee** family, newcomers to the wine business, bought the property in 1970. They

promptly set about restoring and modernizing the rustic wood barns that still serve as the cellars, and with **Michael Lee** as winemaker they launched a series of excellent Cabernets and Zinfandels. Their top wines are the Artist Series Cabernet, with labels based on a painting by a different artist every year. Artists have included **David Lance Goines, Joseph Neary,** and **James Harrill.** They also make Chardonnay from Beltane Ranch grapes and an outstanding Sauvignon Blanc, a blend of grapes from 17 vineyards from Geyserville to Carneros.
♦ Tours by appt daily 10AM-4:30PM. 9592 Sonoma Hwy, Kenwood. 833.5891

95 Smothers Brothers Wine Store Comedians **Tom Smothers,** a Kenwood resident, and his brother, **Dick,** make wines from grapes grown on Tom's Sonoma Valley ranch. The old country store that is now their tasting room pours their wines and a few of their neighbors', too—**Coturri & Sons, Van Der Kamp Champagne Cellars,** and **Pat Paulsen Vineyards** (yes, the last is owned by the comedian of the same name). This is headquarters for all sorts of wine-country condiments, gadgets, and paraphernalia ranging from the silly to the downright practical. Picnic area. ♦ Daily 10AM-4:30PM. 9575 Sonoma Hwy, Kenwood. 833.1010

JAKE'S DELICATESSEN

96 Jake's Delicatessen ★$ This Italian deli with a small kosher section has a counter stocked with an array of cold cuts, salads, cheeses, and desserts. It includes a salad bar and a soda fountain, and they'll bake pizzas to order. You can eat here or have it bagged to take out. ♦ Deli ♦ Daily 8AM-7PM. 405 Warm Springs Rd, Kenwood. 833.1350

97 Wine Country Wagons Visitors are taken by horse-drawn wagon on a cultural tour of several wineries, including **Kenwood** and **Smothers Brothers.** One highlight is the **Kunde Estate,** not open to the public, and their 32,000 square feet of underground caves. A creekside lunch at a private ranch, using Sonoma County products only, comes with the tour. ♦ $40 per person. The three-hour tours leave daily 10AM, May-Oct.

Reservations must be made 48 hours in advance. Kenwood. 833.1202

Cafe Citti

98 Cafe Citti ★★$$ **Luca** and **Linda Citti** are cooking their hearts out at this small, casual Italian takeout and trattoria. At breakfast, try the Eggs Citti: two poached eggs and ham atop homemade *focaccia* with rosemary potatoes on the side. The espresso is good and strong. Lunch features sandwiches on the same focaccia bread along with pasta dishes with a choice of sauces. For picnics, try one of the spit-roasted chickens. Add a couple of salads and a few biscotti or a slice of ricotta cheese torte and you've got a veritable feast. Table service can be slow when it's busy, but the food tastes authentically Italian. Italian groceries, too, for campers and those with kitchenettes. ♦ Italian ♦ M-Sa 8AM-7PM. 9049 Sonoma Hwy, Kenwood. 833.2690

99 Chateau St. Jean One of the best-known boutique wineries of the late seventies, Chateau St. Jean now produces well over 150,000 cases per year and has been owned by the Japanese firm Suntory since 1984. Until very recently, the same masterful winemaker, **Richard Arrowood,** was at the helm all the while. Arrowood concentrated on single-vineyard wines, notably those from five designated vineyards: Robert Young, Belle Terre, Frank Johnson, McCrea, and the estate's 70-acre St. Jean Vineyard. (Arrowood has now opened his own premium winery, **Arrowood Vineyards and Winery,** just up the road.) The 250-acre estate in the shelter of Sugarloaf Ridge was once the preserve of a wealthy businessman; his former living room is used as the tasting room, and visitors can picnic on the lawn in front of the country mansion. The view of the Sonoma Valley from the mock medieval tower is one of the highlights of the self-guided tour. ♦ Tasting, sales, and self-guided tours daily 10AM-4:30PM. 8555 Sonoma Hwy, Kenwood. 833.4134

100 St. Francis Winery and Vineyards The original vineyard, planted in 1910, was part of a wedding gift to **Alice Kunde** (of the prominent grape-growing family) and her husband **Will Behler.** The 100-acre estate is now owned by **Lloyd Canton** and former San Francisco furniture dealer **Joe Martin** and his wife, **Emma.** Don't overlook their fine Merlot (regular and reserve) or the barrel-select estate Chardonnay; the Sonoma Mountain Cabernet earns good marks, too. They also make Johannisberg Riesling, Gewürztraminer, and a sweet Muscat Canelli. The oak tasting room with burgundy awnings features chilled white wines to purchase for a picnic and cold Calistoga water for the kids. From the patio area equipped with picnic tables,

you can enjoy views of the surrounding vineyards. ♦ Fee. Tasting and sales daily 10AM-4:30PM; tours by appt. 8450 Sonoma Hwy, Kenwood. 833.4666

101 Landmark Vineyards Urban sprawl was a factor in owner **William Mabry's** decision to move his winery from Windsor (near Healdsburg) south to Adobe Canyon Rd in Kenwood. The whitewashed California Mission-style complex houses one of the first wineries in the state devoted primarily to Chardonnay. A hands-on winemaker, Mabry has another avocation: racing formula cars at Sears Point Raceway and Laguna Seca. There's a picnic area near the winery's pond. ♦ Tasting and sales daily 10AM-4:30PM; tours by appt. 101 Adobe Canyon Rd, Kenwood. 833.0053

102 Oreste Golden Bear Restaurant ★$$$ The secluded setting at the foot of Mount Hood keeps this largely a local hangout, where Kenwood and Santa Rosa residents come to enjoy the creekside dining and Italian-American food. The menu features a large array of both cold and hot antipasti, such as *cima* (stuffed veal breast with sweetbreads, bacon, and cheese) or *suppli* (deep-fried rice balls stuffed with mozzarella). As for pastas, try the *penne alla putanesca* (with sun-dried tomatoes, anchovies, capers, and spicy black olives) or the ravioli *tutto mare* stuffed with scallops, shrimp, and crab.

Sonoma

Main courses include calamari in white wine, corn-fed New York steak, and *pollo al mattone* (chicken cooked under a hot brick). Best bet: the half chicken grilled with fresh herbs. ♦ Northern Italian/American ♦ M-Tu, Th-Sa 11AM-10PM; Su 11AM-2PM, 2:30-10PM. 1717 Adobe Canyon Rd, Kenwood. Reservations recommended. 833.2327

103 Sugarloaf Ridge State Park The conical ridge that rises behind Chateau St. Jean in the heart of the Mayacmas range is known as Sugarloaf Ridge. Follow Adobe Canyon Rd as it winds into the hills, past Oreste Golden Bear restaurant, to the entrance of this spectacular state park. Archaeologists now believe Sugarloaf Ridge was first inhabited 7,000 years ago. The steep hills of the 2,700-acre park, covered in redwood, fir, oak, and chaparral, offer more than 25 miles of hiking and riding trails. From the park's highest elevations, views extend to Sonoma and Napa Valley. You can even spot San Francisco Bay and the Sierra Nevada from certain places. Near the entrance to the park, look for the remains of old charcoal-burning areas that **Congressman John King Luttrell** used for the production of charcoal in the late 1890s.

The park includes 50 family campsites, each with tent space, barbecue, and picnic tables. There are corrals for horses, too. A rigorous foot trail (Goodspeed Trail) leads to adjacent

Hood Mountain Regional Park, but "good speed" here means several hours of hiking. ♦ Admission. Sunrise to sunset. 2605 Adobe Canyon Rd (3 miles off Hwy 12) Kenwood. For camping reservations, call 800/444.7275

Within Sugarloaf Ridge State Park:

Sonoma Cattle Co. It's fun to tour the park on horseback with knowledgeable guides who can identify the local flora and fauna. They have horses for riders of all levels; children must be at least eight years old. The stables are located on the valley floor. They also schedule moonlight and overnight trips, and offer rides at Jack London State Historic Park. ♦ Daily from 8AM; full-moon rides until 10PM. Reservations required. 996.8566

104 Hood Mountain Regional Park This 1,300-acre park in the Mayacmas Mountains offers hiking and riding trails, campgrounds, and cool picnic sites. Clamber up Gunsight Rock Lookout for heartstopping views of the Sonoma Valley all the way to the San Francisco Bay and, on occasion, the Sierra Nevada. Open for hiking on weekends and holidays in the fall, winter, and spring; closed in summer due to fire hazards. ♦ Day-use fee. Take Hwy 12 off Los Alamos Rd up Santa Rosa Creek Canyon to the steep ridge that marks Hood Mountain Regional Park. Camping information 539.9903/8092; for more information, call 527.2041

Sonoma

105 Adler Fels Founded in 1980 by **Dave Coleman** and his wife, **Ayn Ryan**, whose family had a hand in starting Chateau St. Jean, this tiny winery sits high atop a 26-foot-wide ridge, very near the outcropping of rock that locals have dubbed Eagle Rock (in German, that name translates to adler fels—hence the winery's name). The half-timbered building looks a bit like Rhine or Alsace set down in California.

They're really white-wine specialists, producing Chardonnay, Fumé Blanc, and a late-harvest Johannisberg Riesling; their red wines are less successful. ♦ Tasting, sales, and tours by appt daily. 5325 Corrick Ln, Santa Rosa. 539.3123

106 Oakmont Golf Club This club offers two 18-hole championship courses, both designed by **Ted Robinson**. The east course is considered challenging; the west course is a more leisurely meander. ♦ Daily dawn-dusk. 7025 Oakmont Dr (Hwy 12) Santa Rosa. 538.2454, 539.0415

The Sebastiani family of Sonoma has the largest collection of carved wine barrels in North America.

"Come, come; good wine is a good familiar creature if it be well used; exclaim no more against it."
William Shakespeare

What's in a Bottle?

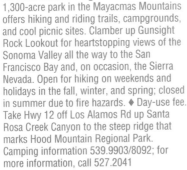

The standard bottle of wine in this country is designed to hold 750 milliliters (that's three-quarters of a liter or four-fifths of a quart). The half bottle (or "split") is, of course, just half that, and ideal for someone dining alone or for a couple who wants to drink a white wine with the first course and a red with the main course. Most wineries also bottle a limited number of magnums—handsome, oversized bottles that hold the equivalent of two bottles of wine (wine ages more slowly in the larger bottles). A series of even larger bottles are occasionally used for red wines, champagnes, and sparkling wines.

Half Bottle Holds 375 milliliters (half the quantity of a standard wine bottle).

Bottle Whether it has the sloping shoulders of a Burgundy-style bottle, the high, rounded shoulders of a Bordeaux-style bottle, or the tall, elongated shape of an Alsace- or German-style bottle, the typical American wine bottle holds 750 milliliters.

Magnum Holds the equivalent of two bottles of wine.

Double Magnum (or **Jeroboam**) Holds the equivalent of four bottles of wine.

Rehoboam Holds the equivalent of six bottles of wine.

Imperial (or **Methusaleh)** Holds the equivalent of eight bottles of wine.

Salmanazar Holds the equivalent of 12 bottles of wine.

Balthazar Holds the equivalent of 16 bottles of wine.

Nebuchadnezzar The granddaddy of them all holds the equivalent of 20 bottles of wine (or a little less, depending on where the bottle was made).

Bests

Laura Chenel
Cheesemaker/Owner, Laura Chenel's Chèvre, Santa Rosa

The Thursday-night farmers market in downtown Santa Rosa.

Tra Vigne's Cantinetta in St. Helena.

A horseback ride at **Annadel State Park** or on the **Bodega Dunes**.

A bicycle ride in the Dry Creek and Alexander Valleys (Healdsburg).

A lazy summer afternoon on the square in Healdsburg Plaza, including a visit to the **Downtown Bakery & Creamery**, **The Raven Theater** (in the evenings), and the **Ravenous Raven** cafe next door.

John Ash & Co. in Santa Rosa for lunch or dinner.

A drive through western Petaluma and Bodega Bay, taking Coleman Valley Rd to Occidental, then over to Freestone—a west-county tour.

Dan Berger
Wine Columnist, *Los Angeles Times*

Sipping a bottle of chilled Navarro Gewürztraminer before a crackling fireplace in a cabin at **Bear Wallow,** hidden in the hills between Philo and the coast of Mendocino. Bear Wallow is a nearly unknown respite from the world: no phones, no TVs, no radio. But it has a one-match fireplace, windows to the trees, fresh air, and a bottle of sherry on the kitchen table of every cabin. Four miles east is Boonville, a lost-in-time town of ultimate charm that has one of the best restaurants in Northern California (the **Boonville Hotel**) as well as some of the best locally grown apples (at **Gowan's Oak Tree**), and real people at the **Horn of Zeese Coffee Shop.** The wines of this region are among the best in the US.

The massive Spanish omelet (with sourdough toast) on a Saturday morning in September at **The Diner** in Yountville. The breakfast at this cafe is the best in Northern California, making the hard bench seats only a minor inconvenience. Don't get there too late or you'll have to wait (and don't miss the fried potatoes or the pancakes).

A walk through **Armstrong Woods** near Guerneville on a spring morning with espresso in a thermos and a sticky bun from the **Downtown Bakery & Creamery** in Healdsburg. (Armstrong Woods, a gem in western Sonoma County, is so little known that even some locals are unaware of it.)

An early morning drive from Santa Rosa west over Coleman Mountain Rd in January, with the wind raking the leaves and newborn lambs frolicking on unsure legs. On the way home, make sure you stop at **Kozlowski's Berry Farm** near Forestville to buy a basket of fresh blueberries—which will never make it back to town alive.

Dinner at **Tra Vigne** in St. Helena preceded by their homemade sardines, home-cured olives, home-baked olive bread dipped in olive oil, and sips of Spottswoode Sauvignon Blanc. Its sister restaurant, **Mustards Grill,** located down the road, may be the best example of California cuisine in the state, but for intensity of flavor Tuscan-style, Tra Vigne has it, with an amazing array of pastas, plus chicken, seafood, and a wait staff both efficient and full of fun. I could eat here three times a week and never get bored.

A night at the modern-eclectic **Stevens Wood Lodge** on the Mendocino Coast, followed the next morning by breakfast at **Café Beaujolais** (reservations required). **Margaret Fox's** amazing morning-food preparations are legendary, so even midweek it's not easy to get a seat here. But the baked goods, scrapple, and even mundane things are cooked to perfection, with freshly ground coffee you can smell up the street.

An impromptu picnic lunch on the lawn in the Sonoma town square with all the accoutrements: a bottle of wine from a local winery; sausages from **Sonoma Sausage Company;** a loaf of sourdough bread still warm from the oven from the **Sonoma French Bakery** across the square; and a block of **Ig Vella's** hard Dry Sonoma Jack Cheese from the cheese shop around the corner. Try the hearty **Haywood** Zinfandel or one from **Gundlach-Bundschu** for a treat with the cheese.

The perfection of **Diane Pariseu's** cooking at calm, quiet **Trilogy** in St. Helena, paired with a bottle of wine from an intriguing wine list and served in splendid tall wine goblets with ultra-thin rims and stems. The word sublime comes to mind....

A Saturday art tour of the Napa Valley, starting with the amazingly diverse **Hess Collection** at the southern end of the valley, followed by an afternoon seminar in the caves at **Clos Pegase,** listening to enthusiastic **Jan Shrem** give his slide presentation on wine as an art form, and art in the world of wine.

A loaf of garlic-herb bread from **Jake's Deli** in Kenwood, a hunk of cheese, and a glass of a local red in Sonoma County's Valley of the Moon at **Jack London State Historic Park** in September. Follow that with a blackberry-picking walk along the side roads.

Zelma Long
President, Simi Winery, Healdsburg

Hiking to the top of **Mount St. Helena** and celebrating with a picnic dinner and good wine, while watching the sun set and the full moon rise.

Lunch at **Terra** in St. Helena.

A weekend at **Sea Ranch,** riding horses and strolling on the beach.

Sunday brunch at **Madrona Manor** in Healdsburg.

The total relaxation of an enzyme bath at **Osmosis** in Freestone.

Walking through the **Pygmy Forest** on the Mendocino Coast.

Shopping for fresh Sonoma County produce at the Santa Rosa Thursday-night street fair and farmers market.

Driving through a wonderland of blossoming trees on Hwy 128 in springtime, between Calistoga and Healdsburg and through Knight's Valley and the Alexander Valley.

Munching on sticky buns and sipping a creamy cafè latté from the **Downtown Bakery & Creamery** in Healdsburg.

Lisa Jang
Bay Bottom Beds, oyster farm, Santa Rosa

David Auerbach's "Carols in the Caves" concerts in St. Helena. Auerbach uses folk instruments from all over the world to play Christmas carols and other holiday music in the storage caves of several wineries. It's a really special way to get the annual dose of Christmas music.

Beautiful routes to travel: Santa Rosa to Calistoga via Mark West Springs Rd, and Sonoma to Santa Rosa via Hwy 12, especially in the early fall.

Pack Jack's in Sebastopol for good ribs. And the noisy and fun **Ma Stokeld's Old Vic** (a pub) in Santa Rosa, which serves good food and great English pastries at very reasonable prices.

Kyoto Koi and Garden Restaurant in Santa Rosa—admire the beautiful koi and great bonsai displays.

The miniature horse ranch in Petaluma for the miniature horses.

Santa Rosa

In 1875 **Luther Burbank** followed up on his older brother's enthusiastic recommendation to leave the East Coast and move to Santa Rosa. And Burbank immediately took a liking to the place. "I firmly believe, from what I have seen, that this is the chosen spot of all this earth as far as nature is concerned," he wrote. For more than 50 years the world-renowned horticulturist labored here in his greenhouse and gardens, producing more than 800 new varieties of fruits, vegetables, and plants.

Santa Rosa was once part of an immense Spanish land grant held by **Doña Maria Ignacia Lopez Carrillo**, the mother-in-law of **General Mariano Vallejo**. Americans first came to Santa Rosa to establish a trading post in 1846, and it was incorporated as a town eight years later.

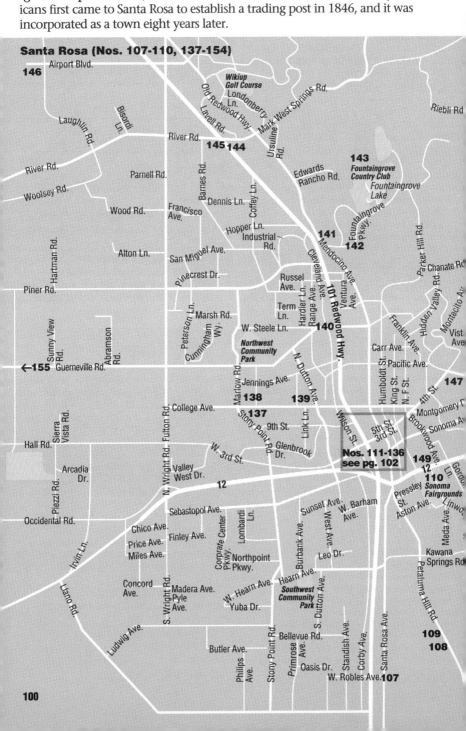

Santa Rosa (Nos. 107-110, 137-154)

Sonoma's county seat, Santa Rosa is home to more than 100,000 people and is just minutes from the Valley of the Moon and a half hour from Healdsburg, in the heart of the Russian River Valley. The city is considered the hub of Sonoma County because most of the main roads cross here.

A quiet town that still retains the atmosphere of another era, Santa Rosa offers a respite for those who find the country a little too quiet, but don't want San Francisco-style nightlife. **Railroad Square**, just west of the freeway in downtown Santa Rosa, is a six-square-block area of restored turn-of-the-century buildings filled with antique stores, shops, and restaurants. And Fourth Street, the main artery of Santa Rosa's restored downtown area, comes alive every Thursday night from May through October with an exuberant farmers market featuring music, street food, and entertainment that attracts folks from miles around.

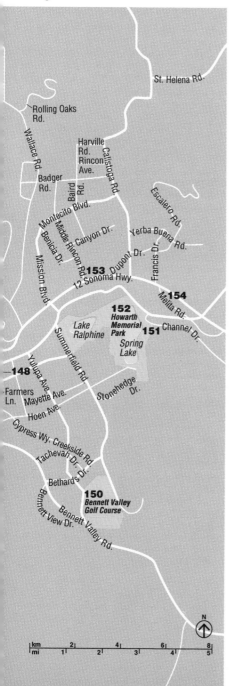

History buffs will want to visit the **Sonoma County Museum** and **Luther Burbank's Home and Gardens.** Across the street from Burbank's home is the **Church Built from One Tree** in Juilliard Park, which was entirely constructed from the lumber provided by one enormous redwood, and now, believe it or not, is a museum devoted to Santa Rosa resident and connoisseur of the strange and wonderful, the late **Robert L. Ripley.** Santa Rosa is surrounded by 5,000 acres of city, county, and state parks offering everything from walking trails and rugged hiking and horseback

Santa Rosa

riding trails to campgrounds and lakes for fishing, swimming, and boating.

Two of Sonoma County's top restaurants, **Matisse** and **John Ash & Co.,** are in Santa Rosa, and lodging includes bed-and-breakfasts, a restored turn-of-the-century hotel in Railroad Square, and several comfortable inns on the northern outskirts of town, including the deluxe **Vintage Court.**

107 Friedman Bros. A Sonoma County fixture, this giant hardware store sells everything from ice chests and portable barbecues to galvanized farm and ranch gates, rural mailboxes, and livestock watering troughs. ◆ M-F 7AM-7PM; Sa 8AM-5:30PM; Su 9AM-4PM. 4055 Santa Rosa Ave, Santa Rosa. 584.7811, 795.4546

108 Crane Melon Barn This farm stand specializes in Crane melons, a luscious, sweet melon first developed by the proprietor's grandfather more than 50 years ago. They also sell string beans, apples, and dried fruit. ◆ Aug-Oct. 4947 Petaluma Hill Rd, Santa Rosa. 584.5141

109 **The Gables** $$ A historical landmark, the imposing 113-year-old Victorian with 15 (count 'em) gables sits in front of a weathered barn on three-and-a-half acres. The six guest rooms, all with a private bath, have Victorian clawfoot tubs and, of course, period decor. The most sought-after accommodation is the two-story cottage in back with a wood-burning stove and a kitchenette so you can prepare produce from the local farmers market. At sunset guests like to congregate on the deck and take in the view. Innkeepers **Michael** and **Judy Ogne** cook up a full-country breakfast, which includes French toast and fruit compote with coconut cream. ◆ 4257 Petaluma Hill Rd, Santa Rosa. 585.7777

110 **Sonoma County Fairgrounds** Summer brings the annual three-week Sonoma County Fair, with hundreds of crafts and homemaking exhibits, plants, flowers, livestock, and wool—and blue ribbons galore. A great way to sample all of Sonoma's bounty. It runs from the latter half of July to early August. ◆ 1350 Bennett Valley Rd, Santa Rosa. 545.4200

At the Sonoma County Fairgrounds:

Sonoma County Fairgrounds Golf Course A nine-hole public golf course; par 29. During the fair, the course is filled with exhibits. ◆ Daily 10AM-7PM. 546.2469

111 **Brother Juniper's Bread Box** This shop sells the justly famous loaves baked at Forestville's Brother Juniper's Café. ◆ M-F 9AM-4:30PM; Sa 9AM-2PM. 463 Sebastopol Ave, Santa Rosa. 542.9012

112 **Juilliard Park** These nine acres in the center of the city were once home to wine-and-fruit broker **C.F. Juilliard,** a Santa Rosa pioneer. The site is now a park with a self-guided tour of 42 varieties of trees. ◆ Santa Rosa Ave and S. A St, Santa Rosa

---

Restaurants/Clubs: Red   **Hotels: Blue**
Shops/ 🌳 **Outdoors: Green**   **Wineries/Sights: Black**

Downtown Santa Rosa (Nos. 111-136)

Robert L. Ripley Memorial Museum

This unusual museum, housed in the historic **Church Built from One Tree,** was made famous by the phenomenally successful cartoonist **Robert L. Ripley.** The entire church was built in 1873 from a single giant redwood from Guerneville. The tree was 275 feet high and 18 feet in diameter and provided 78,000 board feet of wood. Inside is a collection of memorabilia from the archives of the late Santa Rosa cartoonist, whose strip, *Ripley's Believe it or Not,* is read by more than 80 million people in newspapers from 38 countries. You'll find some of his original cartoons, photos of Ripley in outlandish situations and places, his battered old suitcase covered with stickers from his travels, and a lifelike wax figure of the cartoonist sculpted by a blind man. ◆ Nominal admission. Daily 11AM-4PM, summer; M-Tu, Th-Su, winter; hours may vary, so call for information. 492 Sonoma Ave, Santa Rosa. 524.5233

113 Luther Burbank Home & Gardens Visit the home where world-famous horticulturist **Luther Burbank** worked from 1875 to 1926. The gardens where he conducted his experiments are under renovation now, with plans for completion sometime in 1991 to 1993. The docent-guided tour that starts on the half hour is a thoroughly enjoyable ramble through the garden, the greenhouse, and the modified Greek Revival house where his wife **Elizabeth** lived until her death. The carriage house is a mini-museum with

photographs of notables who visited Burbank and drawings of his creations such as the shasta daisy, the russet potato, and the Santa Rosa plum, among others. This brilliant, self-educated man introduced more than 800 new varieties of plants to the world (including over 200 varieties of fruits alone). His objective was to improve the quality of plants and thereby increase the world's food supply. After his death, Congress inducted him into the Hall of Inventors. An annual holiday open house and gift sale is held the first weekend in December. ◆ Nominal fee for tours. Home: W-Su 10AM-3:30PM, Apr-Oct. Tours every half-hour. Memorial gardens: daily 8AM-7PM, year-round. 204 Santa Rosa Ave, Santa Rosa. 524.5445

Illustration from one of Burbank's first nursery catalogs, circa 1887

Santa Rosa

114 Pygmalion House $ This restored Queen Anne cottage is tucked away at the end of a quiet residential street a short walk from Railroad Square (but close to the freeway). There are five reasonably priced rooms, all with private baths featuring old-fashioned clawfoot tubs and furnished with a mix of antiques and reproductions. The full breakfast, which includes fresh fruit and freshly baked muffins and croissants, is served in the large country kitchen. ◆ 331 Orange St, Santa Rosa. 526.3407

115 Days Inn Hotel $$ Part of the dependable chain, this hotel's 140 rooms and suites are furnished in a contemporary style, with either two double-sized beds or one queen-sized bed, cable TV, and private bath. Guests have use of the pool and outdoor Jacuzzi. The hotel is a block from Railroad Square and bordered by the freeway and a residential area. Non-smoking rooms by request. ◆ 175 Railroad St, Santa Rosa. 573.9000

116 Railroad Square Historic District In 1870 the first Santa Rosa-North Pacific train chugged into town, bringing San Franciscans to the countryside. The old depot is now the focus of a newly restored historic district called Railroad Square. The surrounding turn-of-the-century stone and brick buildings have been spruced up to house antique shops, restaurants, and cafes; the depot itself, which was added to the National Register of Historic Places in 1979, is slated for full restoration soon. ◆ Bounded by Third-Sixth Sts, Hwy 101, and Santa Rosa Creek, in Santa Rosa. 578.8478

117 Sonoma County Convention and Visitors Bureau Extensive information on wineries, lodging, restaurants, and activities in all of Sonoma County is offered by an ardent staff. Stop in for maps of the county and Santa Rosa, the Russian River Wine Road, and Sonoma Farm Trails. ◆ M 9:30AM-5PM; Tu-F 8AM-5PM; Sa 10AM-4PM, (also Su 10AM-4PM, May-Oct) Railroad Square (in the old Western Hotel) 10 Fourth St, Suite 100 Santa Rosa. 575.1191

118 Chevy's ★$$ Part of a highly successful chain, this restaurant has an appealing menu of Mexican specialties (see Chevy's on page 79). And if you can handle the summer heat, there's a large deck out back. ◆ Mexican ◆ M-Th, Su 11:30AM-10PM; F-Sa 11:30AM-11PM. Railroad Square, 24 Fourth St, Suite 100, Santa Rosa. 571.1082

119 A'Roma Roasters & Coffeehouse ★★$$ You've just found the best cafe in

Santa Rosa

town, with great espresso, cappuccino, caffè latte, and house specialties. When it's sweltering outside, come in for a refreshing Italian soda, an iced coffee, or one of their frappés of the day. The bright-red French roaster trimmed in brass sits right in the middle of the store, filling it with the heady scent of fresh-roasted coffee; owners **Dayna McCutchen** and **Sandra Young** feature 18 types to choose from. They'll also tempt you with organic fruit pies and other locally made desserts. Wednesday through Friday they feature live music (no cover charge), ranging from flamenco guitar and chamber music to jazz and blues. ◆ M-W 7AM-9PM; Th 7AM-11PM; F 7AM-midnight; Sa 8AM-midnight; Su 8:30AM-5:30PM. Railroad Square, 95 Fifth St, Santa Rosa. 576.7765

120 Hotel La Rose $$ This hotel in a turn-of-the-century stone building (pictured above) in Railroad Square offers moderately priced

accommodations. The 20 rooms all have private baths and country-on-a-budget decor: flower wallpaper, rose comforters, carpeting, and reproduction period furniture. Most bathrooms are on the small side and the views from some rooms are merely of the freeway. But the hotel has a sun deck with a Jacuzzi, air-conditioning, and a pleasant bar downstairs with a fireplace and decorative grape motif. They serve high tea on weekday afternoons. Ask about midweek specials. ◆ Railroad Square, 308 Wilson St, Santa Rosa. 579.3200, 800/579.3247

Within Hotel La Rose:

The Pub at Hotel La Rose ★$$ With its plaid-covered banquettes and high-back upholstered chairs, the hotel's pub looks something like a Scotch bistro, if there is such a thing. The lunch menu includes a nice Cobb salad with curly endive, chicken, avocado, and warm bacon dressing, along with black-bean chili, a hot turkey sandwich, several pasta dishes, grilled sausages with caramelized onions, and mesquite-grilled flank steak. They've got a good array of beers and ales from local microbreweries. Games such as backgammon, dice, dominoes, and cribbage are available to while away the evening. ◆ California/British ◆ Tu-F 11:30AM-2PM, 5:30-9PM; Sa 5:30-9PM. High tea Tu-F 3-5PM. 579.3200

121 Polka Dots Cafe ★$ You got it: Dots and more dots are the theme at this informal diner. For breakfast, order *huevos rancheros*, down-home biscuits and gravy, or an egg sandwich on whole-wheat toast. At lunch, you can get ground beef, turkey, or chicken-breast burgers, as well as old standbys such as a triple-layered BLT, meatloaf, or ham and cheese sandwiches. Light luncheon salads, soups, and chili are also available. And to cool off, try one of their old-fashioned shakes. ◆ Tu-Su 7AM-10PM. Railroad Square, 115 Fourth St, Santa Rosa. 575.9080

121 Consuming Passions At this tiny shop, chocolatier **Thea Baker** presents her handmade chocolates. Choose from truffles, deep chocolate fudge, rich caramels, chocolate-covered cherries, molded chocolate roses—even sugar-free chocolates sweetened with a corn derivative. Mail order available. ◆ Daily 9:30AM-5PM. Railroad Square, 115 Fourth St, Santa Rosa. 571.8380

122 Las Manos This store's appealing collection of ethnic clothing, much of it handwoven cotton or silk, is absolutely suitable for the wine-country climate. You'll find lots of summer frocks, Panama hats, and an interesting selection of accessories such as hand-crocheted wallets from Guatemala and jeweled baseball caps from Thailand. Check the racks upstairs for discounted items and handwoven Guatemalan fabrics. ♦ M-Sa 10AM-6PM; Su 11AM-4:30PM. Railroad Square, 133 Fourth St, Santa Rosa. 578.1649

122 Small Change Bright, colorful clothing for kids and moms-to-be. ♦ M-Sa 9:30AM-5:30PM; Su 11AM-4:30PM. Railroad Square, 127 Fourth St, Santa Rosa. 576.1092

122 Mixx ★★$$$ An up-to-date menu of Italian-style dishes is translated into the California wine-country idiom: carpaccio, *bruschetta, focaccia,* Caesar salad, and handmade ravioli. Sonoma's sun-dried tomatoes get a workout in selections such as *pappardelle* (wide ribbon noodles) with smoked mussels, pancetta, and red Swiss chard or basil fettuccine with smoked chicken, Niçoise olives, and poached garlic. There's a classic *crème brûlée* for dessert. No smoking allowed. ♦ California/Italian ♦ M-Th 11:30AM-2PM, 5:30-10PM; F-Sa 11:30AM-2PM, 5:30PM-midnight. Railroad Square, 135 Fourth St, Santa Rosa. 573.1344

123 Whistlestop Antiques Pack rats will have a ball prowling through this two-story antiques collective for old furniture, kitchenware, costume jewelry, and knickknacks. Some stalls specialize in Art Deco plastic jewelry, fifties cocktail shakers, or sleek chrome furniture and stylish vintage radios. Collectors can also find **Russell Wright** dinnerware (1939-59), and if you love arts-and-crafts furniture, one stall has a well-edited selection of original furniture by **Stickley, Limbert,** and other masters of the genre. ♦ M-Sa 10AM-5:30PM; Su 11AM-4:30PM. Railroad Square, 130 Fourth St, Santa Rosa. 542.9474

124 Earth Options A unique environmental store featuring everything from air filters and biosafe household products to energy-efficient lightbulbs, solar panels, and water-conservation systems. Some things are truly state-of-the-art, such as the Destiny 2000, the world's first production solar-electric sports car, while others are decidedly old-fashioned, like the umbrella-type clothesline from a manufacturer who has been making them for 75 years. Be sure to take home one of their catalogs; it has excellent information on how to make your own home environmentally sound. ♦ M-F 9AM-5PM; Sa 10AM-6PM; Su 10AM-4PM. Railroad Square, 116 Fourth St, Santa Rosa. 542.1990; fax 542.4358

124 Omelette Express ★$ Santa Rosa's casual breakfast spot offers about 50 omelets, from standard combos to vegetarian and seafood, all served with cottage fries. From 11AM on, they serve charbroiled sirloin burgers and classic sandwiches including roast beef, grilled cheddar cheese, and tuna salad. Special kids' menu, too. ♦ M-F 6:30AM-3PM; Sa-Su 7AM-4PM. Railroad Square, 112 Fourth St, Santa Rosa. 525.1690

124 The Clay Company If you're itching to lend your home some of that wine-country chic feel, this is the place to stock up on giant canvas market umbrellas, classic wood Adirondack and garden chairs, baskets, rattan furniture, and more. ♦ M-F 10AM-6PM; Sa 10AM-5PM; Su 11AM-4PM. Railroad Square, 100 Fourth St, Santa Rosa. 527.6110

124 Sweet Potato This novelty store features zillions of crazy cards, silly gifts and gags, off-the-wall books, and whimsical jewelry. If you've been dying to pick up a copy of *Best Places to Kiss in Northern California* or a plastic flamingo for your lawn, your search is over. ♦ M-Sa 10AM-7PM; Su 9AM-6PM. Railroad Square, 100 Fourth St, Santa Rosa. 526.2777

125 La Gare ★★$$$ At this family-owned restaurant in a charming stone building on Railroad Square, you'll find the type of old-style French dishes that have virtually disappeared from trendier menus—standbys such as quiche lorraine, onion soup au gratin, veal medallion *cordon bleu,* duck *à l'orange,* and *filet de boeuf* Wellington. Yet the propri-

Santa Rosa

etors are savvy enough to include a vegetarian special, and they put chocolate decadence (that divine combo of dark chocolate and raspberries) alongside that old favorite, cherries jubilee. ♦ Swiss/French ♦ Tu-Th 5:30-10PM; F-Sa 5-10PM; Su 5-9PM. Railroad Square, 208 Wilson St, Santa Rosa. 528.4355

125 Auntie's Shanty Shop here for antique and reproduction stained-glass lamps in the Tiffany mode. ♦ M-Th 10AM-5PM; F-Sa 10AM-5:30PM; Su 11AM-5PM. Railroad Square, 206 Wilson St, Santa Rosa. 577.8794

125 Richard's Antiques Richard specializes in vintage and antique furniture, with a focus on mahogany, plus accessories and collectibles. ♦ Daily 10AM-5PM. Railroad Square, 204 Wilson St, Santa Rosa. 528.1447

125 Hot Couture Inveterate vintage clotheshounds are sure to get derailed for an hour or two in this emporium stocked with sequined sweaters, forties coats, and glamorous fifties cocktail dresses. For men, they've got old-fashioned tuxedo shirts (great on women, too), and classic jackets and coats à la Bogie. ♦ M-Sa 10AM-6PM; Su 11AM-5PM. Railroad Square, 101 Third St, Santa Rosa. 528.7247

125 Black Swan Antiques Here you'll find leaded glass and silk lamp shades, country antiques, and collectibles. ♦ M-Sa 10:30AM-5PM. Railroad Square, 105 Third St, Santa Rosa. 523.4355

125 Cole Silver Shop The shop for antique silver, including sterling silver flatware. Silver plating, polishing, repairs, and appraisals are also available. ♦ M-F 10AM-5PM; Sa by appt. Railroad Square, 107 Third St, Santa Rosa. 546.7515

125 Antiques, Apples & Art Great for browsing. Small objets d'art, glassware, textiles, lamps.... ♦ Tu-Sa 11AM-5:30PM. Railroad Square, 109 Third St, Santa Rosa. 578.1414

125 Marianne's Antiques Handsome tables, sideboards, armoires, and other large pieces of furniture are the specialty at this spacious antique store. ♦ M-Sa 10AM-5:30PM; Su 11AM-5PM. Railroad Square, 111 Third St, Santa Rosa. 579.5749

126 Sonoma Outfitters This large store features a friendly, knowledgeable staff and a terrific selection of outdoor gear and apparel, including boots, tents, sleeping bags, and packs. If you're heading for the Russian River, check out the bright canoes, and you can test out rollerblades on the oval ring that winds right through the middle of the store. On weekends, a vertical climbing wall is available. The staff is thoroughly versed in all the equipment and gear. ♦ M-Sa 10AM-6PM; Su 11AM-5PM. Railroad Square, 145 Third St, Santa Rosa. 528.1920

Santa Rosa

127 Smith & Hawken For gardeners on a budget, this is the discount outlet for the Mill Valley-based store featuring handcrafted teak benches and tables, French bistro furniture, market umbrellas, ingenious English- and Japanese-made garden tools, and gardening attire. They also carry housewares, linens, Victorian tin dinnerware, candles, and potpourri. Some are overstocks and seconds; all are offered at discounts of up to 70 percent. Pick up one of their mail order catalogs, too. ♦ Daily 10AM-6PM. 4 A St, Santa Rosa. 573.1154

128 Traverso's Gourmet Foods and Wine Since 1929 this Italian deli, opened by two brothers from Genoa, **Louis** and **Enrico Traverso,** has been a treasure trove of local and Italian foodstuffs. They've got a decent selection of local cheese and cold cuts already sliced so you can get in and out fast, plus all the standard fixin's. To stock the pantry, shop for California and Italian olive oils, vinegars, Sonoma County dried tomatoes, and jams. In the well-stocked wine section, vintage photos give a glimpse of Santa Rosa in the thirties and forties. Ask about their used wine shipment boxes for mailing from two to 12 bottles. ♦ Deli ♦ M-Sa 8AM-6PM. 106 B St, Santa Rosa. 542.2530

129 Thursday Night Market From May through October, downtown Sonoma's Fourth Street is closed to traffic on Thursday nights, when it becomes the site of a remarkably successful farmers market. With live music, jugglers, magicians, and lots of street food, it's a nonstop party that attracts people from miles around. Get down with grilled sausages and beer, Preston Point oysters from **Bay Bottom Beds,** and pastries and breads from **Mezzaluna** and **Brother Juniper,** both highly lauded local bakeries. Take home some of the Holy Smokes barbecue sauce and jams from **Kozlowski Farms** in Forestville. The real farmers set up their stalls along B Street, touting their luscious strawberries, goat cheese, spring onions, Santa Rosa plums, and whatever else the season has to offer. Bring a big shopping bag because it's impossible not to get into the spirit of things. ♦ Th 5:30-7:30PM, May-Oct. Fourth St (B-E Sts) Santa Rosa. 539.0345

130 Sonoma Coffee Co. The toasty scent of whole-bean coffees pervades this long, narrow cafe, where a sandblasted brick wall stands in as an informal photography and print gallery. A collection of thermoses sits atop an old Wedgewood stove for the serve-it-yourself house coffee; they also feature espresso drinks and an array of morning pastries. ♦ M-Sa 7AM-11PM; Su 9AM-6PM. 521 Fourth St, Santa Rosa. 573.8022

130 Caffè Portofino Ristorante & Bar ★★$$$ The bar at the front of this cafe is a popular spot for wine tasting. Best bets on the menu are the *bruschetta* (the official classic: toasted bread rubbed with garlic and doused with virgin olive oil), Caesar salad prepared at the table, and slices of fresh Buffalo-milk mozzarella and tomatoes drizzled with olive oil and topped with fresh basil. They make a decent linguine with fresh clams, and their pasta tossed with potato and pesto is just like they do it in Genoa. You can't go wrong with simply prepared grilled items such as fresh salmon or lamb chops served Roman-style with a mint sauce. At lunch they make special *panini* (sandwiches), but they're really more American-style than Italian. Eat inside or on the sidewalk at umbrella-shaded tables. ♦ Italian ♦ M-Th 11:30AM-10PM; F-Sa 11:30AM-11PM. 535 Fourth St, Santa Rosa. 523.1171

131 Treehorn Books This bookstore has a good cookbook section, including the complete works of Glen Ellen food writer M.F.K. Fisher, Michele Anna Jordan's affectionate *Cook's Tour of Sonoma,* and books on California wine-country cooking.

♦ M-Sa 10AM-9:30PM; Su noon-6PM. 625 Fourth St, Santa Rosa. 525.1782

132 Copperfield's Annex You'll find lots of reduced-price books, including cookbooks, wine books, and works on travel, gardening, and art. Check out the big mystery section. ♦ M-F 9AM-9PM; Sa 10AM-9PM; Su noon-6PM. Fourth and D Sts, Santa Rosa. 545.5326

133 Ma Stokeld's Old Vic ★★$ Locals come to this popular hangout for live music in the evenings (folk, jazz, rock, or whatever) plus hearty pub grub and good beer and ale. ♦ Daily 11AM-midnight or so. 731 Fourth St, Santa Rosa. 571.7555

133 The Last Record Store Rock, blues, reggae, classical, and world music have all found a home in this must-stop record store. Both new and used recordings are available, much of it on old-fashioned vinyl. ♦ M-F 10AM-8PM; Sa 10AM-6PM. 739 Fourth St, Santa Rosa. 525.1963

134 Matisse ★★★$$$ Though founder **Michael Hirschberg** recently sold the place to concentrate on his Italian restaurant, **Siena,** and new bakery, **Mezzaluna,** chef **Sheila Parrot** plans to stay on for a while. It's sincerely hoped that she does, since her sensual and vibrant cooking is among the best in the wine country—and truly exceptional in terms of price and quality. The prix-fixe menu changes every day, and Parrot gives you easily a half-dozen choices, all very different. The ingredients are top notch and mostly local. Expect to find fresh shiitake and morel mushrooms in puff pastry, pasta sauced with smoked salmon and cream, or Louisiana duck and sausage gumbo. Main courses may include roasted pork loin with chutney, grilled Petaluma duck with rhubarb sauce, or braised Sonoma rabbit, all served with beautifully cooked vegetables. The setting is hardly glamorous—a simple storefront with banquettes, bistro tables, and Matisse posters on the wall—but the service is definitely classy and the attractively priced wine list is a broad-ranging compendium of French and California wines. All nonsmoking. ♦ French/California ♦ M-F 11:30AM-2PM, 6-9:30PM; Sa-Su 6-9:30PM. 620 Fifth St, Santa Rosa. 527.9797

135 Taj Mahal ★★$$ At last—an ethnic restaurant worth recommending in the wine country. **Abdus Salam** has created a lovely ambience in his Indian restaurant, with white walls, pastel tablecloths, and outdoor dining on the broad sidewalk area in front. Since, according to Salam, they eat fish six days a week in Bengal, you'll find a variety of seafood dishes, such as the king prawns cooked with paprika, tomatoes, onions, and herbs or the grilled filet of salmon with Indian spices. He has four fixed menus in addition to the à la carte items. Strict vegetarians can order an entire menu cooked without oil or dairy products, and you can substitute brown rice for white if you like. ♦ Indian ♦ M-Sa 11:30AM-2:30PM, 5-10PM; Su 10:30AM-1:30PM, 4-9PM. 53 Ross St, Santa Rosa. 579.8471

136 Sonoma County Museum Housed in the old Post Office and Federal Building (built in 1909 by **James Knox Taylor**), the county museum has a permanent collection of 19th-century landscape paintings. Other exhibits change frequently, but all relate to

Santa Rosa

Sonoma County and the North Bay. On one visit, you may find an exhibit of Pomo Indian basketry with fine black-and-white photos of the basket-making process, a show of local woodwork, or an exhibit with a Victorian theme. Check the museum gift shop for books on Sonoma history and architecture,

Sonoma County Museum

DRAWING COURTESY E. ROSS PARKERSON

work from local craftspeople, and souvenirs of Sonoma County. ♦ Nominal admission. W-Su 11AM-4PM. 425 Seventh St (B St) Santa Rosa. 579.1500

137 Bay Bottom Beds Have oyster knife, will travel. If you and a few hungry friends can handle a minimum of 50 oysters, order ahead and pick them up at this Santa Rosa supplier. **Lisa Jang** and her husband **Jorge Rebagliati** cultivate their Miyagi oysters (a variety of Pacific oysters originally from Asia) at Preston Point in Tomales Bay. Harvested to order, the oysters are always pristinely fresh. You also can taste them at the Thursday night farmers market (see page 106). Pick up by appointment only; call at least one day ahead. They can ship by overnight UPS. ♦ 966 Borden Villa Dr #103, Santa Rosa. 578.6049

138 Laura Chenel's Chèvre Owner **Laura Chenel,** Sonoma County's queen of goat cheese, began with a love of the country, a herd of goats, and a passion for chèvre (French goat cheese). After apprenticing with several cheese-making families in France, she launched her Sonoma County goat cheese business in 1979 with dainty rounds of snowy, fresh chèvre, sold plain or rolled in herbs, crushed peppercorns, or paprika. She since has added other types of goat cheese: an ash-covered *pyramide*, an aged *crottin* and *tome* (a firm, dry cheese suitable for grating),

Santa Rosa

and other superb examples of the new American tradition of handcrafted cheese. Widely available at cheese shops and fine markets, Chenel's chèvres are an essential element of any California wine-country picnic. If you're interested in seeing how goat cheese is made, she occasionally gives tours of her cheese-making facility; call for an appointment. Mail order available. ♦ 1550 Ridley Ave, Santa Rosa. 575.8888

139 Ristorante Siena ★★★$$$ This Italian restaurant is the brainchild of the founder of Santa Rosa's best French restaurant, **Matisse.** Here **Michael Hirschberg** concentrates on homemade pasta and seafood dishes. Start with *bruschetta* (grilled bread with assorted toppings) or the mussels prepared Roman-style with white wine, garlic, and parsley. Then try the supple fettuccine with pesto, pine nuts, and Asiago or the penne with roasted tomato, grilled eggplant, and a pinch of oregano. Ravioli may turn up stuffed with smoked salmon or goat cheese and served with a dill and caper sauce or a southern Italian caponata (pickled eggplant and onion). The simply grilled fish dishes are always a good bet, as is the calamari *fritti* (fried calamari) with a garlic-infused lemon

sauce. You also can find more familiar dishes such as veal scaloppine cooked with Marsala and mushrooms, a grilled rib eye steak, or Petaluma duck breast in fresh cherry sauce. All the breads come from Hirschberg's latest venture, a bakery next door called **Mezzaluna.** Siena just started serving breakfast, and the lunch menu includes some interesting sandwiches, burgers, and salads (such as roast chicken, pears, and gorgonzola cheese), half a dozen moderately priced pasta dishes, and individual pizzas. If the weather is pleasant, ask for an outdoor table when you make your reservation. Good list of California and Italian wines. ♦ Italian ♦ M 7AM-2PM; Tu-F 7AM-2PM, 5:30-9PM; Sa 5:30-9PM; Su 10AM-2PM. 1229 N. Dutton Ave, Santa Rosa. 578.4511

140 Redwood Empire Ice Arena *Peanuts* cartoonist **Charles Schultz,** one of Santa Rosa's most eminent citizens, came up with the idea for this Olympic-sized ice skating rink. Open since 1969 (rent your skates here or bring your own), the arena stages a yearly ice show, and includes a coffee shop and ice-cream parlor. The flexible design permits the arena to be converted in just a few hours into a concert theater seating 3,000, and headliners such as **Bill Cosby, Helen Reddy,** and the late **Liberace** have appeared here. Fans of Schultz's long-running comic strip will want to visit the gallery next door. ♦ Daily 6AM-10:30PM. 1667 W. Steele Ln, Santa Rosa. 546.7147

140 Snoopy's Gallery & Gift Shop The world's largest collection of Snoopy memorabilia and merchandise is housed here—and Schultz generously permits Charlie Brown, Lucy, Linus, and the rest of the Peanuts gang to hawk their likenesses here, too. Don't miss the collection of his original drawings and personal photos. ♦ Daily 10AM-6PM. 1665 W. Steele Ln, Santa Rosa. 546.3385

141 Doubletree Santa Rosa $$ Part of a large chain, this hotel offers 252 spacious and pleasantly decorated guest rooms and suites, a terrace bar, and an Olympic-sized pool. The restaurant serves adequate California cuisine. ♦ 3555 Round Barn Blvd, Santa Rosa. 253.7555, 800/528.0444

142 Fountaingrove Inn $$ Understated luxury is the theme at this contemporary inn on the old Fountaingrove Ranch. Each of the 85 rooms and suites is decorated with simplicity and taste, featuring custom-designed furniture and attention to details such as soundproofing, separate dressing alcoves, double closets, and work spaces with modem jacks. Suites feature a Jacuzzi and a dining area. There is a beautifully landscaped pool with a waterfall and an outdoor Jacuzzi. Special weekend wine-country packages bring a double room here into the price range of most B&Bs. ♦ 101 Fountaingrove Pkwy, Santa Rosa. 578.6101

Within the Fountaingrove Inn:

Equus Restaurant & Lounge ★★$$$ The hotel restaurant offers an eclectic seasonal menu encompassing men's club standbys such as oysters Rockefeller and lobster bisque along with a Sonoma Valley salad prepared with fresh local greens, a raspberry vinaigrette, and baked brie. The rack of local spring lamb or the mixed grill (lamb chop, veal medallion, and beef filet served with cottage potatoes and vegetables) is perfect to show off a hearty red chosen from their extensive list of Sonoma County wines. ◆ California ◆ Daily 11AM-9:30PM. 578.0149

143 Fountaingrove Country Club Once owned by the pioneering Japanese winemaker **Kanaye Nagasawa,** who added an Asian touch to the landscape with bonsai trees and stone lanterns, this par-72.8, Ted Robinson championship course opened in 1985. Reserve ahead, as it's very popular. ◆ Daily 6:30AM-dusk. 1525 Fountaingrove Pkwy, Santa Rosa. 579.4653

144 Luther Burbank Center for the Arts The three theaters here are used for guest lectures, concerts, and live theater performances by big-name artists such as **Ray Charles, Johnny Mathis,** and **Barbara Mandrell.** ◆ Call for a schedule of events. Hwy 101 (at River Rd) Santa Rosa. 546.3600

145 Vintners Inn $$$ Set in the midst of vineyards, this 44-room luxury inn blends European style with a California wine-country ambience. Rooms are furnished with pine antiques and quilts, but unlike a B&B, you still get first-class room service, a concierge, TV, and phones. The four Spanish-style, two-story buildings with a red-tile roof face an inner courtyard with a fountain. All of the rooms are good-sized, but those on the upper floor get the view. Suites boast a fireplace, a wet bar, and a refrigerator for chilling wine. The inn also has a sun deck and an outdoor whirlpool bath, and serves a Continental breakfast. ◆ 4350 Barnes Rd, Santa Rosa. 575.7350

Within Vintners Inn:

John Ash & Co. ★★★★$$$$ Save up for a meal at this casual-yet-chic wine country enclave with South-western-inspired decor, entrancing vineyard views, and an exciting menu of Sonoma cuisine. Founder John Ash (who is also culinary director of Fetzer Vineyards' Valley Oaks Food & Wine Center in Hopland) pioneered wine-country cuisine, bringing a diversity of influences—French, Italian, Asian, and Southwestern—to bear on Sonoma's bounty of local ingredients. With Ash's top chef, **Jeff Madura,** at the stoves, the restaurant turns out dishes with both imagination and craft. Start with Hog Island

oysters on the half shell, king salmon cured in fresh herbs, lemon, and Buena Vista sherry, or rillette (a country-style pâté made with Petaluma duck instead of the pork or goose more commonly used in France). Main courses are well-conceived, ranging from rabbit braised in wild honey and balsamic vinegar to marinated and grilled tenderloin of pork served in a raspberry vinegar and shallot sauce. The dry-aged sirloin steak in Jack Daniels sauce studded with wild mushrooms is highly recommended. Much attention is paid to the desserts listed on a separate menu, along with coffees, teas, and spirits. The wine list offers a broad range of Sonoma County vintages, as well as a select few from the rest of northern California. A special reserve list includes older vintages of California wines, plus Bordeaux and Burgundies. ◆ California ◆ Tu-Th 11:30AM-2PM, 5:30-9PM (F until 9:30PM); Sa 5:30-9:30PM; Su 10:30AM-2PM, 5:30-9PM. 4330 Barnes Rd, Santa Rosa. 527.7687

146 Sonoma County Airport Fly from San Francisco, San Jose, or Los Angeles to this county airport served by **American Eagle** and **United Express.** Rental cars are available from Avis and Hertz. ◆ 2200 Airport Blvd. 542.3139

147 Petrini's Market This upscale supermarket features real butchers (how often do you see that anymore?) and a good produce section, and its extensive deli runs along one entire wall—a veritable picnic

supply emporium with barbecued chicken and ribs to go, local and imported cheeses, cold cuts, custom-made sandwiches, and breads from **Costeaux French Bakery** in Healdsburg. Fair selection of Sonoma County wines. ◆ M-Sa 8AM-9PM; Su 8AM-8PM. 2751 Fourth St (Farmers Ln) Santa Rosa. 526.2080

Flamingo

147 Flamingo Resort Hotel and Fitness Center $$ This landmark 1957 hotel on the outskirts of Santa Rosa was recently overhauled and renamed the Flamingo Resort Hotel. They couldn't do much about the architecture (call it nostalgic fifties), but the 137 rooms and suites have been spruced up and the heated Olympic-sized pool is now surrounded by lawns and five tennis courts. Ask about special getaway packages that include dinner in the hotel restaurant and golf, ballooning, or horseback riding. The resort is unique in offering comfortable accommodations at a moderate price with access to a spa and fitness center next door. ♦ 2777 Fourth St (Farmers Ln) Santa Rosa. 545.8530, 800/848.8300

Adjacent to the Flamingo Resort Hotel:

Montecito Heights Health and Racquet Club Guests at the Flamingo can use this state-of-the-art fitness center with weight room, aerobics studio, sauna, steam room, and whirlpool facilities. The club has basketball and volleyball courts and a lighted jogging path for die-hard runners. Massages are also available. ♦ M-F 6AM-10PM; Sa-Su 8AM-7PM. 526.0529

148 Lisa Hemenway's ★★★$$ A graduate of John Ash & Co, Santa Rosa's top restaurant, chef/owner Lisa Hemenway features items from the mesquite grill, including burgers, fresh fish, and daily specialties such as grilled halibut or pan-seared *ono* with pickled vegetables and a ginger beurre blanc. This light, airy restaurant looks very European with its sidewalk seating area, and it's definitely a surprise to find such a savvy restaurant in the midst of a shopping center. Dinner emphasizes dishes like duck in cherry sauce and daily pasta specials such as oriental ravioli in a sesame vinaigrette. You can count on Hemenway's Hungarian nut torte. ♦ M-Sa 11:30AM-2:30PM, 5:30-9:30PM. Montgomery Village, 714 Village Ct (Sonoma Ave and Hwy 12) Santa Rosa. 526.5111

148 Lisa Hemenway's Tote Cuisine ★★$$ Put together a wine-country picnic at this

Santa Rosa deli, a spin-off of Lisa Hemenway's more formal restaurant next door. You can order a set box-lunch menu or create your own as you browse. It's all eclectic fare—and a very welcome change from the standard deli menu. Fill your picnic basket with chile-spiked smoked chicken empanadas, Cajun chicken wings, Greek dolmas, and the *torta milanese*, a savory pie layered with vegetables, meats, and cheese. ♦ M 8:30AM-5PM; Tu-Sa 8:30AM-7PM. Montgomery Village, 710 Village Ct (Sonoma Ave and Hwy 12) Santa Rosa. 578.0898; fax 578.5736

149 Farmers Market The Veterans Memorial Building is the site of a lively Saturday-morning open-air market. Bring your own shopping bag and stock up on farm-fresh eggs, flowers, produce, and herb and vegetable starts for the garden. ♦ W, Sa 9AM-noon. Veterans Memorial Bldg parking lot, Brookwood Ave (Hwy 12) Santa Rosa. 538.7023

150 Bennett Valley Golf Course This 18-hole municipal golf course (par 72) is shaded by trees and surrounded by mountain views. Open to the public for individual, club, and tournament play. ♦ Daily dawn-dusk. 3330 Yulupa Ave, Santa Rosa. 528.3673

151 Spring Lake Park This state park has campsites, restrooms, shower facilities, hiking and equestrian trails, and a 72-acre lake. It's open for swimming and boating during the summer months, and is stocked with catfish, black bass, trout, and bluegill for year-round fishing. Launch your own boat or rent a sailboat, canoe, or rowboat for a modest hourly charge; the lake is a popular spot for windsurfing, too. For more information, call the ranger. ♦ East side of Santa Rosa between Howarth Park and Annadel State Park. Access to the camping side of the lake is available via Newanga Ave. 539.8092, for the campground call 539.8082

152 Howarth Memorial Park Pack up that fishing pole and cooking gear and head for Lake Ralphine in this city-owned and -operated park to catch some lunch—catfish, black bass, trout, and bluegill. The park has picnic and barbecue facilities so you can cook it right here. After-lunch activities include a hiking trail and, for the kids, a playground, a merry-go-round, pony rides, a miniature train ride, and an animal farm. Call for information on renting paddleboats, rowboats, and sailboats. ♦ Daily 6AM-dusk; merry-go-round and other rides (fee) W-Su 11AM-5PM. Summerfield Rd, access from Sonoma Ave or Montgomery Dr, Santa Rosa. 524.5115

153 Rincon Cyclery Bicycles to rent by the hour, the day, or the week. Take one of the new 18-speed mountain bikes up to a trail in nearby Annadel, Sugar Loaf Ridge, or Jack London state parks. Helmets and bike racks are also available. ♦ Daily 10AM-6PM. 4927-H Sonoma Hwy, Santa Rosa. 538.0868

154 Melitta Station Inn $$ Near Annadel State Park on the winding country road that served as the old Sonoma Hwy is a six-room B&B in a restored turn-of-the-century train station. The comfortable inn is filled with American folk art and antiques. Five of the six rooms have private baths, and a full country breakfast (juice, fruit, muffins or bread, and an omelet or another main course) is included. The location, at the head of the Valley of the Moon, is ideal for winery touring by bike or car. ♦ 5850 Melitta Rd, Santa Rosa. 538.7712

155 De Loach Vineyards Noted for their Russian River Chardonnay, **Cecil** and **Christine De Loach** make wines in an easy, accessible style. Their top-of-the-line O.F.S. (for "our finest selection") is a rich, barrel-fermented Chardonnay. They also make Sauvignon Blanc, Fumé Blanc, Gewürztraminer, and White Zinfandel, along with red Zinfandel and Pinot Noir. A few picnic tables are set out with views of the vineyard. ♦ Tasting and sales daily 10AM-4:30PM; tours by appt. 1791 Olivet Rd, Santa Rosa. 526.9111

Building a Better Corkscrew

The humble corkscrew seems to be one common household utensil designers are always attempting to improve. There are dozens of models in use today, ranging from the simple and functional to the whimsical and elaborate. (For an overview of the history of the corkscrew, visit **Brother Timothy's** corkscrew collection at Christian Brothers-Greystone Cellars [see page 49] in St. Helena.) Most corkscrews, in fact, will pull that cork out just fine, but some are harder to use than others. Here's a sampling of some of the most popular models:

The simplest corkscrew is this old standby, the type featured on the Swiss army knife. Center the tip of the corkscrew over the cork, and screw it in clockwise, trying as much as possible to drive it in at a vertical angle. Get a good hold on the bottle—and pull. The cork comes out with a resounding pop—a joyful sound to wine lovers.

This model features moveable wings that look a little like flying buttresses. As you screw down through the cork, the wings slowly rise. Push down on them simultaneously and the cork rises straight out of the bottle.

The handy waiter's pocket corkscrew is small and compact—perfect for picnics. The lever attached to the end of the corkscrew is used to help ease out the cork.

In this clever and eminently portable version, no screw is involved. Instead, two narrow, flexible blades are inserted on either side of the cork (between the cork and the neck of the bottle). It takes some practice to master the rocking motion needed to insert the blades all the way, but this type is better for easing out a damaged, crumbled cork. Pull with a slight twisting motion and the cork comes right out.

The Screwpull is an ingenious design that features a long Teflon-coated screw that slips easily through the dense cork. As you turn it clockwise, the cork slowly rises; no exertion is needed. This is the one foolproof corkscrew. Widely available at wineshops, it comes in both a waiter's version and a tabletop model.

Russian River Valley

To the north and west of Santa Rosa is Sonoma County's fastest-growing wine region, the Russian River Valley, a remarkably diverse landscape of gentle hillsides, apple orchards, sandy river beaches, and prime redwood country. This region is so large, in fact, that it is divided into several subvalleys, formed by the Russian River and its tributaries, each with its own microclimate and appellation.

Explored by the Russians based at **Fort Ross** in the 1840s, the Russian River Valley is much less compact than either the Sonoma or Napa valleys. More than 50 wineries are spread out in many directions, and there is no one wine route to follow; instead, a network of small country roads connects the smaller valleys and appellations of this wine region. This makes much of the area uncrowded and uncongested, so you can make your trip somewhat impromptu.

The **Alexander Valley** extends from Cloverdale south to Healdsburg along the Russian River, which takes a more or less parallel course here with Hwy 101 to the west. This stretch of river offers some of the best canoeing in the area, where you can drift past prime vineyards of Chardonnay and Cabernet. The valley is named for **Cyrus Alexander**, an early settler from Pennsylvania who cultivated grapes and other crops here in the mid-19th century. In the last 20 years, several top-notch wineries have been built in this scenic valley.

To the west is **Dry Creek Valley**, bracketed by serpentine Lake Sonoma to the north and the Russian River to the south. Scattered along its length are a number of small wine producers (many of them require appointments to visit—and it's well worth taking the time to do so). The Dry Creek Valley is first and foremost Zinfandel country, producing some of California's finest. You'll also encounter some excellent Sauvignon Blanc along the way.

Just past the southern tip of Dry Creek Valley the river heads west to the sea and the Russian River appellation, prime territory for Pinot Noir and Burgundian-style wines. Westside Road, which runs south from Healdsburg to meet River Road, is an entrancing country drive dotted with small family wineries, old hop-drying kilns, and a couple of farms where you can buy homegrown fruit, vegetables, and freshly laid eggs. River Road cuts through the redwoods to **Guerneville,** and just before arriving at the town, you'll encounter the **Korbel Champagne Cellars** and a heritage rose garden with more than 300 varieties of old-fashioned roses.

The Russian River Valley also includes two smaller wine appellations within its boundaries: the **Chalk Hill** area to the east, which produces wonderful Chardonnay and Merlot, and the cooler **Green Valley** toward Sebastopol to the southwest, which boasts ideal growing conditions for Pinot Noir and Chardonnay.

The diminutive town of **Healdsburg** is the hub of the Russian River Valley, with the three major subvalleys fanning out from its boundaries. At its heart is Healdsburg Plaza, a Spanish-style square that resembles Sonoma's famous plaza in miniature. You can swim in the Russian River at Healdsburg Memorial Beach, rent a bicycle, or go kayaking on the river. Pack up a picnic lunch, because once on the wine trail, there are few places to eat and it can be a long way back into town. Healdsburg offers the most accommodations in the area, but you can also stay in Victorian bed-and-breakfast inns in **Geyserville** and **Cloverdale** to the north.

You could also make the Russian River resort area near Guerneville your base. It offers a number of family resorts and comfortable bed-and-breakfasts along with sunny river beaches and virgin redwood forests. **Armstrong Woods** is one of the largest preserves of ancient trees in California, and the rugged Sonoma Coast is just a short drive away, making the Russian River Valley one of the most dramatic and appealing wine regions in California.

Windsor

Early settler **Hiram Lewis** thought the landscape in this area resembled the English countryside around Windsor Castle in England, hence the name of this sleepy little township that was established in 1855. For wine-country visitors, Windsor offers a country B&B, a waterslide park, golfing, and kayaking.

156 Martinelli Winery Located on the scenic road to Guerneville and the Russian River, this family-owned winery housed in a rustic, old hops-drying barn produces Chardonnay, Sauvignon Blanc, Gewürztraminer, White Zinfandel, and more, all of which can be tasted here. They also stock a good selection of picnic supplies and local food products. A second barn across the way is home to an art gallery showcasing Sonoma County artists. Picnic area. ♦ Tasting and sales: daily 10AM-5PM; tours by appt. Art gallery: Tu-Su 11AM-4PM. 3360 River Rd, Windsor. 525.0570

156 Z Moore Winery You'll sample Chardonnay, Gewürztraminer, and Zinfandel from a winemaker with experience at Milano and Hop Kiln. Those are the serious wines. Winemaker **Daniel Moore** breaks out a different label for his more lighthearted wines; it's called Quaff. ♦ Tasting and sales daily 10AM-5PM; tours by appt. 3364 River Rd, Windsor. 544.3555

157 Sonoma-Cutrer Site of the US Open and the World Championship Croquet tournaments every year, Sonoma-Cutrer is just as serious about croquet as it is about wine. The winery's three vineyard-designated Chardonnays created by winemaker **William Bonetti** are found on the best wine lists worldwide. Les Pierres is their top wine. ♦ Tasting, sales, and tours by appt. 4401 Slusser Rd, Windsor. 528.1181

American wine is made in more than 30 states, and California's share is about 72 percent.

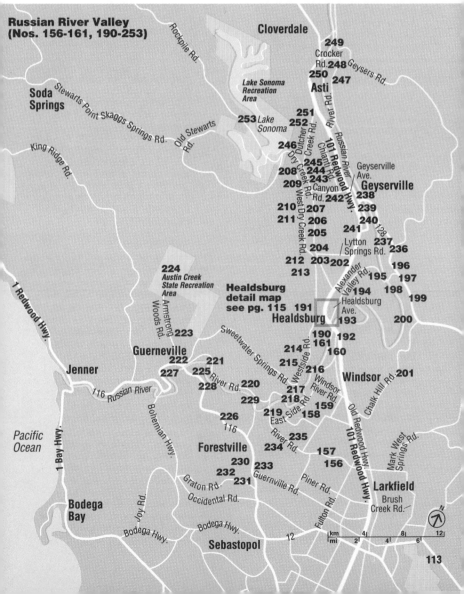

Russian River Valley (Nos. 156-161, 190-253)

113

158 Windsor Golf Club This fairly new 18-hole golf course sits on 120 acres in a country setting of gentle hills. Par 72. ♦ Daily 6:30AM-dusk. Closed the first Monday of every month. 6555 Skylane Blvd, Windsor. 838.PUTT

159 Windsor Waterworks and Slides No turning back now—it's all the way down a 42-foot drop through 400 feet of tunnels, slopes, and hairpin curves to the pool at the very bottom. That's the thrill of the Doom Flume and three other ingenious waterslides. Don't worry; pint-sized aficionados will offer lots of advice on how to get the maximum effect. If you'd rather just swim, the Waterworks also has a large pool and a children's wading pool, plus horsehoe pits, Ping-Pong tables, an electronic game arcade, and a snack bar. Bring your own supplies for a picnic or barbecue. Special weekday rates from 4 to 7PM. ♦ Daily 10AM-dusk, June-Aug; hours vary May-Sep; closed in winter. 8225 Conde Ln (near Windsor River Rd) Windsor. 838.7760/7360

160 California Rivers When veteran canoer **Ann Dwyer** took up kayaking, she quickly became frustrated with the kayak designs then available. No problem—the 65-year-old grandmother simply designed and manufactured her own. Dwyer's Kiwi kayaks are small and light, versatile enough to be safe in all sorts of waters. At her headquarters in Windsor, rent canoes, kayaks, or bicycles by the day or weekend; she offers a discount on weekdays. In addition, Dwyer sells accessories such as waterproof gear bags, sailing rigs, knee pads, and coveralls (look for her own Dragonfly Designs). The store also takes reservations for Kiwi kayak trips and classes (see below).

Russian River Valley

♦ M-Tu, Th-Su 9:30AM-5:30PM. 10070 Old Redwood Hwy, Windsor. 838.7787

Within California Rivers:

KiWi KaYaK co.

Kiwi Kayak Co. **Ann Dwyer** offers day trips and classes for kayakers of all levels. For her weekly Wednesday on the Water series (rated easy), she picks a different spot for kayaking. It could be a section of the Russian River, Tomales Bay, or even the Napa River; sign up for one or several of them. Other easy excursions scheduled for summer nights include paddling on the Petaluma River, Bodega Bay, Russian River, or Lake Sonoma. And once a month throughout the summer Dwyer leads half-day trips along a wild and scenic stretch of the Russian River. Before getting out on the river she'll give you paddling instruction and tips on staying afloat; count on seeing basking turtles, river

ducks, and great blue herons along the way. The trip ends up with a picnic lunch outside Hop Kiln Winery's tasting room on Westside Rd. Also sign up for half-day classes titled "Kayaking for Timid Souls and Others" and day-long classes on more advanced river running and safety skills. Brochure available. ♦ 838.7787

161 Country Meadow Inn $$ Only a few minutes from downtown Healdsburg, this two-story, brown-shingle Victorian farmhouse, now a country bed-and-breakfast inn, was once part of a large farm that stretched to the Russian River. The remaining six-and-one-half acre estate is surrounded by meadows and rolling hills; innkeepers **Sandy** and **Barry Weber** have seeded a hillside with wildflowers and planted an herb garden and strawberry patch. A kitchen garden provides the produce for the three-course country breakfast (fresh or baked fruit, several home-baked pastries, oatmeal-walnut pancakes, or maybe a frittata made with eggs from their own chickens). The inn has five guest rooms, all with private baths, and some with fireplaces and/or whirlpool baths. The pleasant Victorian-era decor features antique furniture and period fabrics. Most romantic is the new garden suite with a king-sized bed, separate sitting area with a fireplace, a sunny atrium, a double Jacuzzi, private entrance, and deck. Guests can cool off in the 16-by-30-foot pool at the edge of a vineyard. No smoking. ♦ 11360 Old Redwood Hwy (Eastside Rd) Windsor. 431.1276

Healdsburg

This town lies at the convergence of three famous viticultural regions—the Alexander, Dry Creek, and Russian River valleys—and there is something here to please every wine-country visitor. Many come for a lazy trek down the Russian River in a canoe rented from **W.C. "Bob" Trowbridge.** Others prefer to cap off a string of visits to local wineries with dinner at restaurants such as **Jacob Horner** or a snack at the **Downtown Bakery & Creamery.** And for history buffs, a stop at the restored Spanish-style **Healdsburg Plaza** and the town's museum is a must.

162 Healdsburg Memorial Beach Park Popular beach and swimming lagoon created by a temporary dam that is erected every Memorial Day and comes down just after Labor Day weekend. Year-round the county park features fishing and canoeing; they have a number of riverside picnic sites, too. ♦ Nominal fee. Daily 7AM-8PM, Memorial Day to Labor Day; 7AM-dusk, the rest of the year. 13839 Old Redwood Hwy, Healdsburg. 433.1625

163 W.C. "Bob" Trowbridge For more than 30 years, Trowbridge has been renting his fleet of silver metal canoes for unguided trips along the Russian River. According to the veteran canoer, this is the most popular canoeing river in the world—and on summer weekends it certainly appears to be. Sign up for any of eight reasonably priced, one-day canoe trips; Trowbridge provides free transportation back to your car. Canoe all the way from Cloverdale to Trowbridge's Alexander Valley Campground or the town of Guerneville, or choose shorter segments in between. One of the most scenic routes starts at the Alexander Valley Campground and winds back to Healdsburg through the heart of the valley and its vineyards, past blue heron rookeries, secret picnic spots, and swimming holes. You don't need to know much about canoeing to set off down the river safely, but bring plenty of sunblock and a hat (sunburns are the biggest hazard). On weekends, sign up for Trowbridge's inexpensive chicken-and-steak buffet barbecue. And if camping along the river sounds appealing, the campground to one side of the Alexander Valley Bridge is an idyllic location, but reserve early. Canoes are rented to swimmers only; reserve ahead, especially on the weekends, and plan to be on the river by 1PM. Buffet barbecue 4 to 7PM weekends. Stop by to pick up a brochure

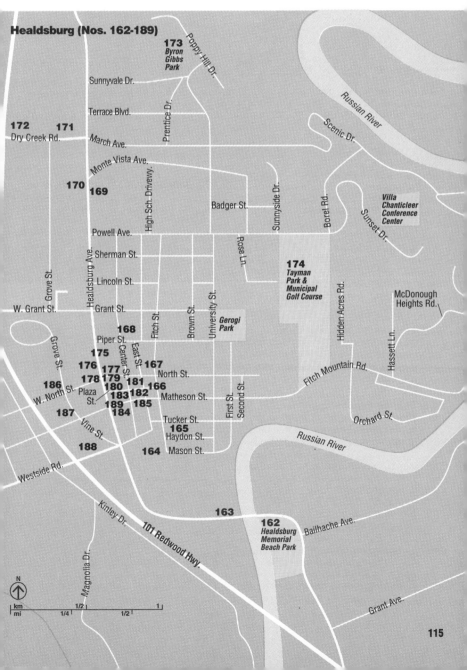

Healdsburg (Nos. 162-189)

listing all the launch sites and locations of their two campgrounds. ♦ Registration daily 8AM-1PM, Mar.-Nov. 20 Healdsburg Ave, Healdsburg. 433.7247

164 White Oak Vineyards Former Alaskan fisherman **Bill Myers** pulled up stakes and opened this winery in 1981. From this functional building in downtown Healdsburg, Myers and winemaker **Paul Brasset** produce Chardonnay, Sauvignon Blanc, Alexander Valley Cabernet, and Dry Creek Valley Zinfandel. ♦ Tasting and sales daily 11AM-4PM. 208 Haydon St, Healdsburg. 433.8429

165 The Haydon House $$ It seems like another era when you walk up to the white picket fence and find guests chatting on the wraparound veranda of this 1912 Queen Anne Victorian (pictured above). The eight rooms have a tranquil ambience, with sunlight filtered through lace curtains, gleaming wood floors, and pastel country prints. Six of the rooms are in the main house; the two least expensive are upstairs and share a hall bath. The **Rose Room** has a private bath and a half-canopied bed covered with an antique crocheted coverlet. The two largest rooms, both in the two-story, Victorian-style cottage behind, feature vaulted ceilings and private baths with whirlpool tubs; the **Pine Room** has

Russian River Valley

a four-poster bed with a Battenberg lace canopy, while the **Victorian Room** is decorated in wicker and Ralph Lauren prints. The full country breakfast may include fresh fruit, homemade muffins, and strawberry crepes. ♦ 321 Haydon St, Healdsburg. 433.5228

166 The Healdsburg Museum Housed in the former 1910 Healdsburg Carnegie Library building, the museum displays the town's historical collection, much of it donated by local families. Permanent displays showcase the culture of the area's Pomo Indians, the Mexican land grant era, the town's founding, and the notorious Westside squatters' wars. They've even managed to find an 1892 people-drawn fire engine. Special exhibits highlighting 19th-century tools, weapons, costumes, and other treasures of the collection change several times a year. At Christmastime, the focus is the annual antique toy and doll exhibit. Check the museum gift shop for reproductions of old-time toys, replicas of Indian crafts, and books

on local history and lore. ♦ Tu-Sa noon-5PM. 221 Matheson St (Fitch St) Healdsburg. 431.3325

167 Camellia Inn $$ **Del Lewand** and her husband **Ray** have been running this elegant B&B in the center of town for just over 10 years. Horticulturist **Luther Burbank** was a family friend of the former owner's, and the camellias (more than 50 varieties) surrounding the house are attributed to him. The Lewands have painted the 1869 Italianate Victorian a lovely pale pink trimmed in cream and a deeper rose; two tall pines flank the entryway, and the low stone wall in front is bordered with roses. The house features a double parlor with a fireplace framed in Minton tiles depicting the seven ages of man from Shakespeare's *As You Like It*. Rooms are named after camellia varieties and are furnished with good antiques and oriental carpets. A favorite of many guests is the **Tiffany Room**, papered in Bradbury & Bradbury hand-silk-screened wallpaper in a pattern of scallop shells, with a queen-sized four-poster bed, a gas fireplace, and a whirlpool tub for two. The two least expensive rooms, upstairs in the main house, share the hall bath. Out back, the swimming pool is surrounded with shade trees and a grape arbor. Buffet breakfast. ♦ 211 North St, Healdsburg. 433.8182

168 Sonoma County Wine Library This special collection at the Healdsburg branch of the Sonoma County Library brings together a wide range of materials on wine-related subjects. The library subscribes to more than 70 periodicals and numbers well over 2,500 books in its collection, ranging from technical works on viticulture and enology to books on wine appreciation and cooking. There's a file containing current information on county wineries. ♦ M-Th 9:30AM-9PM; F-Sa 9:30AM-6PM. Healdsburg Regional Library, Center and Piper Sts, Healdsburg. 433.3772

169 Belle de Jour Inn $$/$$$ Take the drive just across the road from Simi Winery (see page 117) up a hill to this serene retreat overlooking rolling hills to the east. Innkeepers **Tom** and **Brenda Hearn** live in the 1873 Italianate Victorian in front. They've turned the caretaker's cottage into a very private suite with a king-sized bed swathed in Battenberg lace, a Franklin stove, a whirlpool bath for two, and hotel conveniences such as hair dryers and a refrigerator. Three other cottages are nestled alongside, each with a private entrance and view. The **Terrace Room** offers a king-sized bed, a double whirlpool tub, hardwood floors, and a spare, contemporary decor. The snug **Morning Room**, the smallest of the four cottages, has a queen-sized bed, paneled walls, green shutters opening onto a serene country view, a wood-burning stove, and a new shower/steam bath. A full breakfast is served on the deck of the main house, or you can have a breakfast basket set outside your door. The fresh, unfussy decor and the privacy make a welcome alternative to Victorian orthodoxy. ♦ 16276 Healdsburg Ave, Healdsburg. 433.7892

Within the Belle de Jour Inn:

Belle de Jour Vintage Car Tours Sign up for three-hour, chauffered backroads and winery tours in a 1923 Star touring car through the Alexander, Dry Creek, or Russian River valleys—with a catered wine-country lunch to wind up the festivities. Itineraries can be custom tailored to your interests. The Star can also be reserved on an hourly basis (two-hour minimum). ♦ 433.7892

170 Simi Winery Winemaker **Zelma Long** is one of the best. Her regular and reserve wines are well worth seeking out, and the tasting room in Simi Winery (pictured above) will let you sample most of them. Reserve offerings of older vintages of Chardonnay and Cabernet are for sale, too, including a collection of five different bottles in a specially designed wooden box. The tours are well run and informative. Picnic facilities. ♦ Tasting and sales daily 10AM-4:30PM; tours daily 11AM, 1 and 3PM. 16275 Healdsburg Ave, Healdsburg. 433.6981

171 Tip Top Liquor Warehouse Great selection of Sonoma County wines. Shipping available, too. ♦ M-Th, Su 8AM-8PM; F-Sa 8AM-10PM. 90 Dry Creek Rd, Healdsburg. 431.0841

172 Best Western Dry Creek Inn $ A contemporary inn with 103 rooms (choose from a king-sized or two queen-sized beds) and a vaguely Spanish-style decor on a busy street not far from the freeway. If standard comforts such as cable TV and a heated pool are more important than wine-country ambience, this is the place. Continental breakfast included. Ask about special midweek rates. ♦ 198 Dry Creek Rd, Healdsburg. 433.0300, 800/222.KRUG; fax 433.0300

173 Byron Gibbs Park This two-and-one-half acre park has picnic tables and a children's playground. ♦ Hours vary. 1520 Prentice Dr, Healdsburg

Tomb paintings from ancient Thebes depict the grape harvest and winemaking.

Restaurants/Clubs: Red   Hotels: Blue
Shops/ ♥ Outdoors: Green   Wineries/Sights: Black

174 Tayman Park Municipal Golf Course This nine-hole golf course set on 60 acres overlooks the town. Founded in 1922 as the private Healdsburg Country Club by **Colonel C.E. Tayman,** it is now a public golf course. Par 35. ♦ Daily 6:30AM-8PM. 927 S. Fitch Mtn Rd, Healdsburg. 433.4275

175 Western Boot ★$$ You can tuck in down-home portions of steak, ribs, chicken, and seafood at this family-owned restaurant. ♦ Steakhouse ♦ M-Th, Su 11:30AM-2PM, 5-9:30PM; F-Sa 11:30AM-2PM, 5-10PM. 9 Mitchell Ln, Healdsburg. 433.6362

176 Costeaux French Bakery In their newly enlarged premises, Costeaux stacks the display counters with their signature fruit tarts covered with latticed, sugared strips, lemon curd tarts, and dainty pecan tartlets. But it's really their sourdough bread, strawberry-rhubarb pie, and tall bittersweet-chocolate mocha cake that draw raves from loyal fans. The sandwiches on their own bread are fairly standard, but handy for a picnic. Weekend evenings, they offer simple dinner fare such as salads, chili, and pizza at tables set out along the sidewalk. You take your chances with the espresso, though; they just can't seem to get it right.

Russian River Valley

♦ M-W 6AM-6PM; Th-Sa 6AM-9PM; Su 6AM-3PM. 417 Healdsburg Ave, Healdsburg. 433.1913

177 The Raven Theater The flicks change every week at this movie theater, and you can eat before the show at the cafe next door, the Ravenous Raven. ♦ Daily 6 and 8:30PM; matinee on weekends. 115 North St, Healdsburg. 433.5448

177 Ravenous Raven ★$ A great little cafe with an appealing mix of salads, sandwiches, and light entrées. The Sunday breakfast is a nice treat. ♦ American ♦ M, W-F 11:30AM-2:30PM, 5:30-9:30PM; Sa 11:30AM-2:30PM, 5:30-10PM; Su 9AM-8PM. 117 North St, Healdsburg. 431.1770

178 Kendall-Jackson Wine Country Store This is the tasting outpost for Lake County's **Kendall-Jackson** winery and **Cambria Vineyards.** In addition to wine, the store stocks glasses, cookbooks, wine books, and a slew of tempting California gourmet products. ♦ Daily 10AM-5PM. 337 Healdsburg Ave, Healdsburg. 433.9463

PALLADIO

178 Evans/Designs Gallery Evans is the world's largest producer of *raku*, a type of ceramic ware invented by the Japanese potter Chojiro in the 16th century. In this process, the fired pot is removed from a red-hot kiln and heavily smoked, producing a unique, one-of-a-kind glaze. Founder **Tony Evans** and his team of potters have managed to turn raku into production pottery, no mean feat. The decorative pieces are glazed in extravagant colors and metallics; some verge on the gaudy. At any rate, this shop is actually Evans Ceramics' outlet, selling prototypes, seconds, and discontinued stock at reduced prices. ♦ Daily 10AM-5PM. Willow Creek Plaza, 355 Healdsburg Ave, Healdsburg. 433.2502

HEALDSBURG CHARCUTERIE & DELICATESSEN

178 Healdsburg Charcuterie & Delicatessen ★$ In this contemporary deli decorated with bay wreaths and fruit-crate labels, order sandwiches to go or settle in at one of the wooden tables along the big picture window. They roast their own turkey and beef; the homemade meat loaf and the chicken salad are also good bets. They offer a few specials daily and, on Friday night, a supper menu that includes a couple of soups

Russian River Valley

and half-a-dozen entrées, including beef Zinfandel, pork chop *charcutière*, sautéed salmon with lemon butter, *gnocchi* al pesto, and pasta *bolognese*. To take home or thaw out for the grill: frozen sausages from Sonoma Sausage Co. ♦ M, Sa 10AM-5PM; Tu-F 10AM-7PM; Su noon-4PM. 335 Healdsburg Ave, Healdsburg. 431.7213

179 Noah's Ark Owner **Dave Seigle** has collected an engaging menagerie in this animal-kingdom theme store. The critters come in all sorts of guises, from life-sized carvings and stuffed animals to jewelry, puppets, and puzzles. The hippo in the back corner turns into a sofa and the counter up front is shaped like a Sonoma County cow (both available by special order). ♦ M-Sa 9:30AM-5:30PM; Su 10AM-5PM. 320 Healdsburg Ave, Healdsburg. 431.0144

179 Palladio Behind the post-modernist facade lies a stylish design shop specializing in country and garden furniture including wicker chairs, weathered armoires, and stone and iron tables designed by the owners. They have smaller pieces, too, including interesting lamps, willow baskets, and ornate étagères for plants. ♦ Tu-Su 11AM-5PM. 324 Healdsburg Ave, Healdsburg. 431.3325

179 Vintage Antiques Browse for flower vases, cut crystal, silver-back mirrors, and other remembrances of times past. Another place to check again and again in hopes of a fabulous find. ♦ M-Sa 11AM-5:30PM; Su 11AM-4PM. 328 Healdsburg Ave, Healdsburg. 433.7461

179 Off the Plaza You just may find the perfect shade for a favorite lamp in fabric or glass at this specialized shop. Bring in that broken old lamp for repair; they'll even turn vases or other likely candidates into unique tabletop lamps. ♦ M-Sa 10:30AM-5PM; Su 11AM-3PM. 334 Healdsburg Ave, Healdsburg. 433.1906

180 Little Darlins' Diner ★$ A sweet darlin' of a diner decked out in yellow and black. Slide into one of the comfy booths for eggs prepared any which way, home fries, and sausage—maybe even a short stack on the side. At lunch opt for a burger and fries washed down with one of their heroic milk shakes. ♦ M-W, Su 7AM-4PM; Th-Sa 7AM-9PM. 109 Plaza St, Healdsburg. 431.8181

180 Samba Java ★★$$$ **Colleen McGlynn**, who formerly worked at the popular **Stars** restaurant in San Francisco, is the chef at this new restaurant that has taken over the space where the Plaza Grill once reigned. She's brought a breath of fresh air to the sometimes staid wine country with her menus based on Caribbean flavors. The decor picks up the same theme with vibrant paintings, galvanized metal tables, and brightly colored tile accents. Her small yet imaginative menu changes daily and features dishes such as chilled mango and avocado salad, fried plantains, Cuban chicken in citrus and roast garlic, and curried pork loin. McGlynn and co-owner **Jim Neeley** also offer an array of interesting lunchtime antipasta dishes and great burgers and sandwiches served on **Downtown Bakery & Creamery** buns and breads. At breakfast— and this is a must—you can delve into freshly baked pastries such as the divine coconut-sour cream coffee cake or fresh berry muffins. ♦ Caribbean/American ♦ Tu-Su 7:30-11:30AM, noon-3PM, 6:30-9:30PM; F-Sa 6:30-9:30PM. 109 A Plaza St, Healdsburg. 433.5282

181 Terra A little of this, a little of that: Terra is a combination produce store, crafts gallery, wine-tasting bar, and nursery. Look for the products from Ironwood Ridge Ranch, a Sonoma County ranch that specializes in herbs, tomatoes, hot chiles, berries, and flowers grown by intensive French methods. They make their own line of salsas, chutneys, and herb-infused wine vinegars. Out front, you'll find starts for heirloom herbs and vegetables; inside, baskets hold organic baby salad greens. The crafts consist of ceramics and hand-painted silk kimonos, and you'll find the wine-tasting bar all the way in the back. ♦ M-Sa 11AM-5:30PM; Su 11AM-4PM. 324 Center St, Healdsburg. 433.6909

Wine Varieties

Table Wines

Varietals

Red	White
Barbera	Chardonnay
Cabernet Franc	Chenin Blanc
Cabernet Sauvignon	French Colombard
Gamay	Gewürztraminer
Gamay Beaujolais	Johannisberg Riesling
Merlot	Moscato de Canelli
Pinot Noir	Pinot Blanc
Ruby Cabernet	Sauvignon Blanc
Syrah	Sémillon
Zinfandel	White Riesling

Generics

Red	White
Burgundy	Chablis
Chianti	Moselle
Claret	Rhine
Red Table Wine	Sauterne
Rosé	White Table Wine

Appetizer Wines
Madeira
Sherry
White Vermouth

Dessert Wines
Angelica
Cream Sherry
Marsala
Muscat de Frontigan
Muscatel
Port
Tokay

Sparkling Wines
Brut (Driest)
Extra-Sec (Extra Dry)
Sec (Dry)
Demi-Sec (Semi-Dry)
Doux (Sweet)

Within Terra:

Plasberg Wines Here's where you can sample and buy wines from Pacific Port Cellars, Zinful Cellars (makers of Original Zin), Ironwood Ridge Wines, and 10 other local wineries. With the purchase of a souvenir glass, you can taste any six of more than three dozen wines. Case discounts and shipping available. ♦ Same hours as above. 433.2252, 800/487.9463

182 El Farolito $ The standard Mexican menu offers no surprises, but everything from the tamales and enchiladas to the burritos and vegetarian tacos is well prepared and reasonably priced. They've got a nice list of Mexican beers, too. Takeout. ♦ Mexican ♦ Daily 10AM-9PM. 128 Plaza St, Healdsburg. 433.2807

182 William Wheeler Winery Behind the walls of the storefront tasting room is a working winery, founded in 1970 by **Bill** and **Ingrid Wheeler.** The grapes come from the Wheeler's Dry Creek Valley ranch, where 35 of the 175 acres are planted in vines. Winemaker **Julia Iantosca** focuses on moderately priced varietals, including Sauvignon Blanc, Chardonnay, White Zinfandel, and a Dry Creek Valley Cabernet; her latest effort is a Rhône-style red. ♦ Tasting and sales daily 11AM-4PM. 130 Plaza St, Healdsburg. 433.8786

183 Healdsburg Plaza Crisscrossed with walkways and shaded by redwood and palm

Russian River Valley

trees, this lovely plaza that was laid out in 1856 features a gazebo at one end and is the focus of special events throughout the year, including summer concerts, a May wine-tasting festival, and an annual Christmas-tree lighting ceremony. Like Sonoma's historic Spanish-style square, the plaza is bordered by shops and restaurants. ♦ Bounded by Healdsburg Ave and Center St, Matheson and Plaza Sts in Healdsburg

183 The Salame Tree Deli Step up to the counter to order sandwiches to go. You can also order by the pound and make your own on bread from the Downtown Bakery & Creamery. For more substantial picnic fare, they have barbecue chickens (while supplies last). ♦ M-Sa 8AM-7PM; Su 9AM-6PM. 304 Center St, Healdsburg. 433.7224

183 Animal Town This unique children's store features educational toys and games that encourage cooperative play rather than competition. And surprise, surprise, they turn out to be more fun than pedantic. Even grownups might like the reproductions of animal rubber-stamp sets from the late 1800s, the flower and leaf presses, and the ingenious nature games and puzzles. No time to shop? Pick up their extensive mail-order catalog. ♦ M-Sa 10AM-5:30PM; Su 11AM-4PM. 306 Center St, Healdsburg. 433.8855

183 Downtown Bakery & Creamery Lindsey Shere, longtime pastry chef at Berkeley's famous Chez Panisse restaurant and author of *Chez Panisse Desserts,* has graced the plaza with this evocation of an old-fashioned bakery. Everything is top-notch—from the yeasty pecan rolls sticky with caramel to the fruit-drenched sorbets and ice creams. They've got wonderful flour-dusted loaves of bread, a pastry case of fragile tarts, eccentric but irresistible cookies, skillfully baked cakes, and whatever else inspires the chef that day. Don't miss dipping the crunchy biscotti in their cappuccino, and nothing can beat one of their nostalgic milk shakes or sundaes after a canoe ride. They don't have a chair in the place, only a little stand-up marble bar to one side and a single garden bench out front, but the plaza's ample benches and inviting lawn are only a few steps away. ♦ M, W-Sa 7AM-5:30PM; Su

Russian River Valley

7AM-3:30PM. 308-A Center St, Healdsburg. 431.2719

183 Wild Rose This gift shop is filled with scented soaps, lavish wrapping papers, whimsical ceramics, and furniture. To take the chill off a damp fall day, wrap yourself in a handwoven wool and mohair throw. ♦ M-Sa 10AM-5:30PM; Su 11AM-3PM. 308-B Center St, Healdsburg. 433.7869

183 Healdsburg Coffee Co. Sit down with a muffin and a cup of house coffee or a *latte macchiato* (graduated layers of espresso, hot milk, and foam topped with chocolate) at this pleasant little cafe. They also sell a dozen whole bean coffees from **Mountanous Bros.,** the master San Francisco roasters. At lunch they offer a casual menu of salads, soups, and sandwiches, along with Sonoma wines by the glass and juices from The Cherry Tree in Sonoma. Savor your purchase on the plaza, if you like. ♦ M-F 8AM-6PM; Sa-Su 9AM-6PM. 312 Center St, Healdsburg. 431.7941

183 Winston Stanley Florists Stop in this small, elegant florist shop for old-fashioned myrtle and ivy topiaries, fragrant seasonal flowers, and lovely vases. The owners will design gift baskets around a special bottle of wine on request. ♦ M, W-Sa 10AM-5:30PM; Su 11AM-3PM. 320 Center St, Healdsburg. 433.1142

184 Spoke Folks Cyclery Rent 12-speed touring bikes by the day or half-day; helmets are extra. No guided trips, but they have biking maps and will advise on the best route for your interest and fitness level. The Alexander Valley and Westside Rd are both easy rides and favorites with local cyclers. ♦ Tu-Sa 10AM-5PM. 249 Center St, Healdsburg. 433.7171

184 Windsor Vineyards A pioneer in the direct marketing of wines, Windsor sells wines only from their tasting room and by mail order. They produce a wide range, from sparkling wines, Fumé Blanc, and several Chardonnays to Cabernet, Merlot, and Zinfandel, plus late-harvest dessert wines. They'll also provide personalized wine labels (for three or more bottles); order 10 days to two weeks in advance. ♦ M-F 10AM-5PM; Sa-Su 10AM-6PM. 239-A Center St, Healdsburg. 433.2822

184 Levin & Company Bibliophiles will want to save some time to browse the aisles of this used-book store; hardbound copies of the classics share shelves with an eclectic collection of paperbacks in many categories, including travel and gardening. History and architecture buffs may want to pick up a copy of *Historic Homes of Healdsburg*, which provides a self-guided tour of 70 houses representative of local architecture and history. ♦ M-Th 10AM-6PM; F-Sa 10AM-9PM; Su 10AM-5PM. 239-B Center St, Healdsburg. 433.1118

185 Cro-Magnon This gallery and shop specializes in primitive and tribal art from all over the world. You'll find contemporary willow furniture juxtaposed with Anatolian *kelim* rugs, and intricate wood carvings from Asia and Africa. Folk art and primitive jewelry, too. ♦ Tu-Sa 10AM-6PM; Su noon-5PM. 132 Matheson St, Healdsburg. 433.1415

186 Heavenly Down This is the place to find premium white goose-down comforters, pillows, featherbeds, sleeping bags, cotton duvet covers, and natural-fiber linens. The firm does most of their business by mail order, but you can also shop direct at this factory's small outlet, where prices are 15 percent lower. ♦ M-F 9AM-5PM; Sa 11AM-2PM. 419 Allan Ct, Healdsburg. 800/888.DOWN

187 Farmers Market You'll find all the makings of a sumptuous wine-country picnic right here. It's a marvelous, sociable event, and a vibrant showcase for all the countryside's bounty. ♦ Tu 4:30-7PM; Sa 9AM-noon, May-Nov. City Parking Lot, North and Vine Sts, Healdsburg. 431.8409

188 Healdsburg Chamber of Commerce The staff is happy to provide information on lodging, restaurants, and events in the greater Healdsburg area, plus maps of Healdsburg and the Russian River Wine Road, Sonoma Farm Trails, and more. ♦ M-F 8AM-5PM; Sa-Su 10AM-2PM. 217 Healdsburg Ave, Healdsburg. 433.6935

188 Vintage II Antiques This large antiques collective includes more than a dozen members. The stock is constantly changing, so it's worth your while to stop in again and again. They have lots of good stuff, including Irish pine furniture, handsome old ceramic bowls, and other cookware for your country kitchen, handmade quilts and crocheted bedspreads, vintage hats, and old jewelry. In the back is a furniture-repair workshop. ♦ M-Sa 10AM-5PM; Su noon-5PM. 225 Healdsburg Ave, Healdsburg. 433.0223

188 Tre Scalini ★★$$$ The small, sleek Italian restaurant offers *nuova cucina*—that's new Italian cooking prepared with choice local ingredients. The ambience is casual, reservations are a must, and the service is exemplary. **Cynthia** and **Fernando Urroz** present a fat list of Sonoma County wines, but if you bring in one of your recent discoveries, they'll open and pour it for a modest corkage fee. ♦ Italian ♦ M, W-Su 6-10PM. 241 Healdsburg Ave, Healdsburg. 433.1772

189 Toyon Books Visit this plaza bookstore for bedside reading and a nice selection of books on wine and travel with an emphasis on Sonoma County and the North Coast. ♦ M-Sa 10AM-9PM; Su 10AM-6PM. 104 Matheson St, Healdsburg. 433.9270

189 Robinson & Co. This well-stocked cookware store has a small collection of great cookbooks, whole-bean coffees, and imaginative gifts for cooks. They also sell true bay laurel leaves that come from a flourishing bay tree a local woman, now in her seventies, smuggled in as a seedling from France years ago. ♦ M-Sa 10AM-5:30PM; Su 11AM-3PM. 108 Matheson St, Healdsburg. 433.7116

189 Healdsburg Inn on the Plaza $$ The top floor of this Victorian, built as the Wells Fargo bank at the turn of the century, is now a nine-room inn. Most attractive are the large rooms overlooking the plaza, which have sunny bay windows and fireplaces. All guest rooms have private baths, queen-sized brass beds, and the requisite romantic Victorian decor. Early risers will find a Continental breakfast laid out on the breezy veranda at 7:30 every morning; guests can sit down to a hot breakfast at 9. No smoking. ♦ 116 Matheson St, Healdsburg. 433.6991

Below the Healdsburg Inn:

Innpressions Gallery Both fine arts and crafts by North Coast artists are for sale at this compact gallery, which also carries antique prints and jewelry. A special gift show runs every year from October until Christmas. ♦ Daily 11AM-5PM. 110 Matheson St, Healdsburg. 433.7510

189 Kilkenny Bakery This small-town bakery with an Irish twist turns out lots of cookies and decorated cakes. They also have Cornish pasties to take out for a picnic or snack. ♦ Tu-F 7:30AM-6PM; Sa 8AM-5PM; Su 11AM-4PM. 433.0343

189 Friends in the Country Jane Oriel has filled her shop with an enchanting collection of handpainted dinnerware, porcelain tea sets, sumptuous cushions, and throws—all the niceties of life in the countryside of France or Italy displayed with an artist's flair. ♦ M-Sa 10:30AM-5PM; Su noon-4PM. 114 Matheson St, Healdsburg. 433.1615

189 Fabrications This small shop is crammed from floor to ceiling with bright cottons and natural-fiber fabrics for summer frocks or quilt making. You'll find supplies for textile arts, too: needles and quilting templates for patchwork, embroidery hoops and floss, and ribbons and trims for Victorian ribbonwork. The staff is knowledgeable and ready to answer any questions. ♦ M-Sa 10AM-5:30PM. 118 Matheson St, Healdsburg. 433.6243

The Geysers power plant 18 miles east of Cloverdale is the largest geothermal plant in the world and can generate enough power to meet the needs of a million people.

189 Jacob Horner ★★$$$ Healdsburg's old-guard restaurant is named for owner **Jim Gibbons'** great-great-grandfather, an Indiana farmer. The menu reflects an array of culinary influences, as it features pork satay (skewers of Indonesian-style marinated grilled pork with peanut sauce), Mexican nachos, escargots, and calamari *fritti* (deep-fried squid). Main courses concentrate on quality seafood, meats, and poultry from local suppliers. Try the South American-style fisherman's stew laced with lemon and cilantro, the grilled breast of Petaluma duck, or the rack of Sonoma County lamb. Thursday night, **Mark Taylor** plays classical and flamenco guitar music. ♦ California ♦ M 11:30AM-2PM; Tu-Sa 11:30AM-2PM, 5:30-9PM. 106 Matheson St, Healdsburg. 433.3939

190 Piper-Sonoma Cellars Founded just over ten years ago, this California sparkling wine house is owned by the French champagne firm **Piper-Hiedsieck,** which has chalked up almost two centuries in the bubbly business. Piper-Sonoma's modern winery building is notable for the broad terrace in front surrounded by fountains and a moat floating with water lilies. The beautifully landscaped gardens, featured in home-and-garden magazines, make this a popular spot to meet friends for a glass of brut or a walk through the vineyards. Tours of the facility end with a complimentary tasting. The tasting room also sells the firm's Sonoma County brut by the glass or bottle. For a small fee, the tasting-room staff will take you through a technical tasting of each of their sparkling wines: the Brut (a blend of Pinot Noir and

Russian River Valley

Chardonnay), the Blanc de Noirs (made entirely from Pinot Noir), and the Brut Reserve. Top-of-the-line is the Tête de Cuvée, a vintage-dated sparkling wine made in limited quantities from the best Chardonnay and Pinot Noir cuvées each harvest. ♦ Fee. Tasting and sales daily 10AM-5PM; tours with complimentary tasting by appt (usually at 11AM and 2PM) 11447 Old Redwood Hwy, Healdsburg. 433.8843

190 Rodney Strong Vineyards The vineyards come right up to the base of this monolithic structure in buff concrete finished with massive wood beams. Winemaker **Rodney Strong,** a former Broadway choreographer, pioneered direct-mail wine marketing with his first venture, Windsor Vineyards, in the early sixties, and then went on to found this big operation. Strong makes a wide spectrum of wines: Chardonnay, Fumé Blanc, late-harvest Riesling, Cabernet Sauvignon, Merlot, Pinot Noir, and Zinfandel—all available at the tasting room, which also stocks a good

selection of serious wine books. They have picnic supplies (Brother Juniper breads, Molinari salami, and cheese from Sonoma Cheese Co.) plus chilled mineral waters and Rodney Strong whites. The picnic lawn is the site of summer concerts. ♦ Tasting and sales daily 10AM-5PM; tours every half hour. 11455 Old Redwood Hwy, Healdsburg. 433.6511

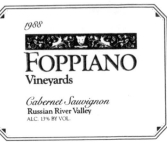

191 Foppiano Vineyards Founder **John Foppiano,** an emigrant from Genoa, began making wine from Russian River Valley grapes as early as 1896. Foppiano remains a family-run winery, with the fourth generation now in charge. The tasting room is a modest clapboard bungalow with an old red-and-white train car sitting behind it. While Foppiano is one of California's oldest wineries, the firm began producing varietal wines under their own label only since 1970. Their best may be the Petite Sirah, closely followed by the Sonoma Cabernet. The Riverside Farm Zinfandel is a good everyday wine for the money. ♦ Tasting and sales daily 10AM-4:30PM; tours by appt. 12707 Old Redwood Hwy, Healdsburg. 433.7272

192 Sotoyome Winery At this small winery perched on a knoll in the Chalk Hill appellation, new owners **John** and **Susan Mitchell** have decided to concentrate on red wines made from grapes grown on their 10-acre estate. They make Petite Sirah, Syrah, and a blush Syrah. ♦ Tasting F-Su 10AM-5PM; tours by appt. 641 Limerick Ln, Healdsburg. 433.2001

193 J.W. Morris/Black Mountain Vineyard A rustic facade and striped awning in the midst of a cluster of industrial buildings mark the home of this small Sonoma winery. A simple wood counter is the tasting bar. Old wine barrels display reasonably priced, everyday varietals from J.W. Morris; owner **Ken Toth** reserves the Black Mountain Vineyard label for his premium estate wines. Former owner and founder **James Olsen** built up a reputation for California ports, and Toth continues to produce a vintage port and a late-bottled vintage port. ♦ Tasting and sales Th-Su 10AM-4PM; tours by appt. 101 Grant Ave, Healdsburg. 431.7015

194 Jordan Vineyard and Winery When Denver oilman **Tom Jordan** and wife **Sally** opened their winery in the Alexander Valley, they created quite a stir in the wine world.

Everybody hurried to see the grandiose French-style stone chateau and to taste their first release, a 1976 Alexander Valley Cabernet, full-bodied and lush—and eminently ready to drink because Jordan had the time and capital to age the wine in his own cellars before releasing it. Later wines have kept to the same high standard set by that first release. Jordan also makes fine estate-bottled Chardonnay. ♦ Tasting and sales M-F 8AM-5PM; tours by appt. 1474 Alexander Valley Rd, Healdsburg. 433.6955

195 **Alexander Valley Campground** This family campground by a beautiful stretch of the Russian River is owned by Healdsburg King of the Canoe, W.C. "Bob" Trowbridge. The 78 sites are suitable for either two tents or a trailer (under 30 feet long). There are canoe rentals and free use of acres of sandy swimming beaches. ♦ Fee. Alexander Valley Rd (at Alexander Valley Bridge) Healdsburg. Reservations required. 433.1320

196 **Jimtown Store** Jimtown is named for **James Patrick,** who settled here in the 1860s and ran a country store first at Soda Rock and then at this spot in the heart of Alexander Valley. When New Yorkers **John H. Werner** and **Carrie Brown** came across the old country store for sale, they decided to move to the wine country and revive the historic Jimtown store. First they hired the Berkeley architecture firm **Fernau & Hartman** to restore the large, lofty space, then they painted it an eye-popping yellow and green and opened for business in the spring of 1991. Stop in for well-made espresso drinks and coffee cake in the morning; on Saturday mornings, look for dried-cherry scones, and on Sunday, cinnamon-caramel buns. The deli counter stocks top-quality cold cuts and housemade salads, including a notable buttermilk cole slaw. The mile-high sandwich layers baked ham, salami, mortadella, provolone, and the store's own olive salad on a baguette. Try their refreshing sports tea (an iced ginseng tea) and the old-fashioned chocolate cake. For kids they offer a special lunch (a peanut butter and Jimtown jam sandwich, celery and carrot sticks, and a Cowboy cookie). There's a sit-down eating area in back, and one corner of the store is stocked with organically grown produce from Tierra Vegetables on Chalk Hill Rd. Call in advance and they'll put together a brown-bag picnic lunch. ♦ M-F 6AM-6:30PM; Sa-Su 8AM-6:30PM; closed M-Tu in winter. 6706 Hwy 128, Healdsburg. 433.1212

197 **Sausal Winery** The Demostene family purchased the 125-acre Sausal ranch in 1956 and began replanting prune and apple orchards with vineyards. In 1973 they turned a building formerly used to dehydrate prunes into a

full-fledged winery, which winemaker **Dave Demostene** initiated with the 1974 vintage, a Zinfandel. Demostene continues to make good Zinfandel, especially the intense and rich private reserve; he also makes a good Cabernet, along with Chardonnay, Sausal Blanc, and White Zinfandel. Older vintages are for sale, too, rereleased for collectors. The tasting room has a shady picnic area on the veranda. ♦ Daily 10AM-4PM. 7370 Hwy 128, Healdsburg. 433.2285

198 **Johnson's Alexander Valley Wines** This small, family-owned winery features **Ellen Johnson** as winemaker. Chardonnay, Pinot Noir, Cabernet Sauvignon, and Zinfandel are her main wines; most of them are sold directly at the winery. ♦ Tasting and sales daily 10AM-5PM. 8333 Hwy 128, Healdsburg. 433.2319

At Johnson's Alexander Valley Wines:

Five Oaks Farm Horse-Drawn Vineyard Tours Longtime Alexander Valley residents **Sue** and **Greg Hannon** offer backroad tours of several Alexander Valley wineries in a horse-drawn surrey. The Hannons act as drivers and guides, taking small dirt roads through the vineyards and stopping to visit three family-owned wineries: Sausal, Alexander Valley Vineyards, and Johnson's Alexander Valley Wines. Choose

Russian River Valley

either a morning wine-tasting excursion followed by lunch, an afternoon wine tasting and an early dinner, or an evening vineyard tour that begins with a wine-and-cheese tasting and ends with dinner at Johnson's Alexander Valley wines. ♦ By advance reservation only Apr-Dec. Six-person minimum. 15851 Chalk Hill Rd, Healdsburg. 433.2422

199 **Alexander Valley Vineyards** Once owned by **Cyrus Alexander,** for whom the Alexander Valley is named, this 250-acre ranch with the original 1841 homestead now belongs to the **Wetzel** family, who produces varietals from grapes grown on the estate. Most of their wines are available only at the tasting room (the age-worthy Cabernet is the one most seen in wine shops). They also make a good Chardonnay and soft, fruity Johannisberg Riesling and Gewürztraminer, plus small quantities of Pinot Noir and Merlot. There is a small shady picnic area beside the parking lot. ♦ Tours by appt. 8644 Hwy 128, Healdsburg. 433.7209, 800/888.7209 (CA only)

200 Field Stone Winery & Vineyards This family-owned and operated winery tunneled into the hillside takes its name from the excavated stones used to construct the rustic facade. Known primarily for their Cabernet and Petite Sirah, this high-quality act also produces Gewürztraminer, Sauvignon Blanc, and a relatively new barrel-fermented Chardonnay. ♦ Tasting and sales daily 10AM-5PM; tours by appt. 10075 Hwy 128, Healdsburg. 433.7266, 800/54.GRAPE

201 Chalk Hill Winery When **Frederick Furth** purchased the Donna Maria Ranch in the Chalk Hill area in 1980, he replanted the vineyards and constructed a barnlike winery building. **Thomas Cottrell** was the first winemaker; in 1991 **David Ramey,** formerly at Matanzas Creek and one of the county's most talented winemakers, took over—it will be interesting to see what he does with the Chardonnay and Cabernet here. The winery also produces a regular and late-harvest Sauvignon Blanc. ♦ Tasting, sales, and tours by appt only. 10300 Chalk Hill Rd, Headsburg. 838.4306

202 Lytton Springs Winery Founder **Richard Sherwin** just happens to own one of the best Zinfandel vineyards in California. Originally planted by Italian immigrants at the turn of the century on a dry-farmed (nonirrigated) hillside, it produces grapes with a rich concentration of fruit and flavor. During the seventies the grapes went to **Ridge Vineyards,** a renowned Zinfandel producer in Santa Clara County, but in 1977 Sherwin decided to make his own wines. One corner of the functional winery acts as an impromptu tasting room, with a bar constructed just in front of a stack

Russian River Valley

of wine barrels; if something is going on in the cellar, you're right there to see it. Try the Sonoma County Zinfandel, especially the private reserve and the Zinfandel made from old vines with even more concentration. They also make Palette (a blend of Zinfandel and Merlot), Cabernet, and late-harvest Gewürztraminer. ♦ Tasting and sales daily 10AM-4PM; group tours by appt. 650 Lytton Springs Rd, Healdsburg. 433.7721

203 Mazzocco Vineyards The first vintage at this family-owned winery was the 1985, and the only wine was a Chardonnay. Today **John Mazzocco** and family produce two barrel-fermented Chardonnays (the best comes from their own River Lane vineyard) and a firmly structured Cabernet Sauvignon. The Zinfandel comes from an 80-year-old vineyard in nearby Dry Creek Valley. The winemaker is **Nancy Steele,** a University of California at Davis graduate who worked at Clos du Val in the Napa Valley before coming here. ♦ Tasting and sales daily 10AM-4PM. 1400 Lytton Springs Rd, Healdsburg. 433.9035

204 Dry Creek General Store Pick up picnic supplies and sandwiches to go, plus cold drinks and snacks. ♦ Daily 7AM-9PM. 3495 Dry Creek Rd, Healdsburg. 433.4171

205 Dry Creek Vineyard Founded in 1972 by Bostonian **David Stare,** who studied enology and viticulture at the University of California at Davis, this winery is a good, steady performer producing first-rate Fumé Blanc and Zinfandel. Picnic tables are set out on an enclosed lawn in the midst of an old-fashioned flower garden. ♦ Tasting and sales daily 10:30AM-4:30PM; tours by appt. 3770 Lambert Bridge Rd, Healdsburg. 433.1000

206 Robert Stemmler Vineyards Founded in 1977 by **Robert Stemmler,** who had worked at Charles Krug and Inglenook in the Napa Valley, and partner **Trumbull Kelly,** this small winery specializes in Pinot Noir and also produces Chardonnay and Cabernet Sauvignon. Sample current releases and some older vintages at the tasting room on Lambert Bridge Rd. Reservations are required for the picnic tables on a deck off the tasting room. ♦ Tasting and sales daily 10:30AM-4:30PM. 3805 Lambert Bridge Rd, Healdsburg. 433.6334

207 Quivira Winery Owner **Henry Wendt** took the name Quivira from a legendary wealthy kingdom, which early explorers believed was situated somewhere in the Sonoma County area. The stark, modern winery is known primarily for Zinfandel and Sauvignon Blanc. The winemaker is **Doug Nalle,** who also produces a terrific Zinfandel under his own label. ♦ Tasting, sales, and tours by appt. 4900 W. Dry Creek Rd, Healdsburg. 431.8333

208 Ferrari-Carano Founded in 1981 by Reno attorney and hotelier **Don Carano** and his wife, **Rhonda,** Ferrari-Carano is housed in a state-of-the-art winery complex at the head of the Dry Creek Valley. Under winemaker **George Bursick,** the winery has been gaining a reputation for their whites, especially the oaky Chardonnay and a well-made Fumé Blanc. They also produce Cabernet, Merlot, and Eldorado Gold (their luscious late-harvest Sauvignon Blanc). All can be sampled in the tasting room with windows looking into the winery. In 1991 they added a spectacular underground barrel-aging cellar, which houses 1,500 French oak *barriques* (60-gallon barrels). Future plans include constructing Villa Fiore next door, an Italianate villa that will serve as headquarters for the winery's ambitious food and wine program (a series of events offering classes and tastings); it will also include a new public tasting room. ♦ Tasting and sales daily 10AM-5PM; tours by appt. 8761 Dry Creek Rd, Healdsburg. 433.6700

209 Preston Vineyards **Lou Preston** first entered the wine scene as a grape grower, and the quality of the grapes coming from his 125-acre Dry Creek Valley estate convinced him to become a winemaker in the late seventies. The winery specializes in Sauvignon Blanc and Zinfandel, producing both a regular and a reserve Zinfandel. They also make aged Syrah, Barbera, and Muscat Canelli dessert wine (which sells out quickly). ♦ Tasting and sales M-F noon-4PM; Sa-Su 11AM-4PM; tours by appt. 9282 W. Dry Creek Rd, Healdsburg. 433.3372

210 Domaine Michel This $7 million estate, owned by Swiss banker **Jean-Jacques Michel** and surrounded by a 100-acre vineyard, produces Chardonnay and Cabernet Sauvignon. ♦ Tours daily by appt. 4155 Wine Creek Rd, Healdsburg. 433.7427

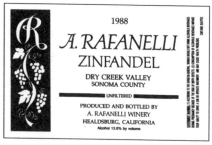

1988

A. RAFANELLI

ZINFANDEL

DRY CREEK VALLEY
SONOMA COUNTY

UNFILTERED

PRODUCED AND BOTTLED BY
A. RAFANELLI WINERY
HEALDSBURG, CALIFORNIA
Alcohol 13.8% by volume

211 A. Rafanelli Third-generation vintner **Dave Rafanelli** still has two of the vineyards his grandfather planted when he first came to this country. The winery is in the redwood barn where Dave Rafanelli's father, **Amerigo,** made wines with little help from modern-day technology. By appointment only, Dave will take you through the winery, explaining how he makes his beautifully balanced Dry Creek Valley Zinfandels and letting you taste the new vintages from the barrel, along with bottled wines. His Zinfandels and Cabernets just keep getting better every year. ♦ Tasting, sales, and tours by appt. 4685 W. Dry Creek Rd, Healdsburg. 433.1385

212 Lambert Bridge Vineyards & Winery When **Jerry Lambert** first bought this property more than 20 years ago, he replaced the existing prune orchards with 76 acres of prime vineyards. The tasting room is a rustic wooden building twined with wisteria in a serene country setting. On damp mornings a big stone fireplace takes off the chill. Sample some of winemaker **Ed Killian's** Fumé Blanc and Chardonnay, along with his best wines, the Merlot and the Crane Creek Cabernet. Reservations are required for the picnic gazebo. ♦ Tasting and sales daily 10AM-4PM. 4085 W. Dry Creek Rd, Healdsburg. 433.5855

213 Bellerose Vineyard Grapes were first planted on this Dry Creek Valley estate as early as 1887. Today's winery, founded by **Charles Richard** in 1979, specializes in three Bordeaux-style wines. The flagship is Cuvée Bellerose (a blend of Cabernet Sauvignon with Cabernet Franc and Petit Verdot). This small but very good producer also makes a Merlot and a Sauvignon Blanc. ♦ Tasting and sales Tu-Sa 11AM-5PM; tours by appt. 435 W. Dry Creek Rd, Healdsburg. 433.1637

214 Madrona Manor $$$ This grand, gabled Victorian inn on the outskirts of Healdsburg includes a first-class restaurant acclaimed for its eclectic wine-country cuisine. Built in 1881 by **John Alexander Patton,** a wealthy entrepreneur and state legislator, the three-story manor boasted 17 rooms, three-and-a-half baths, and seven fireplaces. **John** and **Carol Muir** bought the old mansion in 1981 and after extensive restoration opened it in 1982 as a country inn. Madrona Manor now includes the main house and several other buildings (a total of 18 rooms and three suites). The elegant guest rooms on the mansion's second floor are the best—particularly No. 204, which has a tall, carved wooden bed, a chaise longue, a fireplace, a Victorian clawfoot tub, and French doors opening onto the balcony. Rooms in the carriage house, which dates from 1881, are furnished in a more contemporary (and less attractive) style with hand-carved rosewood from Nepal. In 1991, the inn added a

Russian River Valley

contemporary suite with a king-sized bed, a marble-tiled bath, and a double Jacuzzi. The most secluded unit is the **Garden Suite,** furnished in rattan, with a fireplace, a private garden, and a deck area. Guests can relax in the manor's gracious parlor and music rooms, explore the extensive gardens, or use the swimming pool. A buffet breakfast is served in the dining room or on the outdoor deck. Madrona Manor is also one of the few inns that takes children (the staff will babysit if parents want to dine in the restaurant). The front desk offers full concierge services. ♦ 1001 Westside Rd, Healdsburg. 433.4231

Within Madrona Manor:

Madrona Manor Restaurant ★★$$$$ Directed by the Madrona owners' son **Todd Muir,** who trained at Chez Panisse restaurant in Berkeley, this restaurant serves produce that primarily comes from the inn's extensive kitchen garden. Muir also smokes his fish and meats and makes the breads and pastries. Choose either the five-course prix fixe menu or order à la carte. First courses may include potato blinis with delicate house-smoked salmon, caviar, and dill beurre blanc, or marinated, grilled blue prawns on a bed of tricolored pappardelle (wide-ribbon noodles). For a main course, he offers half-a-dozen choices, ranging from Peking duck served with almond-coconut rice, stuffed chiles, and a rhubarb-honey sauce to salmon steak with sorrel cream sauce and vegetable strudel. Muir never stints on his ingredients and he has an astute flair for unusual flavors. The pastry chef holds to the same high standards, turning out skillful desserts—try the chocolate menagerie, the banana-coconut napoleon, or the sumptuous sorbets and ice creams. On Sundays Muir prepares a special prix fixe brunch with a choice of entrées and desserts. ◆ California ◆ M-Sa 6-9:30PM; Su 11AM-2PM, 6-9:30PM. 433.4231

214 Mill Creek Vineyards This family-owned winery (pictured above) perched on a knoll overlooking their vineyards in the Dry Creek Valley was founded in 1965. The two-story redwood tasting room sits beside the creek, where a wooden mill wheel turns. You can sample the **Kreck** family's full range of varietal wines: Chardonnay, Sauvignon Blanc, Cabernet blush wine, Cabernet, and Merlot. Up a steep path at the back of the property is a large tree-shaded picnic deck with a

Russian River Valley

panoramic view of the Dry Creek Valley.◆ M-F noon-4:30PM; Sa-Su 10AM-4:30PM. 1401 Westside Rd, Healdsburg. 433.5098

214 Middleton Gardens Nancy and Malcolm Skall sell superb organic fruits and vegetables, many of them grown from European heirloom seeds. Drive past the perfect white farmhouse surrounded with a mass of old-fashioned flowers. Ring the bell in front of the barn out back and one of the Skalls will arrive shortly to weigh out garlic braids, French pumpkins, sweet and hot peppers, sweet corn, 20 types of tomatoes, and seven kinds of eggplant. And don't miss Nancy's luscious strawberries; you may have to call ahead to secure a basket or two. Look for Malcolm at the Healdsburg farmers market. ◆ Open when the sign is hung out front. Closed mid Dec-Jan. 2651 Westside Rd, Healdsburg. 433.4755

215 Belvedere Winery Belvedere's top-of-the-line wines are Cabernet Sauvignon or Merlot from the Robert Young Vineyard, Pinot Noir from Winery Lake, and York Creek Cabernet Sauvignon. The winery also produces the

Discovery Series, a line of lower-priced varietals. ◆ Tasting and sales daily 10AM-4:30PM. 4035 Westside Rd, Healdsburg. 433.8236

215 Sonoma Antique Apple Nursery Terry and **Carolyn Harrison** grow more than a hundred types of antique or heritage apple trees (that is, varieties of apples no longer commercially grown but that offer a spectrum of delicate and very different flavors) and over 30 kinds of pear trees. They no longer sell apples or apple juice. The mail-order catalog costs two dollars. ◆ Tu-Sa 9AM-4:30PM, 15 Jan-31 Mar; April-Dec by appt. 4395 Westside Rd, Healdsburg. 433.6420

216 Hop Kiln Winery A brass plaque just outside the immense old building with its three towers reads: "This structure served the important hop industry of California's North Coast region, once the major hop-growing area in the West." Built in 1905 by a crew of Italian stonemasons, it represents the finest existing example of its type, consisting of three stone kilns for drying the hops, a wooden cooler, and a two-story press for baling hops for shipment. Listed on the National Register of Historic Places, the hop-kiln barn was restored and converted to a winery by **Dr. Martin Griffin** in 1974. The tasting room pours the winery's Chardonnay and powerful Gewürztraminer, along with their robust reds. Their two best efforts are the Russian River Petite Sirah and Marty's Big Red (made from four unidentified grape varieties found growing on a remote corner of the property). With its picnic grounds beside a duck pond, this is a popular stop for bicyclists heading to or from the Russian River on Westside Rd. ◆ Tasting and sales daily 10AM-5PM. 6050 Westside Rd, Healdsburg. 433.6491

216 J. Rochioli Vineyards & Winery The Rochioli family has been growing premium grapes since the thirties. They make good Sauvignon Blanc and Pinot Noir as well as Chardonnay and Cabernet Sauvignon. A small gallery offers a changing art show. Bring your lunch, and picnic at tables on an outdoor deck. ◆ Tasting and sales daily 10AM-5PM; tours by appt M-F. 6192 Westside Rd, Healdsburg. 433.2305

Restaurants/Clubs: Red   **Hotels:** Blue
Shops/ ◊ Outdoors: Green   **Wineries/Sights:** Black

On the fertile banks of the Russian River

217 Westside Farms Stop at this restored 1869 Westside Rd farmhouse for free-range fertile eggs and homegrown popcorn. During the summer **Pam** and **Ron Kaiser** sell several kinds of corn, tomatoes, onions, and potatoes. You can also find their products at the Healdsburg and Santa Rosa farmers markets. In addition to farming 40 acres of Chardonnay and Pinot Noir grapes, the Kaisers raise sheep and Angora goats for wool along with the miniature donkeys that are always a big attraction with kids. During their October Farm Pumpkin Fest, they invite the public to visit their family farm with 20 acres of pumpkins, free hayrides, and Indian and decorative corns. ♦ Daily 10AM-5PM, Oct; by appt the rest of the year. 7097 Westside Rd, Healdsburg. 431.1432

218 Davis Bynum Most of the wines available for tasting here are sold only at the winery. Chardonnay, Sauvignon Blanc, and Cabernet are good bets; occasionally they'll offer visitors a special "future wines" barrel tasting. They have a shady picnic area with tables set up at the edge of a cool ravine. ♦ Daily 10AM-5PM. 8075 Westside Rd, Healdsburg. 433.5852

219 Raford House $$ When **Raford W. Peterson** built this two-story farmhouse northwest of Santa Rosa in the 1880s, it was intended to shelter both his family and his ranch hands. Called the Wohler Ranch at the time, the property was surrounded by more than 400 acres of hops, which Peterson processed and shipped to the flourishing beer-brewing industry. In 1981, after a year of restoration work, the house, which now sits on four and a half acres in the midst of vineyards and orchards, was converted to a B&B. Flanked by stately palms, the Raford House, a Sonoma County Historical Landmark, has seven guest rooms, all but one with a private bath and period decor. Two

of the guest rooms have fireplaces; the bridal suite is the most private, featuring a fireplace and its own balcony. Innkeeper **Gina Villaneuve** provides a Continental breakfast. ♦ 10630 Wohler Rd, Healdsburg. 887.9573

Guerneville

This unpretentious little town sits squarely on the site of the logging camp and sawmill **George Guerne** set up in 1865 to cash in on the redwood logging boom. So many trees were felled that the area around what is now Guerneville was referred to as Stumptown; in fact, the center of Guerneville is built right on top of the stumps of centuries-old redwoods. Things stepped up when the San Francisco and North Western Pacific Railroad chugged into town for the first time in 1877. Soon tremendous trainloads of logs and lumber were heading south, and Guerneville became one of the busiest logging centers in this part of the west. When the area was pretty much logged out, enterpreneur **A.W. Foster** came up with the idea of transforming the old logging camps into vacation resorts. And so a tradition was born. Guerneville and the Russian River remain a popular weekend getaway for San Franciscans bent on fishing, camping, and tramping in the redwoods.

Guerneville offers cafes and restaurants, picnic supplies, canoe and boat rentals, and accommodations ranging from family camping sites to resorts for gays and Victorian bed-and-breakfasts. Reservations should be made early, especially from August through October. Annual events include the wildly successful Russian River Jazz Festival in September and the Russian River Rodeo and Stumptown Days in June.

Russian River Valley

220 Ridenhour Ranch House Inn $$ Built in 1906 by **Louis E. Ridenhour,** the turn-of-the-century redwood house was once part of the famed Ridenhour Ranch, which extended for 940 acres on both sides of the Russian River. Now an eight-room B&B, the ranch stands on two and a quarter forested acres just next door to the Korbel Champagne Cellars. Innkeepers **Diane Rechberger** and her Austrian husband, **Fritz,** had a restaurant in Orange County before moving up to the Russian River in 1988. Fritz, who trained as a chef in Europe, cooks up quite a breakfast in the large kitchen. Every morning he bakes at least three pastries and serves them with his own jam, yogurt, and granola. For the main course, he might prepare an omelet filled with duck-apple sausage or scrambled eggs with Bodega Bay smoked salmon. Afternoons, he leaves out a big tray of cookies. Guests can also arrange for him to cook a five-course dinner. The large living room features a 1913 Steinway grand piano, a fireplace, and forest views. The most private accommodation is the **Hawthorne**

Cottage; it has a queen-sized bed, a fireplace, and a window seat for curling up with a good book. In the main house, the cozy **Spruce Room,** with a queen-sized brass bed and an antique English armoire and dresser, has a view of a forest. The rooms actually are more like the guest bedrooms you'd find in a friend's house than the fussy theme rooms whipped up by some B&B owners. For the traveler on a budget, they have two smaller rooms upstairs that share a bath. ◆ 12850 River Rd, Guerneville. 887.1033

221 Korbel Champagne Cellars Nestled among the redwoods, the gabled brick building covered with ivy overlooks gentle, vine-carpeted hills and the Russian River. The winery was founded in 1886 by the three **Korbel** brothers, Czech immigrants who had first gone into the logging business along the Russian River, felling huge redwood trees, cutting them into timber, and crafting them into cigar boxes. They decided to plant vineyards among the redwood stumps on some of the land they had cleared, first concentrating on still wines, distilling some of them into brandy. Soon, however, they decided to produce sparkling wines from European grape varieties. The first shipment of Korbel Champagne was made in the spring of 1882, and the business remained in the family until 1954, when it was purchased by **Adolf Heck,** a descendant of a winemaking family from the Alsace area in France.

Korbel has since extended its vineyards and added new sparkling wines to the Korbel line of nonvintage sparkling wines, which range from brut and brut natural to Blanc de Noir and an all-Chardonnay Blanc de Blanc; they also make a rosé dubbed Rose-Pink Champagne. Korbel Natural was the sparkling wine poured at the 51st Presidential Inauguration in January 1989. Tours here take visitors through the complicated process

of making *méthode champenoise* wines from start to finish and end with a tasting of the firm's wines. From May through September, you can also opt for a tour of Korbel's glorious hillside rose garden, planted with more than 300 varieties of antique roses and a wealth of other old-fashioned flowers and bulbs. ◆ Tasting and sales daily 9AM-5PM; tours until 3PM. 13250 River Rd, Guerneville. 887.2294

222 Russian River Region Information Center Pick up details on Russian River area restaurants, lodging, wineries, recreation, and events. They also sell tickets for some activities. ◆ M-Sa 10AM-5PM; Su 10AM-4PM; hours vary in winter. 14034 Armstrong Woods Rd, Guerneville. 869.9212

222 Little Bavaria ★★$$ In October 1991 this German *biergarten* and restaurant owned by **Walter Seitz,** a native of Frankfurt, celebrated its 10th anniversary. Of course, Octoberfest is the big celebration here, with live entertainment, special beer, sausages, and lots of other celebratory dishes, including a whole roasted pig. The homey restaurant serves traditional German fare such as Bavarian sauerbraten (beef marinated and braised in vinegar and onions) served with homemade *spaetzle* (squiggly egg noodles). Other specialties are roast pork cooked with mustard and spices and traditional sausages served with imported sauerkraut and cabbage. You can also find lighter fare, such as grilled King salmon or lime chicken with wild Sonoma honey. They're open at both lunch and dinner, but if you just want to stop by for a glass of good German beer in the outdoor garden overlooking the river, they offer a menu of appetizers such as prawn cocktails, sausages, and more. ◆ German ◆ M-W 5-9PM; Th 11AM-3PM, 5-9PM; F-Sa 11AM-3PM, 5-10PM; Su 10AM-3PM, 5-10PM. 15025 River Rd, Guerneville. 869.0121

Good Reads on Wine and the California Wine Country

American Wine: A Comprehensive Guide by Anthony Dias Blue (1988; Harper Row)

California Coastal Access Guide by the California Coastal Commission (1991; University of California Press)

California's Great Cabernets by James Laube (1989; Sterling)

California's Great Cabernets: The Wine Spectator's Guide for Consumers by James Laube (1989; M. Shanken Comm.)

California's Great Chardonnays: The Wine Spectator's Ultimate Guide for Consumers, Collectors and Investors by James Laube (Sterling)

The Hiker's Hip Pocket Guide to Sonoma County by Bob Lorentzen (1990; Bored Feet Publications)

The Hiker's Hip Pocket Guide to the Mendocino Coast by Bob Lorentzen (1989; Bored Feet Publications)

Making Sense of Wine by Matt Kramer (1989; Morrow)

Napa: The Story of an American Eden by James Conaway (1990; Houghton Mifflin)

Napa Valley by Charles O'Rear (1990; Collins Publishers)

The New Frank Schoonmaker's Encyclopedia of Wine by Alexis Bespaloff (1988; Morrow)

Parker's Wine Buyer's Guide 1989-1990 by Robert M. Parker Jr. (1989; Simon & Schuster)

The Simon & Schuster Pocket Guide to California Wines by Bob Thompson (1990; Simon & Schuster)

Vintage: The Story of Wine by Hugh Johnson (1989; Simon & Schuster)

The Wines of America by Leon D. Adams (1990; McGraw)

222 **Mike's Bike Rental** This shop carries a full range of bikes and accessories. Sign up for bike rentals by the hour, half day, or full day. No guided tours are offered, but you can get plenty of good advice on favorite spots to bike either along the river or through the redwood groves. ♦ Daily 10AM-5PM; closed Tu-W in winter. 16434 Hwy 116, Guerneville. 869.1106

222 **King's Sport and Tackle Shop** Serious fishers will enjoy trolling here for all sorts of gear and diving equipment. Owner **Steve Jackson** keeps customers up to date with information on river and fishing conditions. He can also arrange sportfishing trips with knowledgeable guides. During the fishing season (which runs roughly from mid-August through February), he opens up as early as 5AM. Summer opening hours are less rigorous: 8AM during the week and 6AM on weekends. Whether you fish or not, you can still find beach gear and attire at this friendly shop. ♦ M-F 8AM-6PM; Sa-Su 6AM-7PM; winter hours vary. 16258 Main St, Guerneville. 869.2156

222 **Johnson's Beach** Every summer a temporary dam goes up to create this swimming lagoon along a sandy stretch of beach. It may be foggy and dreary only an hour away in San Francisco, but at Johnson's Beach it is definitely summer. When you tire of swimming or sunbathing, you can always rent one of the silver aluminum canoes and paddle off into the afternoon. Site of the annual Russian River Jazz Festival in September. ♦ First and Church Sts, Guerneville

222 **Johnson's Beach Resort** $ This family resort sits right on the Russian River beach, from where it's only a short walk into town. The 50 camping spaces are suitable for either tents or RVs; they also have inexpensive rooms, nothing fancy. The campground has hot showers, a laundromat, a picnic area, and access to the river for swimming or fishing. Johnson's rents out boats, too. Daily and weekly rates. ♦ Daily May-Sep. 16241 First St, Guerneville. 869.2022

222 **Sweet's Cafe & Bakery** ★★$$ In the morning stop in for Belgian waffles, omelets, and their own freshly baked pastries and croissants, along with espresso drinks and a special coffee roast. At lunch the kitchen turns out homemade soups, salads, and sandwiches on Brother Juniper's bread (from the bakery in Forestville), as well as eclectic fare such as chicken Thai burritos, a cold salad of cheese tortellini sauced with blue cheese and basil, and a half roast chicken. Desserts are all made right there, including fruit pies and cheesecake. At night they offer special dishes such as *filo*-dough triangles stuffed with goat cheese and vegetables, or sliced pork tenderloin in ginger sauce. Good list of top-notch beers and Sonoma County wines at reasonable prices. On warm days, you can eat outside on the patio. ♦ California

♦ M-Tu, Th 8:30AM-7PM; F-Sa 8:30AM-9PM; Su 8:30AM-4PM. 16521 Main St, Guerneville. 869.3383

223 **Ring Canyon Campground** Just two blocks from the entrance to Armstrong Woods, this family campground has 35 tent sites under the redwoods; trailer sites, too. All have picnic tables and fire rings; a bathhouse provides hot showers. ♦ 1747 Armstrong Woods Rd, Guerneville. 869.2746

224 **Armstrong Redwoods State Reserve** Already a county park by 1917, this reserve of stately redwoods along Fife Creek near Guerneville became a state park in the thirties. The 750-acre property just north of the Russian River offers a number of hikes through the cool, dense forest of virgin redwoods. The easiest is the One-and-a-quarter-mile walk along a marked nature trail, where the highlight is the massive Colonel Armstrong Tree (14 1/2 feet in diameter, 308 feet tall, and estimated to be 1,400 years old). There's also a 1,200-seat amphitheater and a number of shady picnic spots and barbecue pits. After a morning on the river, the serene forest is a heavenly respite from the heat. No overnight camping. ♦ Fee per vehicle. 1700 Armstrong Woods Rd (Hwy 116) Guerneville. 869.2015 or 865.2391

Armstrong Woods Pack Station Laura and **Jonathan Ayers** organize guided horseback rides in the redwood country. Sign up for half-day or full-day rides with a picnic lunch. You can also opt for two- or three-day pack trips by horseback into the wilderness of adjoining Austin Creek State Recreation Area. ♦ Reservations required. 887.2939

Russian River Valley

224 **Austin Creek State Recreation Area** This 4,200-acre wilderness of oak forests, canyons, and sunny glades surrounds Austin Creek and its tributaries. You can camp at Redwood Lake or hike or ride your horse into one of the three remote primitive campsites. The park is sometimes closed in summer because of fire hazards. ♦ Fee per vehicle. 17000 Armstrong Woods Rd, Guerneville. 869.2015 or 865.2391

225 **The Estate Inn** $$ Surrounded by redwood country, this elegant inn, once the country home of a wealthy banker, offers first-class service in the more personal setting of a B&B. Owners **Jim Caron** and **Darryl Notter** have furnished the Mission Revival mansion's 10 guest rooms with discriminating taste and all the comforts of home. The rooms are traditionally, yet not fussily, decorated with good antiques, queen-sized beds, down comforters, reading lights, and armloads of flowers. Each room has a private bath, a telephone, and a cable TV, and most have serene forest views. A lavish breakfast is included. The inn also has a swimming pool, and the Russian River is just a few minutes away. ♦ 13555 Hwy 116, Guerneville. 869.9093

226 Santa Nella House $$ Just across the river from the Ridenhour Ranch House Inn is the Santa Nella House, once the winemaker's residence at the historic Santa Nella Winery. Surrounded by lush redwoods and only a short walk from the river and Korbel Champagne Cellars, the 1870 Victorian features a wraparound veranda where guests can relax after a day's touring. The inn has four guest rooms, all with queen-sized beds, private baths, and fireplaces. Innkeepers **Ed** and **Joyce Ferrington** serve a full country breakfast. ♦ 12130 Hwy 116, Guerneville. 869.9488

227 Duncans Mills As soon as the railroad reached Guerneville in 1877, brothers **Alexander** and **Samuel Duncan** took apart the sawmill they had been running at the tiny coastal community of Bridgehaven, loaded it on a barge, and headed upriver to meet the railroad at this bucolic spot. Today the Victorian Revival village that grew up around Duncans Mills and the old 1880s depot has been refurbished to attract travelers on their way to or from the coast. This charming hamlet with 20 residents is filled with shops, delis, restaurants, and the old general store. ♦ Off Hwy 116

227 Gold Coast Oyster and Espresso Bar Pull into this delightful pit stop along the road to the coast to find well-made espresso drinks and morning pastries. They roast their own whole-bean coffees, and on sunny days you can take your coffee outside to the garden. Weekends, try the grilled, freshly harvested Tomales Bay oysters. ♦ M-F 8AM-

Russian River Valley

5:30PM; Sa-Su 9AM-6PM. Steelhead Blvd, Duncans Mills. 865.1441

227 Duncans Mills General Store This old-time general store dates from the sawmill days in the late 19th century. It still offers everything from picnic supplies, coffee, and pastries to fishing tackle, cookware, and beef jerky for the trail. Campers come in for newspapers and magazines—and to get fishing licenses before heading off for that secret fishing hole. ♦ Daily 7AM-8PM. 25200 Hwy 116, Duncans Mills. 865.1240

227 Casini Ranch Family Campground This huge 120-acre site surrounded on three sides by the Russian River offers great family camping. Each of the 225 campsites (suitable for tents or RVs) has picnic tables and a barbecue pit. **George Casini** and family have turned the old 1862 horse barn into a recreation hall, now used for parties. They've got a mile and a half of beach and plenty of fishing holes, so you can catch trout, silver salmon, or catfish for supper. RV hookups include cable TV. The Casinis have a store, a laundromat, and showers, and can rent you a rowboat or canoe. Weekly rates available. ♦ 22855 Moscow Rd, Duncans Mills. Reservations recommended. 865.2255

228 Monte Rio Every year this tiny riverside community makes the news when San Francisco's Bohemian Club holds their annual Bohemian Days at their 2,700-acre private grove in Monte Rio. The club's members number among the wealthiest and most powerful men in the country (women are allowed in the club now, but can't participate in the Bohemian Days activities). Crowds inevitably turn out to gawk at the rich and famous, such as **Henry Kissinger** and **Ronald Reagan,** as they arrive.

228 Northwood Golf Course Nestled among the gorgeous redwoods along the Russian River just three miles west of Guerneville is this nine-hole golf course. The 3,000-yard course (par 36) was designed in 1928 by **Allister MacKenzie.** ♦ Daily 7AM-7PM. 19400 Hwy 116, Monte Rio. Reservations required. 865.1116

Forestville

This tiny hamlet deep in redwood country is known for the wines produced in the nearby Green Valley appellation and for its many berry farms. Everybody stops at Kozlowski's on the way home from the Russian River to pick up baskets of raspberries and other homegrown products.

229 Burke's Canoe Trips Canoe down the Russian River for 10 miles through the majestic redwood forests from Forestville to Guerneville. The unguided trip takes from three to three-and-one-half hours from start to finish, but most people dawdle along the way, turning it into an all-day affair. Bring an ice chest, pack a picnic, and don't forget the sunscreen and sun hats—it can get blistering hot out there. When you arrive in Guerneville, a shuttle takes you back upriver to your car. They also have a campground with river views under the redwoods, plus a beach for swimming and a picnic and barbecue area. No dogs allowed. ♦ Daily 9AM-6PM, May-Sep; Oct by appt only. 8600 River Rd, Forestville. 887.1222

230 Brother Juniper's Café Founded by the Little Flowers of St. Francis, a religious order dedicated to charitable works, this cafe is named after a 12th-century monk and follower of St. Francis. Baker/owner **Brother Peter Reinhart** bakes and sells his popular homemade loaves of bread here. You can sit inside and enjoy a muffin, Philadelphia sticky bun, or brownie with a cup of coffee or tea. In addition to the bread, make sure you pick up a bottle of Brother Juniper's sizzling homemade barbecue sauce. ♦ M-Sa 9AM-4:30PM. 6544 Front St, Forestville. 887.7908

231 Topolos at Russian River Vineyard
There's no mistaking this winery with its eccentric wooden towers. Winemaker **Michael Topolos** produces decent Chardonnay, Sauvignon Blanc, Zinfandel, and Petite Sirah. Sample them in the tasting room or at the Topolos family's Greek restaurant on the property. ♦ Tasting daily 10:30AM-5:30PM; tours by appt. 5700 Gravenstein Hwy North, Forestville. 887.1575

Also at Topolos at Russian River Vineyard:

Topolos at Russian River Vineyard Restaurant ★$$ If California cuisine shares certain affinities with French or Italian cuisine, why not Greek? After all, they come from the same Mediterranean roots, and the flavors of olive oil, garlic, tomatoes, and fresh herbs are certainly familiar and heart-warming. Enjoy the Topolos family restaurant's hearty Greek food at tables set out on a brick patio area. Begin with the *meze*, a platter of Greek appetizers, or the *saganaki,* imported kasseri cheese flamed right at the table. The Greek salad with crumbled feta cheese and Kalamata olives is always refreshing. Main courses include *spanakopita* (a spinach and feta cheese *filo*-dough pie), prawns Santorini (prepared with tomato, feta, and fresh dill), and roast baby rack of lamb in a tarragon and Port sauce. Desserts include a honey-drenched baklava, chocolate mousse, and berry pies. ♦ Daily 11:30AM-2:30PM, 5:30-9:30PM. 887.1562

231 Kozlowski Farms Famous for their wonderful jams, vinegars, and condiments, the **Kozlowski** family, in business since 1949, runs this shop along the Sebastopol-Guerneville road. In season, you can buy apples by the barrelful and fabulous berries—raspberries, boysenberries, blackberries, loganberries, and blueberries. They also have homemade berry or apple pies (including their special no-sugar pies), individual little berry tartlets, and all sorts of cookies. In all, they make 65 food items—every one of them worth taking home (especially the raspberry white fudge sauce, which comes in a dark chocolate version, too). They'll put together a gift basket of Sonoma County products or ship your purchases anywhere in the continental US. Mail-order catalog is available. ♦ Daily 9AM-5PM. 5566 Gravenstein Hwy (Hwy 116) Forestville. 887.1587

Restaurants/Clubs: Red   Hotels: Blue
Shops/ 🍴 Outdoors: Green   Wineries/Sights: Black

232 Iron Horse Vineyards
This winery is responsible for some of California's top sparkling wines, produced exclusively by *méthode champenoise*. One of the few champagne houses with no French connection, Iron Horse makes four cuvées along with Pinot Noir and Chardonnay. ♦ Sales and tours by appt. 9786 Ross Station Rd, Sebastopol. 887.1507

233 Dehlinger Winery Owner/winemaker **Thomas Dehlinger** produces top-notch Pinot Noir and Chardonnay loaded with flavor from a small, functional winery in the Russian River area. ♦ Tasting and sales M-F 1-4PM; Sa-Su 10AM-5PM; tours by appt. 6300 Guerneville Rd, Sebastopol. 823.2378

234 The Farmhouse Inn $$$ This B&B lies just off River Rd and is nearly hidden in a grove of trees. Designed in the style of English-country row cottages, the inn consists of a turn-of-the-century farmhouse and guest cottages built in the twenties. There are six guest rooms and two suites decorated in restful color schemes of sand and mauve, each with a private entrance, a spa tub, a sauna, and a fireplace. Unlike most B&Bs, rooms at the inn boast phones, refrigerators, and terrycloth robes. And in the common living room, guests can watch satellite TV or choose a film from the inn's movie library to view on the VCR. In fact, unless you feel like it, you needn't venture very far. Spend the day sunbathing around the swimming pool surrounded with formal

English gardens or playing croquet. Innkeeper **Rebecca Smith's** herb and kitchen garden provides ingredients for her full country breakfast. She is also flexible enough to provide a special low-cholesterol or vegetarian breakfast on request and will put together two- or three-day itineraries for guests. ♦ 7871 River Rd, Forestville. 887.7281/3300, 800/464.6642

235 Mark West Vineyards Founded in 1976 by pilot **Bob Ellis** and his wife, **Joan,** the winery is housed in a converted old dairy building. Visitors can sample their full-flavored Gewürztraminer, Riesling, Pinot Noir, and Chardonnay, and picnic on one of three separate lawns (one or more can be reserved for a private group). Along with the usual wine paraphernalia, they also sell impromptu picnic supplies for those who arrive unprepared: cheeses, crackers, salami, and such. ♦ Tasting and sales daily 10AM-5PM; tours by appt. 7000 Trenton-Healdsburg Rd, Forestville. 544.4813

At Mark West Vineyards:

California Carnivores This unusual nursery specializes in carnivorous plants from all over the world. Proprietors **Marilee Maertz** and **Peter d'Amato's** collection includes more than 200 species of Venus flytraps and other bug-chomping plants. And they claim you can find more species here than at London's Kew Gardens. ♦ Daily 10AM-4PM. 838.1630

Geyserville

The little town of Geyserville was founded in 1851 as Clairville Station, a stage stop for visitors on their way to see the famous Devil's Canyon geysers on Geyser Peak, the world's largest geothermal field, 16 miles to the east. Discovered by **William B. Elliott** in 1846, they are not true geysers, but smoking hot springs and hissing steam vents. From the 1860s to the early 1880s, the "geysers" were a prime tourist attraction, and it's remarkable how many people made the difficult journey north to see them—some 3,500 in 1875 alone. **Ulysses S. Grant, Teddy Roosevelt,** and **William Jennings Bryant** were among the notables who visited. But after 1885, when the more spectacular Yosemite and Yellowstone areas became more accessible, the geysers lost much of their allure. Today PG&E and other companies have several large plants up there and the geysers are closed to the public, although you can see their steam in the distance. The town of Geyserville offers two lovely Victorian bed-and-breakfast inns, an old-time Italian restaurant, and several wineries including **Chateau Souverain** and **Lyeth.** At the Geyserville Bridge, you can slip

Russian River Valley

your canoe into the Russian River and paddle through the pastoral Alexander Valley all the way to Healdsburg.

236 Alexander Fruit & Trading Co. Nearly 10 years old, this small, family-owned winery has been forging a reputation for their honest, reasonably priced wines and their innovative gift packages, which combine bottles of wine with the firm's own dried fruits, mustards, jams, and sauces. On summer weekends you can sample most of their wines and food products in the frontier-style tasting room. Owners **Steve** and **Candace Sommer** also sell picnic supplies, including bread, cheese, soft drinks, and their own trail mix. Instead of the usual cellar tour, Sommer himself will take you on a vineyard walk, by appointment only. ♦ Tasting and sales daily 10AM-5PM. 5110 Hwy 128, Geyserville. 433.1944, 800/433.1944; fax 433.1948

237 Murphy-Goode Estate Winery In 1979 **Tim Murphy** and **Dale Goode,** who have more than two decades of grape-growing experience in the Alexander Valley, founded

their own winery. They made only Fumé Blanc and Chardonnay for their first vintage (1985); Merlot and Cabernet were added to the lineup the following year. Try the lush Fumé Blanc reserve—winemaker **Christina Benz** barrel ferments certain lots of Sauvignon Blanc and leaves the wine on the lees to develop a rich aroma and flavor. The tasting-room manager is well informed and will answer questions as she pours the wines; some, like the Fumé Blanc reserve and a late-harvest Muscat, are available only at the winery. Tours include a walk through the vineyards with a discussion of the grapes, along with a visit to the fermentation and aging rooms. ♦ Tasting and sales daily 10:30AM-5PM; tours by appt. 4001 Hwy 128, Geyserville. 431.7644

238 Isis Oasis Lodge $ Follow the signs for Isis Oasis, past Goddess Way to a fanciful Egyptian-style frieze (with mauve and purple accents, no less) and the retreat's main lodge. The Society for Inspirational Studies offers a wide variety of funky accommodations. You can sign up for a teepee, a yurt (that's a Tibetan tent), the tower room, or a little house in the midst of the vineyard. The most private are the yurts and the tower, but midweek you may find yourself the only guest in one of the larger cottages. This 10-acre retreat might be a good choice for a family or a small group on a budget—the vineyard house can sleep eight to 10, the retreat house can fit up to 15 and includes a private hot tub, kitchen, and three baths. The complex also includes a ragtag menagerie (ocelots, llamas, black sheep, and pygmy goats); animal tours are at 11AM. Take a look before you make reservations; this is definitely not to everyone's taste. Bodywork and massage available by appt. ♦ 20889 Geyserville Ave, Geyserville. 857.3524

239 Catelli's, The Rex ★★$$ For 57 years, the Catelli family has been serving hearty Italian-American fare to local residents and visitors. They make all their pastas and age and cut their meats, including an excellent New York steak. In addition to the large set menu, they offer daily specials such as fettuccine Alfredo, pork roast with sage stuffing, beef short ribs, and leg of lamb with rosemary and sage dressing, all dished out in trencherman's portions. The herbs come from their own kitchen garden, and the wine list is long on Alexander Valley creations. ♦ Italian/American ♦ M-F 11:30AM-2PM, 5-9PM; Sa-Su 5-9PM. 21047 Geyserville Ave (off Hwy 128) Geyserville. 857.9904

239 Hope-Bosworth House and Hope-Merrill House $$ **Bob** and **Rosalie Hope** spent more than four years restoring the Hope-Merrill House, the handsome 1870 Eastlake-style Victorian on Geyserville's main street, doing much of the exterior and all of the interior work themselves. It's fascinating to flip through the photo album detailing their meticulous work, which was rewarded with a first-place award for bed-and-breakfasts from the National Trust for Historic Preservation. The stunning hand-silk-screened wallpapers and the carefully chosen antique furnishings make this a very special place. Each of the seven guest rooms has a private bath and a different decor. The largest are the **Victorian** and **Briar Rose** rooms upstairs, with antique beds, bay windows, and chaise longues. Another favorite is the **Bradbury Room,** with a queen-sized bed, a fireplace, and a coffered ceiling papered in an intricate patchwork of patterns. Rosalie and her daughter, who manages the place, are real country cooks. They serve breakfast in the handsome formal dining room, which might include a platter of sausages from the Sonoma Sausage Co., fluffy buttermilk pancakes, and a light, flaky apple tart, still warm from the oven. With advance notice, they can put together a gourmet picnic lunch; the menu changes every week and always includes a bottle of the wine the Hopes make from the tiny vineyard beside the house.

The **Hope-Bosworth House** across the street is furnished in a less formal style; the five guest rooms are smaller and less expensive. However, guests at both houses have use of the large swimming pool and gardens at the Hope-Merrill House. After more than 10 years of running an inn, the Hopes know a lot about the wine country, and will sit down with you to outline a personal tour of small wineries (Bellerose, Pastori, Ferrari-Carano, and Lytton Springs are some of their favorites). ♦ 21253 and 21238 Geyserville Ave, Geyserville. 857.3356

240 Trentadue Winery At this facility with massive red barn doors, the Trentadue family, grape growers in the valley since the early sixties, produces a slew of wines: Sémillon, Carignane, Merlot, sparkling wine, their Old Patch Red (which comes from a patch of 103-year-old vines), dessert wines, and a couple of port-style wines. In the tasting room pick up picnic supplies, cut-crystal wineglasses, and baskets to tote it all to the shady picnic area sheltered by a latticed grape arbor. ♦ Tasting and sales daily 10AM–5PM. 19170 Geyserville Ave, Geyserville. 433.3104

241 Chateau Souverain This startling architectural complex, with a distinctive bluish slate roof meant to evoke a French chateau, started out as Villa Fontaine in 1972 with the Pillsbury Flour folks at the helm. Since then, it has changed names and owners a number of times, and it is now owned by the parent company of Beringer in the Napa Valley. Their roster of white wines include a Carneros reserve and regular Chardonnay, along with Gewürztraminer, Riesling, and Chenin Blanc. They also make Cabernet, Merlot, and Zinfandel. The chateau is home to not only one of the best restaurants in the wine country but also a more casual cafe. ♦ Tasting and sales daily 10AM–5PM. 400 Souverain Rd, Geyserville. 433.8281

Also at Chateau Souverain:

Chateau Souverain Café at the Winery ★★$$ They've really got the right idea with this contemporary cafe with bright paintings on the wall and jazz playing in the background. Open all afternoon, it offers a menu of light, deftly prepared dishes. Enjoy a glass

Russian River Valley

of the chateau's wine with oysters on the half shell, a fruit-and-cheese plate, or a slice of housemade duck pâté at one of the little bistro tables upstairs or down. Or do a little California-style grazing with dishes such as fried calamari with cilantro aioli (garlic mayonnaise), a hefty grilled ham-and-Gruyère-cheese sandwich on walnut bread, or a bowl of steamed mussels and clams. A great place to eat when you get hungry on the wine trail. ♦ W-Su 11:30AM–10PM

Chateau Souverain Restaurant at the Winery ★★★$$$$ The light, airy dining room, with its high-beamed ceiling, fireplace, and pink and mauve decor, makes this restaurant one of the most romantic in the wine country, especially when the full moon rises over the mountains. When it opened in 1987 under chef **Gary Danko,** this winery restaurant quickly gained a reputation for its finely tuned wine-country cuisine. Danko left in 1990 and was replaced by **Patricia Windisch,** a former student of Madeleine Kamman's and chef at Beringer Vineyards in the Napa Valley.

Restaurants/Clubs: Red **Hotels:** Blue
Shops/ 🌳 Outdoors: Green **Wineries/Sights:** Black

Windisch has kept up the same high standards in the kitchen. She takes much of her inspiration from Mediterranean cuisine, and touches of Asia occasionally sneak into her menus. The dinner menu changes every week and includes half-a-dozen appetizers and main courses. She sometimes does wonderful little savory tarts, such as tomato with mushroom and basil, and beautifully composed salads with smoked chicken on a bed of spinach laced with pears, blue cheese, and walnuts. The smoked salmon risotto with wild mushrooms is an ideal accompaniment to a full-bodied white wine. She is particularly inventive with entrées: consider her smoked, beer-battered lobster tail served with avocado remoulade and mango. Red wine buffs should enjoy the Sonoma lamb with mushroom and shallots, or the veal loin cooked in the style of osso buco. Desserts include a masterful *tiramisu* and chocolate-mousse cake along with a homey apple gratin served with ice cream and warm nutmeg-scented cream. Respectable list of Sonoma County wines. ♦ California/French ♦ Tu-W 11:30AM-3PM; Th-Sa 11:30AM-3PM, 5:30-9PM; Su 10:30AM-3PM. 400 Souverain Rd (off Hwy 101) Geyserville. 433.8281

242 Campbell Ranch Inn $$ Drive up to this 35-acre ranch and you're likely to find innkeeper **Mary Jane Campbell** working in the exuberant flower garden she's planted around the swimming pool in front of the suburban-ranch-style inn. She has her own greenhouse on the property and starts many of the plants as seedlings. She's also an avid baker; the breakfast here, served outside on the brick terrace with a view of Geyser Peak, is one of the inn's main attractions. Her

Russian River Valley

pampered guests also get homemade pie or cake as a bedtime snack. The inn has four guest rooms, all with private baths and king-sized beds; most have a private balcony. She also rents out the old bunkhouse as a private cottage with its own deck and fireplace. Guests have use of the tennis court and the hot tub; she has bicycles available, too. And for those who don't want to miss their favorite TV shows, she's just installed a satellite dish and a large-screen television. ♦ 475 Canyon Rd, Geyserville. 857.3476

243 J. Pedroncelli Winery Just down the road from the Campbell Ranch Inn is Pedroncelli Winery. The original winery and buildings were bought in 1927 by **Giovanni Pedroncelli;** his sons **John** and **Jim** are still running the show. Along with the jug wines of their father's day, the Pedroncellis produce a range of Sonoma County varietals. Try the Zinfandel, especially the reserve, and the Cabernet, both good values. They also make Fumé Blanc and Chardonnay, and their latest wine is a brut rosé. ♦ Tasting and sales daily 10AM-5PM; tours by appt. 1220 Canyon Rd, Geyserville. 857.3531

244 Geyser Peak Winery You can't miss the ivy-covered stone building with flags flying overhead. The winery is owned by the Australian producer **Penfolds** and Santa Rosa businessman **Henry Trione.** The once-staid wines are improving, particulary with the 1989 and later vintages of the Reserve Cabernet. Fans of Gewürztraminer made in a softer style should try the winery's version, along with the Riesling and Chenin Blanc, all easy on the wallet. The Estate Reserve Chardonnay is definitely a good buy, as is the Semchard (a blend of Sémillon and Chardonnay). Among the cellar door selections (featured only at the winery) is a late-harvest Riesling.

Geyser Peak also has two walking trails: the first, named for Bay Area walking enthusiast and author Margaret Doss Patterson, leads from Geyser Peak's administration building on the other side of Hwy 101 past vineyards along the lazy Russian River to a shaded picnic area with a barbecue and views of the vineyards and Geyser Peak Mountain (call ahead to reserve the picnic area). The second panoramic hiking trail winds through the vineyards with views of Geyser Peak. ♦ Tasting and sales daily 10AM-5PM. 22281 Chianti Rd, Geyserville. 857.9463

245 Lyeth Winery Captivated by the chateaux and the spirit of Bordeaux on a tour of the French wine regions, **Munro Lyeth** decided to build his own California chateau. After a year-long search for the right property, he purchased this 285-acre estate in the Alexander Valley, which had first been planted with vines in the 1880s. In 1978 Lyeth designed the triple-peaked winery depicted in outline on the winery's label; his first vintage was 1981. The winery makes just two distinguished Bordeaux-style wines: Lyeth Red, a blend of Cabernet Sauvignon, Merlot, Cabernet Franc, and Malbec (all traditional Bordeaux varieties), and Lyeth Ultra White, a blend of Sauvignon Blanc, Sémillon, and a small amount of Muscadelle Bordelaise. ♦ Tasting, sales, and tours by appt M-F 10AM-4PM. 24625 Chianti Rd, Geyserville. 857.3562

246 Lake Sonoma Winery The **Polson** family, who have three decades of experience growing grapes in Sonoma, established this winery in 1977 at the very end of the Dry Creek Valley. The new tasting room built over the underground cellar is 140 feet above the valley floor and affords a view of Warm Springs Dam and the valley. Sample their full range of wines, which includes Chardonnay, Sauvignon Blanc, Chenin Blanc, Cabernet, and Zinfandel, at the bar or out on the veranda. Summer Sunday afternoons (3-6PM) they hold an informal potluck barbecue (they provide the charcoal, grill, and cooking utensils; you bring the rest; by reservation only). ♦ Tasting, sales, and tours daily 10AM-5PM. 9990 Dry Creek Rd, Geyserville. 431.1550

Cloverdale

An agricultural community just 20 miles north of Healdsburg, Cloverdale was settled in the mid-1800s and is home to one of California's oldest newspapers, *The Cloverdale Reveille,* founded in 1879. From Cloverdale, it is only one and a half hours to the Mendocino Coast by way of the Anderson Valley.

247 KOA Kampground One hundred and fifty campsites (55 of them are tent sites) are offered at this well-maintained family campground on 60 acres with a 60-foot swimming pool, a mini-golf course, a couple of fishing ponds, and a completely stocked store. Horses can come along with the family, too. ♦ Fee. 26460 River Rd, Cloverdale. 894.3337

248 Ye Olde' Shelford House $$ A short walk from the Russian River is this charming Victorian B&B (pictured above), built in 1885 by **Eurasthus M. Shelford** on part of a large ranch acquired by his family in 1863. The long porch in front looks west across a sea of vines. The inn offers six guest rooms, three in the main house and three in the carriage house. The two upstairs bedrooms in the main house share a bath, but guests have the entire floor to themselves. All the rooms are furnished with antiques and handmade quilts, giving the inn a cozy country feel. Guests can use the gazebo for wine tasting and picnic lunches, and innkeeper **Ina Saunder** has a few 10-speed bikes and a bicycle-for-two available for her guests. She also cooks a full breakfast every morning. No smoking. ♦ 29955 River Rd, Cloverdale. 894.5956

At Ye Olde' Shelford House:

Surrey & Sip Ye Olde' Shelford House was once a stagecoach stop. Turn back the clock and take a ride in a turn-of-the-century horse-drawn surrey through the scenic backroads of the Cloverdale area, with a wine-country lunch to top off the excursion. ♦ May-Oct. Reservations required. 894.5856

249 Dutcher Creek RV Park This rustic campground is about a half mile west of Hwy 101 and a 10-minute drive or 30-minute bike ride from Lake Sonoma. They have 22 campsites, 10 suitable for tents and another 12 for RVs or trailers, with hot showers, a laundry room, and a picnic area. Call for directions. ♦ Fee. 230 Theresa Dr, Cloverdale. Reservations recommended. 894.4829

249 Vintage Towers Bed & Breakfast Inn

$$ This blue-and-white Queen Anne Victorian sits on a quiet residential street in downtown Cloverdale. Listed on the National Register of Historic Places, the handsome house has a big side veranda overlooking a rose garden and a lawn where guests sometimes play a game of croquet. The entire inn was extensively renovated in 1980 and now features a library furnished with chaise longues, a parlor with a TV, stereo, and phone for guests' use, and a special music room housing owners **Jim Mees** and **Garrett Hall's** collection of vintage radios and Victrolas. The four guest rooms and three upstairs tower suites are beautifully furnished with quality antiques and lavish period fabrics. The largest is the **Vintage Tower** suite, with a sitting room in the five-sided tower, a queen-sized bed, a Victorian clawfoot tub, and Eastlake Victorian furniture. Hall, who worked as a pastry chef in Los Angeles before opening the inn, cooks a four-course breakfast every morning with fine coffees, teas, and, of course, his homemade pastries. ♦ 302 N. Main St, Cloverdale. 894.4535

Russian River Valley

250 Pat Paulsen Vineyards Comedian **Pat Paulsen** and his wife, **Jane,** produce Chardonnay and Cabernet from their 37-acre Cloverdale ranch, along with pleasant quaffing wines dubbed (tongue in cheek) Refrigerator White and American Gothic Red—perfect for a picnic along the Russian River. You can also taste Pat Paulsen wines and those of the **Smothers Brothers** at the Smothers Brothers Wine Store in Kenwood (see page 96). ♦ Tasting and sales daily 10AM-6PM. 26155 Asti Store Rd, Asti. 894.3197

251 Diamond Oaks Vineyard At this small Dry Creek Valley winery, the Diamond Oaks label is used exclusively for the reserve wines, which include Chardonnay, Sauvignon Blanc, and Cabernet; the less expensive Thomas Knight signature is the label for their regular bottling. Taste and compare the two at the winery just south of Cloverdale. ♦ Tasting and sales M-F; by appt Sa-Su 10AM-5PM. 26900 Dutcher Creek Rd, Cloverdale. 894.3191

252 Fritz Cellars Known for their Chardonnay, this small winery named for owner **Arthur J. Fritz** also makes Sauvignon Blanc and Zinfandel; many of the wines are available only at the winery, which is built partly underground for maximum energy efficiency. Visitors may use the picnic area overlooking the creek. ♦ Tasting and sales daily noon–4:30PM. 24691 Dutcher Creek Rd, Cloverdale. 894.3389

253 Lake Sonoma & Warm Springs Dam This serpentine lake, created by the US Army Corps of Engineers to protect the Dry Creek Valley from flooding, was opened in 1985 as a recreational area. The lake and surrounding park total 17,600 acres with 53 miles of shoreline. Just 10 miles from Healdsburg, the area offers wonderful picnic spots, miles of hiking trails, and, in summer, swimming, camping, and fishing. At the Visitors Center you can pick up trail guides and learn a little about the region's wildlife and the Pomo Indians who originally settled the area. During the spawning season (November–March), salmon return to the adjoining Lake Sonoma fish hatchery to lay their eggs; from the second-floor **Interpretive Center,** visitors can watch as eggs are removed from females and incubated for 20 days. The hatchery's rearing ponds are home to the fish until they become six or seven inches long and are released into Dry Creek. ♦ Visitors Center M-F 9:30AM-4PM; Sa-Su 10AM-5PM; closed M-Tu in winter. 433.9483

Within the Lake Sonoma area:

Liberty Glen Campground This campground offers 113 campsites for tents or RVs as well as 15 primitive lakeside sites

Russian River Valley

that can be reached only by hiking or boating. ♦ Reservations required. 433.9483

Lake Sonoma Marina Open to the public, this privately owned marina has boats and 250 boat slips for rent, a boat launch, and parking. ♦ Daily 9AM-5PM, winter; 9AM-9PM, summer. 433.2200

(from left) Indian pink, grass nut, and Indian warrior are a few of the wildflowers that can be spotted along the trails around Lake Sonoma

Restaurants/Clubs: Red   Hotels: Blue
Shops/ 🌿 Outdoors: Green   Wineries/Sights: Black

Allan Temko
Architecture Critic, *San Francisco Chronicle*

Inglenook Winery in Rutherford—grand scale and great spaces.

Beringer Winery in St. Helena—the Rhineland of California.

Christian Brothers Winery in St. Helena—stone architecture of monumental dignity and power.

Hess Collection and Winery in Napa—exquisite restoration and expansion of a historic winery with an adventurous art collection.

Jack London State Park in Glen Ellen—ruins of what had been a magnificent house; a fine place to picnic.

The Plaza in Sonoma—a wonderful public space and town hall; stone mementos of early California, especially the Bear Flag Revolution, surround the square.

The **Vallejo Adobe**, west of Sonoma—the greatest and truest ranch house in Northern California.

Michele Anna Jordan
Caterer/Food Columnist/Author of *A Cook's Tour of Sonoma*

Eating the world's best hamburger at **Rocco's** in Freestone, followed by a two-minute walk to the **Wishing Well Nursery** to watch the three black swans float around the pond with its replica of the Statue of Liberty.

An early dinner at **Tre Scalini** in Healdsburg, followed by a movie or live music at the **Raven Theater,** the best movie house in the North Bay.

A summer dinner on the patio of the **Russian River Vineyards** in Forestville, timed to witness the nightly emergence of the thousands of brown bats that live in the towers of the guest rooms bordering the patio.

Shopping at **Traverso's Gourmet Foods and Wine** in Santa Rosa and being waited on by **Enrico** or **Louis Traverso.**

The **Cabaret Theater,** followed by music from the *Stupid White People* at **Ma Stokeld's Old Vic** in Santa Rosa. The steak-and-kidney pie and a Newcastle Brown Ale draught are the perfect accompaniments.

A romantic dinner at **Le Bistro** in Petaluma.

A private picnic at dawn or dusk at **Bodega Head.**

The rising of the October full moon anywhere at all as long as it overlooks the Valley of the Moon (**Viansa Winery** is a good location).

Browsing through the records—yes, the black vinyl kind—at the **Last Record Store** in Santa Rosa.

A leisurely cheese tour of Sonoma County, beginning at the **Marin French Cheese Factory** in Petaluma, progressing to the **Redwood Hill Farm Goat Dairy** and **Rachel's Goat Cheese** in Sebastopol, **Laura Chenel's Chèvre** and **Joe Matos Cheese Factory** in Santa Rosa, and the **Vella Cheese Factory** and the **Sonoma Cheese Factory** in Sonoma.

Visiting **Madeleine Kamman,** the director at **Beringer Vineyards' School for American Chefs** in St. Helena.

Dinner at **Chateau Souverain** in Geyserville, the best in the area.

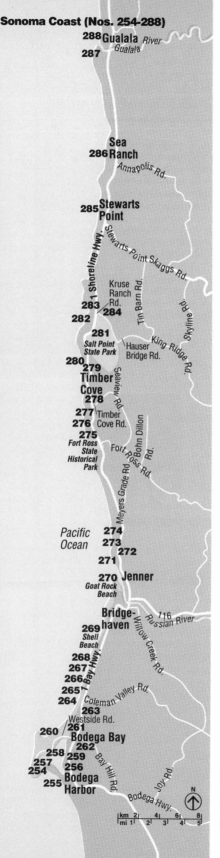

Sonoma Coast

Just an hour's drive north of San Francisco and half an hour west of Santa Rosa lies Bodega Bay and the start of Sonoma's rugged and dramatic coastline—55 miles of pristine beaches, hidden coves, and grassy headlands covered with wildflowers. Home to the Pomo and Coastal Miwok Indians, this section of the coast was largely ignored by the Spanish for two centuries until **Juan Francisco de la Bodega y Cuadro** set anchor here on his way to Alaska and "discovered" the bay that bears his name. The Russians actually established the first white settlements on the coast, building outposts at Fort Ross and Salmon Creek Valley to supply their starving settlers in Alaska with food. But after they had killed off the sea otter population and could no longer support their colonies, they pulled up stakes in 1841. Today this gorgeous area is still sparsely populated, leaving great stretches of uninhabited coastline between small resort towns such as **Jenner** and **Timber Cove.** Most of these hamlets grew up around lumber mills in the mid-19th century as doghole ports, in which lumber was loaded down a chute on the bluffs to ships anchored in the cove below.

More than 5,000 acres and 13 miles of coastline make up the Sonoma Coast State Beach system, which encompasses sandy beaches, salt marshes, underwater reserves and parks, and myriad tide pools. There are more than 20 distinct beaches, separated by rocky outcroppings; the most popular include **Doran Beach** in Bodega Bay, **Salmon Creek Beach** at the mouth of Salmon Creek, **Goat Rock Beach** at the mouth of the Russian River, and **Salt Point State Park** just north of Timber Cove. You can camp at some of the beaches or find lodging in seaside inns. Wherever you stay, the emphasis is on quiet and relaxation, making the Sonoma Coast an ideal weekend retreat. Bring binoculars for bird-watching and spotting wildlife such as harbor seals,

California sea lions, and, if you've timed it right, migrating gray whales. The state park system also includes protected underwater areas for diving. Watch for the brown Coastal Access signs with an illustration of bare feet superimposed on a wave to indicate where it's possible to get down to the beach. For more information, contact the state park office at Salmon Creek Lagoon (707/875.3483) or the Russian River Region information center (707/865.2391).

Bodega Bay

This town (just 68 miles north of San Francisco) is a popular weekend destination for those who enjoy exploring the dunes and beaches, and it's now one of the busiest commercial fishing ports between San Francisco and Eureka. The bay was discovered on 3 October 1775 by the Spanish explorer **Juan Francisco de la Bodega y Cuadro,** for whom it is named. Eighteen years after its discovery, the naturalist **Archibald Menzies,** a member cf an expedition led by **Captain George Vancouver,** disembarked here to collect botanical specimens. Today the area is still rich in flora and fauna, and from November through March, during the annual whale migration, Bodega Head draws many visitors to watch the whales as they pass on their way to or from Baja California.

254 Bodega Head The southernmost tip of a peninsula that extends south from Bodega Dunes, Bodega Head is characterized by high bluffs and steep, craggy cliffs. Bodega Rock, half a mile off shore, is a breeding ground for Brandt's cormorants and western gulls; harbor seals and California sea lions can also be spotted there. During the annual whale migrations, Bodega Head is a prime spot for watching the giant mammals. On clear days the rugged area offers fine views

Sonoma Coast

of the Marin and Sonoma coasts. ♦ End of Westside Rd, Bodega Bay. 875.3540

255 Bodega Marine Laboratory Part of the 356-acre Bodega Marine Reserve is dedicated to the University of California's marine research facility. Docent-guided tours are given once a week, taking visitors through the research laboratories and aquariums. ♦ Tours F 2-4PM. Westside Rd, Bodega Bay. 875.2211

256 Bodega Harbour Golf Links This privately owned, 18-hole course adjacent to the Bodega Bay Lodge was designed by **Robert Trent Jones, Jr.** Trent laid out the course with ocean views from every hole. From the championship tee, the course is 6,200 yards; it is 5,630 yards from the regular tee. Par 70. ♦ Daily 7AM-6PM, summer; 7AM-dusk, winter. 21301 Heron Dr, Bodega Bay. Reservations taken up to 60 days in advance. 875.3538

257 Doran Beach Regional Park at Bodega Bay Just down the road from the Bodega Bay Lodge is a regional park perched on the narrow, two-mile-long spit of sand that separates Bodega Harbour from Bodega Bay. Bird-watchers haunt the salt marshes and the low sand dunes to gaze at sanderlings, willets, snowy plovers, and other shorebirds. The park has ocean and bay access and is a popular spot for swimming and surfing. It's also a good place for clam digging; razor and horseneck clams are just two of the varieties found here. There's an ocean fishing pier, a public boat launch, and a fish-cleaning station, along with picnic tables and restrooms. The park has 128 campsites with space for a car or RV, plus 10 suitable for tents only. ♦ Fee per vehicle. Hwy 1. 875.3540

258 Bodega Bay Lodge $$$ This Best Western inn consists of a  series of two-story, brown-shingled buildings on a secluded, terraced site sheltered by pines and overlooking the salt marshes of Bodega Bay. The showpieces of the main lobby are the massive fieldstone fireplace and two stunning, 500-gallon saltwater aquariums filled with tropical fish, starfish, and coral. All 78 of the inn's rooms have patios or balconies, coffeemakers, and cable TV. They afford views of the salt marsh and the ocean beyond, and most have tiled fireplaces. The decor is clean-cut contemporary with carpeting, matching comforters, and tiled bathrooms. There's a modest-sized swimming pool here and a whirlpool spa that stands beneath a fieldstone-and-redwood gazebo open to the sky. Guests also have use of a redwood sauna and fitness room equipped with Lifecycles and Nautilus equipment. Bicycle down to Doran Beach on one of the inn's complimentary bikes; they'll also put together a basket lunch (you get several choices). ♦ Pool and spa daily 9AM-10PM. Coast Hwy 1, Bodega Bay. 875.3525, 800/528.1234

Restaurants/Clubs: Red   Hotels: Blue
Shops/ 🌴 Outdoors: Green   Wineries/Sights: Black

Within the Bodega Bay Lodge:

Ocean Club Restaurant ★$$$ A complimentary Continental breakfast is served to guests in the dining room, and the restaurant offers both a nightly prix fixe and an à la carte menu that changes monthly. Executive chef **Keith Strellis** concentrates on Sonoma County ingredients with dishes such as Bodega Harbour seafood chowder, boned chicken stuffed with housemade sausage and wild rice, and grilled Petaluma duck quesadilla with pepper jack cheese and avocado chile salsa. Follow that with a fresh little salad tossed with raspberry vinaigrette and the *crème brûlée* or poached pear and local berries served with *crème anglaise*. ♦ California ♦ M, W-Su 6-9PM. Reservations required. 875.3525

258 Lucas Wharf Fish Market and Delicatessen The boats unload their catch right at this wharf, where the fish is cleaned and placed in the market for sale. Picnickers can find smoked salmon, cooked shrimp, pickled herring, and crab meat, along with fresh fish filets or beautiful fresh whole salmon for the grill. They've also got an array of cold cuts, cheeses, giant pickles, pig's feet, and other fare, and will make any of two dozen sandwiches to go. Pick up a jar of the Peloponnese pickled baby eggplant as an appetizer. ♦ M-F 10AM-6PM; Sa-Su 9AM-8PM. 595 Hwy 1, Bodega Bay. 875.3562

Also at the Lucas Wharf Fish Market and Delicatessen:

Lucas Wharf Seafood Bar To one side of the fish market and deli is a bar with oysters and hot seafood to go. Order some fish and chips, shrimp and chips, or, for that matter, calamari or oysters and chips. Spicy Cajun-style shrimp and onion rings are also specialties. They've got iced beers and soft drinks, and a few picnic tables beside the take-out window. ♦ M, F-Su 11AM-5PM, summer; Sa-Su 11AM-5PM, winter. 875.3562

Lucas Wharf Restaurant and Bar ★$$ This is a pleasant spot for a beer or a quick bite. The broad, wooden plank floorboards and old-fashioned wooden chairs give the restaurant a vaguely nautical scheme, but the real decor is just outside the windows: a nonstop view of all the goings-on in the harbor. A bowl of Boston clam chowder will take the chill off, or try the mussels steamed in white wine, shallots, and garlic or the standard Dungeness crab Louis. Entrées include grilled red snapper filet with lemon butter, king salmon with hollandaise sauce, and a deep-fried seafood mix of calamari, prawns, and oysters. They've also got some surf 'n' turf combos and half-pound burgers. Watch for daily specials such as pan-braised sea bass or garlic fettuccine with smoked salmon, scallops, and mussels. ♦ Seafood ♦ M-Th, Su 11AM-9:30PM; F-Sa 11AM-10PM. 875.3522

258 The Tides Wharf Fresh Fish Market The same folks who own The Inn at the Tides developed this uninspiring, touristy complex across the road. They've got a great spot with a long stretch of wharf in front; plunking down buildings better suited to a shopping mall was an unfortunate choice. However, you can pick up a cooked whole crab or oysters for a picnic, fresh fish for the grill, packaged cheeses, and chilled white wines from Sonoma producers. The fish market also has bait and tackle, and there's a gift shop. ♦ M-Th, Su 7AM-8PM; F-Sa 7AM-9PM. 835 Hwy 1, Bodega Bay. 875.3554

Within The Tides Wharf Fresh Fish Market:

The Tides Wharf Restaurant ★$$ This seafood restaurant features everything from fish and chips and grilled or pan-fried fillets to crab cioppino (seafood stew) and deep-fried oysters. They've got a great view of the harbor, but the decor is coffee-shop mundane. At breakfast, you can get the usual egg dishes, hot cakes, and side orders. ♦ Seafood ♦ M-Th, Su 7:15AM-9:30PM; W-Sa 7:15AM-10PM. 875.3652

258 Bodega Harbor Inn $ A very basic motel with 16 rooms in slate-blue bungalows on a hillside overlooking Porto Bodega Marina. All

Sonoma Coast

have small private baths and cable TV. ♦ 1345 Bodega Ave, Bodega Bay. 875.3594

258 Candy & Kites/Harbor Kites When the wind is good, stop here to pick up dual-control stunt kites, beginners' kites, and colorful dragon kites. A series of baskets overflows with saltwater taffy in bizarre flavors: red cinnamon, black licorice, peanut butter. Believe it or not, the taffy comes in sugar-free versions, too. ♦ M-F 10AM-5PM; Sa-Su 10AM-6PM. 1415 Hwy 1, Bodega Bay. 875.3777

258 The Boathouse This seafood snack bar offers fish and chips, clam strips, fried calamari, oysters, prawns, and scallops. Landlubbers can also get cheeseburgers and turkey or roast beef sandwiches. Take out or grab a table on the large deck outside. ♦ Seafood snack bar ♦ Daily noon-9PM. 1145 Hwy 1, Bodega Bay. 875.3495

At The Boathouse:

New Sea Angler & Jaws Sportfishing

The Boathouse offers sportfishing trips on the 65-foot *New Sea Angler* or the 55-foot *Jaws,* which take 49 and 38 passengers, respectively. The larger ship heads out to Cordell Bank, Fanny Shoals, and the Farallon Islands, while the smaller ship specializes in light-tackle rock cod trips. The Boathouse will provide bait and tackle, breakfast, and box lunches if desired. ♦ Daily 7AM-5PM. Reservations required, plus 50 percent deposit. 875.3495

258 *Challenger* **Sportfishing** This firm specializes in sportfishing and deep-sea fishing for salmon, rock cod, and ling cod in their 55-foot *Challenger* boat. They also give one-and-a-half-hour cruises of the harbor on Saturday evenings during the summer, and they host whale-watching expeditions from January through April. ♦ Daily 6AM-9PM; harbor cruises Sa 7-8:30PM, May-Oct. 1785 Hwy 1, Bodega Bay. Reservations required. 875.2474

259 **The Inn at the Tides** $$$ Seen from the road, the brown-shingled guest lodges scattered over the hillside to the east of Hwy 1 look more like

condominiums than an inn. There are 86 guest rooms altogether, every one with a view of the harbor below. Most have tiled fireplaces and all have small refrigerators, coffeemakers, cable TV, and terry robes. The decor is contemporary, though somewhat dated, featuring plush carpeting, print comforters, and suburban-style baths. Guests have use of the outdoor lap pool, whirlpool spa, and Finnish sauna. Complimentary Continental breakfast is served every morning. ♦ 800 Hwy 1, Bodega Bay. 875.2751, 800/541.7788

Also at The Inn at the Tides:

Bay View Room ★$$$ This intimate restaurant, serving a limited California menu five nights a week, looks out on the bay and a terraced flower garden. Choose from half-a-dozen main courses, all served with soup or salad, such as poached king salmon with lemon-chive butter, seared breast of Petaluma duck in gooseberry-orange sauce, and fettuccine lavished with lobster, scallops, and Parmesan cheese. ♦ California ♦ W-Su 6-10PM. Reservations recommended. 875.2751

259 **Nuño's TNT** ★$$ This unpretentious Mexican restaurant serves home-style cooking. Try the nachos doused with Rancher0 sauce and topped with guacamole and sour cream, the oversized quesadilla stuffed with cheese, mushrooms, and green onion, and the Baja-style seafood dishes such as grilled lobster tail served with rice, beans, lime wedges, and flour tortillas. You can also find more conventional burritos, tacos, and enchiladas. They have a children's menu and a nice list of Mexican beers. ♦ Mexican ♦ M-F 11AM-9PM; Sa-Su 11AM-10PM. 1400 Hwy 1, Bodega Bay. 875.2729

259 **Crab Pot** For 20 years now, **Billie** and **Lynn** have been smoking fish and seafood at their bright orange shack with nasturtiums planted all around. Stop by and most likely you'll find aromatic smoke seeping from the door; they use applewood to smoke salmon, tuna, swordfish, sturgeon, and peppered salmon. They'll make up shrimp and crab sandwiches, too, and offer a few chilled wines, mostly from Pedroncelli and Geyser Peak. In season, they also have whole cooked Dungeness crabs. ♦ Daily 9AM-6PM, summer; 9AM-5:30PM, winter. 1750 Hwy 1, Bodega Bay. 875.9970

260 **The Sandpiper Dockside Cafe & Restaurant** ★$$ Stop in for breakfast at this casual cafe, where the service couldn't be friendlier and the bonus is a view of the harbor and bay. They've got eggs served with home fries or hash browns and patty sausage, along with *huevos rancheros* and a dynamite Spanish omelet loaded with salsa, avocado, and sour cream. Another favorite: the omelet made with Dungeness crab and jack cheese. At lunch they serve a clam chowder so thick the spoon stands up in it, salads, fish and chips, burgers, and fresh-fish sandwiches. The dinner menu includes several more ambitious dishes, including snapper Vera Cruz smothered in a cilantro-spiked fresh tomato sauce, linguine with clam sauce, and a New York steak served with tempura prawns. ♦ M-Tu, Th, Su 7AM-8PM; W 7AM-6PM; F-Sa 7AM-9PM. 1410 Bay Flat Rd, Bodega Bay. 875.2278

261 **Branscomb Gallery** The three-level gallery exhibits work by local artists along with those from around the country. Note the wildlife etchings by Mendocino artist **James J.D. Mayhew,** watercolors of Sonoma County landscapes by **El Meyer,** and colored etchings of vineyards and other rural scenes by **Gail Packer.** ♦ Daily 10AM-4PM. 1588 Eastshore Rd, Bodega Bay. 875.3388, 800/548.2439; fax 875.2905

261 Vacation Rentals International $$$ This agency rents out more than a hundred private beach homes, ranging from cabins on Salmon Creek to five-bedroom homes in a country-club setting. Rentals in the Bodega Harbour development include guest privileges at the Bodega Harbour Country Club. Rent for two to three nights or by the week or month. ♦ Daily 9AM-5PM. 1580 Eastshore Rd, Bodega Bay. 875.2221, 800/548.7631

261 Lucy's Whale of a Cookie & Pastry Place Half-a-dozen types of cookies are baked right here. (And unlike most cookies from similar shops, Lucy's are not too sweet!) Try the oatmeal coconut walnut cookie, the chocolate chip macadamia nut, or the classic chocolate chip with walnuts. You can also buy some of the cookie dough to take home and bake, and they carry Thanksgiving coffee beans from Mendocino and jams and jellies from Kozlowski Farms in Forestville. ♦ Daily 8AM-5PM. 1580 Eastshore Rd, Bodega Bay. 875.2280

262 The Bay Hill Mansion $$ This brand-new three-story inn sits high on a hill overlooking the bay and is meant to be a contemporary version of a Queen Anne Victorian. The inn has six guest rooms, each with queen-sized beds, down comforters, and a view; most have shared baths. Innkeeper **Fran Miller** serves a full breakfast each morning in the dining room, which has a view of the bay. ♦ 3919 Bay Hill Rd, Bodega Bay. 875.3577, 800/526.5927

263 Sea Horse Guest Ranch $$ If you're planning on some riding, why not bunk at the B&B on this 700-acre working ranch bordered by Salmon Creek? The suburban ranch-style main house has three guest rooms with private baths and color TVs (two of the bedrooms can be connected to make an impromptu suite). Continental breakfast is included. ♦ 2660 Hwy 1, Bodega Bay. 875.2721

Within the Sea Horse Guest Ranch:

Sea Horse Stables Sign up for guided trail rides through the hills and dunes surrounding Bodega Bay. The one-hour Hill Ride winds past Salmon Creek and returns along a hilly route with views of the coastline. The two-hour Dune Ride crosses over to the sand dunes on the other side of Hwy 1 and provides a look at the harbor and marinas. Beginners are welcome, and the stable has pony rides for kids. Guests at the B&B get a 10 percent discount on rides. ♦ Office: daily 8AM-9PM; riding: 10AM-5PM. Reservations recommended. 875.2721

264 Bodega Dunes State Park & Camping More than 900 acres of gentle rolling sand dunes lie covered with soft mounds of dune grasses here. Monarch butterflies winter in the eucalyptus trees, and you can spot alligator lizards, black-tailed deer, jackrabbits, owls, foxes, and badgers throughout the year. Trails include a five-mile loop for hiking and horseback riding; another trail leads to Bodega Head. The park includes a campground with 98 campsites and has numerous picnic areas. ♦ Fee per vehicle. Hwy 1 (1/2 mile north of Bodega Bay). 875.3483

265 Salmon Creek Beach The Russians established a colony in the Salmon Creek Valley in 1809, growing wheat to support their settlements in Alaska. In 1841, when the sea otter population was depleted and they could no longer support their colonies by hunting, they abandoned the settlement. This popular sandy beach at the mouth of Salmon Creek extends some two miles and includes a shallow swimming area. The creek is a good spot to fish for steelhead trout, and the saltwater and freshwater marshes are filled with wildlife. A trail leads south to Bodega Head. ♦ Hwy 1, north of Bodega Bay

266 Portuguese Beach A steep trail leads to this beach. Restrooms are available. ♦ Off Hwy 1, north of Bodega Bay

267 Duncans Landing In the mid-19th century, this was where the lumber from Duncans' sawmill in Bridgehaven was loaded onto ships waiting below. (The lumber was transported by carts from the sawmill.) The small beach here is accessible via a steep trail. ♦ Hwy 1 (about 1 1/2 miles north of Bodega Bay)

268 Wright's Beach Thirty beachside campsites with fire pits are available here.

Sonoma Coast

 ♦ Fee per vehicle. Hwy 1 (1 1/2 miles north of Bodega Bay) 800/444.7275 for camping reservations

269 Shell Beach This beach is a good spot for observing wildlife. It's directly across from Gull Rock—a nesting area for Brandt's cormorants, western gulls, and pigeon guillemots—and black-tailed deer, rabbits, and gray foxes can be sighted on the grassy headlands. Access trail to the beach. ♦ Hwy 1, north of Bodega Bay. 875.3483

270 Goat Rock Beach This state beach situated at the mouth of the Russian River is one of the most popular along the Sonoma Coast. The sand spit formed as the river empties into the sea is a haven for seals and is rich in birdlife. In summer, fish for ocean smelt; in winter, try the Russian River for steelhead trout. While there is access to the beach on both the river side and the ocean side, swimming is allowed only on the former; sleeper waves, which can surprise the unsuspecting swimmer, make it too dangerous on the ocean side. Picnic areas with fire pits are available. Whale talks are given on Sundays, mid-December through mid-April, during the migration of the gray whale. ♦ Off Hwy 1, north of Bodega Bay. 875.3483

Jenner
This town is perched on a high bluff over-looking the spot where the Russian River ends its journey to the sea. It was a bustling logging town in the latter half of the 19th century, and it started a new life as a summer resort at the turn of the century. Today, Jenner remains a small resort area, popular for its laid-back ambience and the rugged beauty of the cove, where birds and wildlife abound. The Penny Island Bird Sanctuary is home to ospreys, blue herons, and other shorebirds.

271 Seagull Gifts & Deli $ Along with espresso drinks, frozen yogurt, and ice cream, this stand-up snack bar dishes out clam chowder, chili, and sandwiches ranging from peanut butter and jelly to local Willie Bird roasted turkey. You can sit at the nearby picnic tables and watch the kayakers go by on the river. The gift shop looks touristy, but actually carries some good wines—from Dry Creek Vineyards, Dehlinger, Kenwood, Roederer Estate, and Sea Ridge. You can also pick up maps and nature books on whales. ♦ Snack bar ♦ Daily 9AM-5PM. 10439 Hwy 1, Jenner. 865.2594

271 Jenner Visitors Center Stop here for information on any of the Sonoma Coast beaches and parks, as well as maps. The center has a small boat-launching ramp, restrooms, and a few picnic tables. ♦ Sa-Su 10AM-4PM. Hwy 1, Jenner. 875.3483

Sonoma Coast

272 Murphy's Jenner Inn $$ This comfortable and unpretentious inn (pictured above) welcomes you immediately with maroon velvet couches pulled up to a wood-burning stove and books and games ready for whiling away an afternoon. Most of the 11 guest rooms, suites, and cottages are furnished with antiques and quilts and have a warm, lived-in feel. The accommodations range from simple, inexpensive rooms with river views in the Captain's House to suites with a private entrance or deck, a fireplace, and a full kitchen. In addition, the inn has half-a-

dozen private homes for rent, most with dramatic ocean views and fireplaces. The most romantic? **The Haven,** a studio cottage with a fireplace and a hot tub, tucked away in Jenner Canyon. ♦ Daily 10AM-8PM. Route 1, Jenner. 865.2377, 800/732.2377

273 Lazy River Motel $ This funky motel with an overgrown garden decorated with driftwood offers modest accommodations in bungalows perched at the very edge of the sea. The decor is plain and humble, but all five rooms have views and the price is definitely right. ♦ 10625 Hwy 1, Jenner. 865.2409

274 River's End Restaurant and Lodging ★★$$ This small, popular restaurant sits atop a cliff just where the Russian River empties into the sea. **Wolfgang Gramatzki** has attracted a loyal local following for his eclectic cooking, which includes German, Indonesian, Asian, French, and American dishes. Some of his specialties are Bahmie Goreng, a mix of poultry, seafood, and beef satay served with Indonesian vegetable noodles and his own peach chutney; stuffed boneless quail; and veal medallions with the unlikely combination of wild mushrooms and crayfish. For dessert, Wolfgang turns out chocolate mousse spiked with rum and an old English trifle composed of sherry-soaked sponge cake layered with Bavarian cream and wild berries. He's got a nice list of local wines, too. ♦ International ♦ M-Sa noon-9:30PM, Su 10AM-9:30PM, summer; hours vary in winter. Hwy 1, Jenner. 865.2484, 869.3252

Within River's End Restaurant and Lodging:

River's End Resort $$ There are three rooms underneath the restaurant, four pint-sized cabins, and a separate little house with a full-sized kitchen that could sleep up to 15 if you folded out all the couches and cots. The wood-paneled cabins set in a row beside the restaurant are very private and consist of a room with either one or two queen-sized beds, a small shower/bath, and a coffeemaker. Sliding glass doors open onto balconies overlooking the river and the ocean beyond. They also have several campsites and a boat-launching facility. ♦ 865.2484; 869.3252

Fort Ross
In 1741, thirteen years after he discovered the strait that bears his name, Russian admiral **Vitus Bering** sailed to the Aleutian Islands and the Alaskan mainland. The Russians were soon exploiting the region for its sea otters. They established outposts on the Aleutian Islands and eventually ventured south along the California coast with the idea of founding a colony to supply the Alaskan settlers with food. **Nikolai Rézanof,** the

imperial chamberlain, made an exploratory visit in 1806 to buy grain in San Francisco and establish trade relations with the Spanish. That same year an agent of the Russian-American Fur Company named **Ivan Alexandrovich Kuskov** was charged with setting up temporary bases at Bodega Bay and Salmon Creek Valley. In 1812 he returned with a party of 25 Russians and 80 Aleuts and founded Fort Ross on a high, windswept bluff overlooking the sea, a few miles north of the river the Spanish had dubbed the "Russian River" after the people who had explored it. By 1840, the Russians had completely depleted the sea otter population along the coast and abandoned their California outposts.

275 Fort Ross State Historic Park You should first stop at the Visitors Center for a copy of the walking tour of the fort. Then follow the well-marked path down to the old fort, situated on a dramatic bluff above the sea; little kids will probably be making cannon noises inside the blockhouse as you pass. The small redwood chapel with its cupolas topped with crosses is actually a reconstruction of the original chapel, which was built in 1812 and partially destroyed in the earthquake of 1906. The Officials' Quarters bring the era back to life with Russian furnishings and carpentry and metal workshops. Peek into the kitchen, where the silver samovar for making tea is stored. Guided tours are available on weekends. The annual Fort Ross Living History Day, on the last Saturday in July, re-creates a typical day at the fort in 1836. If you walk out the west gate of the compound and head north along the road, you'll pass the Call ranch house (**George W. Call** purchased Fort Ross in 1873) and a secluded picnic area in a grove of trees. Adjacent to the park is an offshore underwater park for divers. ♦ Fee per vehicle. Daily 10AM-4:30PM; guided tours Sa-Su 11AM-3PM. Hwy 1, Fort Ross. 847.3286

276 Fort Ross Lodge $$ This gray, wood-framed lodge set on a hillside overlooking the ocean has been designed so that most rooms have ocean views. All 24 of its modern units have a color TV, a private patio with barbecue, a private bath, a small refrigerator, and a coffeemaker. ♦ 20705 Hwy 1, Jenner. 847.3333

277 Timber Cove Boat Landing On the weekends, this is one busy place, with divers in wetsuits unloading their gear in front and sailors arriving to sling launch their boats into the cove below. You can obtain a fishing license here, buy bait and tackle, or rent scuba diving gear or boats. The nominal day-use fee includes transportation to and from the cove and use of the hot tub. There's a campground (some sites with hookups), and campers have use of hot showers, a hot tub, and laundry facilities. You can also sign up for guided boat tours and fishing or sight-seeing trips. ♦ Day-use fee. M-Th, Su 7AM-6PM; F 7AM-10 or 11PM; Sa 7AM-8PM. Hwy 1. 847.3278

Within the Timber Cove Boat Landing:

Sea Coast Hideaways $$/$$$ The proprietors of the boat landing also rent out seven private homes in and around Timber Cove, ranging from a rustic redwood cabin overlooking the boat landing with beach access to a two-bedroom hillside home with a view of Stillwater Cove. ♦ 847.3278

Restaurants/Clubs: Red   **Hotels:** Blue
Shops/ 🌳 Outdoors: Green   **Wineries/Sights:** Black

Sonoma Coast

Fort Ross Compound

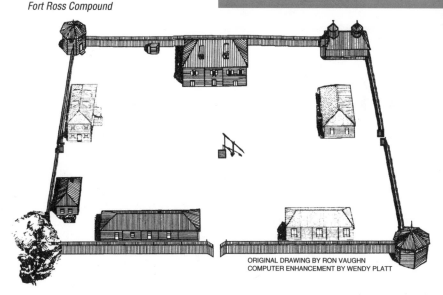

ORIGINAL DRAWING BY RON VAUGHN
COMPUTER ENHANCEMENT BY WENDY PLATT

278 Timber Cove Inn $$$ The Japanese pond where swans and ducks float outside the massive timbered lobby sets the tone of serenity and contemplation at Timber Cove Inn. Everything is very well done, from the sophisticated simplicity of the rooms decorated with Ansel Adams photographs to the large balconies facing the wild, scenic cove. No TVs or phones to disturb you. Just over half of the 47 rooms have fireplaces or wood-burning stoves, and a number have built-in hot tubs. True romantics will like the large ocean-view units with a hot tub either in the room or on the deck—and a shower with a glass wall facing the ocean. ♦ Deluxe ♦ 21780 N. Hwy 1 (three miles north of Fort Ross) Jenner. 847.3231; fax 847.3704

Within the Timber Cove Inn:

Timber Cove Inn Restaurant ★★$$ A few steps down from the bar is the inn's dining room. With its expansive views of the sea, lofty ceiling, and stone walls, it's a dramatic spot for dinner. ♦ Continental ♦ M-Th 6-9:30PM; F-Sa 6-10PM. 847.3231

279 Stillwater Cove Regional Park You'll find a wealth of wildflowers in this park, not to mention ospreys nesting between the cove and Salt Point in the tops of redwood and fir trees. If you take the hiking trail, which runs along Stockhoff Creek, keep an eye out for the Fort Ross schoolhouse, built in Greek Revival style in 1885. There are lots of good picnic areas, as well as a campground with 23 sites available on a first-come, first-serve basis. A stairway provides access to the beach. ♦ Fee per vehicle. Hwy 1. 847.3245, 524.7175

Sonoma Coast

279 Stillwater Cove Ranch $ A former boys' school, this two-decade-old inn offers modestly priced accommodations on a ranch where peacocks, sheep, and deer wander the grounds. One building houses the spacious east and west rooms, both with fireplaces, kitchenettes, and two double beds. Rustic wooden chairs are pulled up in front of the fireplace, and there's a broad veranda in front. The two white cottages are smaller, but both have a fireplace and two double beds. Two other rooms feature king-sized beds; one has a fireplace. Groups of fishermen or divers often rent the **Dairy Barn,** a bunkhouse furnished with eight bunks, a full kitchen, and two showers (bring your own linen for this bargain accommodation). ♦ Daily 8AM-8PM. 22555 Hwy 1 (3 miles north of Fort Ross) 847.3227

"Wine makes daily living easier, less hurried, with fewer tensions, and more tolerance."
Benjamin Franklin

279 Salt Point Lodge $ The name sounds fancy, but this is really a 16-room motel with moderately priced accommodations, not easy to find along the Sonoma Coast. Rooms have a standard contemporary decor and distant ocean views; all have private baths and one has a private hot tub, while another has a fireplace. There is also an outdoor hot tub and sauna. ♦ 23255 Hwy 1 (3 miles north of Fort Ross) 847.3234

Within Salt Point Lodge:

Salt Point Lodge Bar & Grill ★$$ This family restaurant features a solarium bar with an ocean view. The breakfast includes omelets and other egg dishes, while at lunch they concentrate on burgers, sandwiches, and fish and chips. The dinner menu offers seafood dishes and meats barbecued over mesquite: prime rib bones, half chickens, and country ribs, all served with the house barbecue sauce. You can also get a grilled steak or a burger, or try the salad bar. ♦ American ♦ M-Th 9AM-9PM; F 9AM-9:30PM; Sa-Su 8AM-9:30PM. 847.3234

280 Ocean Cove Store & Campground This campground has 80 sites with fire pits; 30 are beside the ocean with great views. ♦ 23125 Hwy 1. 847.3422

281 Salt Point State Park In the past, the Kashaya Pomo and Coast Yuki Indians would take up summer residence here to gather the salt they used to preserve fish—hence the name. The 4,300-acre park is now a National Archeological District because of several ancient Indian sites. It offers a wide variety of terrains, from redwood groves and a pygmy forest of stunted cypresses to craggy bluffs and tide pools. There are lots of secluded picnic areas and campsites at Gerstle Cove and Woodside campgrounds (see below). The park has trails for hiking and horseback riding. It is also an underwater park, and diving is permitted offshore. Guided whale-watching walks available in winter. ♦ 25050 Hwy 1. 847.3221

Within Salt Point State Park:

Gerstle Cove Campground This campground has 30 family campsites with picnic areas and fire pits. Gerstle Cove is an underwater preserve; no form of marine life within its boundaries may be removed or disturbed. (They're trying to allow the depleted abalone population to recover.) ♦ Hwy 1, Salt Point State Park. 847.3221

Woodside Campground Also a part of Salt Point State Park, this campground has 79 campsites plus 20 walk-in sites and 10 primitive sites that are accessible only by hiking or biking. Check in at Gerstle Cove Campground. ♦ Hwy 1, Salt Point State Park. 847.3221

282 Stump Beach Located in Salt Point State Park, this beach is a good spot to observe the breeding of cormorants. No camping is allowed, but there are picnic facilities with fire pits. ◆ Hwy 1 (one mile north of the main entrance to Salt Point State Park) 847.3221

283 Fisk Mill Cove Also in Salt Point State Park, this beach has picnic facilities with fire pits and several trails along the bluffs that lead to the beach below. ◆ Hwy 1, just south of Kruse Ranch Rd. 847.3221

284 Kruse Rhododendron Reserve
Spectacular in the spring, this 317-acre reserve shelters a second-growth redwood forest and a large stand of native California rhododendrons. Some of the shrubs are 20 feet high, and when they are in bloom, mid-April to mid-June, it is quite a sight. No picnic facilities; five miles of hiking trails. ◆ Day-use only. East of Hwy 1, off Kruse Ranch Rd. 865.2391, 847.3221

285 Stewarts Point An important doghole lumber port in the mid-19th century, this is where cut lumber was loaded down a chute to the ships waiting below. The Skagg's Springs Rd is a scenic, but very slow route over to Dry Creek Valley near Healdsburg and the surrounding wine country. ◆ Hwy 1 at Stewarts Point-Skaggs Springs Rd

286 The Sea Ranch Lodge and Golf Links
$$$ In 1964 this magnificent 5,000-acre property was acquired by Hawaii-based Castle & Cook, who did extensive environmental studies before developing the site as a second-home community. The first condominiums were designed by the architectural firm of MTLW (Charles Moor, William Turnbull, Donylyn Lyndon, and Richard Whitaker), and their simple, elegant designs, with shed roofs and natural wood interiors, set the tone for much of the other building that followed. Fortunately, a guest lodge was included in the plans so visitors also can enjoy the serenity and beauty of this unspoiled landscape. All of the rooms have views of the sea; most have natural wood paneling and a rustic, modern decor, with patchwork quilts, bentwood rockers, and window seats. The complex includes tennis courts, a heated swimming pool, and a sauna. Even if you're not planning to stay here, stop by the bar and sit for a while in front of this unsurpassed view of the headlands and the sea beyond. ◆ 60 Sea Walk Dr, Sea Ranch. 785.2371, 800/842.3270

Within the Sea Ranch Lodge:

The Sea Ranch Restaurant ★$$ The beautiful dining room, which has views of the bluffs and the sea, is simply and elegantly

furnished. There are no surprises on the breakfast or brunch menus, and lunch features such standard fare as a chef's salad, seafood pasta, burgers, and several sandwiches. The dinner menu changes seasonally and pretty much sticks to the straight and narrow, a grilled New York steak, veal scaloppine, and chicken cordon bleu. ◆ California ◆ M-F 8-10:30AM, 11:30AM-2:30PM, 6-9PM; Sa-Su 8AM-2:30PM, 6-9PM. 785.2371

Sea Ranch Public Access Trails Within
this enormous private reserve are five trails to the beach below, with parking areas west of Hwy 1. Look for the brown California access signs to Walk-On Beach, Shell Beach, Stengel Beach, Pebble Beach, and Black Point Beach. In addition, there is a trail into Sea Ranch from Gualala Point Regional Park and another that runs along the bluffs from the same park.

286 Ram's Head Realty Vacation Rentals
Sea Ranch home rentals are available for two days to a week or more. They range from small redwood cabins to large luxury homes. ◆ Annapolis Rd, Sea Ranch. 785.2427

286 Sea Ranch Escapes This company rents Sea Ranch properties for the weekend, week, or month. ◆ 60 Sea Walk Dr, Sea Ranch. 785.2426

286 Sea Ranch Vacation Rentals More private homes at Sea Ranch can be rented here. ◆ Box 88, Sea Ranch, 785.2579

287 Sea Ranch Golf Course Just south of the
Gualala River is this privately owned, nine-hole championship golf course designed by **Robert Muir Graves.** It boasts an ocean view from every hole. ◆ Daily 7AM-dusk; driving range: daily 7AM-5PM. 785.2467, 800/842.3270

288 Gualala Point Regional Park This park is another prime spot for winter whale-

watching, and for bird-watching and wildlife spotting throughout the year. Look for great blue herons, pygmy owls, shorebirds, deer, jack rabbits, and gray foxes. Cormorants can be seen offshore on Gualala Point Island. The 75-acre park has river and ocean access, and includes 19 campsites with picnic facilites and fire pits, available on a first-come, first-serve basis. ◆ Visitors Center M, F-Su 10AM-3PM. Hwy 1, one mile south of Gualala. 785. 2377

The tomb of King Tutankhamem (who died in 1,352 BC) included 36 amphoras of wine meant to accompany his spirit on its journey to the afterlife.

The first member of the University of California faculty to teach viticulture was Professor Eugene Hilgard who started instructing in 1880.

Restaurants/Clubs: Red   **Hotels:** Blue
Shops/ 🌳 Outdoors: Green   **Wineries/Sights:** Black

Mendocino County's Hopland-Ukiah Wine Road

From Cloverdale in the Russian River Valley, it's a short jaunt north on Hwy 101 to the tiny township of **Hopland** and the dozen or so wineries scattered along the highway close to town and up towards **Ukiah.** A rural, sparsely populated area, this part of **Mendocino** has enjoyed a Renaissance of winemaking in the last two decades. Hopland, the improbable center of it all, was a hop-growing region hit by an economic slump when hops (the flavorful dried flowers of the hop vine) went out of fashion in American beer brewing in the 1950s. The most visible presence of the town's new-found prosperity is the **Fetzer** tasting room, a former high school turned into an attractive wine-tasting station and shop featuring local products (it's the first building on the left as you drive through the three-block town). Several of the other local wineries also have opened tasting rooms in Hopland. If you have the time, drive out to the back roads and visit wineries such as **McDowell, Hidden Cellars,** or tiny **Whaler Vineyards,** which are set in a bucolic, rugged landscape. More wineries are strung along the highway all the way to Ukiah, the county seat. And north of **Lake Mendocino,** a few more remote, small wineries are tucked into the folds of Redwood Valley.

In between a few visits to favorite wineries, it's easy to fit in some bicycling around the wine country or even some water sports on Lake Mendocino. And from Hopland or Ukiah, you can drive over the mountains to **Clear Lake,** visiting wineries such as **Kendall-Jackson** in **Lakeport** and **Konocti** in **Kelseyville** on the Mendocino side of the lake. Depending on which route you take, it's a half-hour to 40-minute drive one way. This part of Mendocino is also home to two of the few producers of pot-still brandies (the same process used in the Cognac region of France). **Jepson** produces brandy and wine and you can see the copper alambic (or distilling aparatus) when you visit (alas, you cannot taste the brandy there). The second producer is **Germain-Robin,** and while they are not open for visitors, you can purchase their brandy at the Fetzer tasting room in Hopland. Look for Jepson and Germain-Robin brandies on local wine lists.

If you're visiting on a weekend, be sure to make a reservation for a guided tour of **Fetzer Valley Oaks Food & Wine Center,** a remarkable, 50-acre complex with a showcase organic garden devoted to the study of food and wine. In Ukiah, the **Grace Hudson Museum and Sun House** is definitely worth seeing. As for lodging, try the three-story, Victorian **Thatcher Inn** in Hopland or a bed and breakfast in Hopland or Ukiah. A little-known alternative is **Vichy Hot Springs** east of Ukiah, a historic hot-springs resort that was recently refurbished. (They also bottle the naturally effervescent mineral water under the Vichy Springs label.)

Hopland-Ukiah Wine Road

Good restaurants around here are rare. There's the **Thatcher Inn** for California cuisine, or the **Hopland Brewery** for casual pub fare and live music at night. The wine road in this area is compact enough for you to spend the morning visiting the tasting rooms in Hopland and a couple of nearby wineries and still have time to lunch in the charming town of Boonville.

For information on Mendocino County parks, call 937.5804; for camping reservations, call 800/444.7275; and for vacation home rentals, contact Mendocino Coast Reservations by writing to Box 1143, Mendocino CA 95460, or call 937.5033 or 800/262.7801.

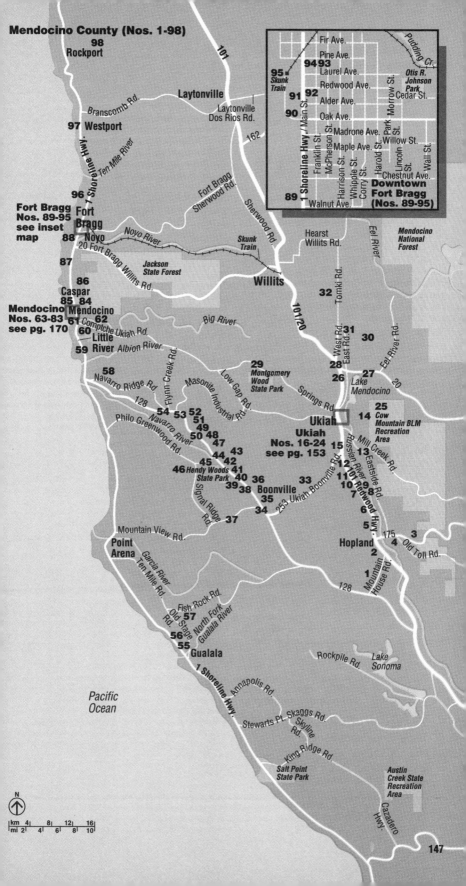

Mendocino County (Nos. 1-98)

98 Rockport

Laytonville

Branscomb Rd.

97 Westport

Laytonville Dos Rios Rd.

101

162

Ten Mile River

1 Shoreline Hwy.

Fort Bragg Sherwood Rd.

96

Fort Bragg Nos. 89-95 see inset map

Fort Bragg

88 Novo

20 Fort Bragg Willits Rd.

Novo River

Sherwood Rd.

Skunk Train

Hearst Willits Rd.

Mendocino National Forest

Eel River

87

Jackson State Forest

86

Caspar

85 84

Mendocino Nos. 63-83 see pg. 170

61 62

Mendocino

Comptche Ukiah Rd.

60

Little River

59

Albion River

Willits

32

Tomki Rd.

West Rd.

East Rd.

31 30

101/20

Big River

58

Navarro Ridge Rd.

128

Flynn Creek Rd.

Low Gap Rd.

Masonite Industrial Rd.

29 Montgomery Wood State Park

Springs Rd.

28 26 27 Lake Mendocino

Eel River Rd.

20

54 53 52 51 49 50 48 47 44 43 45 42 46 Hendy Woods State Park 41 40 39 38 36 35 34 37

Navarro River

Philo Greenwood Rd.

Signal Ridge Rd.

Ukiah

Ukiah Nos. 16-24 see pg. 153

33

Boonville

253 Ukiah Boonville Rd.

25 Cow Mountain BLM Recreation Area

14 15

Mill Creek Rd.

Russian River

Eastside Rd.

13 12 11 10 9 8 7 6 5

101 Redwood Hwy.

Mountain View Rd.

Point Arena

Garcia River

Ten Mile Rd.

Fish Rock Rd.

Old Stage Rd.

57

56

55

Gualala

North Fork Gualala River

3 175 4 Old Toll Rd.

Hopland

2

1

128

Mountain House Rd.

Rockpile Rd.

Lake Sonoma

Pacific Ocean

1 Shoreline Hwy.

Annapolis Rd.

Stewarts Pt. Skaggs Rd.

Skyline Rd.

King Ridge Rd.

Salt Point State Park

Austin Creek State Recreation Area

Cazadero Hwy.

N

km 4 8 12 16
mi 2 4 6 8 10

Inset: Downtown Fort Bragg (Nos. 89-95)

Fir Ave.

Pine Ave.

94 93

Laurel Ave.

95 Skunk Train

Redwood Ave.

91 92

Alder Ave.

90

Oak Ave.

Madrone Ave.

Maple Ave.

89

Walnut Ave.

1 Shoreline Hwy. / Main St.

Franklin St.

McPherson St.

Harrison St.

Whipple St.

Corry St.

Harold St.

Park

Lincoln St.

Chestnut Ave.

Willow St.

Wall St.

Pudding Cr.

Otis R. Johnson Park

Cedar St.

Morrow St.

Downtown Fort Bragg (Nos. 89-95)

147

Hopland

Just three blocks long, Hopland is billed as the gateway to the Mendocino wine country. It is surrounded by vineyards, with the majority of the valley's wineries strung out along Hwy 101 north of Hopland all the way to Ukiah and the Redwood Valley beyond. To make their products more easily accessible to visitors, several of the wineries have installed tasting rooms right in town. **Fetzer Vineyards** is the most prominent, but you'll also find **McDowell, Hidden Cellars,** and **Dunnewood,** plus a few antique shops and the restored **Thatcher Inn.**

Before the arrival of white settlers in the early 1850s, Pomo Indians lived in the area around Hopland. The entire Sanel Valley was granted to **Fernando Féliz,** who had come from Pueblo San José south of San Francisco, and the town of Sanel grew up around his home there. The township, first called Sanel, was established in 1859 and named after an Indian village that once occupied a nearby site on McDowell Creek. By the mid-1860s the surrounding area had become the prime producer of hops for the brewing industry, and in 1887, Sanel was renamed Hopland in honor of its best-selling crop.

Despite a setback during Prohibition, farmers continued to grow mainly hops until the fifties, when the market diminished and it made more sense for most of them to replant their fields with pear and prune orchards and grape vineyards. The town was a quiet backwater until Fetzer Vineyards opened their tasting room complex in 1977 (and frankly, even today you wouldn't exactly call it a hopping town).

DUNCAN PEAK
Vineyards

Mendocino County
Cabernet Sauvignon 1988
Produced by Hubert Lenczowski

BOTTLED BY DUNCAN PEAK WINE COMPANY, UKIAH, CA
ALCOHOL 12.5 PERCENT BY VOLUME

1 Duncan Peak Vineyards This tiny winery makes just one wine: a Cabernet Sauvignon from grapes grown on a few hillside acres on the edge of Sanel Valley near Hopland. Owner **Hubert Lenczowski** produces only 500 cases of handcrafted Cabernet each year. ♦ Tasting and tours by appt only. 14500 Mountain House Rd, Hopland. 744.1129

2 Milano Winery When winemaker **Jim Milone** founded this winery in 1977, he incorporated the old barn-like hop kiln his grandfather and father had built into the winery. The weathered redwood structure houses the tasting room, where you can sample their Chardonnay, Cabernet Sauvignon, and Zinfandel. Also try their special late-harvest dessert wines, if there's still any left by the time you get around to visiting. One standout: in 1985 they produced a true ice wine (made from berries that had been left on the vine to shrivel and concentrate their sugars, and then frozen in the field). The bottle is incised with snowflakes and grapes; available in very limited quantities. Almost all of Milano's wines are sold directly at the winery. ♦ Tasting daily 10AM-5PM; tours by appt. 14594 S. Hwy. 101, Hopland. 744.1396

At Milano Winery:

Private Reserve Cottage $$ Jim and Pat Milone offer a self-contained cottage for rent on the Milano Winery property. It stands all by itself just off the drive, but it's not really secluded. It has a small private yard, barbecue, and bicycles. They'll also take guests out for a walk through their 64-acre vineyard and a tour of the winery. ♦ 744.1396

3 McDowell Valley Vineyards A beautiful four-mile drive east on Hwy 175 takes you to McDowell Valley, where this small family winery is installed in a low-slung redwood building outfitted with banks of solar panels. The world's first solar-heated winery was designed and built by vintners **Richard** and **Karen Keehn** in 1979. Part of their property had been planted in Syrah and Grenache grapes in the twenties, and these vines, perhaps the oldest in California, go into McDowell's Les Vieux Cépages (the old varietals). They make a graceful Grenache Rosé in the style of Provence's Tavel; a cuvée called Le Trésor (a Syrah/Grenache blend), which takes its inspiration from Châteauneuf-du-Pape and Gigondas from the Rhône Valley; and they've just introduced a rich, concentrated Syrah. In addition, they make a wonderful Fumé Blanc (Sauvignon Blanc with a little Sémillon blended in), and both a regular and an estate reserve Chardonnay. They also have lots of fans of their rich, berry-like Zinfandel from old vines, aged in small oak barrels. Their two generic white and red table wines are ideal for a casual picnic or barbecue. The redwood tasting room on the top story of the winery boasts an entrancing view of the valley. You can also sample their wines at the Grapevine Tasting Group room in downtown Hopland. ♦ Tasting and sales Sa-Su 10AM-5PM; tours by appt. 3811 Hwy 175, Hopland. 744.1053

4 Fetzer Valley Oaks Food & Wine Center The dynamic Fetzer family designed this culinary research center in 1984. To date, more than 50 acres have been developed, including a spectacular four-and-a-half-acre organic garden and an experimental organic vineyard. Open to the public only on weekends, the garden is planted with more than 1,000 varieties of fruits, vegetables, herbs, and ornamental and edible flowers. The center also includes conference rooms and a state-of-the-art demonstration kitchen where weekend cooking classes are hosted. The culinary director is **John Ash,** who owns **John Ash & Co.,** a wine-country restaurant in Santa Rosa. Some classes are taught by Ash, others by a roster of celebrated guest chefs. For guided tours of the winery and garden, as well as information on cooking classes, write or call Joel Clark. ♦ Docent-led tours of the garden Sa-Su by reservation. 13601 East Side Rd, Hopland. 744.1250

5 Made in Mendocino, Inc. Next door to the Fetzer tasting room is a cooperative gallery featuring the work of 40 Mendocino artists and artisans, staffed by the members themselves. A wide range of media is displayed here, from photographs and paintings of the Mendocino landscape to handwoven baskets, textiles, and hand-thrown pottery. You can find smaller gift items, too, such as jewelry in silver, ceramic, or glass. ♦ Daily 10AM-5PM. 13500 S. Hwy 101, Hopland. 744.1300

5 Fetzer Vineyards While Fetzer's winery is actually several miles north in the Redwood Valley, the Fetzer family has transformed the former downtown Hopland high school into a tasting center for their wines. Founded in 1968 by the late **Bernard Fetzer** and his wife **Kathleen,** 10 of their 11 children now work full-time for the firm. In recent years, they have guided Fetzer through a period of tremendous growth, and the winery is now making more—and better—wines than ever. They've been experimenting in developing methods for farming grapes organically (that is, without the use of pesticides or chemicals) and they may introduce an organic wine soon.

Winemaker **Paul Dolan,** who has been with Fetzer since 1977, introduced the Fetzer Reserves in 1990, and the wines are top-notch; try the Fetzer Reserve Cabernet or the late-harvest Riesling. The Barrel Select Vintage wines are vinified vineyard by vineyard (meaning the grapes from different vineyards are not mixed) and they're selected by the barrel. The tasting complex is set up like a series of shops, with the tasting bar at the end of a large room. Check the small wine library for bottles of Fetzer reserve, older vintages, and special bottles such as double magnums. You'll also find Germain-Robin brandy, picnic supplies, cookbooks, herb vinegars, virgin olive oils, and all sorts of local food products. A cooler holds chilled white wines, plus organic Chardonnay and Cabernet grape juice from **The Tinman** in Anderson Valley. There's also a deck and a grassy area adjoining the tasting room where you can sit and enjoy a snack with a glass of wine. ♦ Tasting and sales daily 9AM-5PM. Hopland Tasting Room, 13500 S. Hwy 101, Hopland. 744.1737

6 Dunnewood Vineyard This charming, blue-and-white Victorian house (pictured above) is home to the Dunnewood Vineyard tasting room. Ceiling fans turn overhead and braided rugs on the floor give it a welcoming, homey feel. Step up to the tasting bar to sample Sauvignon Blanc, Chardonnay, and Cabernet. Winemaker **George Phelan** also makes Merlot and Pinot Noir. A second tasting room is located in Vintners Village in St. Helena (Napa Valley). ♦ Daily 10AM-5PM. 13450 S. Hwy 101, Hopland. 744.1728

6 John Carpenter's Hopland Antiques Inveterate browsers won't be able to resist poking around the cluttered rooms of this antique shop. They've got a little bit of everything—and more than a little bit of vintage and estate jewelry; antique fishing lures and reels; fine, old China; and cast iron doorstops. ♦ Daily 9AM-4PM or by appt. 13456 S. Hwy 101, Hopland. 744.1023

6 Mendocino Woolens This shop has a marvelous selection of natural-fiber clothing and gifts. You can choose from classic plaid woolen shirts and jackets from Pendleton Mills, flannel shirts, and cozy shearling slippers. They produce their own line of handwoven clothing, blankets, and throws, and you can buy handwoven cloth by the yard, already blocked and ready to sew. They also make their handwoven woolens into ponchos and capes, bomber jackets, and sport coats. If you're searching for something absolutely unique, they take custom orders, too. ♦ Daily 9AM-5PM. 13420 S. Hwy 101, Hopland. 744.1110

6 Hopland Superette & Liquor A modest, family-owned grocery and liquor store where

you can find basic picnic fare, chilled drinks, and some local wines. ♦ Daily 8:30AM-8PM. 13400 S. Hwy 101, Hopland. 744.1171

7 Olive Branch Antiques and Collectibles This charming corner shop displays lots of glassware and bric-a-brac in the windows. You'll discover old costume jewelry, antique furniture, and the occasional handmade quilt, along with old locks, Victorian doorknobs, tools, and toys. ♦ M-Sa 10AM-5PM. 13380 S. Hwy 101, Hopland. 744.1502

Restaurants/Clubs: Red   **Hotels:** Blue
Shops/ ♥ Outdoors: Green   **Wineries/Sights:** Black

8 Grapevine Tasting Group There's a spacious tasting room here for McDowell and Hidden Cellars wineries (see pages 8 and 12 for details on their wines). Since these two wineries are off the beaten track, they decided to open a tasting room for travelers driving through Hopland on Hwy 101. Die-hard fans can search out the wineries themselves for a visit during limited hours or by appt. ◆ Daily 10AM-5PM. 13441 Hwy 101, Hopland. 744.1516

8 Thatcher Inn $$ This striking, many-gabled hotel first opened in 1890 as a rest stop for travelers heading by stage or train from San Francisco to the Oregon border on the old Redwood Highway. At the time, the stagecoach horses were kept in an old barn behind the hotel and rooms were lit with kerosene lamps and candles. The drivers occupied the tiny rooms at the very top of the hotel, and Pomo Indians tended the vegetable gardens and livestock. After an $800,000 restoration, the old Victorian hotel, named for its former proprietor, **W.W. Thatcher,** reopened in 1990.

The 21 rooms, all with private baths, are furnished with original and reproduction antique furniture. The bridal suite features a queen-sized bed dressed in pink satin and lace with matching armoire and a large bay window draped in lace curtains; the spacious bathroom has a Victorian clawfoot tub with brass shower fittings. Other nice suites include the **Ornbaum Room,** (No. 12), which is located at the back of the hotel and looks

Hopland-Ukiah Wine Road

out over the patio and pool, and the **Milone Room,** (No. 15), which has a brass bed and a clawfoot bathtub tucked in a corner. The hallways of the hotel are lined with gilt-framed photos of old Hopland and local families. Downstairs, there's a lovely library room panelled in Philippine mahogany, just the place to enjoy a toddy from the hotel bar's wonderful collection of single-malt scotches, brandies, cognacs, and Armagnacs. Be sure to try a taste of Germain-Robin or Jepson, both locally distilled, fine brandies. The hotel has lower mid-week rates and special weekend getaway packages that include double guest-

room accommodations, a bottle of sparkling wine, and dinner and breakfast for two in the hotel dining room. No children allowed as overnight guests. ◆ 13401 Hwy 101, Hopland. 744.1890

Within the Thatcher Inn:

Thatcher Inn Restaurant ★★$/$$ The Thatcher does breakfast proud with freshly-squeezed orange juice, omelets, and French toast, all served with home fries and a choice of toast, buttermilk cream biscuits, or homemade muffins. The most popular breakfast item is their hazelnut cornmeal griddle cakes, served with real maple syrup. At lunch you can find well-made burgers, club sandwiches, and fish and chips made with a beer batter, along with an array of salads. Have breakfast or lunch outside on the back patio, furnished with ornate white Victorian garden furniture and shaded by an 800-year-old oak tree.

Dinner offers more sophisticated fare. As an appetizer or first course, try the grilled tiger prawns marinated in olive oil, garlic, and lemon-lime juice, or Laura Chenel's Sonoma goat cheese enrobed in bread crumbs and served warm over a salad of delicate greens. Entrées include poached, fresh salmon with Hollandaise sauce; fresh ocean pasta del mar (with a mix of shellfish); and filet mignon (corn-fed aged beef) maître d'hotel. All entrées come with Swiss cheese fondue, the soup of the day, salad, vegetables, and potatoes or rice pilaf. Wednesday is family night, featuring an inexpensive prix fixe menu with a choice of two entrées. ◆ California ◆ Daily 8AM-2PM, 5:30-9:30PM. 744.1890

9 Hopland Brewery Brewpub & Beer Garden ★$ When California changed its laws to permit breweries to sell directly from attached taverns, **Michael Laybourn, Norman Franks,** and **John Scahill**—all avid home brewers—put their heads together and decided to open a brewery and brew pub in Hopland, the center of the old hops industry. After adding master brewer **Don Barkeley** and **Michael Lovett** to the partnership, they formed the **Mendocino Brewing Company** and, in 1983, opened the first brew pub in California since Prohibition. (It was only the second in the nation.)

Installed in the old-brick Hop Vine Saloon Building, just across from the Thatcher Inn, the brew pub is one of the prime attractions of Hopland. It's a casual place, something like a rustic English pub, with an outdoor beer garden shaded with a grape arbor and hop vine trellis. They produce four brews, all made in the traditional manner with one hundred percent malted barley, whole hops, pure yeast culture, and water. Peregrine is the lightest, an ale brewed with pale malt and Cascade hops, while medium-bodied Blue Heron Pale Ale has a slightly bitter finish. Black Hawk Stout is made from fully roasted black malt, and their most popular brew is their amber, full-bodied Red Tail Ale. They've got eats, too: appetizers such as buffalo wings and soft pretzels, plus burgers, BLTs, and other sandwiches, even a tofu veggie sandwich. They also have local wines, and the nightly live music—which runs the gamut from blues to country—has become a big drawing card. A shop at the back sells all sorts of beer paraphernalia: etched glass Mendocino Brewing Co. mugs, baseball hats inscribed with the name of your favorite brew, Red Tail Ale T-shirts and sweatshirts, along with a nice, tall pint glass, and nifty coasters. ♦ Daily 11AM-9PM. Tours by appt. 13351 S. Hwy 101, Hopland. 744.1361, 744.1015

9 The Cheesecake Lady The Cheesecake Lady hails from Philadelphia. She moved her business out west in 1982 and now sells to restaurants and cafes all over northern California, with all her goods baked at the large kitchen behind this Hopland cafe. In the morning, stop in for espresso drinks and her freshly baked croissants, Danish pastries, and bagels. You'll also find a slice of her superlative cheesecake uplifting any time of the day. She makes as many types of cheesecake as local vintners make wine, but the hands-down favorite is the original sour cream version made with a graham-cracker crust and topped with sour cream. The more adventurous might like to explore the peach melba cheesecake or the version topped with white chocolate and toasted almonds. One of the best is the espresso cheescake, which has a chocolate-cookie crust and sour cream topping. The ladies in back also whip up deep chocolate tortes layered with butter creams and mousses. For the flower-child-at-heart (and they're are a lot of them 'round these parts), they bake carrot cakes. ♦ M-F 7:30AM-6PM; Sa-Su 9:30AM-5PM. 13325 S. Hwy 101, Hopland. 744.1441

10 Hopland House $$ **Alice** and **Gene Gildenmeister** have been running this B&B for a little more than four years. They have five guest rooms (three with private bath, two with shared) in a California bungalow on the outskirts of Hopland. Rooms all have queen-sized beds and a quiet country decor, with antiques and flowered coverlets. They serve a full breakfast every morning that might include juice, fresh fruit salad, homemade blueberry muffins, and French toast with sausage patties. ♦ 12900 S. Hwy 101, Hopland. 744.1404

Margaret Fox, Chris Kump, Tricia Priano
Café Beaujolais, Mendocino

An early morning jog or walk along **10-Mile Beach,** north of Fort Bragg.

A canoe trip up **Big River** in Mendocino.

The **Mendocino Coast Botanical Gardens** in Fort Bragg.

Steelhead fishing.

Ocean kayaking.

A picnic on the headlands in Mendocino.

Riding the **Skunk Train** from Fort Bragg to Northspur.

A walk to the waterfalls in **Russian Gulch State Park.**

A trip to any of the rhododendron nurseries in Fort Bragg at the end of April and May.

Wine tasting along Route 128 from Boonville to the coast.

A hike up the ecological staircase at **Jug Handle State Park** in Caspar.

Bird's-Eye Views: Where to See Mendocino and Lake Counties from the Air

Whether you prefer to drift over the wine country in a hot-air balloon or soar silently above in a glider, here's how you can get that high in the sky (30- to 60-minute rides cost about $95 to $145 per person; the two Sonoma Valley-based ballooning companies

Hopland-Ukiah Wine Road

offer rides over the Ukiah area near Lake Mendocino):

Airborn of Sonoma County Balloon rides followed by a champagne brunch. ♦ Box 1457, Healdsburg CA 95448. 433.3210, 800/339.8133 (CA only)

Crazy Creek Soaring Glider rides in southern Lake County. ♦ Middletown Glider Port (north of Midddletown on Hwy 29) 18896 Grange Rd, Middletown CA 95461. 987.9112

Sonoma Thunder Wine Country Balloon Safaris Flights followed by a champagne celebration. ♦ 4914 Snark Ave, Santa Rosa CA 95409. 538.7359, 800/759.5638

Ukiah

The Ukiah area was once part of the Yokayo land grant, which extended from the southern end of Ukiah Valley to the northern end of Redwood Valley and was ceded to Mexican militia captain **Cayetano Juarez** by his government in 1846. Some historians say **John Parker** was the area's first white settler; other accounts credit **Samuel Lowry** as the first homesteader, staking out what is now the corner of Main and Perkins Sts in 1856. An influx of settlers arrived within the next year or two, attracted by the climate and fertile soil. Grain was the first crop planted, followed by fruit trees, tobacco, grapes, and hops for the brewing industry. Hops soon became the major crop in the area and you can still see some of the old drying kilns in the countryside. The spelling of Yokayo (an Indian word meaning "deep valley") was soon changed to Ukiah. In just a few years the town emerged as the region's chief commercial center and in 1859 it became the county seat. It has a small downtown, with many businesses strung along State St and a Victorian residential area. Of primary interest to most visitors is the **Grace Hudson Museum and Sun House.**

11 Jepson Vineyards When Chicago businessman **Robert S. Jepson Jr.** founded his winery just north of Hopland, he decided early on to specialize in just three products: Chardonnay, champagne, and brandy. The Chardonnay is barrel fermented and aged in small oak barrels; his Mendocino champagne, made entirely with Chardonnay grapes, is produced by the méthode champenoise traditionally used in the Champagne region of France. To distill the brandy, he acquired an alambic pot still, just like those used to produce the famous French brandies, and distills his spirits from French Colombard, the same grape used in cognac. You can taste everything but the brandy at the new fieldstone-and-wood tasting room on the property; in fine weather they have tables set outside. Their Sauvignon Blanc, called "Château d'Alicia," is sold only at the winery. Tours include the winery and the copper alambic (but you may not see anything in operation because they distill only one month a year). ♦ Tasting and sales daily 10AM-5PM; tours available weekends and by appt. 10400 S. Hwy 101, Ukiah. 468.8936

13 Whaler Vineyards Russ and **Annie Nyborg** specialize in Zinfandel at their tiny winery on 24 acres near Ukiah. Their first vintage was 1981 and after 10 years they're still fascinated with this intriguing grape, turning out wines in several different styles. It's fun to visit the weathered redwood barn that houses the winery, and in the small barrel-aging room you can hear how one family managed to live out their dream of becoming vintners. The ship on the Whaler label is from the Viking Museum in Oslo, Norway. Norwegian-American Russ Nyborg works as a bar pilot, directing large ships into San Francisco's harbor, and the entire family is very much a seagoing group. ♦ Tours by appt. 6200 Eastside Rd, Ukiah. 462.6355

Hopland-Ukiah Wine Road

12 Tijsseling Winery At this family-owned winery managed by **Dick Tijsseling** (his mother **Alida** owns the estate), you can taste two sparkling wines (a brut and a blanc de blancs) and a full range of bone-dry varietal wines, from Chardonnay and Sauvignon Blanc to Cabernet and occasionally some Petite Sirah. These are what Tijsseling likes to call his "weekend wines." He and winemaker **Fred Nickel** also make their "weekday wines" (softer, with less oak-aging), which bear the Mendocino Estate label. These less expensive wines include Chardonnay, Sauvignon Blanc, Cabernet, and both white and red Zinfandel. ♦ Sa-Su 11AM-5PM, Jun-Sep; other days and months by appt. 2150 McNab Ranch Rd, Ukiah. 462.1810

14 Hidden Cellars Winery In 1981, **Dennis Patton,** a local farmer and avid home winemaker, decided to turn pro. With money borrowed from friends and a garage converted into a microwinery in a hidden mountain canyon, he made his first award-winning wines. His production has grown in leaps and bounds, and he is now well known for his Sauvignon Blanc and rich, supple Zinfandels. He also makes a Chardonnay from organically grown grapes. But the wine

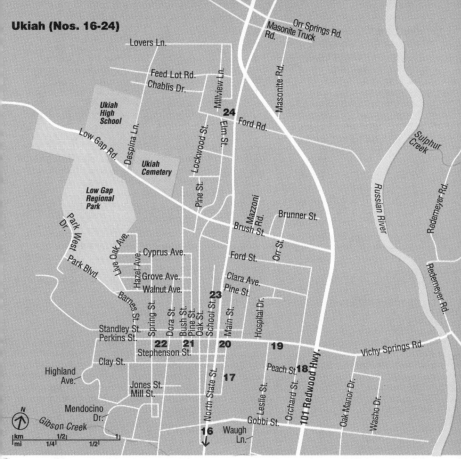

that always stops tasters in their tracks is his Chanson d'Or, a lush, apricot-and-honey-scented dessert wine made from a blend of Sémillon and Savignon Blanc. You can also sample his wines at the Grapevine Tasting Group in downtown Hopland. ♦ Tours by appt; closed Jan-Feb. 1500 Ruddick-Cunningham Rd. Ukiah. 462.0301

15 Parsons Creek Winery From a no-frills warehouse just south of Ukiah, owner/winemaker **Jesse Tidwell** produces two well-crafted Chardonnays (Mendocino and Sonoma) and a Riesling. ♦ Tasting and tours by appt only. 3001 S. State St, Ukiah. 462.8900

16 Moores' Flour Mill & Bakery Make a run into Ukiah for bread, flours, and other basics at this unique shop. Through a window in the back, you can see the century-old mill wheel grinding out beautiful whole-grain flours. Try the whole wheat for baking bread, and you can also buy big bags of unbleached and specialty flours such as cornmeal, polenta, and rye. Even if you don't bake, pick up a bag of their buttermilk or buckwheat pancake mix—the best you'll ever taste. The store is also a minimuseum of old flour sacks with their quaint logos. ♦ M-F 8AM-6PM; Sa 9AM-6PM. 1550 S. State St, Ukiah. 462.6550

17 Grace Hudson Museum and Sun House The Grace Hudson Museum (1986) and Sun House (1911), along with Hudson-Carpenter Park, occupy four-and-a-half landscaped acres in the middle of downtown Ukiah. Bring a picnic lunch and then visit the museum dedicated to artist **Grace Hudson**

Hopland-Ukiah Wine Road

(1865-1937) and her husband, anthropologist **Dr. John W. Hudson** (1857-1936). Hudson was known for her portraits of the local Pomo Indians and the museum has many of her graceful studies of Indian life. It includes a collection of Pomo art and artifacts of anthropological interest, many of them collected by the Hudsons. The museum also shows the work of local artists. The Sun House next door, the home where the Hudsons lived and worked, can only be visited in the company of a docent, but it's worth taking the half hour required to do so. ♦ W-Sa 10AM-4:30PM; Su noon-4:30PM; also open Tu in summer. 431 S. Main St, Ukiah. 462.3370

153

Sun House Docent-led tours of the Sun House, an arts and crafts-style bungalow built for the Hudsons by architect/artist **George Wilcox,** depart from the museum about every half hour. A California Historical Landmark, the lovely redwood house is filled with the personal touches of the couple; Grace designed the lanterns, painted a folding screen with a Mendocino landscape, and designed the hooked rugs. Pomo baskets and other Indian artifacts reflect the Hudsons' fascination with California Indian culture. Grace's studio has been left just as it was, with her easel set up to paint a portrait in the north light. John Hudson, a physician, devoted much of his life to studying and documenting native Indian cultures.

18 Ukiah Farmers Market Shop for farm-fresh produce at this twice-weekly market. ♦ Tu 4-6:30PM; Sa 8AM-noon, June-Oct. Orchard Shopping Center, Orchard St (E. Perkins St-Kings Ct) Ukiah

19 Chamber of Commerce Information available on restaurants, lodging, wineries, recreation, and other activities in the Ukiah Valley. ♦ M-F 9AM-5PM. 495-E E. Perkins St, Ukiah. 462.4705

20 Main Street Wine and Cheese Now located on S. State St, Main Street Wine and Cheese still carries the same well-edited selection of imported and domestic cheeses and local wines. Pick up assorted picnic fixings or order one of the generous sandwiches to go. ♦ M-F 7AM-6PM; Sa 8AM-5PM. 113 S. State St, Ukiah. 462.0417

21 Sanford House Bed & Breakfast $$ If Ukiah's motel row on State St is not your style, there is an alternative: this gracious bed and breakfast in a quiet residential neighborhood. The stately Queen Anne Victorian was built in 1904 as the home of **Senator John Bunyon Sanford,** a longtime California state legislator. Innkeepers **Dorsey** and **Bob Manogue** have five guest rooms, each with a private bath and air conditioning, decorated with good antiques and custom fabrics and wallpapers. As a particularly nice

Hopland-Ukiah Wine Road

touch, the Manogues will serve your Continental breakfast either in the dining room or bring the tray to your bedroom. A typical breakfast may include freshly squeezed juice, fruit, homemade muffins and breads, and coffee or tea. ♦ 306 S. Pine St, Ukiah. 462.1653

22 Held-Poage Memorial Home and Research Library To get a better sense of Mendocino county history, visit this research library housed in a Queen Anne Victorian (pictured above), once the home of Mendocino County Superior Court **Judge William D.L. Held** and **Ethel Poage Held.** Dedicated to the collection of archival

materials relating to the county's history, the library contains more than 5,000 volumes and a wonderful collection of historical photographs, along with documents and maps. ♦ Tu, Th, Sa 1:30-4PM and by appt. Mendocino County Historical Society, 603 W. Perkins St, Ukiah. 462.6969

23 The Coffee Critic Linda Neder-Mountanos, who has a well-known coffee store in San Mateo, has just opened another branch here in Ukiah. She and husband **Mark Mountanos,** a coffee broker, have a vineyard nearby. She buys the coffee green and roasts each variety herself in small batches. In her new location, she has the room to put up all the coffee memorabilia—old tins, signs, and more—to make this attractive space more of a coffee museum and store. Stop in for a great cup of java, and beans to take home for your own coffeemaker. ♦ M-F 7:30AM-5:30PM; Sa-Su 8AM-5PM. 476 N. State St, Ukiah. 462.6333

24 Discovery Inn $ Inexpensive motel lodging just one mile from downtown Ukiah. The 154 rooms with standard contemporary decor feature queen-sized beds, cable TV, a stereo, and direct-dial phones. In summer, the swimming pool offers respite from the heat; there's also a sauna, whirlpool, and tennis court. If you plan to stay for a few days, ask about rooms with kitchenettes or the executive suites. ♦ 1340 N. State St, Ukiah. 462.8873

Vichy Springs

25 Vichy Springs Resort & Inn $$ This mineral springs resort and its famous mineral-water baths were established in 1854. It was named after Vichy Springs in France, because the naturally effervescent waters surging forth from miles beneath the surface are very similar to those in Europe. The resort, now a California landmark, was quite well known in the 19th century, attracting the likes of **Mark Twain, Robert Louis Stevenson,** and Jack London. Teddy Roosevelt and pugilists **John L. Sullivan** and "Gentleman" Jim Corbett took to the waters here, too. The hot springs resort's new proprietors, **Gilbert** and **Marjorie Ashoff,** completely refurbished the inn and Olympic-sized swimming pool, and in 1989 reopened the 700-acre property for overnight guests and recreational activities, such as hiking, picnicking, and mountain biking.

You can stay in one of the guest rooms in the inn, which dates back to the 1860s, or rent one of the two cottages on the property—they were built in 1854 and are said to be among the oldest existing buildings in Mendocino County. The other alternative is to buy a pass and spend the day relaxing by the pool, soaking in the mineral-water tubs, or hiking up to the Old Cinnabar mine shaft or the fern-shrouded falls. A dozen rooms are strung along a broad veranda; most have queen-sized beds (Nos. 11 and 12 have twin-sized beds). They're pleasant, simply decorated rooms, with natural wood floors, print coverlets, and throw rugs; each has a private bath/shower. Think rustic retreat more than luxury. The one-bedroom, blue cottage has a queen-sized bed and sofa bed, and a wood-burning stove in the living room area, plus a full kitchen. The larger, white cottage is furnished with a long, overstuffed couch, a wood-burning stove, and a beautiful thirties-era gas stove. There's a large, shady porch in front and a gas barbecue. The resort has eight indoor and outdoor bathing tubs (in pairs, so you can chat with a friend), a therapeutic massage building, and that Olympic-sized pool (also filled with mineral water). One- or one-and-a-half-hour Swedish massages or foot reflexology massage are available by appointment. The Ashoff's also bottle the mineral water under the Vichy Springs label—the very same water President George Bush served at the 1991 president's dinner at the White House. Future plans include a restaurant at the resort. ◆ 2605 Vichy Springs Rd, Ukiah. 462.9515

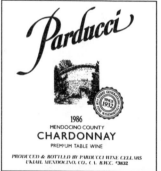

1986
MENDOCINO COUNTY
CHARDONNAY
PREMIUM TABLE WINE

PRODUCED & BOTTLED BY PARDUCCI WINE CELLARS
UKIAH, MENDOCINO, CO., CA. B.W.C. #3832

26 Parducci Wine Cellars After first starting a winery in Cloverdale, **Adolph Parducci** moved north to Ukiah in 1931 to found this family winery in which three generations of Parduccis have now worked. Their tasting room, a white, Spanish-style building, is just north of Ukiah, and offers the full gamut of moderately priced wines from this popular producer. The Merlot and the Barbera are only sold at the winery. The tasting-room complex also houses a gift shop with lots of wine glasses, decanters, wine buckets, and other related paraphernalia. Upstairs is an art gallery with changing exhibits of Mendocino country art. In back is a picnic area with tables and umbrellas set out on a sheltered patio. ◆ Tasting, sales, and tours daily 9AM-6PM; until 5PM in winter. 501 Parducci Rd, Ukiah. 462.WINE

27 Lake Mendocino Recreation Area Ten miles north of Ukiah is this recreational lake that was created when the **Army Corps of Engineers** dammed the Russian River at the mouth of the Coyote Valley in 1958. The 1,822-acre lake, bordered by foothills, is a popular destination for boating, water skiing, wind surfing, and swimming. The lake has two large boat launches and protected beaches for swimming, plus nearly 300 family campsites and a hundred picnic sites, each with tables and a barbecue pit. In season, there's lots of good fishing for striped bass, large- and small-mouth bass, crappie, bluegill, and catfish. Miles of hiking paths wind through the foothills surrounding the lake, which also includes 689 acres of protected wildlife habitat. ◆ Entrances off Hwy 101 at Calpella; off Hwy 20, east of 101; or on Lake Mendocino Dr, off N. State St, Ukiah. Recreation area office, 1160 Lake Mendocino Dr, Ukiah. Reservations recommended for camping. 462.7581

Within the Lake Mendocino Recreation Area:

Pomo Visitor Center To learn more about Native American traditions and Lake Mendocino, visit this center located in the Pomo Day-Use Area at the north end of the lake. Built by the Army Corps of Engineers in the shape of a ceremonial dance house, it is operated by a local Native American council. The exhibits, films, and programs provide information about local Indian ways. ◆ Hours vary seasonally; call for information. Mendocino Lake, Marina Dr, Ukiah. 485.0570

Lake Mendocino Marina This privately owned marina offers ski boats, pedal boats, and fishing boats for rent; they have slip rentals for those who want to bring their own. The store sells bait and tackle as well as marine and camping supplies. There's

also a snack bar with burgers and sandwiches, and a picnic area with barbecues. ◆ Daily Apr-Oct. Off Hwy 20 at Marina Dr, Calpella. 485.8644

28 Weibel Champagne Cellars Locals say Weibel's tasting room resembles an upside down champagne glass. You decide while sampling one of the sparkling wines from this longtime producer. This facility was founded in 1973, but the firm had already been making sparkling and other wines in Alameda before moving north. The parking lot is set up for RVs, and guests are welcome to stay overnight in their campers. ◆ Tasting and sales daily 9AM-5PM. 7051 N. State St, Redwood Valley. 485.0321

28 Broiler Steakhouse ★$$ According to the locals, the best prime rib in Mendocino County is served here, as well as steaks, baked potatoes, bread, and all the salad you can eat. ◆ Steak ◆ M-Sa 5-10PM; Su 4-10PM. 8400 Uva Dr, Redwood Valley. 485.7301

29 Montgomery Woods State Park There's a self-guided nature trail through groves of redwoods in this 700-acre park, as well as several picnic sites with tables. Day use only. ◆ Orr Springs Rd (11 miles NW of Ukiah) Orr Springs. Call Mendocino State Parks for information, 937.5304

30 Olson Vineyards When retired electronics engineer **Donald Olson** and his wife **Nancy** first moved to the Redwood Valley in 1971, they sold their grapes to other wineries, and only began making their own wines in 1982. Now they produce Chardonnay, Sauvignon Blanc, Riesling, and a special blend of Riesling, Chenin Blanc, and a French Colombard called Glacier. Red wines include Petite Sirah, Cabernet, and Zinfandel. Olson is one of a growing number of producers of organic grapes in Mendocino County. ◆ Tasting and sales daily 10AM-4PM. 3620 Road B, Redwood Valley. 485.0323

31 Lolonis Winery Tryfon Lolonis emigrated to the Redwood Valley in 1915, and by 1920 he was already planting vineyards. Grapes from the original Zinfandel vines go into the wines his son **Ulysses** makes today. ◆ Tasting by appt only. 2901 Road B, Redwood Valley. 485.8027

32 Frey Vineyards Owned by the Frey family—that is **Paul** and **Marguerite Frey** and their 12 children—this small winery on a 145-acre ranch was constructed bit by bit with salvaged timber from the old Garret Winery in Ukiah. The vineyards are cultivated organically, and winemaker **Jonathan Frey** makes only small amounts of several different varietals. Gewürztraminer, Grey Riesling, and Sauvignon Blanc compose the whites. Reds include Cabernet, Syrah, and Zinfandel. Frey Vineyards is only one of about a dozen wineries in California that are certified organic farmers. ◆ Tasting and tours by appt only. 14000 Tomki Rd, Redwood Valley. 485.5177, 800/345.3739 (CA only)

Bests

Evan Goldstein
Director, School of Service and Hospitality, Calistoga

The breathtaking and awesome **Petrified Forest** (the world's largest) in Calistoga.

The **Anderson Valley Wine Country**—underrated compared to Napa and Sonoma.

Drinks at **Auberge du Soleil**, where you'll get the best mid-valley view of Napa.

The South Terrace at **Sterling Vineyards** for the best north and south view of the Napa Valley.

Lunch or dinner at **Rissa Oriental Café** in St. Helena—great food, price, and ambience.

The town of Sonoma—it has retained its sleepy charm.

Dry Creek Valley for the most European feel in the North Coast wine country.

Ana's Cantina in St. Helena—lots of local color and the only place open past 10PM.

Where to Sleep: The **Sonoma Mission Inn**—worth the price! **St. Orres** in Gualala—romantic, and great food, too (go in the off-peak season).

Where to Eat: Lunch at the **Calistoga Inn**—outside when it's sunny. **Terra** in St. Helena has the best food in Napa Valley. **Matisse** serves the best food in Santa Rosa. Brunch at **The Diner** in Yountville.

Wineries to See: Napa Valley's **Château Montelena, Silverado Vineyards, Sterling,** and **Stags Leap Wine Cellars** (any that need reservations are always more personal). Sonoma's **A. Raffanelli, Robert Stemmler, Dry Creek,** and **Jordan.** Mendocino's **Navarro, Husch,** and **Roederer Estate.**

Jean Harris
Retailer

Visit **Fort Ross State Park** in Sonoma—the site of an early Russian fur-trading settlement where you'll see old buildings, storerooms, a chapel, a small museum, and a gift shop with Russian books and artifacts. Picnic at the compound on an isolated dune, and spend the night at **Fort Ross Lodge.**

Watch the sunset from the bar in the **Timber Cove Inn.** Walk across *all* the dunes behind the inn for a visit to another planet. (There are incredible rock formations and a sacred Indian burial ground, so approach with proper reverence.)

Two miles north on Hwy 1 is **Stillwater Cove State Park.** Walk the path to the beach and watch the divers collect the best abalone in the world. Across the highway, climb the stairs to the parking lot, and take the trail to the left for a visit to an unspoiled ancient redwood grove.

Continue north to **Kruse Rhododendron Park** and visit **Fisk Mill Beach.**

Go north again to Albion. If you're getting hungry, **Ledford House** and the **Albion River Inn** offer good food and spectacular views .

The **Glendeven Lodge** at Little River is a great place to spend the night. Visit the art gallery at the inn.

The **Little River Cafe** sells nice picnic lunches.

Manchester State Beach is perfect for a good stroll.

And, of course, **Café Beaujolais** in Mendocino is great any time of day.

Anderson Valley

Just north of Cloverdale in Sonoma, take Hwy 128 west towards **Boonville** and the **Anderson Valley** for a tour of one of the most pleasurable wine roads in California. There's no four-lane super highway here to carve up the landscape, but a fairly narrow, country road that dips and turns with the topography, more or less following the course of the **Navarro River** through this ravishing 25-mile-long valley and then through the redwoods to the Mendocino coast. It's an unforgettable drive, meandering past apple orchards, weathered farmsteads, and the hamlets of **Philo** and **Navarro** where three or four buildings mark the towns. The wineries are all strung along the main route, so there's no getting lost on back-country roads. And there's also no reason to hurry, since these tasting rooms stay open to a civilized five o'clock or later, and it may take a half hour at most to drive from one end of the valley to the other. The best company for the road is Philo's KZYX (90.7 FM), one of the smallest public radio stations in the country, playing a mixed bag of great music: rock, jazz, classical, folk, and country.

First stop is Boonville, where you can lodge at the comfortable **Boonville Hotel** (which also has one of the best restaurants in the region), and sample the Anderson Valley brew at the **Buckhorn Saloon.** The burg also has several secluded bed-and-breakfasts and a historical museum in the little red schoolhouse at the north end of town.

Then come the wineries, renowned for their crisp, dry whites, especially Chardonnay, Riesling, and Gewürztraminer, all grapes that thrive in the cool growing conditions of Anderson Valley. Pinot Noir does well, too, but the valley is gaining world recognition for its sparkling wines, with **Scharffenberger** and **Roederer Estate,** owned by the French champagne house Louis Roederer, leading the way. All of which means you can do some very interesting wine tasting in this little valley. In fact, as you travel along this wine road sampling the local varieties, you may discover that you really *do* like dessert wines after all.

The valley was apple country long before vineyards were ever planted, and it remains a prime apple-growing region. Many of the farms have switched over to commercial growing methods in recent years and added antique apple varieties to their repertoire. September and October are the best months for apples, but year-round you'll find apple juice and other apple products. **The Apple Farm** in Philo is a great source for organic cider and chutneys, while **The Tinman** offers tastings of apple juices made from different varieties. And just down the road is a three-star produce stand, **Gowan's Oak Tree,** where you can find all of summer's bounty.

Every inch of this valley is gorgeous, so the ideal plan is to stay at the Boonville Hotel or one of the rustic B&Bs for a day or two before heading for the coast through 15 miles of redwoods and the **Navarro River Redwood State Park.** At the coast, you have your choice: Head south seven miles to **Elk,** or north to **Albion, Little River,** and the town of **Mendocino.**

Boonville

During the early years of this century, the Anderson Valley was still fairly remote, and few travelers made their way to this tiny community strung along the narrow, country road. To amuse themselves and totally mystify the rare stranger that did show up, the folks in Boonville developed an elaborate language of their own called "Boontling." Much of it is bawdy stuff—or at least what would have passed for bawdy in those days.

It's been the subject of scholarly study (you can pick up a popular book about Boontling in town) and you can still see a few signs of it around. The **Boonville Hotel** and the **Buckhorn Saloon** across the street are the two main places to eat; the hotel and several bed-and-breakfast inns offer lodging. Be sure to pick up a copy of *The Anderson Valley Advertiser,* an eccentric local newspaper filled with passionate debate on a number of subjects.

33 The Toll House

$$ When you take Route 253 over the mountains from Ukiah Valley, a few miles before Boonville and the Anderson Valley you'll pass a farmhouse on your right. Set on a 360-acre ranch, the 1912 house with its big front porch and veranda out back has a new life as a comfortable bed-and-breakfast inn and restaurant.

Guests have the run of the ranch, which is home to two llamas and six sheep; proprietors **Barbara McGuiness** and **Betty Ingram** will point out the best paths for hiking. The decor is blissfully free of knickknacks and Victoriana, with large, comfy sofas in the living room and a serene, pale color scheme. Upstairs are three pleasant, sunny rooms. One is decorated in Provençal prints, another in shades of peach and cream with eyelet curtains hanging in the windows. A larger room at the back of the house is the most private, with its own entrance and deck. It also features a handcrafted willow bed, an ornate, hardwood armoire, a fireplace, and a deep Jacuzzi. If you really want to get away from it all, you can rent their chalet in the midst of the inn's garden down by the Navarro River in Philo. The chalet has its own kitchen, and guests are welcome to pick vegetables from the inn's showplace organic vegetable garden. Any of the inn's guests may visit the garden and spend the afternoon at its mile-long, private beach. Breakfast at the inn includes caffè latté served in small bowls (just like the French serve it in the country), juice, freshly baked scones and other pastries, their own homemade preserves, a fruit plate, and perhaps poached eggs with sautéed chard and apple-smoked bacon. ♦ 15301 Hwy 253, Boonville. 895.3630; fax 895.3632

Within the Toll House:

The Toll House Restaurant ★★$$$ This restaurant opened in the summer of '91 with **Ross Brown,** a veteran of San Francisco's

Anderson Valley

Zuni Café, at the stove. He's interested in food with a Mediterranean bent and uses local ingredients as much as possible; in the fall, the restaurant features game on the menu. All the produce comes from the owners' **Nessgram Farms** in Philo. Go down to the river and visit this wondrous six-acre organic garden, which was two years in the planning. To give you an idea of the bounty here, there are 10 types of strawberries, plus two kinds of *fraises de bois* (tiny wild strawberries), dozens of culinary herbs and fragile greens, and rows upon rows of flowers for cutting.

Naturally, Brown follows the seasons in his menus, which change every week. Start with a bowl of crimson-tipped radishes from the garden or golden zucchini soup swirled with pesto. Entrées may include fresh local grilled salmon with coriander-seed-and-chive-blossom dressing or roasted poussin (a small chicken) accompanied with toast slices spread with a Provençal anchovy paste, grilled fennel, and onions. If all this sounds a touch too exotic, they've got an excellent grilled rib eye steak. This satisfying meal might end with a comforting peach-and-berry crumble or a nectarine-and-cherry crostata (Italian open-face tart). The wine list is strong on Scharffenberger and Roederer sparkling wines and other North Coast selections. In the summer, outdoor dining is available.
♦ California/Mediterranean ♦ Th-Sa 6-9PM; Su 10AM-2PM, 6-9PM. (The restaurant plans to open for lunch in summer of '92.)

34 Rookie-To Gallery
Featuring pottery, jewelry, textiles, and sculpture, primarily the work of local craftspeople. ♦ Daily 10AM-5:30PM, May-Dec; call for winter hours. 14300 Hwy 128, Boonville. 895.2204

34 Boonville Hotel
$$ The eight simple but wonderfully stylish guest rooms upstairs at the historic Boonville Hotel are a real surprise. Designed by owner **John Schmitt** and his wife, **Jeannie Eliades,** the decor is Shaker-like in its simplicity and the thoughtfulness that has gone into the design. The rooms are filled with beautifully crafted details, such as the marble star set into the bathroom tile, the hand-crafted, steel shower curtain rod, and the natural-wood Venetian blinds. One room even has handblown water glasses. When they took over the hotel several years ago, the upstairs was virtually gutted. Instead of going to furniture showrooms, they sought out a handful of local artisans, proposing that they each create a bedroom set. One room has a geometric blonde-wood-and-ebony bed and matching armoire. Another features a whimsical four-poster metal bed made by **Stevan Derwinski,** who has his studio out back. The same room features pale, satiny, wooden floors and an extra-large oval tub. The most spacious are the two suites with tall French doors opening onto a broad, second-floor balcony. The smaller but equally comfortable room No. Four gets the morning sun and has a queen-sized bed and shower. Come downstairs in the morning to find a

buffet Continental breakfast laid out in the sunny dining room (freshly squeezed juices, fruit, and warm, crumbly scones served with sweet country butter and homemade jams). Eat it there or take it onto the patio beside the garden. You can also just stop in to buy dried apple wreaths, organic cider vinegar, apple butters, and chutneys from **The Apple Farm** (owned by John's sister **Karen,** who also helps out in the kitchen). ♦ Hwy 128 (at Lambert Ln) Boonville. 895.2210

Within the Boonville Hotel:

Boonville Hotel Restaurant & Bar

★★$$$ Schmitt learned to cook in his family's popular Yountville restaurant, **The French Laundry.** Here he indulges his love for the vibrant flavors of Southwest cooking with a little Italian and American regional tastes thrown in for good measure. The restaurant is eminently cheerful and fun to boot. Start with a homemade soup or one of the individual pizzas topped with pancetta (unsmoked Italian bacon), goat cheese, olives, and thyme, or maybe potato, garlic, rosemary, and Teleme cheese. They make a great Caesar salad and a dynamite burger. Grilled items are excellent, too, such as the fresh fish served with an avocado-and-lime salsa or the Spencer steak (a little fattier—and tastier—than rib eye) served with grilled red onions and pasilla chile butter. Desserts are just as festive. Try the Mexican chocolate ice cream and cookies or the semolina pudding and berries. The Sunday lunch becomes quite an event, with cheese biscuits and honey butter, plus *huevos con chorizo* with fresh tortillas or an omelet with roasted tomato-oregano salsa, apple-smoked bacon, and Jack cheese. Finish it all off with a divine shortcake loaded with peaches, raspberries, and blueberries, all swimming in a pool of cream. Good list of beers and local wines.

The bar is a lively place at night, a local hangout with good conversation, good music, and wines by the glass. And terrific espresso and sassy repartee from the waiters make this the highlight of the Anderson Valley.♦ Eclectic ♦ W-Sa 6-9PM; Su 11AM-2PM, 6-9PM. 895.2210

Also at the Boonville Hotel:

Boonville Farmers Market You can find organically grown produce and armloads of hollyhocks and roses at this local farmers market, which began in 1991. ♦ Sa 9AM-noon, June-Oct. 895.2210

35 Buckhorn Saloon A funky saloon and local hangout that serves pub grub with California flair including fresh fish, fish and chips, burgers, and Porter-steamed sausages. Forget about wine here and order one of the eight kinds of beer and ale on tap, all brewed downstairs at the Anderson Valley Brewing Co. (If you want to see how they make that stout, ale, or porter, they give a brief tour in the late afternoons.) The saloon also hosts an annual **Gooseberry Festival** the second weekend in July. It's a gooseberry contest for the largest berry and the best gooseberry pie and jam, among other things. ♦ Pub Grub ♦ M-Tu, Th-Su 11AM-10PM. 14081 Hwy 128, Boonville. 895.2337

35 Horn of Zeese Coffee Shop "Horn of zeese" you might ask? That means a cup of coffee in the local Boonville lingo. And you got it, this is the place for a quick caffeine jolt. Note the sign over the booth outside: "buckey walter" (otherwise known as a phone booth). ♦ M-Th 6:30AM-2PM; F-Su 6:30AM-8PM. 14025 Hwy 128, Boonville. 895.3525

36 Boont Berry Farm Store Stop here for picnic fare (sandwiches, cold cuts, vegetarian dishes, etc.) and freshly baked goods, along with produce and berries from the Boont Berry Farm. Coming soon: their own line of jams and jellies. ♦ M-Sa 10AM-6PM. 13981 Hwy 128, Boonville. 895.3576

37 Faulkner County Park This 40-acre park off twisting Mountain View Rd is strictly for day use. There's a 1/4-mile long nature trail through wild azaleas and redwood groves, plus several picnic areas, a few with barbecue pits. ♦ Two miles west of Boonville on Mountain View Rd. For information, call 463.4267

38 Anderson Valley Historical Society Museum One mile north of Boonville, look for the Little Red Schoolhouse on the south side of the road. If the flag is flying out front, this homespun museum dedicated to the history of the valley is open. The one-room Conn Creek schoolhouse dates from 1891; the museum also includes a model sheep-shearing shed. Exhibits are set up to demonstrate different aspects of everyday life in the early days of the valley. Pieced together with donations from local families, the museum's collection includes old farming tools, everyday objects, and furniture. The Pomo Indian baskets and stone tools on display were all found in or

around Anderson Valley. ♦ F-Su 1-4PM; longer summer hours vary. Hwy 128, Boonville. 895.3207

The last decade has seen the emergence of a number of small wineries in California. In 1979, there were just 400 bonded wineries; by 1990, there were more than 750.

Restaurants/Clubs: Red	Hotels: Blue
Shops/ ♥ Outdoors: Green	Wineries/Sights: Black

39 Anderson Creek Inn B&B $$ Set in the redwoods off Hwy 128, this comfortable ranch-style inn has two creeks running through the 16-acre property, and three llamas, a miniature horse, and a dozen horned sheep from Wales have the run of the place. Innkeepers **Rod** and **Nancy Graham** have three guest rooms and one suite, all with king-sized beds, private baths, and a fresh, contemporary decor. Only the suite has a fireplace, but all have views of meadows and redwoods. Breakfast might include eggs Benedict, freshly baked banana bread, melon, and local apple juice, served at separate tables rather than family style. There's a swing on the 300-year-old oak tree out back and a large pool. Borrow a bike and make the easy ride into town down the frontage road, past apple orchards and blackberry fields. ♦ 12050 Anderson Valley Way, Boonville. 895.3091

40 The Tinman *The Wizard of Oz* was owner **George Bergner's** favorite book as a child, and so when it came time to name his apple juice company, he dusted off the valiant character. Tinman signs along the road give you just enough time to make the turnoff for this wooden hut, which offers freshly pressed apple juices to taste at the bar. The store manager will start you off with Gravenstein, then move on to MacIntosh, Golden, and Tasty (the last a blend of Jonathan, Pippin, and Spartan apples). Then she'll give you a taste of cider, warmed and spiced. (One of the best is Dorothy's, a blend of Golden Delicious, Jonathan, and Pippin.) The nonalcoholic Cabernet, Pinot Noir, and Chardonnay juices can be served at lunch or brunch. If you liked the hot apple cider, ask

Anderson Valley

for their recipe, which includes a stick of cinnamon, cloves, and a dash of nutmeg, allspice, and cardamom—but the real secret is the apple juice itself. Look for jams and vinegars from **Kozlowski Farms** in Sonoma and organic dried herbs from **McFadden Farms** in Potter Valley. You can buy the juice by the case and they will ship anywhere in the US. ♦ Daily 10AM-5:45PM, summer; 10AM-4:45PM, winter. Hwy 128, Boonville. 895.2759

41 Obester Winery This is the Anderson Valley outpost of Obester Winery, which started in 1977 in Half Moon Bay on the coast south of San Francisco. Ever since Grandpa Gemello taught **Paul Obester** and his wife **Sandy** how to make wine in their garage, they haven't looked back. The Obesters traditionally concentrated on white wines, but they're now focusing more on red and have planted some Sangiovese, the grape used in Tuscany's top red wines and a relative newcomer to California. At the homey tasting room in a yellow 1923 house, sample their Chardonnay and Sauvignon Blanc (especially the barrel-fermented version from Ferrington Vineyard), the Monterey County Riesling produced at their original Half Moon Bay winery, and the Anderson Valley Gewürztraminer. They make a light Zinfandel and a Pinot Noir aged in small oak barrels, and Gewürztraminer grape juice and organic apple juice from their Anderson Valley farm is also for sale here. Stock up on their beautifully packaged herbal wine vinegars and extra-virgin olive oil. Chilled wines are available for a picnic in the gazebo. ♦ Tasting and sales daily 10AM-5PM; tours by appt. 9200 Hwy 128, Philo. 895.3814

42 Indian Creek County Park An easily accessible, lovely spot for a picnic along the creek; there are also self-guided nature walks among the coast redwoods. ♦ One mile northwest of Boonville on Hwy 128. For information, call 463.4267

42 Philo Pottery Inn $$ Built entirely of heart redwood, this 1888 house, once an old stagecoach stop, makes a thoroughly appropriate and charming bed and breakfast. Innkeeper **Sue Chiverton** has four guest rooms in the main house (two with private baths, two with shared), although the little, one-room cottage with a wood-burning stove, detached private bath, and its own back porch is everybody's favorite. For breakfast Chiverton might serve fresh melon, whole wheat buttermilk pancakes, chicken-and-apple sausages, and fresh blackberry muffins from the inn's own blackberry patch. The word pottery in the name of the inn comes from the original owners, who were potters and had a gallery on the premises. ♦ 8550 Hwy 128 Philo. 895.3069

43 Scharffenberger Founded in 1981 by **John Scharffenberger,** this winery is now affiliated with the French champagne houses Champagne Pommery and Champagne Lanson. Scharffenberger was the Anderson Valley's pioneer in mèthode champenoise wines (sparkling wines). Today he and winemaker **Willis Tex Sayer** produce four cuvées: a toasty, beautifully balanced non-vintage brut made from a blend of 70 percent Pinot Noir and 30 percent Chardonnay, an elegant vintage Blanc de Blancs made entirely from Chardonnay, a nonvintage brut rosé made primarily from Pinot Noir, and a subtly effervescent nonvintage Crémant. Made from a blend of grapes simliar to that used in the nonvintage Brut, the Crémant was created for the White House to serve at the 1988 Moscow summit. Taste them all at the winery's new Philo tasting room in a remodeled farmhouse. It will be set up like a cafe, so you'll be able to go off on your own to enjoy a glass at one of the tables or in the side garden. In the future, they may sell picnic lunches, too. The discrete new winery building, designed by **Jacques Ullman** of Sausalito, who also designed the Roederer Estate, sits behind the office and tasting room. ♦ Tasting and sales daily 11AM-5PM; tours by appt. 7000 Hwy 128, Philo. 895.2065

44 Gowan's Oak Tree For more than 60 years the Gowan family has been selling their homegrown produce at this white clapboard roadside stand, one of the Anderson Valley's main attractions. Stop here for fresh-pressed cider and apples from their own orchards, which you can see as you drive up. They've got peaches, plums, apricots, and whatever else is in season, such as green beans, sweet corn so fresh it's practically covered with dew, vine-ripened tomatoes, and cucumbers for pickles. In hot weather, they've got apple and berry popsicles; in winter, hot spiced cider. And in a shady grove out back, there's a couple of picnic tables and a swing for kids, making this a great rest stop on the drive to the coast. ♦ Daily 8AM-6PM, June to early March. 6350 Hwy 128 (2 ½ miles west of Philo) 895.3353, 895.3225

Restaurants/Clubs: Red   **Hotels:** Blue
Shops/ 🌳 Outdoors: Green   **Wineries/Sights:** Black

45 The Apple Farm Karen Schmitt, husband Tim Bates, and their children live right in the midst of the organic apple orchard where they grow about a dozen varieties of antique and heirloom apples. At harvest time (September through October) they have apples galore, but all year round you can stop by for their subtle, organic apple-cider vinegar, apple butters, and chutneys. They also make lovely dried-apple wreaths, and the bundled apple twigs are terrific for barbecues. A large room, something like a rustic loft-studio, is available for rent above the apple-drying barn. It has a wood-burning stove, view of the trees, and a large deck out front. ♦ Open when their sign is hung out front or by appt. 18501 Greenwood Rd, Philo. 895.2333

46 Hendy Woods State Park From the highway, following a ridge to the south, a tall grove of enormous redwoods, so dark they almost look black against the sky, marks this 805-acre state park. Gentle Giant Trail (a self-guided, half-mile trail) leads visitors through groves of old-growth redwoods harboring trees more than 1,000 years old and 270 feet tall. For another self-guided walk, ask for the Discovery Trail map at the park. Bring a picnic to enjoy beside the Navarro River; there are also hiking paths and trails along the river. The park has 92 campsites suitable for tents, trailers, and RVs, and it has day-use facilities. ♦ Enter park on Greenwood Rd a half mile west of Hwy 128. 895.3141, 800/444.7275

ANDERSON VALLEY, MENDOCINO
Pinot Noir
1987
NAVARRO
Vineyards
PRODUCED AND BOTTLED BY NAVARRO VINEYARDS
5601 HWY 128, PHILO, CA. CONTAINS SULFITES

47 Navarro Vineyards This small, family-owned winery founded in 1974 specializes in white wines; their sole red is Pinot Noir, made either in a traditional Burgundian style or as a fresh, young wine called Pinot Noir Nouveau. Navarro is known for its classic dry Gewürztraminer, among the best in the state, but also try the elegant and complex Chardonnay Première Reserve and the excellent late-harvest White Riesling. The tasting room here is quite small and there are basically no tours, but it's hard to find a friendlier welcome (owner **Ted Bennett** himself pours the wines most Sundays and his wife, **Deborah Cahn,** is usually there on Friday and Saturday).

Navarro's wines are sold only at the winery and at a few selected restaurants; most of it is sold by mail. Also note the bottled grape juice that comes in a wine bottle with the handsome Navarro label. Outside the small, wooden building is a redwood deck with brightly colored umbrellas overlooking a landscape of vineyards and rolling hills—a peaceful spot for a picnic. A few more tables are sheltered under an arbor shaded with grapevine leaves. ♦ Tasting and sales daily 10AM-6PM; until 5PM in winter. 5601 Hwy 128, Philo. 895.3686

48 Greenwood Ridge Vineyards The redwood building with a distinctive, tall roof (inside it resembles a wooden teepee) is surrounded by a vineyard originally planted in 1972. The winery gets its moniker from a ridge that was named for the **Caleb Greenwood** family who settled the area in the 1850s. By coincidence the owner is **Allan Green,** a graphic designer and wine aficionado, who came to the Anderson Valley in the early seventies. Today he and winemaker **Van Williamson** produce off-dry (semi-sweet) White Riesling (and, in certain years, a sweet late-harvest White Riesling), along with Chardonnay, Cabernet, Pinot Noir, and a Zinfandel from the 70-year-old Scherrer Vineyard near Healdsburg in the

Anderson Valley

Russian River Valley. They've set up several picnic tables down by the pond and visitors can stretch out on the lawn. Since 1983, the last weekend in July is dedicated to their annual California Wine Tasting Championships. Food, wine, live music, and sun are the components of this spirited event, in which novice tasters and experienced professionals alike try to identify a series of wines by varietal type. ♦ Tasting and sales daily 10AM-6PM, summer; 10AM-5PM, winter. 5501 Hwy 128, Philo. 895.2002

49 Roederer Estate When the prestigious 200-year-old Champagne firm Roederer (maker of Cristal and Brut Premier) decided to establish a California estate, **Jean-Claude Rouzaud** spent more than two years researching sites in the late seventies before choosing the Anderson Valley. With its long, cool growing season, the climate is remarkably similar to that of Champagne. Local residents are very happy with the winery's low-key design, which fits unassumingly into the hillside. In fact, the large, state-of-the-art structure is built partially underground to better maintain the cellars' cool temperature. The estate's French winemaker, **Dr. Michel Salgues,** worked for seven years to develop the vineyards and hone his skills before releasing Roederer Estate's first wine, the Anderson Valley Brut, in October 1988. Made from a blend of Pinot Noir and Chardonnay, it spends 20 to 24 months aging on the yeasts.

Tours of this first-class operation give a good overview of the complicated process of making sparkling wines by the traditional méthode champenoise. The tasting room, which features an antique French bistro bar topped with zinc, is furnished with comfortable banquettes and iron-and-tile tables. The 200-year-old terracotta tiles on the floor come from an old château in France. ♦ Tasting and sales M, F-Su 11AM-4PM, May-Sep; by appt, Oct-Apr. 4501 Hwy 128, Philo. 895.2288

50 Husch Vineyards Founded in 1971, Husch is the oldest winery in Anderson Valley. In 1979 the **Oswald** family purchased it from the Husch family, and currently five members of this third generation farming family are involved in various aspects of the winery. The tasting room is a rustic redwood shack covered with climbing roses and it is hosted by one of the friendliest and most knowledgeable staffs around. More than six people at the bar is a tight fit, but you can take your glass of wine out to the sun deck. Nearby picnic tables are also set up under a vine-covered arbor.

The wines are all well made, and offer one of the best values in Mendocino County. The whites range from barrel-fermented and oak-aged Chardonnay and a dry Sauvignon Blanc to a dry, Alsatian-style Gewürztraminer and an off-dry Chenin Blanc. Reds include a good Pinot Noir and a firmly structured Cabernet (look for the North Field Select bottling). The grapes for their Pinot Noir, Gewürztraminer, and Chardonnay come from their vineyards in Anderson Valley, while the Sauvignon Blanc, Chardonnay, Cabernet, and Chenin Blanc hail from their warmer Ukiah vineyards. After tasting Husch wines, guests are welcome to stroll through the vineyards. ♦ Tasting and sales daily 10AM–6PM; until 5PM in winter. 4400 Hwy 128, Philo. 895.3216

51 Christine Woods Vineyards After spending 20 years as a home winemaker, **Vernon Rose** decided to take the plunge in 1980 and move from Walnut Creek, east of San Francisco, to the 40-acre property he bought as a vacation site in 1966. With classes in winemaking and viticulture at the University of California at Davis under his belt, he made his first commercial Chardonnay in 1982—and it won a gold medal at the Mendocino County fair when it was released. He also makes Cabernet Sauvignon, Merlot, and a Gamay Beaujolais. The name "Christine Woods" comes from an early settlement called Christine in honor of **Christine Gschwend,** who was the first white child born in Anderson Valley. Remnants of the old road to Christine Woods can still be seen on the property. ♦ Daily 10:30AM–6PM, summer; M, Th–Su 11AM–5PM, winter. 3155 Hwy 128, Philo. 895.2115

1987

HANDLEY

Anderson Valley
BRUT ROSÉ

Anderson Valley Sparkling Wine, Alc. 12.5% by vol.
Produced and bottled by Handley Cellars, Philo, CA

52 Handley Cellars **Milla Handley,** great-great granddaughter of beer-brewer **Henry Weinhard,** studied enology at the University of California at Davis and worked at Chateau St. Jean before founding Handley Cellars in the basement of her home near Philo in 1982. (She and husband **Rex McClellan** have since moved into larger quarters.) A rich, complex, barrel-aged Chardonnay is her best known wine, but she also makes a fine Sauvignon Blanc from grapes grown on the Handley family's Dry Creek Valley vineyard in Sonoma, a spicy, off-dry Gewürztraminer, and a small amount of sparkling brut three parts Pinot Noir to one part Chardonnay, aged on the yeasts for 24 to 36 months. Her rosé, made from Pinot Noir grapes and a touch of Chardonnay, is an ideal picnic wine. A couple of wines, such as her Pinot Noir and late-harvest Riesling, are available only at the winery. Sample them all at the sunny tasting room decorated with folk art from around the world.

Just outside the tasting room is a garden courtyard for picnics, and she has planted vines between the tasting room and the house to demonstrate different kinds of trellising. Call a couple of days ahead for tours with Milla herself; she may take you out into the vineyard where she has an experimental block of vines or stay in the cellar to do some barrel sampling and talk about Gewürztraminer, Riesling,

and sparkling wines. ♦ Tasting and sales daily 11AM–6PM; until 5PM in winter; tours by appt. 3151 Hwy 128, Philo. 895.3876

53 Floodgate Store & Grille ★$$ This little roadside cafe in a blue-gray clapboard building with a peaked roof is an appealing spot for lunch or a casual dinner. Look for the neon "Eats" over the front door. Inside, there's a wood-burning stove, patchwork quilts on the walls, wood tables, and chairs painted in primary colors. At lunch you can get homemade soups, a great BLT on bread baked at Brother Juniper's Bakery in Forestville, a grilled buffalo burger on a bun, and the wonderful smoked duck breast salad with apples, pecans, and Gorgonzola cheese. Dinner features freshly made soups and delectable appetizers such as steamed mussels with wine or an artichoke served with roasted garlic mayonnaise. Each entrée comes with a green salad, fresh vegetables, and potatoes. Choose from a grilled, center-cut pork chop or loin lamb chops with a Sicilian eggplant salad. Or how about Chinese barbecue smoked chicken breast glazed with plum sauce or a South American barbecue roast? They also offer one or two vegetarian entrées, which could be something like a black-bean chili or a vegetable lasagna. And for dessert there's Texas fudge pie, an irresistible raspberry-macaroon sundae, Anderson Valley pie (with in-season Anderson Valley fruit such as pears or apples), and more. The wine list features North Coast wines. For the Sunday brunch the kitchen turns out French toast scented with Grand Marnier and served with fresh berries and chicken-apple sausages; a satisfying crab, Gruyère cheese, and chive omelet; and, in season, grilled venison and eggs with potatoes. ♦ Eclectic ♦ M 11:30AM–2:30PM, W 5:30–8:30PM, Th–Su 11:30AM–2:30PM, 5:30–8:30PM, summer; Th–Su 11:30AM–2:30PM, 5:30–8:30PM, winter. Hwy 128, Navarro. 895.3000

54 Navarro River Redwood State Park As you drive from Boonville or Philo past the last of the wineries and enter a thick redwood grove, you'll pass this state park on the left, a 12-mile corridor of redwoods extending from the river to a little north of the highway. In 1991 more than 600 acres of Navarro redwoods were added to the original 22-acre

Paul Dimmick State Park to create this spacious park, which offers visitors numerous activities, including swimming in the Navarro River, fishing for steelhead, and lots of hiking trails. The Paul Dimmick campground is set up for overnight camping, with 30 sites suitable for tents or RVs. The primitive campground has flush toilets and water in summer (pit toilets only in winter) and is available on a first-come, first-serve basis. ♦ Hwy 128, west of Navarro. For more information, call 937.5804

The Mendocino Coast

From the Anderson Valley wine country, it's only a 30- to 40-minute drive—every bit of it scenic—to the coast at **Albion**, where the Navarro River opens into the sea. Head north, and 10 minutes later you'll arrive at the area's prime attraction, the Victorian village of **Mendocino**. All along the North Coast, particularly south of Mendocino, are dramatic coves and secret, sheltered beaches inset with tiny seaside villages such as Albion, **Little River,** and **Caspar**. These hamlets were once the centers of the logging industry, which became a booming business after the Gold Rush increased San Francisco's population and created a demand for building materials.

With no super highway straight to the coast, this area has remained relatively inaccessible; it's a three-and-a-half to four-hour drive from San Francisco by way of Hwy 101 and Hwy 128 through the Anderson Valley. And the drive from the city up the Coast Hwy (Route 1) is an even more arduous (though beautiful) trek, taking up to seven hours on the twisting, narrow road. So when people come to the Mendocino coast, it's usually for more than a couple of days. The idea is to find a hideaway near the sea and indulge in some relaxed, quiet pleasures—walking in the forests of **Van Damme State Park** or any of the many coastal parks, or strolling along the headlands with an eye out for seals and, from November through April, the migrating whales. There are a few tourist-oriented diversions, it's true, such as the **Skunk Train** to **Willits** and a few small museums with displays of local history, but most people end up abandoning their planned activities and revel in doing nothing at all except simply enjoying the scenery.

Gualala

The local Indians used to call this area Walali, meaning "where the river meets [the sea]," until the Spanish started calling it Gualala. Nowadays, you might hear some of the locals call it "Walala" (a combination of the two names), but don't let that confuse you. Gualala is still the town's official name.

Like most of the cities along this coast, Gualala was once a thriving lumber port where schooners were loaded with timber bound for San Francisco. With its river beaches and good fishing spots, Gualala is a haven for anglers and nature lovers. Travelers who want to spend time exploring the local beaches can find very reasonably priced lodging at the old-time **Gualala Hotel.** The town is also home to **St. Orres,** one of the best restaurants along the North Coast and definitely worth a detour.

55 Gualala Hotel $ The year 1903 is proudly inscribed on the front of this historic two-

story hotel that resembles an old-West movie set. It was actually built to house lumber-mill workers and stagecoach travelers. The 19 rooms upstairs have their original dainty proportions and most share a bath, just as they did in the old days. Reserve ahead for one of the five rooms with private baths and ocean views. The unfussy period decor—patterned wallpaper, old-fashioned water basins, bouquets of fresh flowers—is charming. The accommodations are inexpensive, and a Continental breakfast is included with the room's price. ♦ Route 1, Gualala. 884.3441

Within the Gualala Hotel:

Gualala Hotel Restaurant ★$$ Breakfast at the Gualala includes omelets, French toast, and hot cakes, and the lunch menu is mostly sandwiches. The large Italian-American dinners feature fresh seafood and are served family-style in a gold-hued dining room. Entrées range from fresh salmon and deep-fried oysters or scallops to chicken cacciatore, meat-stuffed ravioli, and rib eye steak. A children's menu is available, and Saturday is prime-rib night. There's also a lively bar. ♦ Italian/American ♦ M-Th, Su 7AM-2PM, 5-9PM; F-Sa 7AM-2PM, 5-9:30PM. Reservations recommended for the weekend. 884.3441

56 The Food Company Stop here for a take-out picnic that's prepared on the spot. Choices include salads, sandwiches, and pastries baked fresh daily, plus hot entrées. Patio seating is also available. ♦ M-F 11AM-7PM; Sa-Su 11AM-8PM. 884.1800

The 1915 Panama Pacific International Exposition held in San Francisco was the first major American wine competition in which Cabernet Sauvignon wines were judged as a separate category.

56 Old Milano Hotel $$ Overlooking the sea at Castle Rock, this two-story white Victorian trimmed in green was built in 1905 and is on the National Register of Historic Places. Rooms have been furnished with antiques and most have ocean views. The **Luccinettis,** who built the Old Milano, lived in the master suite, which features a sitting room and a separate bedroom. Guests have use of the lovely music room and the parlor and its stone fireplace; there's also a hot tub set in front of the ocean. The full breakfast can be served in your room or in the parlor. ♦ 38300 Hwy 1, Gualala. 884.3256

Within the Old Milano Hotel:

Old Milano Hotel Restaurant ★$$$ Only dinners are offered here, which are served in the wood-paneled Victorian-era dining room decorated in shades of rose. Starters may include house-cured gravlax (salmon), steamed mussels, or a salad of local greens. All entrées come with soup and vegetables; choose from dishes such as roasted quail with fresh blackberry sauce or grilled pork tenderloin served with homemade plum chutney. A vegetarian entrée is usually available, too. ♦ Calfiornia ♦ Tu-Su 6-9:45PM, summer; W-Su 6-9:45PM, winter. Reservations required. 884.3256

57 St. Orres $$ One of the few inns on the North Coast that combines appealing accommodations with a first-class restaurant. The Russian-influenced architecture—marked by elaborately carved wooden balustrades, stained-glass windows, and ornate towers capped with copper domes—is the four-year project of craftsmen **Ted** and **Eric Black**. The hotel, built in 1976, has eight guest rooms upstairs, all with shared baths; two have ocean views and French doors opening onto the balcony, while the less expensive side rooms overlook the gardens or trees. Scattered over the large property are also 10 very private and unique cottages, some along a creek and others at the edge of a redwood forest. One favorite is the modest **Wildflower,** a rustic cabin with a double bed nestled in a loft, a wood-burning stove, a cookstove, and an outdoor hot-water shower. The **Sequoia** cottage features a carved balustrade, queen-sized bed, fireplace, and an ocean view. The largest, **Pine Haven,** is a mini-domed building with two redwood decks, an ocean view, and a stone fireplace. There's also the Japanese-style cottage, **Wake Robin.** ♦ 36601 Hwy 1, Gualala. 884.3303

Within St. Orres:

St. Orres Restaurant ★★★$$$ The inn's dramatic dining room is in one of the Russian-style towers, and has a soaring three-story ceiling. Tables are set with elegant flower arrangements and handsome dinnerware, and the service is attentive. In the kitchen, chef **Rosemary Campiformio,** who is also part-owner of the hotel, turns out inventive fixed-price, three-course meals, and you can also order à la carte. Appetizers might include a sumptuous venison paté, Stilton cheese wrapped in filo, or a sea urchin mousse. The menu changes daily, but Campiformio's selection of appealing entrées leaves most diners struggling over what to finally order, and choices may vary from venison in a wild huckleberry and Zinfandel sauce to grilled quail marinated in tequila and garlic that's served with yam and green onion pancakes. Very good all-California wine list, too. ♦ Northern California ♦ Daily 6-9:30PM, summer; Tu, Th-Su 6-9:30PM, winter. Closed the first two weeks of December. Reservations required. 884.3335

56 Whale Watch Inn by the Sea $$$$ This

contemporary inn is set on two acres at the edge of the sea just north of Anchor Bay and offers 18 luxurious accommodations in five separate buildings, all with ocean views, private baths, and oceanfront decks. Each features queen-sized beds with down comforters; most have fireplaces, whirlpool baths or saunas, and skylights; some have kitchens. The most luxurious is the **Bath Suite,** which features handcarved furniture, a fireplace, and a two-person whirlpool bath at the top of a spiral staircase, with a view of the Pacific. Continental breakfast is served in your room. ♦ 35100 Hwy 1, Gualala. 884.3667

57 Mar Vista Cottages $$ A dozen white-clapboard cottages are set at the edge of a redwood forest just north of Anchor Bay. Choose from one- or two-bedroom housekeeping cottages, all with a queen-

sized bed, and some with additional double or twin-sized beds. Several have fireplaces or outdoor decks. The eight-acre property also includes a picnic and barbecue area, hot tub, and a path to the beach. ♦ 35101 Hwy 1, Gualala. 884.3522

Restaurants/Clubs: Red   **Hotels:** Blue
Shops/ ♦ Outdoors: Green   **Wineries/Sights:** Black

Albion

Homesick for Britain, **Captain William A. Richardson,** former port captain of San Francisco and a large landholder on the Mendocino coast, dubbed this coastal village Albion, the ancient name for Britain. Richardson also built the town's first sawmill in 1853, just where the Albion River meets the sea.

58 Fensalden Inn $$ Just off Hwy 1 on Navarro Ridge Rd, this bed-and-breakfast inn (pictured above) is set on 20 acres of land, with views of the ocean on the other side of the road. Originally built as a stagecoach stop in the 1860s, the structure now houses four guest rooms and a two-room suite with a fireplace, all with private baths. The property's water tower has also been converted into two guest rooms, and a bungalow has just been added that can sleep four and has a full kitchen. Guests can gather in the living room around the fire or the grand piano. And in the morning, innkeepers **Scott** and **Frances Brazil** serve breakfast with freshly baked muffins and pastries in the dining room or, if you prefer, in your room. ♦ Navarro Ridge Rd (7 miles south of Mendocino off Hwy 1) Albion. 937.4042

59 Albion River Inn $$/$$$ A series of contemporary cottages strung across a dramatic piece of real estate overlooking the ocean composes this popular Mendocino retreat. Every room (complete with a private bath) has a knockout view through the large windows or from the deck. Most have fireplaces and/or Jacuzzi tubs, and range from rather small rooms to large suites. The decor has been kept fairly plain, but it's definitely more condo style than rustic cottage. ♦ 3790 N. Hwy 1, Albion. 937.1919

Within the Albion River Inn:

Albion River Inn Restaurant ★$$$ At the very end of the row of cottages is the

inn's restaurant, a large, simply tailored room that boasts that same spectacular view of the headlands and the sea beyond, which is particularly lovely at sunset. Start with a fresh seafood chowder or a green salad; then try the grilled prawns, the marinated game hen served on a bed of polenta, or the grilled New York steak served with caramelized onions and mushrooms and either a black

pepper or a Dijon mustard sauce. Specials might include grilled King salmon or roasted pork loin. They have quite a good list of North Coast wines from hard-to-find producers such as Dehlinger and Williams & Selyem. ♦ California ♦ Daily 5:30-9:30PM

Little River

Like many of the small cities up and down the coast, Little River was once a bustling logging and ship-building town. Now it's a quiet, charming hamlet dotted with quaint inns that's certainly worth a visit, particularly for a stroll through the lush trails in **Van Damme State Park** and a boat ride through the Big River estuary.

60 Heritage House $$$ Dating from 1877, this New England-style lodge is perhaps the most well known on the Mendocino Coast, and it offers lots of privacy and outstanding ocean views from many of the rooms and cottages. The inn includes a huge range of accommodations, from moderately-priced rooms to large, costly suites and cottages. The cottages overlooking the cove are the most popular, and many are reserved months in advance. ♦ Closed Dec-Jan. 5200 Hwy 1, Little River. 937.5885

Within the Heritage House:

Heritage House Restaurant ★★$$$ Diners gather under the beautiful chandeliered ceiling to enjoy a prix-fixe meal and a view of the coast. Entrées might include seared Pacific swordfish, pan-roasted breast of duck, or sautéed petrale sole. Be sure to listen to the sommelier's recommendations. No smoking. ♦ Daily 8-11AM, 6-9:45PM. Reservations required. Jacket required at dinner. 937.5885

Heritage House Limosine Service Wine-country tours custom tailored to your interests are offered, or you can just hire a car to take you out to some secluded spot for a picnic. ♦ 937.5885

61 Mendocino County Airport This small airstrip can accommodate private aircraft—and certainly a small plane is the fastest and most convenient way to arrive in Mendocino, if you can afford it. The airport also handles car rentals and chartered small planes. ♦ Little River, 14 miles south of Fort Bragg. 937.5129

61 The Victorian Farmhouse $$ Ginger-bread scrolls and curlicues adorn this Victorian bed-and-breakfast house that was originally built in 1877 as a residence. Innkeepers **George** and **Carole Molnar** have 10 guest rooms, some in the main house and some in the row of cottages set along the hill to one side of the original farmhouse. All the rooms have queen- or king-sized beds, private baths, and either ocean or forest views. They are furnished with period antiques, and some have fireplaces. In the morning, the Molnars will deliver breakfast to your door if you'd rather enjoy it in the privacy of your room. ♦ 7001 N. Hwy 1, Little River. 937.0697

61 Konstantin ★$ This sweet, little cottage tucked in the trees beside the road serves dinners a few nights a week and take-out fare for picnics. The sandwiches, made on homemade foccacia or baguettes, are great: choose from black-forest ham, grilled chicken breast, or French salame, and more, with a choice of homemade condiments. Salads range from Russian potato salad to a Greek orzo pasta-and-feta cheese salad. You can put together a fine cheese plate to accompany a bottle of wine, too. Entrées at dinner include roasted chicken with fresh herbs, grilled game hen, roast-duck lasagna, or baked rabbit. Specialties (which must be ordered several days in advance) include paella valenciana loaded with seafood, a Spanish-style fish stew, and Peking roast duck. They'll also cater a special dinner or put together a custom picnic with a day or two's notice. ♦ Mediterranean/American ♦ Takeout by appt; dinner W-Su 6PM. 7675 Hwy 1, Little River. Reservations recommended. 937.1636

61 Little River Inn $$/$$$ A white New England-style farmhouse (pictured above) built in the 1850s now serves as the inn's office, while lodgings are spread out in bungalows and cottages throughout the hillside grounds. All of the 55 units have private baths, and many have balconies overlooking the sea; a few face the other way, with views of the golf course in back. The more expensive rooms also have fireplaces. While the location is ideal and the staff helpful and warm, the decor fails to inspire, with mundane carpeting, drab curtains, sliding-glass patio doors, and a general

suburban look. The inn includes two championship tennis courts and a nine-hole golf course right on the property. ♦ 7751 N. Hwy 1, Little River. 937.5942

At the Little River Inn:

Little River Inn Restaurant ★$$ A casual place for breakfast or dinner, where the tables by the windows get a glimpse of the ocean. Breakfast focuses on Swedish hot cakes, egg dishes, and omelets, while the dinner menu offers a dozen regular entrées along with daily specials. Everything is served with freshly made soup or salad, vegetables, rice or potatoes, and either crunchy, homemade bread sticks or warm biscuits. Choose from the broiled swordfish filet marinated in tequila and lime juice or the grilled prawns rolled in bread crumbs and chopped hazelnuts. Consider also the summer supper of chicken-and-turkey sausage served with polenta and vegetables or the charbroiled New York steak. Saturday night is prime-rib night. ♦ California ♦ M-Th 7:30-10AM, 6-8:30PM; F 7:30-10AM, 6-9:30PM; Sa 7:30-11AM, 6-9:30PM; Su 7:30AM-1PM, 6-9:30PM. 937.5942

Little River Golf & Tennis Club Regulation nine-hole golf course with a driving range and putting green. Golf carts are available, and the pro shop can set you up with golf togs and equipment. ♦ Daily 7AM-dusk. 937.5667

61 Little River Market Cheese, cold cuts, cold drinks, Häagen-Dasz, ice cream, and a collection of local wines. ♦ M-Th 8AM-7:30PM; F 8AM-9PM; Sa 8:30AM-9PM; Su 8:30AM-7:30PM. 7746 N. Hwy 1, Little River. 937.5133

61 Little River Restaurant ★★$$$ Adjoining the post office is this very cozy spot, with no more than half a dozen tables and no view to speak of. The attraction is the well-prepared food and the pleasure of dining in such an intimate and friendly setting. Start with baked brie wrapped in filo or prawns in a champagne beurre blanc. Entrées, which come with garden soup, salad, and freshly baked breads, include poached salmon in a tarragon cream sauce, broiled quail in a hazelnut sauce, and roasted duck in a sauce made with apricot vermouth. The small dessert menu usually includes fresh fruit ices and a chocolate amaretto mousse.

Mendocino Coast

♦ California/French ♦ M, F-Su, seatings available at 6 and 8:30PM. 7750 N. Hwy 1, Little River. Reservations recommended. 937.4945

Restaurants/Clubs: Red   **Hotels:** Blue
Shops/ ♥ Outdoors: Green   **Wineries/Sights:** Black

61 Van Damme State Park This beautiful park covers some 1,826 acres of dramatically diverse landscape. The Visitors Center at the head of the park can give you trail maps and information; pick up some bird- or fern-finder guides to take on the hike along the lush Fern Canyon Trail, which is definitely worth a stroll and is also a great place for an early-morning jog. Another prime attraction is the Pygmy Forest, where the acidic, compacted soil has stunted cypresses and pines; some of the mature trees are just a foot tall. The park also has 74 campsites suitable for tents or RVs and they are very popular; reserve ahead. Ten additional campsites can be reached only by hiking in. ♦ Fee per vehicle. Dawn to dusk. At Little River just 3.5 miles south of Mendocino. 937.0851, 800/444.7275

61 Glendeven Inn $$/$$$ This two-acre property on the east side of Hwy 1 was first settled by **Isaiah Stevens** in 1867; he built the New England-style farmhouse the same year. The handsomely renovated farmhouse and the restored old hay barn, plus a new building with four suites with fireplaces, make up this inn. Altogether there are ten guest rooms; some are larger than others and range in price from moderate to expensive. They're all furnished in a country style, with a mix of antique and contemporary pieces, and all have private baths. Innkeepers **Jan** and **Janet deVries** serve a Continental breakfast (juice, fruit, homebaked pastries, and coffee or tea) either in the room or in the main house, which features an attractive, large living room with a fireplace and grand piano. ♦ 8221 N. Hwy 1, Little River. 937.0083

Within Glendeven Inn:

Gallery Glendeven A gallery of fine art and crafts from local artisans. ♦ M-Tu, Th-Su 10AM-5PM. 937.0083

61 Rachel's Inn $$ In the early 1980s **Rachel Binah** renovated an old 1860s farmhouse and turned it into a welcoming bed-and-breakfast. Not only are all the rooms

Mendocino Coast

comfortable and quite private, she is a great cook and turns out wonderful, generous breakfasts served family-style around a long wooden table. The main house has four guest rooms, three upstairs and a secluded garden room with its own entrance downstairs. A textile artist who is now active in the ocean sanctuary movement (fighting against offshore oil drilling), Binah has

furnished the rooms in quiet colors and with some of her own artwork. All have queen-sized beds and private baths. In addition, a contemporary barn beside the house is equipped with four private large guest rooms and suites on three levels. They've got most of the conveniences of a small, first-class hotel—fireplaces, good reading lamps, private baths. The suites have a wetbar and a refrigerator, along with Murphy beds for extra guests and families. The furniture includes either French-style sofas and chairs or pretty wicker, and most of the rooms have views of the meadow and headlands beyond.

From Binah's door are two great walks: one down to the beach in front of Van Damme State Park, the other a long hike on the headlands, through pines and meadows where deer and other wildlife abound. Binah has set out hay bales at the point the path meets the sea, so guests can sit and watch the seals and sea lions below. ♦ Mendocino (2 miles south of Mendocino at Little River) 937.0088

62 The Stanford Inn by the Sea $$$ Also known as Big River Lodge, this 260-room inn stands on a bluff overlooking Big River and the ocean. Aside from great views from all the rooms, the large hillside estate features an organic garden and a new greenhouse with a large Olympic-sized pool, a spa, and a sauna. Rooms come with coffeemakers and all sorts of nice touches, including four-poster beds (queen- or king-sized), fireplaces, and VCRs (and a videotape library of classic and current movies). The buffet Continental breakfast consists of freshly-squeezed orange juice, warm rolls and croissants, yogurt, fruit, and coffee or tea. Innkeepers **Joan** and **Jeff Stanford** permit guests to bring their pets, as long as the critters are well behaved—in fact, a few llamas roam the property. ♦ Pool and greenhouse daily 8AM-11PM. Hwy 1 and Comptche-Ukiah Rds, Mendocino. 937.5615

Also at The Stanford Inn by the Sea:

Catch A Canoe & Bicycles Too! Both guests and non-guests can rent kayaks or canoes to explore the Big River estuary, rated Class 1, a gentle river suitable for the novice. However, it's still advisable to get information on tides and river conditions before setting off. The office also rents mountain and touring bicycles, and will suggest various routes. ♦ Daily 9:30AM-5:30PM. 937.0273

Village of Mendocino

This Victorian village, perched at the very edge of a high bluff overlooking the ocean and flanked on three sides by the wild sea, has captured the imagination of visitors from all over the world. A protected historical area with Cape Cod-style architecture, Mendocino resembles a New England village set down beside the Pacific. In fact, in the popular television series "Murder She Wrote," Mendocino appears as the fictional town, Cabot Cove, Maine. Many of the town's old homes have been turned into bed-and-breakfast inns, restaurants, shops, and galleries. And the headlands, with their marvelous vistas of the sea, have remained just as they were in times past.

Legend has it that the name Mendocino means "path to the sea," but the cape may actually have been named for the Spanish captain who discovered it in the 16th century, or perhaps after his ship. At any rate, the town had its start in 1852, when German immigrant **William Kasten**, apparently the sole survivor of a shipwreck off the coast, washed up on a nearby beach. With no rescue in sight, he built himself a cabin on the headlands and had been living there for almost two years when a ship finally ventured into the bay. The sailors on that vessel noted the vast redwoods surrounding the cape, and **Henry Meiggs,** a lumberjack then working in Bodega Bay to the south, organized a party of men to head up the coast and begin logging operations. In 1853, after much difficulty, they constructed a sawmill, and Mendocino (then known as the town of Big River) was launched as a logging center.

By 1865, the fledgling metropolis had a population of 700 and a number of hotels and rooming houses for the loggers. Most of the grander homes were built in the 1870s and 1880s for lumber barons and bankers. Mendocino remained a logging town up until the thirties, when economic depression shut down operations. In the fifties, artists discovered the picturesque little town, and it became an artists' community much like California's Laguna Beach or Carmel.

63 Mendocino Café ★$$ A charming little cafe with blue tables and bright paintings that serves eclectic fare. For breakfast there are such items as huevos rancheros, a Thai scramble (eggs laced with stir-fried vegetables and rock shrimp), and cornmeal waffles. Lunch may include Thai burritos made with smoked meats and homemade Thai chili sauce, quesadillas with black beans, Greek salads with feta cheese and olives, or a series of well-made sandwiches such as the tasty smoked chicken with garlic mayonnaise or the Cajun-spiced sautéed snapper with tartar sauce. The dinner menu adds pasta dishes from Italian and Asian traditions, plus blackened rock fish, steamed shellfish, barbecued ribs, and a decent steak. For dessert, try the fresh local blackberry pie or nectarine-berry cobbler. Good list of beers and North Coast wines. In fine weather, ask to be seated on the deck out back.
♦ Eclectic ♦ M-W, F-Su 7:30AM-9:30PM; Th 1:30-9:30PM. 10451 Lansing St, Mendocino. 937.2422

63 The Sea Gull of Mendocino ★$$ This spot is a Mendocino landmark, famous for its live music, which is scheduled every night but Wednesday. Downstairs is a cozy cafe with low ceilings and booths. Breakfast fare includes buttermilk pancakes, omelets, and scrambled eggs. At lunch they serve sandwiches on grilled French bread, burgers, and salads. Dinner continues with the casual theme: pepper steak, charbroiled chicken, and seafood, as well as some lunch items such as sandwiches and cheeseburgers. They also have a short children's menu. Upstairs is a large room with a natural-wood peaked roof and a long bar at one end with a scattering of tables in front—a relaxing place for a beer or a glass of wine. ♦ American ♦ M-Th, Su 8AM-9PM; F-Sa 8AM-10PM. Lansing and Ukiah Sts, Mendocino. 937.2100

64 Mendocino Gold Unusually nice jewelry, much of it contemporary and handcrafted, plus Australian fire opals, colored stones,

Mendocino Coast

and a selection of wedding rings. ♦ Daily 10AM-5PM. Lansing and Ukiah Sts, Mendocino. 937.2018

64 Mendocino Chocolate Company This tiny shop is heady with the aroma of deep, dark chocolate. Famous for their truffles, which they make in more than two dozen flavors, this homey chocolate company has a few other specialties: Mendocino toffee is a butter toffee dipped in light chocolate and rolled in toasted almonds, while the Mendocino Breakers are chocolate caramels dipped in light chocolate, almonds, and white chocolate. They'll box up special assortments and ship them home, too. ♦ Daily 10AM-5:30PM. 10483 Lansing St, Mendocino. 937.1107

64 Mendocino Bakery Pizza by the slice, garlic, and onion bialys, along with an assortment of hefty pastries, muffins, and scones. Take your espresso or cappuccino outside on the deck to the side. ♦ Daily 8AM-7PM. 10483 Lansing St, Mendocino. 937.0836

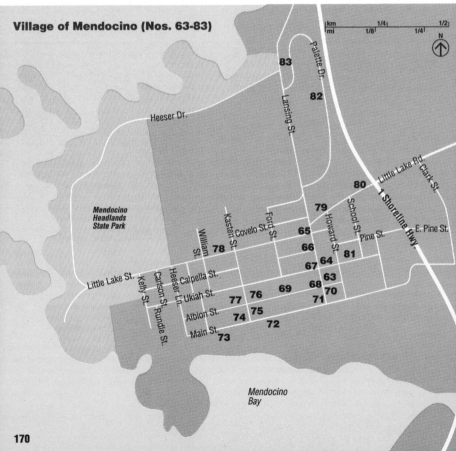

64 Rainsong Shoes The emphasis here is on comfort and style, with lots of good walking shoes, serious tennies, dress shoes, and boots. The Aerosole shoes are good-looking, comfortable, and moderately priced. The slippers shaped like little piggies, Angora cats, or schnauzers just might tickle someone's fancy. ♦ Daily 10AM-5PM. 10483 Lansing St, Mendocino. 937.1710

64 Mendosa's Merchandise & Market A full-service market with plenty of picnic supplies such as cheese, cold cuts, barbecued chicken, and Mendocino County wines, including already chilled whites. The hardware division next door stocks fishing equipment, barbecues, picnic baskets, enameled camp cookware, and corkscrews. ♦ Daily 9AM-9PM. 10501 Lansing St, Mendocino. 937.5879

65 The Cheese Shop The best picnic supplier in town. Stop here for imported and domestic cheeses, cold cuts, and a bottle of North Coast wine. They've got condiments galore, from Mendocino mustard and special chutneys to locally made jams and jellies. You can get some great classic deli sandwiches made, and when the weather is damp, a bowl of the housemade barley or carrot-ginger soup is ideal. Salads are more interesting than usual deli fare; you might find tabbouleh (a Middle Eastern bulghur wheat salad), a celery root salad, or a well-made coleslaw. The store is also crammed with all sorts of gourmet gift items, kitchen gadgets, and accessories. ♦ Daily 10AM-6PM. Little Lake and Lansing Sts, Mendocino. 937.0104

The pigments in wine are the same pigments that cause the red and blue colors of most fruits and flowers.

Village of Mendocino (Nos. 63-83)

66 The Village Art Gallery Watercolor landscapes of Mendocino, gift cards, and more make up this yellow-and-white wooden house with flower boxes of nasturtiums planted in front. ♦ Daily 10AM–5PM. 10540 Lansing St, Mendocino. 937.2787

67 Masonic Temple Now the Savings Bank of Mendocino County (established in 1903), this white wooden building with its single soaring steeple (pictured at right) was first built as the Masons Lodge in 1866 by **Erik Albertson**, the first Worshipful Master of Mendocino Lodge No. 179. Albertson also sculpted the statue of Time and the Maiden, sitting atop the steeple, from a single redwood trunk. ♦ Lansing and Ukiah Sts

68 Temptations Gallery A large gallery divided into three sections: fine art, jewelry, and glass. It's the last that's the most interesting, featuring hand-blown vases and bowls in swirls of colors and subtle shapes made by master glassblowers. ♦ Daily 10AM–5PM. 10466 Lansing St, Mendocino. 937.0610

68 Mendocino Cookie Company Very sweet, freshly-baked cookies, including a double chocolate chip, plus espresso and coffee drinks to go. ♦ Daily 10AM–5PM. 10450 Lansing St, Mendocino. 937.4843

68 Tote Fête Stop here for sandwiches; there are at least a dozen kinds, including homemade chicken salad, meat loaf, and turkey, avocado, and jack cheese. There's also pizza by the slice, their own rosemary-and-garlic focaccia bread, and an array of salads. Try to stop here a little before the lunch hour, since the place is tiny and a line often forms outside the door. ♦ M-Th, Sa 10:30AM–7PM; Su 10:30AM–4PM. 10450 Lansing St, Mendocino. 937.3383

68 Down to Earth: A History & Nature Store If visiting the Mendocino coast has inspired you to further study nature, this is the place to find books on local flora and fauna, science and nature games, and some purely recreational or silly items such as the California map T-shirts and the ship-in-a-bottle kits. They also have relief maps of California and the San Francisco Bay. ♦ Daily 10:30AM–5PM. 10450 Lansing St, Mendocino. 937.1447

68 Shibui Necessities and Accessories Folk art from around the world, including old copper vessels, cushions made from flat-woven kelim rugs, ethnic jewelry, and Indian block-printed textiles. There are some fine Indonesian baskets and Chinese and Japanese teapots, too. ♦ Daily 10:30AM–5PM. 10450 Lansing St, Mendocino. 937.5613

69 Old Gold This elegant shop, furnished with Oriental carpets, palms, and orchids, specializes in antique jewelry and wedding rings. They have some top-notch pieces, such as an 18K ruby-and-diamond Victorian

Masonic Temple

bracelet, an 18K floral, diamond cluster brooch by Cartier from the forties, and an English Victorian opal-and-diamond ring. They also carry some contemporary pieces

Mendocino Coast

and a large array of wedding rings. ♦ Daily 10:30AM–5PM. Albion and Lansing Sts, Mendocino. 937.5005

"I feast on wine and bread and feasts they are."
Michelangelo

Restaurants/Clubs: Red **Hotels:** Blue
Shops/ ♥ Outdoors: Green **Wineries/Sights:** Black

69 The Book Loft Follow the little path lined with nasturtiums to this cozy bookshop, where you can find a self-serve samovar of herbal tea and two chairs pulled up to the wood-burning stove (put on a headset and listen to some of the music tapes). Good selection of works from local authors and gardening and travel books, mysteries, and best-sellers, plus a smattering of used books. ◆ Daily 10AM-6PM. 45006 Albion St, Mendocino. 937.0890

70 Kelley House Museum Mendocino pioneer **William Kelley's** house has been restored and is now a museum of the cultural life and history of this seaside town. It is also the headquarters for Mendocino Historical Research, Inc., which operates the museum and has compiled impressive archives of historical photos and research material. They've also done extensive work on the grounds, planting native California plants and old-fashioned flowers. ◆ Nominal donation. M, F-Su 1-4PM, or by appt M-F. 45007 Albion, Mendocino. 937.5791

71 Mendocino Headlands State Park Visitor Center This park, which encompasses the headlands in and around the town of Mendocino, uses a two-story 1857 residence, originally built for **Bursley Ford,** co-owner of one of the town's first sawmills, as a visitors center. Stop here for information on Mendocino and books on its history, nature, wildlife, and the sea. They've got tide charts, maps, field guides to tide pools and birds, and, of course, books on spotting whales. In fact, the house is a favorite observation point during the annual migration of the California gray whale. Pop in to see the large model of Mendocino circa 1890, created in 1990 by **Leonard Peterson**. A couple of rooms are set up with exhibits on the logging and seafaring days of Mendocino. Outside, the park has picnic tables with views of the headlands. ◆ Daily 10AM-5PM. 735 Main St, Mendocino. 937.5397

Mendocino Coast

Bread and wine are united by chemistry as well as history. Before the advent of purified yeast (what we buy in small packets at the supermarket), sometimes a baker's bread would rise, sometimes it wouldn't. So breadmakers started frequenting the local brewhouse or winery to borrow active beer or wine yeast in order to make their loaves rise. Today, a few wine-country bakers have revived this tradition of making grape-yeast bread, which has an unusual, tangy taste.

72 Bay View Café ★$$ Light casual fare served almost all day, including omelets, pancakes, and French toast for breakfast. At lunch it's a short menu of sandwiches, burgers, fish and chips, omelets, and salads. Dinner is only a bit fancier, with pasta and steaks added to the list. The entrance is up the watertower stairs to a dining room with an outdoor deck and a great view of the ocean. ◆ Daily 8AM-3:30PM, 5-9PM. 45040 Main St, Mendocino. 937.4197

72 Mendocino Cyclery and Outfitters Touring and mountain bike rentals are available by the half-day or day. They'll send you off with a helmet and a map of suggested rides; no guided tours are available. Visit the headlands, the Pygmy Forest, or loop through the farms and the redwoods. Most rides are one-to-four hours long, and it's advisable to pack a picnic lunch, preferably a sandwich from Café Beaujolais. ◆ Daily 10AM-5PM. 45040 Main St, Mendocino. 937.4000

72 Out of This World Big and little kids will have fun browsing through this space-age store, which features maps of the heavens and earth, star charts, and celestial music tapes. They have several powerful telescopes set up inside, so you can gaze out at the headlands and beyond. Owners **Marilyn Rose** and **James Blackstock** have a sister store called **Down to Earth,** which features everything to do with nature and our home planet, of course. ◆ Daily 10AM-6PM. Albion and Lansing Sts, Mendocino. 937.3335

72 Mendocino Dry Goods Canning jars, wildflower seeds, and gardens-in-a-box from the heirloom seed company Le Marché, plus pick-up sticks, puzzles, and other amusements for the country life. ◆ Daily 10:30AM-5PM. 45050 Main St, Mendocino. 937.1226

72 The Irish Shop A small house at the back of a brick walk features woolens and cottons from Ireland and Scotland. Look for natural cotton, crocheted or hand-knitted throws, tweed sport coats and caps, along with teatime necessities such as shortbread, imported jams, and teas. ◆ Daily 9:30AM-5:30PM. 45050 Main St, Mendocino. 937.3133

Restaurants/Clubs: Red   Hotels: Blue
Shops/ 🍴 Outdoors: Green   **Wineries/Sights: Black**

72 Highlight Gallery A large two-story gallery with some paintings, small sculptures, ceramics, and hand-turned and hand-carved wooden bowls made with exotic hardwoods. There are some beautiful jewelry boxes, and a small collection of handcrafted furniture is exhibited upstairs. ♦ Daily 10AM-5PM. 45052 Main St, Mendocino. 937.3132

72 Mendocino Hotel & Garden Suites $$$ This 1878 false-front hotel sits right on Main St and has an unobstructed view of the sea. There are a number of buildings in back, including the 1852 **Heeser House** and an acre of gardens. The accommodations here cover a wide range of prices, from simple European-style rooms with shared baths (the hotel provides a bathrobe) and twin- or double-sized beds; rooms with private baths, queen-sized beds, and wood-burning stoves; to deluxe rooms and large suites. There are 51 in all, most decorated with Victorian antiques and each completely different because of the decor, the view, a balcony, or a garden in front. The most luxurious are the three Heeser Garden suites, all with fireplaces, spacious modern bathrooms, and king- or queen-sized beds with an extra sofa bed for the family. ♦ 45080 Main St, Mendocino. 937.0511, 800/548.0513

Within the Mendocino Hotel:

Mendocino Hotel Restaurant ★$$$ The new chef here is **Colleen Murphy,** formerly head chef at the Little River Inn. The hotel actually has two restaurants: Breakfast and lunch are served in the informal garden room filled with plants, while dinner is served in the more formal dining room. For breakfast, they offer Belgian waffles with olallaiberries, pecan pancakes with pear marmalade, omelets, and other egg dishes. Lunch features moderately priced sandwiches, burgers, and salads. Dinner entrées, all served with soup and salad, include linguine tossed with a mix of seafood and a garlic-and-white wine sauce, roasted free-range chicken, loin of lamb with rosemary glaze, or grilled New York steak. For dessert, try the deep-dish olallaiberrie pie, served with homemade vanilla ice cream. That same ice cream goes into the sinfully rich hotel sundae, which is topped with melted chocolate truffles and honey-roasted pecans. ♦ American ♦ Daily 8AM-2:30PM, 6-9:30PM. 937.0511

72 The Mendocino Ice Cream Co. Winner of a gold medal at the California State Fair, this shop does a brisk summer business in ice-cream cones, scooping out more than two dozen of their own homemade ice cream flavors into regular or waffle cones. Try the Black Forest (chocolate, bing cherries, and chocolate chips) or the Macadamia nut brittle. They've also got sundaes and shakes. Eat it all here in one of the wooden booths or take your cone out for a stroll along Main Street. ♦ Daily 10AM-5PM. 45090 Main St, Mendocino. 937.5884

72 The Courtyard They have big blue bowls with high rims for mixing bread dough and lovely pottery pie plates for sale here. There are also spices, country crafts, and cookware to choose from. ♦ Daily 10AM-5PM. 45098 Main St, Mendocino. 937.0917

72 Golden Goose I & II The opulent beds on display will tempt all weary shoppers to plop themselves down here. A good place to shop for featherbeds, duvets, down pillows, fine Austrian linens, or even an antique bed or armoire. ♦ Daily 10AM-5PM. 45094 Main St, Mendocino. 937.4655

73 Mendocino Art Center Showcase This gallery features local artists and a wide variety of media and crafts. Shop here for handwoven shawls and mufflers, marbled silk scarves, handthrown dinnerware, ceramics, woodcuts, prints, and paintings. ♦ Daily 10:30AM-5PM. 560 Main St, Mendocino. 937.2829

73 Crossblends A tiny shop crammed with everything to do with quilting—framed, embossed paper quilts, wrapping paper in

quilt patterns, patchwork greeting cards, books on quilting, and a collection of antique and contemporary patchwork quilts. ♦ Daily 10AM-5:30PM. 45156 Main St, Mendocino. 937.4201

According to the *Book of Genesis*, the patriarch Noah was the world's first vintner.

73 The Collector Although it's not the same as finding your own on the beach, all manner of sea shells and minerals can be found here. It's not exactly the collection to set a true connoisseur's heart afire, but you can find some beautiful shells to use as paperweights or to hold to your ear for a sound of the sea. Shells begin at 10 cents. ◆ Daily 10:30AM-5PM. 45160 Main St, Mendocino. 937.0888

73 Creative Hands of Mendocino Handmade gifts and clothing from a group of local artisans. Don't overlook the imaginative stuffed animals—from penguins to dragons—from the Soup Factory in Elk. ◆ Daily 10AM-5PM. 45170 Main St, Mendocino. 937.2914

73 Artists Co-op of Mendocino Seven local artists run this gallery that features landscape paintings. They work in a variety of media, including pastels, oils, watercolors, and acrylics. Every two months a well-known guest artist is showcased. ◆ Daily 10AM-5PM. 45270 Main St, Mendocino. 937.2217

73 Mendocino Jams & Jellies A small, blue cottage at the very end of Main Street is home to **Marilyn Douglas'** Mendocino Jams & Jellies, which she makes in sumptuous variety. You can usually taste three or four of the jams here, including an apricot jam, a sour-cherry jam, blueberry preserves, and a super wild-blackberry jam. Douglas also makes several mustards, as well as positively sinful dessert toppings—a deep, dark fudge sauce, a buttery praline pecan sauce, and a chocolate sauce spiked with rum. Bring on the ice cream. And since those jars are heavy, she'll pack up your purchases and ship them home to you. Mail order available. ◆ Daily 10AM-5PM. 440 Main St, Mendocino. 937.1037

74 Chocolate Moosse The best place in town to relax over an espresso or dessert—especially if you can grab one of the Adirondack armchairs set out on the side lawn. Settle in with a good book and enjoy the setting. Not only does the kitchen turn out great Belgian-chocolate mousse pie and an irresistible dark-chocolate Blackout cake, they serve ice cream with hot fudge sauce, homemade

Mendocino Coast

soups, apple-wood smoked salmon on a bagel with cream cheese, pâté and bread, quiche, and garden salads. Beer and Mendocino wines, too. All the dishes are available for takeout if you'd rather transport your picnic to the headlands. ◆ M-Th 11:30AM-9PM; F-Sa 10AM-11PM; Su 10AM-9PM. 390 Kasten St, Mendocino. 937.4323

74 Blue Heron Inn $ Just as you enter the Chocolate Moosse, there's a narrow staircase to the right; up those stairs is this moderately priced inn with a duet of cozy rooms furnished with down comforters, feather pillows, and bouquets of freshly cut flowers. The **Bay Room** has a view of rooftops and the ocean, while the smaller **Sunset Room** has a window desk facing the ocean; the rooms share a bath. There's also an attached cottage with a fireplace and a private bath and entrance. Breakfast includes fresh-squeezed orange juice, warm croissants or homemade coffee cake, and coffee or tea. ◆ 390 Kasten St, Mendocino. 937.4323

75 The Gallery Bookshop This is where you can find *The New York Times,* the *San Francisco Chronicle,* and the *New York Review of Books,* plus an intriguing mix of good reading (and not just the usual bestsellers). The shop is clearly owned by folks who love to read; they'll special order and are ready to advise on what's new or best in a number of subjects. You can also find a good collection of books on the history of Mendocino and northern California. ◆ M-F 10AM-6PM; F-Sa 10AM-9PM. 319 Kasten St, Mendocino. 937.2665

75 Bookwinkle's Childrens Books If you have kids—or even know any kids—head to this shop for a well-chosen selection of children's books. It's incredible how many titles they've managed to fit in this small store, even including a few foreign-language tomes. ◆ Daily 10AM-6PM. Kasten and Albion Sts, Mendocino. 937.KIDS

76 Wind & Weather All the instruments to investigate and stay tuned to the weather are displayed in this converted water tower. Choose from barometers, thermometers, and chronometers, as well as special weather radios. They've got all manner of weathervanes, too, from the whimsical to the classical. Add your name on the mailing list to receive their annual catalog. ◆ Daily 10AM-5PM. 45080 Albion St, Mendocino. 937.0323

"Nothing more excellent or valuable than wine was ever granted by the gods to man."   **Plato**

Restaurants/Clubs: Red   Hotels: Blue
Shops/ 🍃 Outdoors: Green   **Wineries/Sights:** Black

Wildflowers of the Wine Country

The wine country encompasses a wide variety of terrain, from lush valley floors and stony hillside slopes to rocky coasts, river banks, and wetlands. An abundance of wildflowers are found in all of them, and their diversity ensures there's almost always a plant in bloom. Here are some of California's most popular wildflowers.

California Poppy—*Eschsholtzia californica*

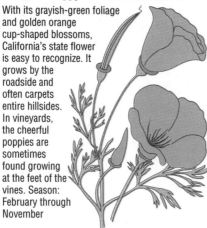

With its grayish-green foliage and golden orange cup-shaped blossoms, California's state flower is easy to recognize. It grows by the roadside and often carpets entire hillsides. In vineyards, the cheerful poppies are sometimes found growing at the feet of the vines. Season: February through November

California Rhododendron—*Rhododendron californicum*

and Pacific Rhododendron—*Rhododendron macrophyllum*

These broad-leafed evergreen shrubs grow from 3 to 15 feet or more in height, blossoming in springtime with large, lightly freckled rose flowers in big, showy clusters. Visit the **Kruse Rhododendron Reserve** on the Sonoma coast to see this native flower in all its splendor. Season: April through June

Cobweb Thistle—*Cirsium occidentale*

This is one thistle that attracts a number of admirers, including butterflies, honey bees, and hummingbirds. The spiky plants, which grow to one-and-a-half to two-feet tall, have prickly leaves and tufted flowers ranging from crimson to light purple. Sand dunes are a favorite habitat, but it can also be found inland. Season: April through July

Douglas Iris—*Iris douglasiana*

Named for David Douglas, a botanist who did extensive collecting in California in the 1830s, the Douglas Iris comes in many shades, from cream and yellow to blue and delicate tones of lavender and mauve. In coastal redwood forests, the two-feet-tall

plants can sometimes be found in large colonies, an entrancing sight when in bloom. Season: March through June

PATRICIA KEELIN

Farewell-to-Spring
Clarkia amoena

So-called because its first bloom in June heralds the end of spring. This annual wildflower is found primarily in oak groves. It's also known as Godetia and Summer's Darling. The large, open blossoms are deep pink or lavender with a darker rose or crimson spot on each petal. Season: June through August

Larkspur—*Delphinium*

Many species of larkspur abound in northern California and are easy to recognize, with their tall, slender stems covered with large blue to deep purple blossoms. In profile, the blossoms resemble spurs and, indeed, the Spanish name for this graceful flower is *espuela del caballero* (the horseman's spur). Some varieties are poisonous to livestock. Season: March through July

Lupine—*Lupinus*

This common wildflower derives its name from *lupus* (or wolf), because it was once considered destructive to the soil. Lupines are abundant and come in many sizes and colors, including several shades of blue, white, and yellow. One of the prettiest is called "sky lupine" for its bright, clear color. Its rounded leaves grow in clusters of 3, 5, or 7, depending on the variety, and the delicate flowers grow in tiers off a central stem. Season: April through June

Mendocino Coast

Queen Anne's Lace—*Daucus carota*

The showy blossoms of this common roadside wildflower are flat and arranged in clusters with a minuscule purple flower at the center. Seen up close, the blossom resembles a snowflake or a Victorian lace parasol, and along some roads, the wildflower is so abundant it forms a dazzling, lacy border. Season: May through September

76 MacCallum House $$ This ornate 1882 Victorian was built as a honeymoon haven for **Daisy Kelley** (daughter of lumber magnate **William Kelley**) and her husband **Alexander MacCallum**. The house, together with its carriage house, cottage, barn, and water tower, features 22 guest rooms. Most of the rooms in the main house have shared baths, while the more expensive—and larger—rooms have private facilities. All are furnished in period with treasured antiques. The greenhouse has been turned into a rustic redwood cottage with skylights and a wood-burning stove. Guests can also stay in the water tower, which has a room on each of its three floors with ocean views, two queen-sized beds, and a private bath. The fanciest accommodations are in the restored old barn, which features an upstairs suite with a private deck. Continental breakfast includes orange juice, coffee, fresh fruit, scones, and muffins—light fare that's ideal before a vigorous walk on the headlands. When you've worked up a real appetite, head for Café Beaujolais (see page 177) for a hearty country breakfast. ◆ 45020 Albion St, Mendocino. 937.0289

Within the MacCallum House:

MacCallum House Restaurant ★★$$$ Under separate ownership, the restaurant downstairs offers dinner in the formal dining room or the more casual cafe and bar area. Start with one of the homemade soups such as seafood chowder or a potato-garlic soup swirled with parsley pesto. The emphasis here is on pasta dishes such as the feathery light spinach and ricotta gnocchi or the pappardelle (wide ribbon noodles) with braised rabbit sauce. Main courses may include half a free-range chicken, grilled Pacific king salmon, or lamb chops marinated in rosemary and garlic and served with mint pesto. For dessert, don't pass up the peach crisp or one of the housemade ice creams. Good list of North Coast wines. ◆ California/Mediterranean ◆ M-W, Th-Su 5:30-9PM. 937.5763

77 Eclectic This gallery, specializing in Mexican folk art, has a fine collection of whimsical handcarved and painted wooden animals from Oaxaca's best artisans. Take home a turtle waving its arms, a

Mendocino Coast

fire-breathing dragon, or a wonderful pig with a green snout and ears. Some of the animals are set out in the sculpture garden behind the gallery. ◆ Daily 10:30AM-4:30PM. 10460 Kasten St, Mendocino. 937.5951

Restaurants/Clubs: Red   Hotels: Blue
Shops/ 🍴 Outdoors: Green   **Wineries/Sights: Black**

GALLERY FAIR

77 Gallery Fair A fine selection of crafts from local and other northern California artisans. Expect to find handcrafted jewelry and superb handmade furniture. Everything is very special (and rather costly) here, from the beautifully crafted lingerie cabinet by **Charles Beresford** to the whimsical "jazz dancer" cabinet in English brown oak and curly maple by **Hank Holzer,** with curving legs and an arched torso. **Robert Erickson** will even make a hardwood rocker to your measurements. ◆ Daily 10AM-4PM. Kasten and Ukiah Sts, Mendocino. 937.5121

77 John Dougherty House $$ The severe facade of the John Dougherty house, built in 1867, reveals little of its charming interior. There's a small living room with sofas pulled up in front of the fireplace and a large veranda with views of the town and the bay beyond. The **Captain's Room** upstairs has an even better view from its private veranda, and the sloping ceiling gives it a cozy feeling. Like the **First Mate's Room,** it has a private bath and is decorated with pine antiques and a double-woven, blue-and-white bedspread. Innkeepers **Marion** and **David Wells** also have a two-room suite with a wood-burning stove, a four-poster bed, and a veranda with a view. Another room with a four-poster bed is installed in the water tower; this one has a sitting room and a private bath. They also have two garden cottages, both with a sitting room, private bath, and veranda. ◆ 571 Ukiah St, Mendocino. 937.4431

78 Mendocino Art Center In the fifties, with its studios, summer study programs, and performing arts, the Mendocino Art Center became a hub for artists of many types. Today educational and recreational programs are offered in painting, drawing, ceramics, woodworking, and textiles that draw students from around the country. This is also home to the **Helen Schoeni Theater,** which houses the Mendocino Performing Art Center. A sculpture garden is on the grounds. ◆ 45200 Little Lake St, Mendocino. 937.5818

79 Reed Manor $$$$ If you'd really rather be in a condominium than in rustic Mendocino, this new bed-and-breakfast is located on a spectacular piece of real estate overlooking the town. The five guest rooms are furnished with every convenience of big-city life—color TVs (one room even has a second TV in the bathroom for viewing from the tub), VCRs, refrigerators, wet bars, telephones, and answering machines. The rooms and suites are huge, and the decor is straight out of a furniture showroom, with glitzy French-style furniture, cedar-lined closets, and more. Telescopes are set up on the balconies. For ultimate privacy, Continental breakfast supplies are stocked in each room. ♦ 44950 Little Lake St, Mendocino. 937.5446

80 Joshua Grindle Inn $$ Set on two acres overlooking the village, this inn (pictured above), originally built in 1870 by town banker **Joshua Grindle,** has faithful clients who come back year after year The main house has five guest rooms; two more are in a rear cottage, and the water tower out back has been converted to three rooms. Much of the decor follows a nautical theme, with blue and white colors predominating, and paintings of sailboats and ships scattered about. All have private baths, and some have wood-burning fireplaces. The **Nautical Room** is quite nice, and comes complete with a queen-sized bed, ship's table, and ocean view. The **Library Room** features a four-poster queen-sized bed, a fireplace framed in original tiles, and a floor-to-ceiling bookcase. And the three rooms in the water tower, stacked one on top of the other, are charming. Innkeepers **Arlene** and **Jim Moorehead** serve a full breakfast on a 150-year-old pine harvest table in the kitchen. ♦ 44800 Little Lake Rd, Mendocino. 937.4143

81 Sweetwater Gardens Here's the spot for indulging in a hot tub and sauna (there's even a large tub and sauna for groups). Swedish/Esalen massage and deep-tissue bodywork are available by appointment. The best deal is the "Rub-a-Dub" special: on Monday, Wednesday, and Friday, you get a free hot tub after your massage. ♦ M-Th 2-11PM; F-Su noon-midnight. 955 Ukiah St, Mendocino. 937.4140

81 Café Beaujolais ★★★$$-$$$ The author of two best-selling cookbooks, *Café Beaujolais* and *Morning Food,* owner/chef **Margaret Fox** is famous for the sumptuous country breakfasts she serves in this lovely Victorian. Highlights include the silver-dollar buttermilk pancakes with local blueberries and andouille sausage, buttermilk and cornmeal waffles (the best you'll ever taste!) with real maple syrup, and a Thai chicken and ginger-sausage omelet with goat cheese and peppers.

The simply furnished dining room with its beribboned wallpaper and antique chairs is the perfect setting for Fox's down-home cooking. At lunch she features savory homemade soups, such as the Ukrainian beet soup or black-bean chili, along with individual pizzas baked in a wood-fired oven, a dynamite grilled hamburger made with naturally-raised beef and topped with roasted pasilla peppers and goat cheese, and great salads. Be sure to save room for dessert, such as her famous panforte di Mendocino (a dense, nut-studded, Italian-style confection) and the deep-chocolate mousse-cake with strawberry sauce. At dinner, Margaret's husband, **Chris Kump,** takes over the stove offering a menu of nouveau California dishes with Asian touches, including seared sea scallops with coconut milk and black-chanterelle mushrooms, and a spicy smoked Thai beef salad. Also, try the roasted free-range chicken with pecan-and-brandied prune stuffing or the rib eye steak Bordelaise (most of the meats and poultry come from local sources). Monday night features a "Beau Thai" prix-fixe menu of Thai dishes.

The garden around the house is surrounded with drought-tolerant shrubs, edible and cutting flowers, lots of herbs, and long-blooming antique roses that have been a labor of love for years. Call ahead to sign up for one of the monthly garden tours given by landscape designer **Jaen Treesinger,** followed by lunch at the cafe. ♦ California ♦ M, Th-Su 8:30AM-2PM, 6:15-8:45PM; closed 6 Jan-mid March. 961 Ukiah St, Mendocino. Reservations recommended. 937.5614

Also at Café Beaujolais:

The Brickery ★★★$ This wood-fired oven is Chris Kump's project, built brick-by-brick by hand and decorated with tiles he brought back from Provence after a visit to the French teacher and cookbook author Simone Beck. It sits in the middle of the garden and is busy turning out wonderful breads and pizzas. The breads change every day (from a repertoire of more than a dozen), and might include a Mendocino sourdough leavened with wild yeasts, a sourdough rye that includes a little Red Seal Ale, an Austrian sunflower bread, and a buckwheat bread with hazelnuts. The sandwiches made on those breads are the best in town. You can also order an individual pizza (10 versions to choose

from, such as pancetta, artichoke hearts, and tomato or roasted eggplant , garlic, mozzarella, and goat cheeses) and retire to the garden tables or take it out for a beachside picnic. ♦ Pizza and breads ♦ M-W 11:30AM-3:30PM; Th-Su 11:30AM-7:30PM

"A bottle of good wine, like a good act, shines ever in the retrospect."   **Robert Louis Stevenson**

Mendocino Farmers Market Café Beaujolais also hosts a farmers market every Friday afternoon where you can find fresh fruit, vegetables, flowers, and many of the makings of a picnic supper or lunch. ♦ F 3-5PM, May-Sep

82 Hill House $$$ The television series "Murder She Wrote" made this hilltop hostelry famous when it used the inn as one of its regular settings. It has 44 guest rooms, most furnished with brass beds, reproduction antiques, and lace curtains—all of which sound innocent enough, but the effect is just a bit dowdy. The views are quite good, though. ♦ 1071 Palette Dr, Mendocino. 937.0554

Within Hill House:

Hill House Restaurant ★$$/$$$ The dining room offers wonderful views and a rather classic menu. The specialty is beef Wellington, but they also have a New York pepper steak and grilled center-cut pork chops on the menu, along with several pasta dishes, grilled filet of salmon, and prawns flamed in brandy. A more casual menu is served in the Spencer Lounge: soups, salads, pasta, and sandwiches. Breakfast includes straightforward egg dishes, omelets, Belgian waffles, and their own corned-beef hash. ♦ Daily 7-10AM, 11:30AM-2:15PM, 6-9PM

83 Agate Cove Inn $$ Sallie and Jake McConnell-Zahavi moved from the worlds of fashion and advertising in New York to innkeeping at this secluded spot overlooking Agate Cove. The hillside property, with an extensive flower garden of old-fashioned varieties, has cottages scattered over the grounds; all but one have a fireplace and a private deck where you can settle in to watch the ocean. Most of the 10 rooms have four-poster or canopy beds, an attractive country decor, TVs, and a private bath. There is also a breakfast room at the inn with an old wood-burning stove and a spectacular view

Mendocino Coast

of the sea. Breakfast is a cheerful, sociable affair with the couple both working at the stove, cooking up omelets, eggs Benedict, or French toast along with sausage and ham. Jake's specialty is homebaked bread served with country jams. He started baking bread at the inn, and just four months after making his first loaf, he won the blue ribbon for

breadbaking at the 1988 Mendocino County Fair. ♦ 11201 Lansing St, Mendocino. 937.0551

Within Agate Cove Inn:

Academy of Wine **Norm Roby,** a San Francisco wine journalist and former dean of the California Culinary Academy, sponsors several inexpensive seminars on wine appreciation at Agate Cove. Topics, offered on a rotating basis, include wine identification, major wines of the world, red wines of the West Coast, and regional characters. ♦ W, Sa 4-5:30PM. For more information, write to: Academy of Wine, Box 932, Mendocino CA 95450.

84 Russian Gulch State Park This park includes acres of redwood groves, spectacular ocean views, and 12 miles of hiking trails, including a path along the headlands where visitors encounter an ocean blowhole (a hole in the rocks in which water emerges with tremendous force, resembling a whale's spout). There are some entrancing views of the village of Mendocino along the way, and some trails head inland to meet the enormous Jackson State Forest to the east. The park has specially marked trails for horseback riding and bicycling. There are also 30 campsites, plus a small camp for equestrians. ♦ Fee per vehicle. 2 miles north of Mendocino on Hwy 1. Reservations recommended for camping. 937.5804, 800/444.7525

85 Caspar Pass through this quiet town, with its white, steepled church, and a scattering of old cottages and farmhouses, and it's hard to imagine that it was once the site of one of the busiest lumber mills along the Mendocino coast. So much lumber was produced here, in fact, that the **Caspar Lumber Company,** which closed in 1955, ran its own fleet of ships to sail it down to San Francisco.

86 Jug handle State Reserve This park is home to the five-mile **Ecological Staircase Trail,** a hike through a series of 100-foot-high terraces cut out of the landscape by waves eons ago. Each "step" is 100,000 years older than the next, and at the end of the trail is the Pygmy Forest with dwarfed cypress and pine trees. Pick up a brochure at the ranger headquarters before setting off. ♦ One mile north of Caspar on Hwy 1

Fort Bragg

Founded as a military outpost to supervise the Mendocino Indian Reservation, Fort Bragg later became an important logging and fishing town and the largest city along the Mendocino Coast. It's a working-class town and has little of Mendocino's carefully preserved charms except for the row of restored buildings and historic facades located where Hwy 1 turns into Main Street.

Otherwise you'll just see rows of motels, gas stations, and stores. However, Fort Bragg is home to the **Skunk Train,** which departs from the refurbished California Western Railroad Station twice a day for the trip to Willitts, 40 miles to the east (see Skunk Train on page 180).

87 Mendocino Coast Botanical Gardens It took retired nurseryman **Ernest Schoefer** 16 years to clear the 47 acres he bought on a bluff overlooking the ocean at Fort Bragg. He purchased the property three decades ago to create a showcase botanical garden. He made the trails and planted rhododendrons and other flowering plants. May is the best time to visit, when the rhododendrons and roses are in full bloom. Major plant collections here include heathers, succulents, ivies, and camelias, so there is always something of interest to look at—in all, the garden is home to several thousand varieties of native and cultivated plants. In 1982, 17 acres were purchased by the Mendocino Coast recreation and park district, and the gardens are now supported by donations and a volunteer staff. You can follow a trail onto the headlands, where it's possible to see the gray whales on their annual migration. If you want to make an afternoon of it, they have a shady picnic area. ♦ Admission. Daily 9AM-5PM, Mar-Oct; 10AM-4PM, Nov, Feb. 18220 N. Hwy 1, Fort Bragg. 964.4352

88 Noyo Harbor This working fishing village at the mouth of the Noyo River is a good spot to watch the boats enter and leave the tiny harbor. There's also a public boat-launching ramp and a sandy beach beneath the highway. It's fun to go down and have a look, maybe stopping for fish and chips or smoked salmon. Every Fourth of July, Noyo Harbor is the site of what's billed as the world's largest salmon barbecue. ♦ South end of Fort Bragg

Also at Noyo Harbor:

Misty II Charters Sport-fishing and whale-watching expeditions. ♦ Daily by reservation. 964.7161

Lady Irma II Sport-fishing and whale-watching expeditions. ♦ Daily by reservation. 964.3854

Sea Pal ★$ Order some fish and chips to enjoy on the outdoor deck with a view of the harbor and the boats. Sea Pal is also a fresh seafood market where you can buy fresh fish for the barbecue or smoked salmon for a picnic. Takeout available, too. ♦ Fish market: daily 10AM-6PM; fish and chips: daily 11:30AM-6PM. 32410 Harbor Dr, Fort Bragg. 964.1600

89 Georgia Pacific Nursery Look for the greenhouses and nursery on the left as you drive into town. When operating at full capacity, this working nursery contains two million coastal redwood and Douglas fir trees. Visitors can learn about reforestation management and today's lumber business on self-guided tours. The site also includes nature trails with trees labeled with identification plaques. Picnic tables are available, and a free packet of redwood seeds is sent to each family that visits. ♦ M-F 9AM-4PM, Apr-Nov. N. Main St, Fort Bragg. 964.5651

90 Georgia Pacific Lumber Mill Tours Georgia Pacific is the largest private employer on the Mendocino Coast and part of one of the largest forest products companies in the world. Logging is an explosive issue in Mendocino and anyone concerned about it should see how a lumber mill is operated. One-hour tours are offered about three times a day during the summer, where visitors don hard hats and safety glasses to observe the manufacturing of lumber from redwood logs. You'll see the bark stripped away and follow the logs through the mill. Children over age eight are welcome. ♦ By appt M-F, June-Aug. Follow the signs to a parking area at the end of Oak Ave (west of Hwy 101) Fort Bragg. 964.5651

91 The Guest House Museum The home of **Charles Russell Johnson,** founder of the Union Lumber Company, has been turned into a museum filled with photos, artifacts, and memorabilia from Fort Bragg's days as a logging and lumber center. ♦ W-Su 10AM-4PM, Apr-Oct. 343 N. Main St, Fort Bragg. No phone

92 Egghead Omelettes of Oz ★$ This tiny storefront cafe offers more than 40 omelets, in addition to pancakes, eggs Benedict, and other breakfast dishes, along with freshly squeezed orange juice and espresso drinks. For lunch, the Egghead features salads, sandwiches, and half-pound burgers. ♦ Daily 7AM-2PM. 326 N. Main St, Fort Bragg. 964.5005

92 Carol Hall's Hot Pepper Jelly Company Try Hall's line of hot pepper jellies, which come in four varieties, along with Mendocino mustard, Russian mustard from **Konstantin** in Little River, and all sorts of dressings and

condiments, plus coffee beans from **Thanksgiving Coffee,** the celebrated local roaster. ♦ M-Sa 10AM-5:30PM; Su 10AM-5PM. 330 N. Main St, Fort Bragg. 961.1422

Restaurants/Clubs: Red   Hotels: Blue
Shops/ ♠ Outdoors: Green   **Wineries/Sights:** Black

92 Fort Bragg-Mendocino Coast Chamber of Commerce This storefront office offers good advice on what to see and do along the North Coast. ♦ M-F 9AM-5PM; Sa 10AM-4PM. 332 N. Main St, Fort Bragg. 964.3153

93 Fort Bragg Farmers Market Everyone from backyard growers to high school agriculture students to farmers sets up shop here to hawk fruits, vegetables, and flowers. The market is run by **Main Street,** a state program that revitalizes and preserves historic downtown areas. They draw the crowds with their produce (almost all organically grown), which is sold just hours after being picked. ♦ W 3:30-5:30PM, May-Oct. Laurel Ave and Franklin St, in front of City Hall, Fort Bragg. 961.0360

94 Round Man's Smokehouse For fans of smoked meats and poultry, it's hog heaven here at this family-run smokehouse. Up front is **Joy Kauffman,** and in the back is her husband **Mike Kauffman** at the smoker, turning out smoked Chinook salmon, albacore, and black bass (he buys his fish straight off the boats and cuts them up himself), plus some terrific peppered salmon jerky. For picnics, consider the small specialty hams, boned and lean, or the smoked chicken breast, both fully cooked and ready to eat. They've got spicy German sausage made from pork shoulder and beef chuck, and for a great, lean BLT, Kauffman takes beef brisket and gives it the same cure as bacon, and then thinly slices it. All of their smoked products are vacuum-packed for a shelf life of six to eight weeks. Mail order available. ♦ M-Sa 10AM-5:30PM; Su 1-5PM. 137 Laurel Ave, Fort Bragg. 964.5954,

94 The Restaurant ★$$ Just around the corner from Round Man's Smokehouse is this savvy restaurant, where you can get a sandwich made with Round Man's smoked turkey breast, avocado, and fontina cheese, or a burger and a salad. Somebody in the kitchen must be Italian, because they offer a typical Tuscan dessert—a glass of vin santo

Mendocino Coast

(an amber dessert wine) with biscotti cookies; there's also an assortment of housemade sorbets to choose from. At dinner, the creative cooks turn out Mediterranean fare along with a few Asian-style dishes. Start with bruschetta (toasted bread rubbed with garlic and topped with basil and shallots) or sea scallops with leeks,

garlic, and thyme. Then you might like to sample their Thai-style shrimp in a fiery curry sauce or their Asian seafood stew, or perhaps penne with artichokes, mushrooms, and peppers. It's an informal, pleasant restaurant and a welcome respite from the crowds in Mendocino. ♦ California ♦ M-Tu, Sa 5-9PM; Th-F 11:30AM-2PM, 5-9PM; Su 9AM-1PM, 5-9PM. 418 N. Main St, Fort Bragg. 964.9800

94 North Coast Brewing Co. ★$$ A handsome cream-color building trimmed in green right on Main Street is headquarters for this local brew pub. Step up to the bar for a glass of Scrimshaw, a Pilsner-style beer; Old No. 38, a dry stout; or the firm's best known brew, the Red Seal Ale, a copper-red pale ale. You can eat light or hearty, choosing from a menu of sophisticated pub grub. Try the Texas-style Championship Chili (made with no beans), the Cajun black beans and "dirty" rice, and the half-pound burgers served with fries. They've got a great mixed grill of prawns, chicken, and spicy sausage, served with black beans and rice, along with grilled local salmon and a one-and-a-half-pound slab of spareribs slathered in the pub's own barbecue sauce. For dessert, there's Mendocino Mud Cake, a fudgy confection topped with whipped cream, or a fruit cobbler. ♦ Pub Grub ♦ Tu-Sa 2-11PM. 444 N. Main St, Fort Bragg. 964.BREW

95 Skunk Train Named for the noxious fumes the early gas engines gave off, this narrow-gauge railroad has been making the run from Fort Bragg to Willits since 1911. Step up to the spiffy restored train station in downtown Fort Bragg for tickets for the six-to-seven hour round trip through 40 miles of redwood forest and mountain passes. On the way, the train crosses 31 bridges and trestles. Less avid railfans can also just sign up for a half-day trip, traveling only to Northspur and back. Refreshments, such as hot dogs and cold drinks, are available at the Willits Station. ♦ Daily except Thanksgiving, Christmas, and New Year's Day. Trains leave Fort Bragg at 9:20AM and 1:35PM and depart Willits at 8:50AM and 1:45PM. California Western Railroad Depot, foot of Laurel Ave, Fort Bragg. Reservations required. 964.6371

96 MacKerricher Beach State Park Just three miles north of Fort Bragg lies this state park blessed with one of the longest stretches of sandy beach in California. Picnic among the dunes, and there are miles of trails for hiking and biking. From November through April, follow the wooden boardwalk to the whale-watching platform. One of the favorite activities here is to explore the tidepools along the coast and to observe the seals from the rocks. The park includes 143 sites for camping. ♦ 3 miles north of Fort Bragg on Hwy 1. 937.5804

97 Westport Fifteen miles north of Fort Bragg is the coastal town of Westport, with its rich heritage of New England-style architecture left over from the days when this was the largest seaport between San Francisco and Eureka. Once the railroad from Fort Bragg to Willits was completed in 1911, the seaport lost its importance. Now it's better known as the gateway to Mendocino's **Lost Coast,** the wild stretch of seashore north of Westport where Hwy 1 turns inland. The only access to the coast is a dirt road that travels 21 miles into the Sinkyone Wilderness State Park.

98 Sinkyone Wilderness State Park This 1,576-acre park on the Lost Coast is rugged country, unspoiled and unsettled, with unforgettable ocean views, secret beaches, and secluded campsites. Inside the park are two dozen back-country campsites, which can only be reached by hiking. Camping in vehicles is permitted only at **Usal Beach,** at the southern end of the park. The primitive campsites each have a picnic table and a barbecue pit; for further details contact the park ranger at the Visitors Center in a turn-of-the-century house at Needle Rock. ♦ 50 miles north of Fort Bragg via Hwy 1 and County Rd 431. For more information, call 946.2311

Bests

Denise Lurton Moullé
Wine Broker, Berkeley

Restaurant: **Mustards Grill** in Yountville—a relaxed ambience and good wines.

Overnight accommodation: **Meadowood Resort** in St. Helena (on the weekdays).

Winery: **Joseph Phelps** in St. Helena—bring a lunch from the **Oakville Grocery** and sit outside the winery with a bottle of their wine and enjoy the view.

Breakfast: **Doidges** in St. Helena.

Shopping: The **Olive Oil Factory** in St. Helena.

There She Blows: California Marine Mammals to Spot from the Coast

California Sea Lion—*Zalophus californianus*

The playful California sea lion, with its distinctive, sharp bark, can reach seven feet in length. The males weigh a hefty 700 to 900 pounds and the females range from 200 to 500 pounds. This sleek, whiskered marine mammal with a pronounced brow has a rich dark-brown coat; the females are a bit lighter in color. The sea lions' agile, rotatable flippers and their adaptability to training have made them a hit at circuses and aquatic shows. Sea lions are gregarious and curious, and will come right up to boats and skin divers to investigate.

Harbor Seal—
Phoca vitulina

These pale silver-gray seals with dark spots and whiskers are generally four to six feet long and weigh 200 to 300 pounds. They belong to the family phocidae, which is characterized by the absence of ear flaps and by flippers that cannot rotate forward, making their movement on land awkward. Among the shiest of seals, they keep to themselves, basking on sand-bars or offshore rocks at low tide. Much quieter than the sea lion, they sometimes slap the water sharply with their flippers and vocalize in snorts and hisses.

California Gray Whale—*Eschrictius robustus*

These large sea mammals range in length from 35 to 50 feet and can weigh anywhere from 20 to 40 tons. They are actually black in color; patches of barnacles and scars give their skin a gray appearance. Every year the whales make a great migration from their summer feeding grounds in the Arctic Sea all the way down to Baja California to breed. It takes them three months to travel each way (an astonishing 12,000-mile round trip), and they cruise at about four to five miles per hour, sometimes traveling 20 hours at a stretch. They head south from December through February and return to the north from March through April. As they pass by the Sonoma and Mendocino coasts, they can be spotted from the headlands.

Killer Whale—*Orcinus orca*

Also known as orcas, killer whales are members of the family delphinidae, and like other members of this group of cetaceans, they have a prominent dorsal fin. Easily recognized by its black-and-white markings, the orca is found most commonly from Monterey Bay north to the Aleutian Islands, and often travels in pods of 5 to 30 animals.

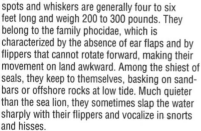

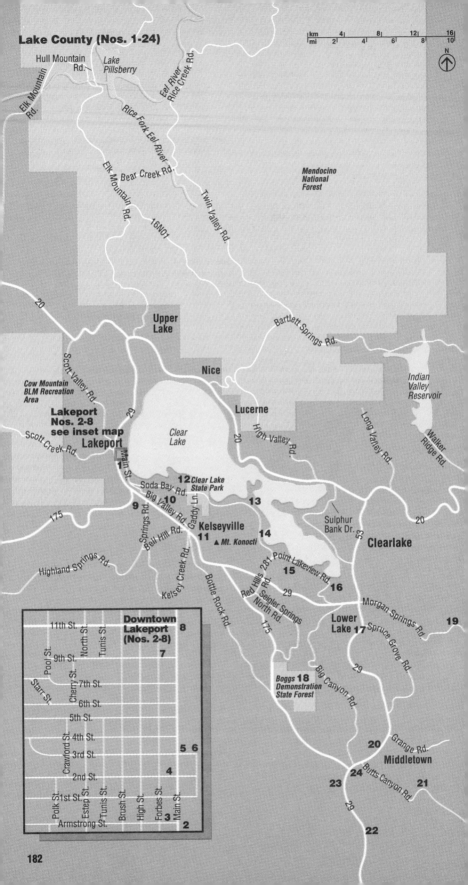

Lake County (Nos. 1-24)

Hull Mountain Rd.

Lake Pillsbury

Eel River Rice Creek Rd.

Elk Mountain Rd.

Rice Fork Eel River

Bear Creek Rd.

Elk Mountain Rd.

16N01

Twin Valley Rd.

Mendocino National Forest

20

Upper Lake

Bartlett Springs Rd.

Nice

Scott Valley Rd.

Cow Mountain BLM Recreation Area

Lucerne

Indian Valley Reservoir

Lakeport Nos. 2-8 see inset map

Scott Creek Rd.

Lakeport

29

Clear Lake

High Valley Rd.

20

Long Valley Rd.

Walker Ridge Rd.

1 Main St.

12 Clear Lake State Park

Soda Bay Rd.

Gaddy Ln.

13

10

9

Big Valley Rd.

Springs Rd.

Bell Hill Rd.

175

Kelsey Creek Rd.

Highland Springs Rd.

11 Kelseyville

▲ Mt. Konocti

14

Sulphur Bank Dr.

53

20

Clearlake

231 Point Lakeview Rd.

15

16

Bottle Rock Rd.

Red Hills Rd.

Seigler Springs North Rd.

29

175

Morgan Springs Rd.

19

Boggs **18** Demonstration State Forest

Big Canyon Rd.

Lower Lake **17**

Spruce Grove Rd.

29

20 Grange Rd.

Middletown

23 **24** Butts Canyon Rd. **21**

29

22

km 4 8 12 16
mi 2 4 6 8 10

N

Downtown Lakeport (Nos. 2-8)

11th St.

North St.

Tunis St.

8

Pool St.

9th St.

7

Cherry St.

7th St.

Starr St.

6th St.

5th St.

Crawford St.

4th St.

3rd St.

5 6

2nd St.

4

Polk St.

1st St.

Estep St.

Tunis St.

Brush St.

High St.

Forbes St.

Main St.

3

2

Armstrong St.

Lake County

Due north of the Napa Valley and east of Mendocino County, Lake County is dominated by **Clear Lake**, California's largest natural lake and the county's main tourist attraction. With no big cities and only a sprinkling of towns, most on the shores of the lake, this region offers visitors the great outdoors in a wine-country setting. The feeling around here is small town and rural, comfortable and unpretentious. Ask a question and you'll get a conversation—on wine, weather, or the state of the country. Even more refreshing, you won't find busloads of tourists crowding you at the tasting bar or rabid connoisseurs bent on putting yet another notch in their wine-tasting belts. It's hard to get too fast-paced or competitive about visiting wineries here because there are only a handful—a few lie on the Kelseyville/Lakeport side of the lake (about a half hour's ride over the Mendocino border), and a few more are located at the southern end of the lake near Middletown and the Napa border.

Winery visits in Lake County will fit easily into a day of golfing, boating, or hiking among the redwoods. And this is the site of one of California's newest parks, **Anderson Marsh**, a large wetlands nature preserve rich in Indian history and wildlife habitats. The lake's great fishing (lots of bass, catfish, and crappie) is one of the county's biggest draws. So catch that fish, pop that cork. This could be the life.

While there may be only a handful of wineries now, this is not a new region for wine. Grapes were planted as early as the 1870s in Lake County, and just after the turn of the century when people flocked to the lakeside resorts, the county boasted 36 wineries. Then, just like today in the Napa Valley and Sonoma, the rich and the famous were getting involved in winemaking. The celebrated English actress **Lillie Langtry** bought an estate in Guenoc Valley in the 1880s and proceeded to bring a winemaker over from Bordeaux to make her wines. Before things really got going, though, Prohibition closed the wineries, and farmers had to turn to other crops. It's only been a few decades since the vineyards were replanted with grapevines, but in that short time, Lake County has re-established itself as an up-and-coming wine region. It's still very small, however, accounting for less than five percent of the total wine grapes grown in the North Coast.

One way to visit Lake County wineries is to make a day trip, starting from **Guenoc Winery** in Middletown and following the lake to Kelseyville and Lakeport. **Kendall-Jackson** is the best known of the wineries here, and it has a lovely tasting room with picnic grounds. If you decide to stay overnight to take in the sights, resorts along the shores of Clear Lake offer a wide variety of lodging, from the luxurious **Konocti Harbor Resort and Spa** on Soda Bay to several moderate and inexpensive family resorts.

Lakeport

This small lakeside town of 5,000 residents was officially incorporated in 1889, but its history begins 40 or so years earlier during the Gold Rush when would-be miners passed through on their way to the fabled mines. After the rush was over, some came back to the lakeshore to settle. The town used to be called Forbestown after early settler **William Forbes,** but the name was changed to the more descriptive Lakeport a year before it was incorporated.

A quiet place with a relaxed, small-town feeling, Lakeport becomes an almost bustling center during the summer, when tourists come to the Clear Lake area for fishing, boating, watersports, and wine tasting. The month of June brings the **Lakeport Revival**, a festival of classic cars, motorcycles, and boats. The big draw in July is the **Lake County Rodeo** at the county

fairgrounds, followed by the **Lake County Fair** in late August and early September.

Restaurants/Clubs: Red   Hotels: Blue
Shops/ Outdoors: Green   Wineries/Sights: Black

1 Lake County Visitor Information Center The dynamic, interested staff has the low-down on everything about Clear Lake and its surroundings. The Visitor Center also has a great view of the lake from the parking lot. ♦ M-F 8AM-5PM; Sa 10AM-6PM; Su 10AM-3PM, summer; call for shorter winter hours. 875 Lakeport Blvd, Vista Point, Lakeport. 263.9544, 800/LAKESIDE (CA only)

2 Lakeport Chamber of Commerce Information on Lakeport and Lake County lodging, restaurants, activities, and events. ♦ M-F 9AM-5PM. 290 S. Main St (Martin St) Lakeport. 263.5092

3 Mt. Konocti Brewing Company ★$ This cozy brew pub was founded in 1991. Brewmaster **Ed West** produces Lupoyoma lager (named after a legendary Indian princess), Konocti brown ale, and Ka-ba-tin (the Indian name for Clear Lake) amber ale. All are available on tap at the bar; you can even try them with potato skins, fried zucchini, and chips and salsa. The lunch menu offers hamburgers, sandwiches, and salads, while the dinner menu includes charbroiled steaks and pasta dishes. Live music is occasionally scheduled. ♦ Daily 11AM-10PM, summer; M-Sa 11AM-10PM, winter. 101 S. Main St (First St) Lakeport. 263.8944

4 Lake County Museum Housed in a stately 1870 Georgian building that was the county seat until 1958, this museum has a wonderful collection of local Indian artifacts, including intricate Pomo baskets, polychrome baskets adorned with feathers, arrowheads, and tools. Historic photos provide a glimpse of how the lake and town looked in the days of steamships and old spas. There's a collection of old clocks, gems, and, upstairs, old musical instruments are displayed in a reconstructed music room. ♦ W-Su 10AM-3:45PM; closed Su in winter. Old courthouse, Main St, Lakeport. 263.4555

5 Bicycle Rack A full-service bike shop with sales and repair service. **Brian** and **Norma Aldeghi** also rent mountain bikes and single-speed bikes by the half or full day. No tours available yet. ♦ M-F 10AM-5:30PM; Sa 10AM-4PM. 350 N. Main St, Lakeport. 263.1200

6 Park Place ★★$ Partners **Nancy Zabel** and **Barbara Morris** had just the right idea when they put together this popular cafe five years ago. A garden at a friend's farm

supplies the vegetables, herbs, and greens—all picked fresh every morning. The menu concentrates on light fare, including soups, salads, sandwiches, and a few special daily entrées. You can eat inside at one of the booths or take your food outside onto a deck with a view of the lake. None of the food here is ordinary fare. The soups are all made with their own good stocks, such as the fresh mushroom soup with thyme and cream and Nancy's Italian vegetable soup (everybody's favorite), which is chock-full of whatever vegetables are in season. They also make their own pasta and top it with an array of homemade sauces. There's always a New York steak on the menu, as well as fresh fish such as grilled sea bass with ginger butter. And for dessert, don't hesitate to order the blackberry sorbet (the blackberries are from their own patch). Best of all, they serve throughout the afternoon, so you can stop by whenever your body cries out for food after a spell of wine tasting. ♦ M-Th, Su 11AM-9PM; F-Sa 11AM-10PM. 50 Third St, Lakeport. 263.0444

6 On the Waterfront Rentals of jet skis, pedal boats, ski boats, water skis, and fishing boats. ♦ Daily 9AM-6PM (winter hours vary) 60 Third St, Lakeport. 263.6789

7 The Forbestown Inn $$ Just a block from the lake, this B&B dates from 1869, when Lakeport was still known as Forbestown. Furnished with oak antique furniture, the inn has just four guest rooms, most with shared baths. The largest is the **Barlett Suite,** with a king-sized bed and a private sitting area. The **Sayre Room** features a queen-sized bed and a private bath with a Victorian clawfoot tub; like the **Henry McGee Room,** it adjoins the library. The grounds of the 127-year-old house have lots of trees and a secluded garden with a large pool and hot tub. Instead of insisting on breakfast at a certain time, innkeepers **Jack** and **Nancy Dunne** try to fit in breakfast with their guests' plans; not only that, they ask what you'd like to eat the night before. Choose from omelets with bacon, ham, or sausage on the side, eggs Benedict, which Nancy serves up with homemade hollandaise sauce, or Jack's sourdough Belgian waffles. They also offer afternoon tea with desserts, and have bicycles available to guests who want to ride into town or along the lakeshore. ♦ 825 Forbes St, Lakeport. 263.7858

8 Skylark Motel $$ Reserve early for this moderately priced, lake-front motel with 45 comfortable and conventionally-decorated units. Accommodations include poolside rooms, housekeeping cottages with one or two bedrooms (rented by the day, week, or month), and fancier suites (some with kitchens) in a one-story building with lake views and patios. They also have a boat-launching ramp and dock. ♦ 1120 N. Main St, Lakeport. 263.6151; fax 263.7733

Clear Lake, the largest natural lake in California, was known to the Indians in the region as "Hok-has-ha" and "Ka-ba-tin," names given to it by two different tribes.

1990
Vintner's Reserve
Chardonnay
CALIFORNIA

ALCOHOL 12.5% BY VOLUME

9 Kendall-Jackson Winery The tasting room in the little bungalow welcomes visitors with masses of potted flowers and a picnic gazebo overlooking the neatly manicured vineyards. When San Francisco attorney **Jess Jackson** began growing grapes in Lake County in 1974, he was no greenhorn, having been involved in farming all his life. He sold his grapes to Fetzer in Mendocino County, but only until he could build his own winery. He opened his winery in 1982, and the enterprise quickly grew both in size and reputation. The roster here includes several barrel-fermented Chardonnays, Johannisberg Riesling, and excellent Sauvignon Blanc. Reds run the gamut from Cabernet and Zinfandel (including several fine vineyard-designated wines from old mountain vineyards) to an exciting new Syrah. He also makes the brass-colored Grand Finale, a select, late-harvest dessert wine devised from a Sémillon/Sauvignon Blanc blend. Kendall-Jackson has just opened a second tasting room in downtown Healdsburg (in the Russian River Valley). ♦ Tasting and sales Tu-Su 11AM-5PM. 700 Matthews Rd, Lakeport. 263.5299

Konocti
1980
LAKE COUNTY
CABERNET SAUVIGNON
PRODUCED & BOTTLED BY KONOCTI WINERY
KELSEYVILLE, LAKE COUNTY, CALIF., B.W. 4929 • ALC. 12.5% BY VOL.

10 Konocti Winery Situated in a former walnut orchard a little north of Kelseyville, this winery may lack a bit in ambience, but it makes up for it with well-made, attractively priced wines. Konocti was started in 1979 by a group of small Lake County grape growers who mostly focused on red varietals. Since white wines were particularly strong on the market at that time, they developed blush wines first, but lately they've been concentrationg on premium varietals. Winemaker **Steven Reeder,** a University of California at Davis graduate who worked at several east coast wineries before coming to Konocti, produces Fumé Blanc, Riesling, and Chardonnay, along with Merlot, Cabernet Sauvignon, and a Cabernet blush wine. Guests are welcome to use the large lawn and shaded picnic area and inspect the small demonstration vineyard. ♦ Tasting and sales M-Sa 10AM-5PM; Su 11AM-5PM. Hwy 29 (at Thomas Dr) Kelseyville. 279.8861

11 Holdenried Farms This attractive country gift shop is stocked with antiques, collectibles, snowy linens, candles, handmade pottery, and baskets stuffed with samplings of wine, dried pears, kiwi, honey, wild rice, walnuts, and other goodies. Owners **Marilyn** and **Myron Holdenried,** fifth-generation Lake County farmers, grow Bartlett pears and wine grapes. Mail order available. ♦ M-F 10AM-5:30PM; Sa 10AM-4PM. 3940 Main St, Kelseyville. 279.9022

11 Loon's Nest ★$$ A casual spot with a menu that changes every day, but usually features an excellent steak, such as the Black Angus filet mignon, along with herb-and-garlic-encrusted lamb chops or yakitori pork tenderloin. Fish dishes get equal time on the menu, too. Look for broiled King salmon, sautéed Mexican gold prawns, or grilled Alaskan lobster tail topped with a pesto crust. There's always a big demand for the prime rib, which is served on weekends only. ♦ M-Sa 5:30-9PM; closed M, Su in winter. 5685 Main St (at Hwy 29) Kelseyville. 279.1812

12 Clear Lake State Park Each year thousands of people visit this spectacular park at Soda Bay on the southwest shores of beautiful Clear Lake, the largest natural lake in California. The park covers a diverse terrain, from 1,400-foot elevations all the way down to lake level. There are four developed campsites, plus numerous picnic sites and several miles of hiking trails. The three-mile **Dorn Trail,** rated moderately strenuous, winds through forests of oak and chapparal to emerge now and then in fields of wildflowers; the easy 1/4-mile self-guided **Indian Nature Trail** is designed to show visitors some of the tribe's in-depth knowledge of native plants. The picnic area along the east side of Cole Creek has tables and barbecues, and if you're lucky, you might catch a crappie or a large-

Lake County

mouth bass to cook up for lunch. (The Department of Fish and Game periodically restocks the lake so the fishing is usually very good.) Indigenous fish include blackfish, Sacramento perch, and tule perch. The park also has some fine swimming beaches and boat launches. Stop at the Visitors Center (west of the boat-ramp parking lot) for more detailed information about lake resources and activities. A large aquarium will introduce you to some of the fish that live in Clear Lake. ♦ Fee per vehicle. Entrance to the park is by way of Soda Bay Rd, north of Kelseyville. Call 800/444.7275 to make campground reservations up to eight weeks in advance. Or call 800/852.5580 to receive mail-in reservation forms.

Within Clear Lake State Park:

Cole Creek Campground Set in the shade of oaks and cottonwoods next to an open meadow, this campground is very popular during the hot summer months. The individual campsites are flat, suitable for tents and RVs (up to 21 feet long).

Kelsey Creek Campground A fairly new addition to the park, this campground has several sites right on the shoreline, and every one of its 65 sites has a lake view. Each will accommodate a tent or RV (up to 34 feet long). Campers with lakeside sites may pull their boats onto the beach. Reserve early for this campground area; spaces go quickly.

Lower Bayview Campground Located in a shady grove of oaks and buckeyes, this campground features some sites with good views of the lake. It is also quite close to the swimming beach. Each of the 21 sites has a flat area for a tent; the parking spaces are not suitable for campers and trailers. Shower facilities for this campground are located at the entrance to the Upper Bayview Campground.

Upper Bayview Campground Several of the sites here can accommodate trailers or RVs (up to 21 feet long). The campground also has a number of large tent sites.

13 Buckingham Country Club This nine-hole golf course sits at the foot of the extinct volcano, Mount Konocti. The golf course and clubhouse restaurant are open to the public and the resort's guests. ♦ Daily 7AM-dusk. 2855 East Lake Dr (off Soda Bay Rd) Kelseyville. 279.4863

14 Konocti Harbor Resort and Spa $$/$$$ The fanciest place to stay in these parts is the 250-room resort at the foot of Mount Konocti on the shores of Clear Lake. All the rooms have a pleasant, if unexciting, contemporary decor with phones, cable TVs, and air conditioning. And even in the lowest price range, some rooms have a view. The resort

also has beach cottages, apartments, and suites that will sleep one to four people. Deluxe apartments feature king-sized beds (or two double beds), a sofa bed in the living room, a kitchen, and a large balcony. Every

four units has a barbecue. The most secluded are the **Haven** apartments with two double beds and a full kitchen. The beach cottages are the most popular, and are set on a large lawn that leads down to the lake. If decor is important to you, consider the fancier apartment suites furnished with whitewashed pine.

Not only can the staff arrange for fishing, boating, water skiing, and other aquatic sports, the resort just added a multi-million-dollar spa. The tennis complex (eight regulation courts) overlooks the lake, and a pro is on hand to teach you the basics or help you brush up on your backhand. Two championship swimming pools ensure that it's never too crowded to swim, and they've got a couple of wading pools for children. The resort also provides a playground, a recreation center for teenagers, and a miniature golf course. There's a fully equipped marina with boat rentals, a boat-launch ramp and hoist, a fueling station, and a bait-and-tackle shop. Golfers get preferred starting times at any of the local courses. During the summer, the resort sponsors concerts (everything from country music to classic rock) and offers special room rates for concertgoers. ♦ 8727 Soda Bay Rd, Kelseyville. 279.4286, 800/862.4930

Also at Konocti Harbor Resort:

Konocti Princess During the summer months this 64-foot, Mississippi-style paddle-boat sails out of the Konocti Harbor Resort marina for a two-hour tour of Clear Lake. She's a double-decker with room for a hundred passengers, and as she moves along at a stately pace, the captain will point out the sites. ♦ W, F 2-4PM, Sa 2-4PM, 6-8PM, July-Sep

Dancing Springs Health and Fitness Spa This new spa in its own building at Konocti Harbor Resort offers a number of half-and full-day spa packages at very affordable prices (that is, compared to the luxury resorts in Napa or Sonoma). You can sign up for individual massages or facials, even an herbal body wrap, or forgo all that and head straight for the spa's steam room, sauna, and whirlpool. Day-use privileges also include exercise classes, workouts in the fitness room, and use of the lap pool (a small fee is charged for both hotel and non-guests). And to top off the experience, you can get your hair done, take a private make-up lesson, or get your legs waxed. And for true hedonists, they offer an almond-mint body scrub and special honey-mango or seaweed bubble baths. ♦ M-F 6AM-10PM; Sa 8AM-10PM; Su 8AM-6PM. Reservations recommended for massages, facials, and spa packages. 279.4261, 800/862.4930

Mount Konocti, the massive volcanic cone that rises 4,200 feet above Clear Lake, is still classified as an active volcano, though it has been quiet for some 10,000 years.

Glass Menagerie

There's more to the wineglass than what meets the eye. For example, do you know why the long, slender stem of the wineglass was developed? To allow you to hold the glass without cupping your hand around the wine, which would affect the temperature of this sensitive liquid. And why are wineglasses made of clear glass? So you can see the color of the wine, which, to the practiced eye, reveals much about the wine's age. In general, the bigger (or more full-bodied) the wine, the larger the glass should be; this is to ensure there's enough air and space for the wine to develop its bouquet or aroma. Many other wineglass features have been developed to suit certain wine varieties and to enhance your appreciation of wine. Here are some of the basic shapes:

Champagne Flute

The familiar saucer-shaped champagne glass is, in fact, the worst possible vessel for serving sparkling wines; the bubbles escape too fast. Champagne should be served in a narrow wineglass, and the ideal shape is the slender flute pictured at left.

White Wineglass

This simple shape, which narrows slightly at the top to focus the bouquet of the wine, is perfect for serving white wines. It's also a good choice for aperitif wines, rosés, and blush wines, as well as light, young red wines.

Bordeaux Glass

This glass is taller than the white wine model but also narrows slightly at the top. It has enough room for a full-bodied, complex red wine to develop its bouquet.

Burgundy Glass

Even larger than the Bordeaux, this glass has a modified balloon shape so that a robust red has room to aerate and develop its full bouquets.

Brandy Snifter

This is the classic shape for serving brandies and cognacs and often comes in several sizes. However large the glass, only a small amount of brandy should be poured at a time so you can warm the spirit by cupping the bowl with your hands.

Restaurants/Clubs: Red   **Hotels:** Blue
Shops/Parks: Green   **Wineries/Sights:**

Konocti Landing Restaurant ★★$$$ The resort's formal dining room offers entrées ranging from Caribbean prawns to whiskey peppercorn filet mignon and Australian rock lobster. Top it all off with their chocolate suicide (a chocolate-lover's paradise with a tart raspberry sauce). ♦ M-Th, Su 5-9PM, F-Sa 5-10PM, winter; M-Th, Su 5:30-10PM, F-Sa 5:30-11PM, summer. Reservations recommended. 279.4286

15 Clear Lake Riviera Golf Course Another nine-hole course at the base of Mount Konocti. No restaurant; also open to the public. ♦ Daily 7AM-dusk. 10200 Fairway Dr, Kelseyville. 277.7129

16 Anderson Marsh State Historic Park One of California's newest state parks, this site is rich in Indian artifacts and wildlife. It was inhabited by Native Americans for more than 10,000 years. Anderson Marsh at the southern end of Clear Lake embraces more than 50 percent of the lake's remaining wetlands. A paradise for bird watchers, the marsh counts numerous American bald eagles among its feathered residents. More than 151 species have been identified in the park, including herons, marsh wrens, mallard ducks, and great egrets.

The best way to observe the marsh's wildlife is by boat, and some are available to rent (call Garner's Resort, 994.6267, and Shaw's Shady Acres, 994.2236). You can also hike through Redbud Audubon Society's McVicar Preserve (a 170-acre wildlife preserve). The Audubon Society hosts a nature walk on the first Saturday of every month at 9AM, but you can take the hike on your own and finish at the picnic tables at the end of the trail. ♦ F-Su 10AM-4PM. (These are the official hours, but the park is accessible every day of the week. During off hours, park across the highway from the entrance between Lower Lake and Clear Lake on Hwy 53.) 994.0688 or 279.4293

17 Stuermer Winery Scientist **Daniel Stuermer** picked up his family and moved to Lake County in 1977 to build a small winery and grow grapes on a 53-acre ranch. The original name, Lower Lake Winery, was changed to Stuermer Winery a few years ago; under that label he produces Sauvignon Blanc and a nice Cabernet. A wider range of wines is marketed under the label Arcadia, but it's all made right here. Wine tasting is available only when the Stuermer Winery has a sale. ♦ Call for sale dates. Hwy 29 (one south mile of Lower Lake) Lower Lake. 994.4069

Lake County

18 Boggs Demonstration State Forest The purpose of this park is to demonstrate forest management practices; ask the ranger for a tour if you're interested. Otherwise you can just enjoy the groves of pine and fir on this ridgetop site on Boggs Mountain. The forest has miles of trails for hiking, horseback riding, and mountain biking. There are 14 primitive campsites with tables and fire rings; you can park near the campsites. The campground is operated on a first-come, first-serve basis only. ♦ One mile north of Cobb on Hwy 175, at the State Fire Station sign. 928.4378

19 Homestake Mining Company's McLaughlin Mine During the tourist season, the Homestake Mining Co. offers tours of McLaughlin Mine, one of the largest working gold mines in the country, on Friday and Saturday at 11AM. The interesting one-

and-a-half hour tour demonstrates how the mine extracts one ounce of gold from seven tons of ore. ♦ F-Sa 11AM, May-Sep. Morgan Springs Rd. Reservations required. Call the Lake County Visitor Information Center for reservations 263.9544, 800/525.3743

20 Crazy Creek Soaring The new Middletown Glider Port with its 4,000-foot grass strip is home to this company's experienced glider pilots. You can sign up for a ride high above the Lake County landscape or take gliding lessons. And for those who own their own gliders, they'll tow your plane aloft. ♦ Daily 9AM-5 or 6PM. Middletown Glider Port, Hwy 29, Middletown. 987.9112

Deciphering a Wine Label in Nine Easy Steps

sometimes, but not always, indicate that fact by placing the name of the vineyard on the label. By law, 95 percent of the grapes should come from the named vineyard.

5 The **appellation** (place of origin) specifies the geographic area where the grapes were grown. It can be as simple as "California," in which case 100 percent of the grapes must come from that state. For a county designation, 75 percent of the grapes must be from that county. To have a more specific viticultural appellation, such as "Stag's Leap" or "Guenoc Valley," 85 percent of the grapes must come from the area indicated.

6 The wine type in California is most often the **grape variety,** such as Chardonnay, Merlot, or Zinfandel, and 75 percent of the grapes used to make the wine must be the stated varietal. If the wine is made from a blend of grapes, the label may bear a generic name, such as "Table Wine" or the more old-fashioned terms "Chablis" or "Burgundy," which were borrowed from wine regions in France and bear little resemblance to wines from those two regions.

7 What is listed on this section of the wine label varies from bottle to bottle, but generally it provides information about the wine **producer and bottler.** When this line says "produced and bottled by," the winery made the wine and watched over it until it was bottled, but a large percentage of the grapes were purchased. If it only says "bottled by," the winery probably bought the finished wines and blended them at their cellar before bottling. "Grown, produced, and bottled by" is essentially the same as "estate bottled."

8 This is the **trade name** and address of the wine bottler.

9 The **alcohol content** of the wine is listed here (plus or minus 1¹/₂ percent), and it cannot exceed 14 percent for most wines. Dessert wines may not be more than 21 percent alcohol by volume.

♦ The terms **"reserve," "special reserve,"** and **"private reserve"** may be added to a wine label by the producer to indicate a special wine—one that comes from a particular cask or that has been aged a little longer, for example.

1 This can be either the **brand name** or the name of the wine producer (some producers bottle wines under several different brand names).

2 The term **"estate-bottled"** indicates that the wine was made entirely from grapes grown or controlled by the producer, and was created and bottled by the producer.

3 The **vintage** is the year that at least 95 percent of the grapes used to make the wine were grown and harvested. Not all wines have a vintage date, in which case the wine inside the bottle is a blend of wines from different vintages (a typical practice for

making champagne and port). Wine without a vintage date does not mean it's an inferior wine.

4 When the grapes come from a special **vineyard** or section of a vineyard that consistently yields a particularly high quality of grape, the producer will

21 Guenoc Winery Six miles east of Middletown lies this large estate, once owned by British actress **Lillie Langtry,** who bought the property in the 1880s as a country retreat. She thought she'd try her hand at winemaking and imported a winemaker from Bordeaux, but Prohibition intervened before they could really get the experiment off the ground. When the current owners, **Bob** and **Orville Magoon,** bought the 23,000-acre estate and built their well-equipped winery in 1982, they decided to feature Lillie's portrait on their labels. There's a view of the vineyards and Langtry's Victorian house from the winery and tasting room. Hoist a glass of the Cabernet to her memory and vision. Guenoc also produces dry, crisp Chenin Blanc, Sauvignon Blanc, and several inexpensive Zinfandels. ◆ Tasting, sales, and tours Th-Su 10AM-4:30PM. 21000 Butts Canyon Rd, Middletown. 987.2385

22 Horne Winery One of the newest additions to Lake County's wineries, Horne is the first winery you'll encounter on the drive north on Hwy 20 from the Napa Valley. It is owned by the **Horne** family, who have been grape growers for more than 15 years and now offer their wines to the public at their new tasting room just south of Middletown. Most of the grapes come from their 180-acre ranch. The winery focuses on Sauvignon Blanc and Chardonnay. ◆ Tasting and sales W-Su 11AM-5PM; Sa-Su only in winter. 22000 Hwy 29, Middletown. 987.3743 or 987.3503

23 Lake County Visitor Information Center Information on everything about Lake County, Clear Lake, and their surroundings—including, of course, Lake County wineries. ◆ M, Th-Su 10AM-6PM, May-Sep. 21337 Bush St, Middletown. 987.0707, 800/525.3743

24 Channing Rudd Cellars This very small winery started out in founder **Channing Rudd's** home in Alameda (near Oakland) in 1976. A graphic designer with a love for good wine, Rudd designed his own label, and moved up to Lake County in 1982 to produce Chardonnay and Cabernet. ◆ Tasting and sales by appt. 21960 St. Helena Creek Rd, Middletown. 987.2209

Small but Select Wineries

This guide to the wine country features a selective list of wineries; not every winery is listed, since many have a very limited visiting policy or simply don't have the facilities to receive visitors. That doesn't mean they should be left out of your wine-country experience. Keep the following producers in mind when you're browsing in wine shops or are confronted with an extensive California wine list in a restaurant. They are well worth seeking out.

Napa Valley:

Buehler Vineyards (Cabernet)

Diamond Creek Vineyards (Cabernets from Volcanic Hill, Red Rock, Gravelly Meadow)

Dominus Estate

Dunn Vineyards (Cabernet from Howell Mountain and Napa)

Far Niente Winery (Chardonnay)

Forman Vineyard (Cabernet and Chardonnay)

Grace Family Vineyards (Cabernet)

Livingston Wines (Cabernet)

Neyers (Chardonnay)

Opus One

Spottswoode Winery

Steltzner Vineyards (Cabernet, Sauvignon Blanc, late-harvest Gewürztraminer)

Stony Hill Vineyard (Chardonnay)

Sonoma Valley:

Clos du Bois

Kistler Vineyards (Chardonnay)

Las Montañas Winery

Laurel Glen Vineyard (Cabernet)

Nalle Winery (Zinfandel)

Sugarloaf Ridge Winery

Wildcat Wines

Williams Selyem Winery (Pinot Noir)

Russian River Valley:

Balverne Winery and Vineyards

Domaine Laurier

Duxoup Wine Works

Hanna Winery

Joseph Swan Vineyards

La Crema

Pommeraie Winery

John Scharffenberger
President, Scharffenberger Cellars, Philo

Hendy Woods State Park near Boonville—the best stand of old-growth timber; an easy 30-minute hike.

Cloverdale Coffee & Ice Cream Co.—an oasis for the traveler on Hwy 101; great coffee.

Floodgate Store and Grille in Navarro—best food in the Anderson Valley.

Philo Pottery Inn—best B&B in Anderson Valley; quiet, comfortable, and friendly.

Highland Ranch in Philo—a rustic, relaxing dude ranch high up in the Redwood forest.

History of the Wine Country

Native American tribes lived in this fertile California paradise for thousands of years, thriving off the bounty of the land by hunting, fishing, and gathering. Many tribes shared the area, including the Miwok, Wappo, Pomo, Yuki, and Wintun.

1542—After repeated attempts by Spaniards **Hernán Cortés** and **Viceroy Antonio de Mendoza** to explore the coast north of Mexico, **Juan Rodríguez Cabrillo** first sights Alta (upper) California.

1579—Englishman **Sir Francis Drake** and his ship, *The Golden Hind,* find safe harbor at Drake's Bay near Point Reyes in Marin County.

1603—Mexican explorer **Sebastián Vizcaíno** sets off from Acapulco to explore the coast of Northern California and changes many of California's old Spanish place-names along the coast.

1775—Spanish explorer **Juan Francisco de la Bodega y Cuadra** discovers the bay that now bears his name (Bodega Bay, about an hour and a half north of San Francisco).

1776—The San Francisco Mission and Presidio is founded.

1808—Russian fur traders explore Bodega Bay on the Sonoma coast.

1811—The Russians build Fort Ross on the coast just north of the Russian River, and hunt for sea otter.

1821—California becomes a far-flung province of independent Mexico.

1822—The Russians build the Fort Ross Chapel with hand-hewn redwood.

1823—The first recorded expedition is made into Napa County when **Padre José Altimira** scouts sites for his northernmost California missions. He selects Sonoma and founds Mission San Francisco Solano de Sonoma, bringing Mission grapes with him to plant in the fertile valley.

1834—**General Mariano Guadalupe Vallejo** secularizes the mission and establishes a presidio in Sonoma; one year later, he lays out the Sonoma plaza.

1836—**George C. Yount,** a pioneer from North Carolina, receives the Rancho Caymus land grant: 12,000 acres in the heart of what is now the Napa Valley and the town of Yountville.

1841—**Cyrus Alexander** is given a 120-acre land holding in the Russian River region that is eventually named after him.

1843—The impoverished English surgeon **Edward Turner Bale** marries General Vallejo's niece and receives the Rancho Carne Humana land grant, encompassing the whole northern Napa Valley.

1846—The Bear Flag Revolt. General Vallejo is imprisoned and an independent California Republic is

History

proclaimed; 25 days later, the American flag flies over Sonoma.

1847—While tracking bear, hunter **William B. Hackett** discovers the geysers in the Russian River Valley and describes his find as "the gates of the inferno."

1848—Gold is discovered at Sutter's Mill in the foothills of the Sierra Nevada, heralding the Gold Rush.

1850—California gains its statehood.

1852—German immigrant **William Kasten,** lone survivor of a shipwreck off the Pacific coast, is washed ashore and builds a cabin in the area now known as Mendocino.

1857—After tasting General Vallejo's wines, **Agoston Haraszthy** realizes the potential of winemaking in the region and soon founds Buena Vista, California's oldest winery.

1857—**Lieutenant Horatio Gates Gibson** is ordered to establish a military post on the Mendocino Indian reservation; the site of that military post is now the city of Fort Bragg.

1858—Millionaire **Samuel Brannan** purchases a tract of land in the Napa Valley to establish a hot-springs resort and plant a vineyard. Ten years later he establishes the town of Calistoga.

1861—**Governor Downey** commissions Agoston Haraszthy to go to Europe and bring back cuttings of European grape varieties. Haraszthy returns from his venture with 100,000 cuttings of 300 varieties.

1864—The first formal vintage celebration in California history is held at Agoston Haraszthy's Pompeian-style villa near Sonoma; guests of honor are General and Mrs. Mariano Guadalupe Vallejo.

1869—The transcontinental railroad is completed and California wines are shipped to the Midwest and the East Coast.

1871—Prospector **Charles Evans** excavates the Petrified Forest near Calistoga, and is thereafter known as "Petrified Charlie."

1874—A destructive root louse called "phylloxera" begins to attack Sonoma vineyards planted with European vines and eventually destroys much of California's vineyards before it is discovered that vines can be grafted onto native American rootstock resistant to the pest.

1876—The **Beringer Brothers** establish their winery in St. Helena.

1878—**Luther Burbank** moves from Massachusetts and begins his horticultural experiments in Santa Rosa.

1880—**Robert Louis Stevenson** and his bride, **Fanny,** spend their honeymoon in a deserted miner's cabin on the slopes of Mount St. Helena, an experience the author memorializes in his book, *The Silverado Squatters.*

1888—**Lillie Langtry,** the Victorian English actress, purchases an estate in the Guenoc Valley and imports a winemaker from Bordeaux.

1895—**Samuele Sebastiani** makes his first wine, a Zinfandel.

1906—The Great San Francisco Earthquake hits; the epicenter is near Santa Rosa.

1909—Author **Jack London** settles permanently at his Glen Ellen estate, Beauty Ranch.

1919—National Prohibition is voted into law and hundreds of wineries close throughout California.

1933—Prohibition is repealed, but only a handful of wineries that produce sacramental wines or wines for medicinal uses are still in operation.

1935—The University of California at Berkeley's Department of Viticulture and Enology, the leading research and training institute in winemaking and viticulture, moves to the University of California at Davis.

1937—The completion of the Golden Gate Bridge opens a new era of business and travel between San Francisco and the North Coast.

1938—**André Tchelistcheff,** wine consultant extraordinaire, arrives in California from Europe.

1943—Newspaperman **Frank Bartholomew** buys the old Buena Vista Winery and brings it back to life.

1950s—A handful of abandoned wineries are acquired, mostly by outsiders moving to the wine country from San Francisco.

1956—**James D. Zellerbach,** owner of Hanzell Winery, decides to try aging his wines in French oak barrels from Burgundy, creating a trend among local vintners.

1964—**Jack** and **Jamie Davies** buy the Schramsberg Winery near Calistoga.

1966—**Robert Mondavi** builds his winery in Oakville, ushering in a new winemaking era in the Napa Valley.

1968—Americans now drink more dry table wine than dessert wine.

1975—The French Champagne house of Moët-Chandon builds its Napa Valley winery, Domaine Chandon.

1976—The famous Paris Tasting, organized by Paris wine merchant **Steven Spurrier,** changes the world's preconceptions that California produces inferior wines; a blind tasting of Chardonnay and Cabernet Sauvignon is conducted with an expert panel of French tasters and results in top honors for two Napa Valley wines: the 1973 Château Montelena Chardonnay and the 1973 Stag's Leap Wine Cellars Cabernet Sauvignon.

1979—The first vintage of Opus One is launched. The branchild of **Robert Mondavi** and the late **Baron Philippe de Rothschild** of Mouton-Rothschild, Opus One becomes the inspiration for a number of Bordeaux-style wines to come.

1980s—Foreign investment in the California wine country increases. Producers from Europe enter into joint ventures with American vintners or establish their own California-based wineries.

1991—Attempting to balance the state's budget, California legislators increase the excise tax on wine production from 1 cent to 20 cents per gallon (still much lower than the US average of 70 cents). To the consumer this equals about a 10-cent increase per bottle.

Wine Talk

acidity: Refers to a wine's tartness. Acidity comes from a grape's natural acids and keeps wine from spoiling during the fermentation and aging processes.

aerate: To allow a wine to breathe (come in contact with air) by decanting. You can also aerate a wine by swirling it around in a glass, thereby releasing its aromas.

age-worthy: Describes a wine that has the potential to age. What determines age-worthiness is the varietal, the vintage, the style of vinification, and the balance of tannins, acids, and fruit in the wine. Not all wines are suited for aging.

aging cellar: Where wines in a cask or bottle are aged. Traditionally, the cellar or cave was underground or tunneled into a hillside, where a steady, cool temperature was naturally maintained. Today it can be any structure that is dark and has temperature control that's suitable for aging wine.

appellation: The geographic region a wine's grapes are grown in. To be classified by state, such as "California," 100 percent of the grapes used for the wine must come from that state. For a county designation, such as "Sonoma County," a minimum of 75 percent of the grapes have to come from that area. And for a more specific American Viticultural Area (AVA) designation, such as "Guenoc Valley" or "Anderson Valley," at least 85 percent is required.

aroma: The fragrance of a wine (it's reminiscent of the grape from which it was made). It can be sensed through smelling and tasting.

barrel-fermented: When wine has been fermented in small oak barrels, instead of the usual stainless-steel tanks. The technique requires more skill, but results in a wine with a more complex flavor.

barrique: The name for a type of wooden barrel used in the Bordeaux region of France. Made of oak, the small barrel holds 225 gallons of wine and is widely used by California winemakers, particularly for aging Chardonnay, Cabernet Sauvignon, Merlot, and Pinot Noir.

blanc de blancs: White wine, particularly a sparkling wine, made from white grapes. The term originated in the Champagne region of France to distinguish more delicate champagnes from those made with both white and red grapes.

blanc de noirs: White wine made from "black" or dark grapes (i.e., red grapes). In Champagne, France, where the term originated, it refers almost exclusively to Pinot Noir. The color of the grapes resides in the skins; if the juice is separated immediately from the skins, the juice will remain clear. In California, blanc de noirs also refers to

Glossary

so-called blush wines, such as White Zinfandel or Cabernet, which are tinged with color.

blend: A wine created from several grape varietals (e.g., a Cabernet Sauvignon and Merlot blend or a Sémillon and Sauvignon Blanc blend). A wine can also be a blend of wines from different vintages.

blind tasting: When a group of wine "tasters" meet to compare a selection of wines. The participants know which wines are featured in the tasting, but they don't know what order the wines are being poured into their glasses. In a double-blind tasting, the wines as well as the order of the pouring are unknown. In both situations, the wines are usually disguised in plain brown paper bags until their identities are revealed at the end. This is done so the tasters' ratings and comments will not be influenced by the label or by any previous knowledge of the wine producer.

blush wine: The term used in California to describe the pale rose-colored wines made from Zinfandel, Cabernet Sauvignon, or Pinot Noir. These are really blanc de noirs, that is, white wines made from red grapes.

body: The way a wine feels on your tongue. Body may range from thin and light to full and heavy. Heaviness results from a wine's solids (sugars, glycerine, and pigments).

Bordeaux-style: (See meritage.)

botrytis or botrytis cinerea: A beneficial mold known as noble rot (or, in French, *pourriture noble*) that creates tiny pinpricks on the grapeskin. As the liquid content of the grape evaporates, the sugar content becomes increasingly concentrated, so much so that when the grapes are crushed and the wine is fermented, not all of the sugar is transformed into alcohol. A certain amount of residual sugar remains, creating a dessert wine, such as late-harvest Riesling.

bouquet: The fragrance or scent of a wine that develops from the aging process. It tastes and smells more pronounced in a bottle of mature wine.

brut: This French term for very dry champagne is widely used in classifying sparkling wines throughout the world. Champagnes range from sweet to very dry. See "Wine Varieties" on page 119.

cask: A large wooden container, usually oak, built much like an oversized barrel with oval or round heads joined by curved staves. Casks are generally used to age or store wines. Sometimes the face of the barrel is ornately carved.

cave: The French word for cellar. Also refers to the tunnels hollowed out of hillsides used as aging cellars.

cellar: Where wines are made, stored, and aged. It can also refer to the act of storing wine while it ages.

crush: The period immediately after the harvest when the grapes are shipped to the winery, crushed, and made into wine; it's also another term for the grape harvest itself.

Glossary

current release: The most recent vintage on the market. For white wines it is usually the previous year, but for red wines it can be two or more years earlier, depending on how long a particular maker ages each wine before releasing it to the marketplace.

cuvée: A French term that denotes a particular lot or blend of wine. It can be wine from a special barrel, such as Stag's Leap Wine Cellars' famous Cask 23 Cabernet Sauvignon, or a special blend that has a higher proportion of grapes from an especially good vineyard or from a particular variety.

decanting: The process of pouring wine from the bottle into another container. This is only necessary if the wine has sediment on the bottom.

dessert wine: Sweet wines, such as a late-harvest Riesling or Gewürztraminer, that are served with dessert or as dessert.

dry wine: Wines that lack sweetness; generally means those with less than 0.5 percent residual sugar.

enology: The art and science of wine production. This field covers every aspect of producing wine, from the harvest and pressing of the grapes to the fermentation, aging, and bottling of the wine. An enologist is professionally trained in this science.

estate wines: Wines made from grapes grown by or supervised by the winery estate instead of grapes bought by the estate on the open market. The idea is that if the winemaker has control over the quality of the grapes, and all goes well, the quality of the wine should be consistent from year to year.

fermentation: The segment of wine production in which the sugar in grape juice is turned into alcohol by the enzymes in yeast.

fining: The process of clarifying wine by adding clay, raw egg whites, or gelatin. These products drag the wine's suspended particles to the bottom of the tank.

French oak: When a winery boasts that a particular wine has been aged in French oak, this refers to the barrels (or *barriques*) and the wood they are made from. Currently, a French oak barrel costs more than $500; the barrel imparts an oaky flavor to the wine for only a few years, so it can be quite an investment. After a few years have passed the barrels are called "neutral."

generic wines: These wines do not come from one specific grape variety. The wine's name, such as Chablis or Burgundy, reflects that it's a general type of wine. A generic wine is different from a *varietal* or *proprietary* wine.

horizontal tasting: A tasting in which all the wines come from the same year or vintage. Participants rank the wines and try to distinguish the characteristics of the wines of that particular year.

jug wine: Inexpensive wines sold in jugs that are of a lower quality than bottled wines. They are usually generic, but may be a varietal wine.

late-harvest: Wines made from extremely ripe grapes and/or grapes affected with the mold, botrytis cinerea.

lees: The sediment young wines develop in a barrel or tank as a result of fermentation or aging. When the wine is transferred to another container or "racked," which happens several times before it is bottled, the lees remain behind. Sometimes a wine is deliberately left "on the lees" for a period of time in order to develop a more complex flavor.

library wines: Wines that come from the winery's "library" of older vintages. These are sometimes offered for tasting, so that visitors can get a sense of how wines evolve as they age, and many are sold only at the winery.

magnum: A large bottle that holds the equivalent of two regular bottles of wine. Preferred by connoisseurs because the wine ages more slowly in the larger bottle, resulting in more complex flavors.

meritage: The name used for Bordeaux-style blends of California wines, in which the predominant grape is below the 75 percent minimum required to bear a varietal label, yet the quality of the wine is such that calling it mere "table wine" would be a disservice. To honor these top-notch blends of Cabernet Sauvignon, Merlot, Cabernet Franc, and other varieties for reds, or Sauvignon Blanc and Sémillon for whites, the term *meritage* (which combines the words merit and heritage) was coined. (The word was chosen from a national contest that attracted more than 6,000 participants and was won by Neil Edgar of Newark, California.)

méthode champenoise: The traditional method of making sparkling wine in the Champagne area of France in which a special cuvée (or blend) is bottled, and a precise amount of sugar and yeast is added to induce a second fermentation inside the bottle, thereby trapping the bubbles that are a by-product of the fermentation process.

microclimate: Refers to a vineyard's particular combination of soil, angle of exposure to the sun, slope, altitude, weather, temperature, and other factors, all of which influence the quality of the grapes.

nonvintage: Describes a wine that bears no particular vintage date. For example, many brut champagnes or sparkling wines are nonvintage, because they are actually a blend of wines from more than one year.

nose: The scent of a wine as determined by smelling alone. This is different from *aroma* and *bouquet,* which can still be sensed after tasting.

old vines: Grapevines that are typically more than 50 years old and are prized for the quality of grapes they produce. Old vines produce fewer grapes, but they have a more concentrated flavor. Young vines are more vigorous and produce more, but the grapes aren't as rich in flavor.

phylloxera: The plant louse that ravaged the world's vineyards in the late-19th century. The pesky insect actually comes from America's East Coast (where the native grapevines were resistant to its attack) and was accidentally introduced to Europe in 1860 when it arrived in the roots of vine cuttings exported for experimental purposes. It was not until most of the vineyards of Europe and later Russia, South Africa, Australia, New Zealand, and California (where European varietals had been planted) had been destroyed that scientists came up with a solution: grafting European grape varieties onto disease-resistant American rootstock. This is still the practice today.

press: The winemaking apparatus that recovers the juice after the grapes have been crushed, and the wine after the fermented must (pulp, seeds, and skins) has been discarded.

proprietary: A winery's exclusive right to the brand name created for its own use. Examples include Trefethen's Eschol Red and White and the Opus One created by the Mouton-Rothschild and Robert Mondavi collaboration.

rack: The process of clarifying wine by transferring it from one storage container to another.

reserve or private reserve: This term has no legal definition in California and is often used to denote a producer's top-flight wines. A reserve may be a special blend or come from a special vineyard; in some cases the term is used to designate wines that are aged longer before release.

residual sugar: The grape sugar that is unfermented in a wine.

rootstock: The stem and root of a non-fruit-producing grapevine to which wine-grape varieties are grafted. Growers choose a rootstock according to its level of pest-resistance (see phylloxera) and other qualities that will benefit the grafted grapevine.

second or secondary label: In addition to their premium line, many wineries produce a second line of wines under a different label. These may be less expensive wines or wines made in a different style.

single vineyard: Designates a wine made from grapes grown in one particular plot or block of vines.

sparkling wine: A wine that has gone through a second fermentation, resulting in bubbles.

sweet wine: Wine that generally has at least one percent residual sugar. Sweetness becomes noticeable at about 0.5 percent residual sugar.

tannin: The cause of a wine's astringency (this is what makes your mouth pucker), this compound comes from grape skins, seeds, and stems.

varietal: The specific grape used to make a wine, such as Cabernet Sauvignon or Chardonnay. In California, a wine bearing a varietal name must include at least 75 percent of the named grape.

vertical tasting: All the wines presented at the tasting come from one estate. Tasters compare different vintages (or years) to understand how the wines age and how consistently the estate performs under varying conditions.

vinification: The conversion of fruit juice into wine through the fermentation process.

vintage: The year the grapes were picked and the wine was produced. Champagne and sparkling wines are often nonvintage wines—that is, they are made from a blend of wines from different years.

vintner: One who takes part in the process of making wine.

viticulture: The cultivation of grapes for wine production.

Index

Q

R

S

T

Index

Index

Y

Z

Restaurants

Only restaurants with star ratings are listed below. All restaurants are listed alphabetically in the main (preceeding) index. Always call to ensure a restaurant has not closed, changed its hours, or booked its tables for a private party.

★★★★

★★★

★★

Index

Features

Index

Credits

Research & Writing
S. Irene Virbila

Editor
Rebecca Poole Forée

Associate Editor
Karin Mullen

Contributing Editor
Mona Behan

Editorial Assistants
Margie Lee
Daniela Sylvers

Word Processing
Jerry Stanton

Art/Research Assistant
Claudia A. Goulette

Administrative Assistant
Stacee Kramer

Designer
Tom Beatty

Map Designer
Kitti Homme

Production Assistants
Michael Blum
Cheryl Fitzgerald
Gerard Garbutt
Patricia Keelin
M. Kohnke
Chris Middour

Film Production
Digital Pre-Press
International

Printing and Otabind
Webcom Limited

Special Thanks
Cyrus Highsmith
Ann Kook
Pat McKelvey
Stuart L. Silberman
Lynne Stiles

ACCESS®PRESS

President
Mark Johnson

Director
Maura Carey Damacion

Project Director
Mark Goldman

Editorial Director
Rebecca Poole Forée

Acknowledgments
Ron Batori
BMUG
Nancy Brown, Brown-
  Miller Communications
Marion Cunningham
Elisabetta Currado
Sandra Dijkstra
Alice Erb
Kathleen Fitzgerald
Lise Friedman
Angelo Gaja
Evan Goldstein
Dick Grace
Helen Gustafson
John Harris
Jacqueline Killeen
Wendell Lee
Jean Linsteadt
Bob Long
Paul Marcus
Mendocino County
  Vintners Association
Denise Lurton Moullé
Napa Valley Vinters
  Association
Napa Valley Wine Library
E. Ross Parkerson
Ruth Reichl
Amy Rennert
Russion River Wine Road
Terril Schorb
Fred Seidman
Stan Sesser
Michael Singer
Sonoma County Wine
  Library
Sonoma County Wineries
  Association
Sonoma Valley Visitors
  Bureau
Jan Steubing
Susan Subtle
John Thoreen
Helen Turley
Patricia Unterman
Bob Waks
Jean Wolfe Walzer
Alice Waters
Jack Weiner
John Wetlaufer
The Wine Institute
The Wine Spectator
Rosalie Wright

Oak Street store, Napa

DRAWING BY KATHLEEN FITZGERALD